THE INTERNATIONAL LEGAL PROTECTION OF PERSONS IN HUMANITARIAN CRISES

The instinctual desire to support those in need, irrespective of geographic, cultural or religious links, is both facilitated and overwhelmed by the extent of information now available about the multiple humanitarian crises which occur on a daily basis around the world. Behind the images of devastating floods and earthquakes, or massive forced displacements resulting from armed conflicts, is the all-too-real suffering faced by individuals and families. From the 2004 Indian Ocean Tsunami to the ongoing conflict in Syria, recent years have seen an increasing debate regarding the international legal mechanisms to protect persons in such humanitarian crises.

This book argues that an *acquis humanitaire* is identifiable through the interconnected web of existing and emerging international, regional and national laws, policies and practices for the protection of persons caught up in humanitarian crises. Indeed, the humanitarian imperative to alleviate suffering, wherever it may be found, permeates various branches of international law, and is reflected in the extensive humanitarian activities undertaken by states and other actors in times of armed conflict, population displacement and disaster. This book argues that by clarifying the conceptual framework and normative content of the *acquis humanitaire*, gaps and lacunae can be identified and the overall protection of persons strengthened.

Studies in International Law: Volume 67

Studies in International Law

Recent titles in this series

Democratic Statehood in International Law: The Emergence of New States in Post-Cold War Practice
Jure Vidmar

International Law and the Construction of the Liberal Peace
Russell Buchan

The OIC, the UN, and Counter-Terrorism Law-Making: Conflicting or Cooperative Legal Orders?
Katja Samuel

Statelessness: The Enigma of the International Community
William E Conklin

The Reception of Asylum Seekers under International Law: Between Sovereignty and Equality
Lieneke Slingenberg

International Law and Child Soldiers
Gus Waschefort

The Contractual Nature of the Optional Clause
Gunnar Törber

Non-State Actors in International Law
Edited by Math Noortmann, August Reinisch and Cedric Ryngaert

The Rule of Law at the National and International Levels: Contestations and Deference
Edited by Machiko Kanetake and André Nollkaemper

Human Rights Obligations of Non-State Armed Groups
Daragh Murray

Security and International Law
Edited by Mary E Footer, Julia Schmidt and Nigel D White

Complicity and its Limits in the Law of International Responsibility
Vladyslav Lanovoy

Complicity in International Criminal Law
Marina Aksenova

For the complete list of titles in this series, see the 'Studies in International Law' link at www.hartpub.co.uk/books/series.asp

The International Legal Protection of Persons in Humanitarian Crises

Exploring the *Acquis Humanitaire*

Dug Cubie

•HART•
OXFORD • LONDON • NEW YORK • NEW DELHI • SYDNEY

HART PUBLISHING
Bloomsbury Publishing Plc
Kemp House, Chawley Park, Cumnor Hill, Oxford, OX2 9PH, UK

HART PUBLISHING, the Hart/Stag logo, BLOOMSBURY and the Diana logo are trademarks of Bloomsbury Publishing Plc

First published in hardback, 2017
Paperback edition, 2019

A catalogue record for this book is available from the British Library.

Library of Congress Cataloging-in-Publication data

ISBN: HB: 978-1-84946-800-8
PB: 978-1-50993-131-6
ePDF: 978-1-50990-403-7
ePub: 978-1-50990-404-4

Typeset by Compuscript Ltd, Shannon

For Niamh, Aoibhe and Elsie

Acknowledgements

As with any book, numerous people have kindly given their time, expertise and encouragement over the course of the past few years. My awareness of and interest in the emerging field of international disaster law was first sparked by David Fisher of the IFRC over seven years ago while I was still working for the Irish Red Cross Society. Subsequently, my PhD supervisors at University College Cork (UCC), Siobhán Mullally and Siobhán Wills, expertly guided me through the process of developing my research and academic skills, and have consistently provided me with support while simultaneously challenging me to critique my work. I would similarly like to thank my PhD examiners André Nollkaemper and Owen McIntyre for encouraging me to develop the concept of an *acquis humanitaire* into this monograph.

I first presented my initial thoughts on the *acquis humanitaire* at the fourth International Four Societies Conference on 'International Law and Disasters' at UC Berkeley in September 2012, at the kind invitation of the American Society of International Law and generously hosted by David Caron. At the conference I benefitted greatly from discussion, debate and insights from other participants, including Kirsten Bookmiller, Claire Clement, David Caron, Michael Kelly and Anastasia Telesetsky, as well as editorial comments on my chapter introducing the *acquis humanitaire* in the subsequent publication.[1] I must also specifically thank Marlies Hesselman for our engaging debates and discussions around the core concepts of accountability and the full cycle of protection as we developed our joint paper on the human rights implications of disasters for the *Netherlands Quarterly of Human Rights* (2015).

As this monograph took shape, I received detailed comments and critiques from colleagues at Queen's University Belfast; in particular I would like to thank Bal Sokhi-Bulley, Luke Moffett and Thérèse Murphy for sharing their expertise and time to review various chapters. Likewise, Thérèse O'Donnell at the University of Strathclyde provided detailed and challenging questions on the concept of the protection of persons, and Kirsten Bookmiller provided excellent feedback on international disaster laws. I also received insightful comments from my colleagues at the UCC

[1] D Caron, M Kelly and A Telesetsky (eds), *The International Law of Disaster Relief* (Cambridge University Press, 2014).

School of Law Research Colloquium on the concept of protection; in particular I would like to thank Sean Butler, Maria Cahill, Steve Hedley, Irene Lynch-Fallon, Patrick O'Callaghan and Conor O'Mahony. Bill Asquith at Hart Publishing has provided consistent support and understanding, despite the slippage in delivery date and ever-expanding word count. The law is stated as of 30 September 2016. As always, any errors or omissions remain my own.

Finally, I would like to thank my wife and family, to whom this book is dedicated, for enduring the long hours as I worked on this manuscript.

Contents

Part III: Concluding Observations

List of Acronyms

ALNAP	Active Learning Network for Accountability and Performance in Humanitarian Action
AU	African Union
ASEAN	Association of South-East Asian Nations
CESCR	Committee on Economic, Social and Cultural Rights (UN)
CIL	Customary International Law
CPA	Coalition Provisional Authority (Iraq)
CRC	Convention on the Rights of the Child
DRR	Disaster risk reduction, prevention and preparedness
ECHR	European Convention on Human Rights
ECtHR	European Court of Human Rights
ESCR	Economic, Social and Cultural Rights
HFA	Hyogo Framework for Action 2005–2015
HRC	Human Rights Council (UN)
IACHR	Inter-American Commission on Human Rights
IASC	Inter-Agency Standing Committee
ICCPR	International Covenant on Civil and Political Rights
ICDO	International Civil Defence Organisation
ICESCR	International Covenant on Economic, Social and Cultural Rights
ICJ	International Court of Justice
ICRC	International Committee of the Red Cross
IDLO	International Development Law Organisation
IDP	Internally Displaced Person
IDRL	International Disaster Response Laws
IFRC	International Federation of Red Cross and Red Crescent Societies
IHL	International Humanitarian Law
IIHL	International Institute of Humanitarian Law

ILC	International Law Commission
IOM	International Organization for Migration
MNF-I	Multi-National Forces-Iraq
MSF	Médecins Sans Frontières
NGO	Non-Governmental Organisation
UDHR	Universal Declaration of Human Rights
UNDRO	Office of the UN Disaster Relief Co-ordinator
UNGA	UN General Assembly
UNHCHR	UN High Commissioner for Human Rights
UNHCR	Un High Commissioner for Refugees
UNICEF	UN Children's Fund
UNISDR	UN Office for Disaster Risk Reduction
UNITAR	UN Institute for Training and Research
UNOCHA	UN Office for the Co-ordination of Humanitarian Affairs
UNSC	UN Security Council
WFP	World Food Programme

Table of Cases

European Court of Human Rights

International Criminal Court

International Criminal Tribunals

International Court of Justice

Other Courts and Arbitrations

Table of Selected Legislation and Related Documents

Conventions, Treaties, Charters and Agreements

Decisions and Regulations

Reports, Resolutions and Decisions from UN Bodies

UN Security Council Reports

UN Security Council Resolutions

UN General Assembly Resolutions

International Law Commission documents

Other Materials

Introduction

> In the past, there was a tendency to accept misery—especially that of other people—with resignation. There was an acceptance of the excessively facile explanation of inevitable destiny. Nowadays, it is true, the total sum of suffering which afflicts the world has certainly not diminished and in some regions it is on the increase. The sense of human solidarity has developed however and people are more aware of the duty of combating distress wherever it manifests itself, and no matter how disproportionate to it are the means available.
>
> Jean Pictet, 1979[1]

The sentiments expressed by Jean Pictet nearly 40 years ago in his examination of the fundamental principles of the Red Cross Movement have equal applicability today. The sense of human solidarity and need to combat distress remain powerful motivators for large sections of the population, whether fighting rising flood waters from damaging a neighbour's house, or making a financial donation to assist strangers on the other side of the world.[2] Yet, even more so than in 1979, we are all too aware of the extent of human suffering from war, terrorism and disasters through the constant bombardment of traditional and social media and our own lived experiences. In many respects, the humanitarian context has changed dramatically since the end of the Cold War, with a global war on terror, mega-disasters such as the 2004 Indian Ocean Tsunami, evolving threats arising from well-financed non-state armed groups, mixed refugee-migrant flows within countries or across international borders, and the potentially catastrophic impacts of global climate change. Concomitantly, an increasingly complex web of organisations and relationships within and between states has developed, providing a body of laws, policy and practice addressing various aspects of what can broadly be termed 'humanitarian assistance'.

The instinctual desire to support those in need, irrespective of the geographic, cultural or religious connections between those affected and those assisting, is both facilitated and overwhelmed by the extent of information now available about the multitude of humanitarian crises which occur on a daily basis around the world. From a small-scale flood which

[1] J Pictet, 'The Fundamental Principles of the Red Cross: Commentary' (May–June 1979) 210 *International Review of the Red Cross* 130, 146.

[2] See, eg, D Forsythe, 'Contemporary Humanitarianism: The Global and the Local' in R Wilson and R Brown (eds), *Humanitarianism and Suffering: The Mobilization of Empathy* (Cambridge University Press, 2009) 58–87.

devastates the crops and livelihoods of a village, to armed conflicts which result in the displacement of millions of people and comprise numerous armed factions, one must always keep in mind the all-too-real suffering faced by individuals and families. As stressed in an urgent appeal by a coalition of over 160 humanitarian organisations and UN agencies in January 2016, the long-running Syrian conflict has resulted in 13.5 million people in need of humanitarian assistance in Syria alone—'That is not simply a statistic. These are 13.5 million individual human beings whose lives and futures are in jeopardy.'[3] This appeal for action by the international community was made '[i]n the name of our shared humanity … for the sake of the millions of innocents who have already suffered so much … and for the millions more whose lives and futures hang in the balance'.[4] Recognising the range of emergency scenarios which may prompt large-scale suffering and the need for international solidarity and action, the UN World Health Organisation (WHO) has defined a 'humanitarian crisis' as:

> An event or a series of events representing a critical threat to the health, safety, security and/or well-being of a community or other large group of people, usually over a wide area. Armed conflicts, epidemics, famine, natural disasters and other major emergencies may all involve or lead to a humanitarian crisis.[5]

This monograph takes this descriptive definition of a 'humanitarian crisis' as the starting point for examining how international law, policy and practice regarding such events are evolving. However, there is a risk of lurching from one crisis to the next, either as a humanitarian actor working on the ground, or as a source of academic enquiry. Hilary Charlesworth has questioned the focus on 'crises' as a means of developing international law, arguing that such an approach leads to a restricted series of questions which 'shackles international law to a static and unproductive rhetoric'.[6] Moreover, Charlesworth argues that, from an academic point of view, a focus on the most recent crisis can lead to a lack of analytical progression from one event to the next, and an inability to see the larger picture.[7] Such a critique is valid and gives pause for thought. Over the course of

[3] *An Appeal to End the Suffering in Syria*, UNICEF, 21 January 2016, https://medium.com/@&UNICEF/an-appeal-to-end-the-suffering-in-syria-44d803e494b#.hvo0xuiwd.

[4] ibid.

[5] World Health Organisation, *Risk Reduction and Emergency Preparedness: WHO Six-year Strategy for the Health Sector and Community Capacity Development* (WHO, 2007) 7.

[6] H Charlesworth, 'International Law: A Discipline of Crisis' (2002) 65 *Modern Law Review* 377, 377. See also B Authers and H Charlesworth, 'The Crisis and the Quotidian in International Human Rights Law' (2013) 44 *Netherlands Yearbook of International Law* 19, which defines 'crises' as: 'either situations presently unregulated by international law or ones that overwhelm the regulatory capacity of the international system to which the law must nevertheless respond', 20–21.

[7] Charlesworth, 'International Law', above n 6, 384.

this book, I will argue that there is a common conceptual and operational thread running through our preparations for and responses to a broad range of different humanitarian crises—from internal armed conflicts and UN-mandated military interventions to natural disasters and forced displacement arising from global climate change. Yet since each distinct 'crisis' (large or small) provides an example of the implementation of international norms, it remains necessary to review state and humanitarian actors' practice in particular operational settings to fully understand how law influences humanitarian responses (if at all). The country and thematic examples presented over the course of this book are therefore intended to reflect key elements of the legal and operational issues arising from specific humanitarian crises, but are not case studies in the strict sense. Readers may well be able to identify counter-examples where, for instance, the right to adequate housing was achieved after a natural disaster, or sexual and gender-based violence in a refugee camp was effectively addressed. The case examples should therefore not be considered as representative of all humanitarian activities, but as providing sources of information on specific aspects of law, policy or practice in a particular country and humanitarian crisis.

The humanitarian imperative, as elaborated by the International Red Cross Movement, contends that action should be taken to prevent or alleviate suffering arising out of humanitarian crises wherever they may occur.[8] Yet reflecting the range of stakeholders involved, the moral, philosophical and practical application of humanitarianism is a contested field. Nevertheless, there is generally a broad consensus on the humanitarian principles which underpin the actions of states, the UN and non-governmental agencies in their preparations and responses to humanitarian crises. As succinctly set out in UNGA Resolution 46/182, humanitarian assistance is of 'cardinal importance for the victims of natural disasters and other emergencies [and …] must be provided in accordance with the principles of humanity, neutrality and impartiality'.[9]

The fundamental principle of humanity forms the core of humanitarian action, while the concept of human dignity is increasingly recognised as a foundational principle of international human rights law. The interplay between these humanitarian and human rights principles highlights the synergies and potential conflicts between their theoretical and practical application, and also the conceptual origins of different bodies of international law. As argued by Françoise Hampson and Noam Lubell before

[8] Proclamation of the Fundamental Principles of the Red Cross, Resolution VIII, XXth International Conference of the Red Cross, Vienna, 2–9 October 1965.

[9] Strengthening of the Coordination of Humanitarian Emergency Assistance of the United Nations, UNGA Res 46/182, 19 December 1991.

the Grand Chamber of the European Court of Human Rights, there is no single rule to determine the interplay between the two regimes of international humanitarian and international human rights law.[10] As a result, one must examine each scenario on a case-by-case basis to determine the applicable international obligations. This is particularly true when examining the protection of persons in times of humanitarian crises, which can be viewed from an operational perspective (with protection programmes forming a key part of many humanitarian organisations' activities), and also as a legal basis (with the concept of protection taking centre stage in international humanitarian, human rights, refugee and disaster law). The former UN independent expert on human rights and international solidarity, Rudi Muhammad Rizki, identified international solidarity as a precondition to human dignity, which he asserted as 'the basis of all human rights'.[11] Moreover, he argued that such solidarity is not limited to international aid or humanitarian assistance but also includes sustainability in international relations and the peaceful coexistence of all members of the international community. Nevertheless, Rizki also noted that 'there is a large gap between assertions of international solidarity in theory and their reflection in practice'.[12]

Drawing on my own experience of working in refugee protection and humanitarian action for, inter alia, the UN High Commissioner for Refugees, the International Organization for Migration and the Irish Red Cross Society, this book aims to provide both a conceptual understanding and a practical exposition of the range of instruments, policies and practice of relevance to humanitarian action.[13] Therefore, Part I first examines the contested notion of 'humanitarianism' from a theoretical and operational perspective, before introducing the concept of an *acquis humanitaire* which incorporates aspects of law, policy and practice from a range of binding and non-binding sources across several existing branches of international law. Fundamental to the *acquis humanitaire* is the application of the international principle of 'protection'. Therefore, drawing on Walter Kälin's concept of a cycle of protection,[14] alongside Elizabeth Ferris's categorisation of physical, humanitarian and human rights

[10] *Hassan v United Kingdom*, ECtHR, Application 29750/09, Grand Chamber Judgment of 16 September 2014, para 95.

[11] HRC, *Report of the Independent Expert on Human Rights and International Solidarity, Rudi Muhammad Rizki* (5 July 2010) A/HRC/15/32, para 58.

[12] ibid, para 6.

[13] For discussion of the concept of 'humanitarian action', see ch 1, Section II.

[14] W Kälin, *Report of the Representative of the Secretary-General on the Human Rights of Internally Displaced Persons: Addendum on Protection of Internally Displaced Persons in Situations of Natural Disasters* (5 March 2009) A/HRC/10/13/Add.1.

protection,[15] I will argue that while both needs-based and rights-based approaches to humanitarian action are valid operational stances to take, all humanitarian programming can and should incorporate the human rights principles of empowerment, participation, non-discrimination and accountability into their design and implementation. It follows that accountability mechanisms, whether political, legal, administrative, professional and/or social, are an essential element of effective and responsive humanitarian action.

At its heart, this book aims to reflect the call for action set out in advance of the first-ever inter-governmental World Humanitarian Summit in 2016, which envisaged:

> a world whose fundamental humanity is restored, a world where no one confronted by crisis dies who can be saved, goes hungry, or is victimized by conflict because there is not enough political will or resources to help them.[16]

However, such earnest words need to be backed up by legal obligations. Therefore, Part II sets out key examples of binding law and non-binding norms applicable to protection and material assistance activities during humanitarian crises from a variety of branches of international law. But this monograph is not a textbook, and cannot cover all the legal instruments relating to international and non-international armed conflicts, human rights, refugees, or the expanding body of texts relating to natural and human-made disasters, particularly at the bilateral or regional levels.[17] Nevertheless, the central argument presented is that there are important commonalities between the overarching fundamental principles underpinning humanitarian activities in armed conflicts, forced displacement and natural or human-made disasters, and the resultant operational measures taken by states and other humanitarian actors. It follows that we should examine the similarities (and differences) between competing bodies of international law relating to the protection of persons in times of humanitarian crises. As noted by Guglielmo Verdirame: 'Only by examining the norms and practice under various branches of international law can one begin to identify the legal regulation of humanitarian assistance.'[18]

[15] See E Ferris, *The Politics of Protection: The Limits of Humanitarian Action* (Brookings Institution Press, 2011).

[16] World Humanitarian Summit secretariat, *Restoring Humanity: Synthesis of the Consultation Process for the World Humanitarian Summit* (New York, United Nations, 2015) viii.

[17] For a recent example, see the *Central American Protocol for the Shipment, Transit and Reception of Humanitarian Assistance*, adopted by the Coordination Center for the Prevention of Natural Disasters in Central America (March 2016).

[18] G Verdirame, 'Testing the Effectiveness of International Norms: The Provision of Humanitarian Assistance by the UN and Sexual Apartheid in Afghanistan' (2001) 23 *Human Rights Quarterly* 733, 741.

In 1980, Peter MacAlister-Smith, one of the early norm entrepreneurs promoting the legal regulation of disaster responses, queried whether the progressive development of a general international relief law was desirable or feasible.[19] In the intervening years, there has been an exponential growth in both humanitarian activities and legal and policy instruments. At the most simplistic level, I am proposing a 'law of humanitarian assistance', in other words recognition of the interconnected web of existing and emerging provisions across international law which aim directly at providing material support and legal protection for people caught up in humanitarian crises.[20] However, as will be explained over the course of this book, I do not favour this phrase as it is replete with contradictions. So it should be stressed at the beginning of this work that I am not proposing a new unified body of international law. Not only is this conceptually unnecessary, I do not believe that it would advance our understanding or the actual protection of persons in such challenging situations. What I am proposing is that academics and practitioners need to view a wide range of laws, policy and practice as falling within the same sphere of influence, namely the long-standing and instinctive desire to provide support and assistance to people in times of exceptional need.[21]

The French term *'acquis'*, meaning 'accepted' or 'established',[22] gained prominence through its use to describe the body of common rights and obligations arising within the European Union, and has since been applied to the law and practice of both the Council of Europe and the World Trade Organization. This book argues that an emerging *acquis* of humanitarian action is evidenced by the activities undertaken by states and other humanitarian organisations in times of armed conflict, displacement and disaster, and by the similarities in the underlying principles that permeate multiple branches of international law. By understanding this coherence, and delineating the *acquis humanitaire*, I believe we can help minimise the gaps and lacunae that currently exist for the protection of persons in humanitarian crises. As stated by UN Secretary-General Ban Ki-moon at the close of the 2016 World Humanitarian Summit:

> The participants have made it emphatically clear that humanitarian assistance alone can neither adequately address nor sustainably reduce the needs of over 130 million of the world's most vulnerable people. A new and coherent approach

[19] P MacAlister-Smith, 'Human Rights and Disaster Relief' (1980) 5 *Holdsworth Law Review* 173, 179.

[20] For discussion of the 'international law of humanitarian assistance,' see Verdirame, 'Testing the Effectiveness', above n 1, 738.

[21] For an excellent series of articles on various aspects of humanitarianism, see Wilson and Brown, *Humanitarianism and Suffering*, above n 2.

[22] J-B Ormal-Grenon and N Pomier (eds), *Oxford Hachette French Dictionary* 3rd edn (Oxford University Press, 2001) 10.

> is required based on addressing root causes, increasing political diplomacy for prevention and conflict resolution, and bringing humanitarian, development and peacebuilding efforts together.[23]

By elaborating some of the key legal and non-legal sources behind the provision of material assistance and protection activities in humanitarian crises, it is hoped that this book will contribute to the development of such a new and coherent approach.

[23] 'Chair's Summary by the United Nations Secretary-General' in *Standing Up for Humanity: Committing to Action*, final version, World Humanitarian Summit, Istanbul, 23–24 May 2016 (2016) 4.

Part I

Conceptual Framework

1

Setting the Scene: Humanitarianism in Context

I. THE FOUNDATIONS OF HUMANITARIANISM

A. Inter-disciplinary Understandings of 'Humanitarianism'

ALTHOUGH THE TERM 'humanitarian' came into widespread use at the beginning of the nineteenth century, the range of harm and suffering envisaged has varied over time. Originally, humanitarians were considered to be anyone engaged in a broad range of social development activities, from the international abolition of slavery to domestic concerns such as improved labour conditions, the temperance movement and the protection of children in rapidly spreading urban slums.[1] A revised understanding of 'humanitarianism' arose from the specific focus on the victims of war promoted by Henri Dunant and the newly established International Red Cross Movement in the 1860s, which directly influenced our modern understanding of humanitarianism as predominantly cross-border actions taken to support victims of war, displacement or disaster in other countries (as opposed to the domestic humanitarianism of the nineteenth century). Michael Barnett has identified three ages of humanitarianism, namely: 'imperial humanitarianism' covering the early nineteenth century until the Second World War; 'neo-humanitarianism' from the Second World War until the end of the Cold War; and 'liberal humanitarianism' from the end of the Cold War to the present.[2]

In a world encompassing a multitude of humanitarian actors, including states, the UN, non-governmental humanitarian agencies, for-profit organisations and even the military, words such as 'charity', 'mercy' and 'compassion' sit next to 'rights', 'accountability' and 'responsibility'. So the philosophical, cultural and theological development and analysis of

[1] For an engaging account of the development of humanitarianism, see M Barnett and T Weiss, 'Humanitarianism: A Brief History of the Present' in M Barnett and T Weiss (eds), *Humanitarianism in Question: Politics, Power and Ethics* (Cornell University Press, 2008) 1–48.

[2] M Barnett, *Empire of Humanity: A History of Humanitarianism* (Cornell University Press, 2011) 29.

humanitarianism provides a fascinating and rich area of research, reflecting the numerous academic understandings of 'humanitarianism', as well as divergent operational approaches between humanitarian actors.[3] This monograph, however, is intended primarily to provide an analysis of the legal instruments and obligations behind international responses to humanitarian crises arising from armed conflict, forced displacement and disasters, rather than the philosophical or theological motivations of different actors.[4]

Nevertheless, it is impossible to fully understand such legal texts and frameworks without an awareness of the broader contextual debates about humanitarianism in general. Building on their historical analysis of humanitarianism, Michael Barnett and Thomas Weiss have examined the so-called 'forces of humanitarianism'. Barnett and Weiss argue that both the meaning and practice of humanitarianism have been shaped by three key forces, namely the forces of destruction, production and salvation.[5] The forces of destruction include acts of violence which endanger lives, safety and security, principally from war and technological advances but also from natural hazards. Ranged against these forces of destruction are the productive capacities of states and the world as a whole, and a collective commitment to provide salvation from suffering. The forces of salvation therefore consist of moral discourses, religious beliefs, ethical commitments and international norms to help distant strangers. Barnett has furthermore argued that individuals and communities generally wish to see themselves as loving, compassionate and good, and so respond to horrific suffering as a means to reinforce this self-image.[6]

Seen from this perspective, international legal approaches to humanitarianism should aim to minimise the forces of destruction (for example by regulating the means and methods of warfare, or legislating for disaster risk reduction measures such as improved building codes in earthquake zones), while simultaneously promoting the efficient production (that is, delivery) of humanitarian relief, and supporting activities undertaken to protect the inherent dignity of all humans based on ethical, religious, moral and legal norms. Yet there are clear limitations to the normative and

[3] The work of Hugo Slim is particularly effective in merging these various stands. See, eg, H Slim, 'Relief Agencies and Moral Standing in War: Principles of Humanity, Neutrality, Impartiality and Solidarity' (1997) 7(4) *Development in Practice* 342.

[4] For a critique of humanitarianism from a legal perspective, see generally D Kennedy, *The Dark Sides of Virtue: Reassessing International Humanitarianism* (Princeton University Press, 2004).

[5] M Barnett and T Weiss, *Humanitarianism Contested: Where Angels Fear to Tread* (Routledge, 2011) 17–23. See also Barnett, *Empire of Humanity*, above n 2, 22–29, which recognises an additional source of influence in technology, which impacts our capacity for destruction, production and salvation, 29.

[6] Barnett, *Empire of Humanity*, above n 2, 26–27.

practical influence of legal instruments. David Kennedy has argued that international humanitarians often view documents and networks as having an 'inherent humanitarian potency', and warns against an uncritical drive for greater global governance via the production of new instruments and techniques as this 'often comes at a cost to analysis of the substantive results of their use'.[7]

In contrast to Barnett and Weiss's progressive narrative, a more pessimistic view of 'humanitarianism' is captured by the journalist and author David Rieff, who claims that humanitarianism is a marginal activity in the face of the horrors of war and crises:

> [The] reality is clear to anyone who watches the evening news. There is no letup in the horror, no shining new order in which refugees are treated properly and victims of war get shelter, medical care, and food. Better to say we have good intentions, we care, we want to help, and to persuade ourselves that our good wishes are sooner or later going to be transformed into good outcomes.[8]

Having reported on some of the bloodiest armed conflicts of recent times, including Bosnia, Rwanda and Afghanistan, Rieff's cynicism towards humanitarian actors and international law is perhaps understandable, despite its analysis based on political realism:

> As long as the debate is restricted to one about what the laws are, and what they should be, the moral high ground is easy to hold. The law is the law, after all. But once political arguments have to be advanced and defended, things become less cut-and-dried. It is such a saving idea, the law. The problem is that taking refuge in saving ideas rarely ends up saving anyone. To negotiate the terrain between norms and facts, there is only politics.[9]

Rieff's perspective on the appropriate scope and role of humanitarianism, the law and humanitarian actors is fiercely contested, and for good reason. Craig Calhoun has argued that Rieff aims to 'pull humanitarianism back toward its root in ancient ideas of charity, urging more attention to simply and immediately alleviating suffering and less to human improvement'.[10] Barnett and Weiss go further and accuse Rieff of romanticising the history of humanitarianism by equating it with colonialism and imperialism, and

[7] Kennedy, *Dark Sides of Virtue*, above n 4, 119. Scott Veitch goes further, and argues that the law itself can legitimise extensive suffering, for example the sanctions regime against Iraq during the 1990s. See S Veitch, *Law and Irresponsibility: On The Legitimation of Human Suffering* (Routledge-Cavendish, 2007).

[8] D Rieff, *A Bed for the Night: Humanitarianism in Crisis* (Vintage Press, 2002) 87.

[9] ibid, 76.

[10] C Calhoun, 'The Imperative to Reduce Suffering: Charity, Progress, and Emergencies in the Field of Humanitarian Action' in Barnett and Weiss, *Humanitarianism in Question*, above n 1, 74–75.

denying how the concept and practices of humanitarianism have changed over time along with the changing face of the world.[11] International law likewise evolves and adapts to new challenges and power structures, although the normative force of law can be used for harm as well as good.[12] Anne Orford has challenged international lawyers to engage in self-reflection and to consider alternative perspectives to traditional narratives, for example surrounding military humanitarian interventions and the NATO bombing of Kosovo in 1999.[13] In trenchant language, Orford argues that 'international lawyers who celebrate the globalization of human rights, while avoiding any analysis of the ways in which human rights are used to justify highly inhumane and violent acts of intervention, legitimize brutal acts of exploitation and violence'.[14]

Yet, even though political scientists, journalists, sociologists, lawyers and international relations experts have extensively examined the impulses and outcomes of humanitarianism, a consistent focus of such examinations has been on humanitarianism in times of war, rather than peacetime emergencies. Historically, this could potentially be understood due to an underlying fatalism as to the supposed divine origin and uncertainty surrounding natural disasters such as earthquakes and volcanic eruptions.[15] The first recorded instance of states providing international humanitarian assistance occurred following the devastating 1755 Lisbon earthquake and tsunami,[16] an event which had a profound impact on public consciousness at the time.[17] It is therefore no surprise that the Swiss jurist and philosopher, Emer de Vattel, acknowledged the legal, ethical and moral obligations arising from natural or human-made disasters a mere three years later. In 1758 Vattel argued that 'when the occasion arises, every Nation should give its aid to further the advancement of other Nations and save them from disaster and ruin, so far as it can

[11] Barnett and Weiss, 'Humanitarianism: A Brief History', above n 1, 10.

[12] See for example Veitch, *Law and Irresponsibility*, above n 7.

[13] Orford highlights three main bodies of international legal scholarship, namely: feminist approaches to international law; New Approaches to International Law (NAIL); and Third World Approaches to International Law (TWAIL). See A Orford, 'Muscular Humanitarianism: Reading the Narratives of the New Interventionism' (1999) 10 *European Journal of International Law* 679, 706. See also H Charlesworth, 'International Law: A Discipline of Crisis' (2002) 65(3) *Modem Law Review* 377.

[14] Orford, above n 13.

[15] It should be noted that the widely used phrase 'natural disaster' is rightly contested—a natural hazard only becomes a 'disaster' when it impacts on human lives, livelihoods and property. See Section II.C below.

[16] J Hutchinson, 'Disasters and the International Order: Earthquakes, Humanitarians, and the Ciraolo Project' (March 2000) 22(1) *International History Review* 1, 4.

[17] For example, a key event in Voltaire's 1759 satire on optimism, *Candide: or The Optimist*, occurs when Candide and his mentor, Dr Pangloss, witness first-hand the destruction caused by the Lisbon earthquake and tsunami.

do so without running too great a risk'.[18] It was another hundred years before Henri Dunant's *Memory of Solferino* likewise ignited public consciousness to the need for coordinated responses to the suffering caused by war.[19] Such sentiments have distinctly modern equivalents. Intentionally or otherwise, more than 240 years after Vattel's pronouncement, the UN Committee on Economic, Social and Cultural Rights closely mirrored his argument when they concluded:

> States parties have a joint and individual responsibility, in accordance with the Charter of the United Nations and relevant resolutions of the United Nations General Assembly and of the World Health Assembly, to cooperate in providing disaster relief and humanitarian assistance in times of emergency, including assistance to refugees and internally displaced persons. Each State should contribute to this task to the maximum of its capacities.[20]

In spite of the challenges of predicting where the next war, forced displacement or major hurricane will hit, Vattel and Dunant's recognition of a state's obligations towards its own citizens and those of other countries highlights the long-standing awareness that even if crises cannot be predicted or prevented, the suffering caused by such events can be mitigated.[21] Despite the forces of pain and destruction that people and nature can generate, the humanitarian impulse to provide protection and assistance to those in need has resounded down through the centuries.

B. The Humanitarian Imperative: To Prevent and Alleviate Human Suffering

The modern concept of the 'humanitarian imperative' can be traced to the XXth International Conference of the Red Cross in 1965, which adopted the seven fundamental principles of the Red Cross Red Crescent Movement.[22] The first principle adopted was that of 'humanity', which states:

> The International Red Cross and Red Crescent Movement, born of a desire to bring assistance without discrimination to the wounded on the battlefield,

[18] E de Vattel, *The Law of Nations or the Principles of Natural Law Applied to the Conduct and to the Affairs of Nations and of Sovereigns*, text of 1758, Books I–IV, vol iii, 114. For discussion of Vattel's positivism and support for humanitarian interventions, see A Hurrell, 'Vattel: Pluralism and Its Limits' in I Clark and I Neumann (eds), *Classical Theories of International Relations* (St Martin's Press, 1996), in particular 242–45.

[19] H Dunant, *A Memory of Solferino*, 1862 (American Red Cross, 1939, 1959).

[20] CESCR, *General Comment No 14: The Right to the Highest Attainable Standard of Health* (11 August 2000) E/C.12/2000/4, para 40.

[21] Vattel, above n 18, 114.

[22] The seven fundamental principles are: humanity; impartiality; neutrality; independence; voluntary service; unity; and universality. The principles of voluntary service, unity and universality relate primarily to the internal working and structure of the International Red Cross Movement, www.ifrc.org/en/who-we-are/vision-and-mission/the-seven-fundamental-principles.

> endeavours, in its international and national capacity, to prevent and alleviate human suffering wherever it may be found. Its purpose is to protect life and health and to ensure respect for the human being.[23]

The non-binding principle of humanity set out by the Red Cross mirrors several key themes running through various branches of international law, namely: non-discrimination; balancing humanitarian considerations with military necessity; and protecting and respecting human dignity. The Red Cross's fundamental principles were swiftly followed in 1969 with the operational Principles and Rules for Red Cross Disaster Relief, which reaffirmed that: 'The Red Cross in its endeavour to prevent and alleviate human suffering, considers it a fundamental duty to bring relief to all disaster victims.'[24] This concept of a humanitarian imperative, which asserts that a wide range of governmental and non-governmental actors have a duty to provide assistance, has since been broadly accepted as a moral and ethical obligation by many humanitarian actors. For example, the influential *Sphere Handbook*'s Humanitarian Charter not only affirms the primacy of the humanitarian imperative, but argues that nothing should override the principle; while simultaneously noting that although the principles of the Charter reflect international law, they 'derive their force ultimately from the fundamental moral principle of humanity'.[25]

Such an approach raises challenging questions regarding whether the humanitarian imperative can or should trump international law. Does human suffering allow states to intervene in the domestic affairs of another country? If yes, what is the level of harm required before such an intervention is warranted; and can such an intervention ever entail the use of military force? As the Independent International Commission on Kosovo famously concluded, the NATO military intervention in Kosovo in 1999, undertaken ostensibly for humanitarian purposes, was 'illegal, yet

[23] *Proclamation of the Fundamental Principles of the Red Cross*, Resolution VIII, XXth International Conference of the Red Cross, Vienna, 2–9 October 1965. See 'Resolutions Adopted by the XXth International Conference of the Red Cross' (November 1965) 56 *International Review of the Red Cross* 573.

[24] Art 2, *Principles and Rules for Red Cross Disaster Relief*, Resolution XXIV, XXIst International Conference of the Red Cross, Istanbul, 6–13 September 1969. The Principles and Rules have subsequently been amended on five occasions, most recently in 1996. See 'Resolutions of the 26th International Conference' (January–February 1996) 310 *International Review of the Red Cross* 72.

[25] The Sphere Project, *Humanitarian Charter and Minimum Standards in Humanitarian Response* 3rd edn, April 2011, 20. First published in 2000 by a coalition of non-governmental humanitarian agencies, and subsequently updated twice, the *Sphere Handbook* provides a comprehensive set of standards and indicators for the provision of humanitarian assistance. The Humanitarian Charter centres on three overarching principles: the right to life with dignity; the right to receive humanitarian assistance; and the right to protection and security.

legitimate'.[26] As discussed further in chapter four, the appropriate balance between the potentially competing principles of state sovereignty and humanitarianism remains elusive. Following the Kosovo intervention, the G77 Group of States stressed that humanitarian assistance should be provided 'in full respect of the sovereignty, territorial integrity, and political independence of host countries, and should be initiated in response to a request or with the approval of these States'.[27] Conversely, other states have explicitly adopted the language of the humanitarian imperative. For example, the Swedish government's Humanitarian Aid Policy states: 'The goal of the government's policy is to help to save lives, alleviate suffering and maintain human dignity for the benefit of people in need who are, or are at risk of becoming, affected by armed conflicts, natural disasters or other disaster situations.'[28]

The concept of a humanitarian imperative has also attracted criticism on the basis that it focuses on the duty of humanitarian organisations rather than the rights of those affected.[29] Arguing against the concept, Hugo Slim maintains that humanitarian organisations have attempted to provide an imperative gloss to the principle of humanity as a means of establishing a moral absolute, thereby presenting humanitarianism as 'a non-negotiable, almost genetic and biological force'.[30] Elsewhere, Slim has argued that humanitarianism as a whole has a decidedly Kantian influence, comparing the humanitarian imperative with Kant's categorical imperative. As Slim notes, if one brings this argument into the practical world of humanitarian action, a Kantian humanitarian sees humanitarian action as an end in itself, so would object to the suspension of a therapeutic feeding programme for political reasons (such as the human rights record of the affected state's government), as opposed to suspension for purely needs-based reasons.[31] As discussed in more depth in chapter three, this

[26] Independent International Commission on Kosovo, *The Kosovo Report* (Oxford University Press, 2000) 186. For a comprehensive review of the arguments surrounding the illegality of the military intervention, see N Rodley and B Çali, 'Kosovo Revisited: Humanitarian Intervention on the Fault Lines of International Law' (2007) 7(2) *Human Rights Law Review* 275.

[27] *Declaration of the South Summit*, Group of 77 South Summit, Havana, Cuba, 10–14 April 2000, para 54.

[28] Swedish Ministry of Foreign Affairs, *The Government's Humanitarian Aid Policy*, Government Communication 2004/05:52 (16 December 2004) 5.

[29] Slim, 'Relief Agencies', above n 3.

[30] ibid, 346.

[31] For discussion of the Kantian nature of humanitarian obligations, see H Slim, 'Claiming a Humanitarian Imperative: NGOs and the Cultivation of Humanitarian Duty', paper presented at the Seventh Annual Conference of Webster University on *Humanitarian Values for the Twenty-First Century*, Geneva, 21–22 February 2002, 4–5. For an analogous discussion of international human rights law and Kant's categorical imperative, see P Capps, *Human Dignity and the Foundations of International Law* (Hart Publishing, 2010) 115–117.

tension between needs-based and rights-based approaches to humanitarian activities continues to influence and divide opinion on which is the most effective approach to alleviate suffering in a crisis setting.[32]

It is precisely because the humanitarian imperative is a moral or ethical obligation, not a legal obligation on states or humanitarian agencies, that each actor is able to interpret the concept based on their own institutional or philosophical stance. From a transnational legal perspective, such interpretations are part and parcel of the on-going dialogue between interested parties regarding the applicable international norms.[33] The former Deputy Director-General of the ICRC has described the humanitarian imperative as 'an obligation to provide unconditional assistance, wherever and whenever it is needed',[34] although noting that the primary responsibility rests with the affected state. Meanwhile, Jacqui Tong of Médecins Sans Frontières has argued that the humanitarian imperative is to 'alleviate the suffering of a vulnerable population out of respect for human dignity'.[35] Of note, UNICEF has described the humanitarian imperative in the following terms:

> Human suffering must be addressed wherever it is found, with particular attention to the most vulnerable in the population, such as children, women, the displaced and the elderly. The dignity and rights of all those in need of humanitarian assistance must be respected and protected. The humanitarian imperative implies a right to receive humanitarian assistance and a right to offer it.[36]

Considering UNICEF's mandate as one of the primary protection agencies of the UN, such high-level acknowledgement that the humanitarian imperative entails human rights obligations for states prompts yet more questions regarding the need to distinguish between moral, ethical and legal obligations. As set out in Part II, there are a broad range of binding and non-binding sources for states and humanitarian agencies to rely upon in operationalising the humanitarian imperative. One could therefore argue that international law is currently in the process of crystallising a binding legal right to humanitarian assistance in all humanitarian crises. Conversely, such transnational interactions and interpretations may simply reinforce the non-binding moral or ethical responsibilities of

[32] See ch 3, Section II. See also D Curtis, *Politics and Humanitarian Aid: Debates, Dilemmas and Dissension*, Humanitarian Policy Group Report 10, Overseas Development Institute, April 2001.

[33] H Koh, 'Transnational Legal Process' (1996) 75 *Nebraska Law Review* 181.

[34] B Schweizer, 'Moral Dilemmas for Humanitarianism in the Era of "Humanitarian" Military Interventions' (September 2004) 86(855) *International Review of the Red Cross* 547, 548–49.

[35] J Tong, 'Questionable Accountability: MSF and Sphere in 2003' (2004) 28(2) *Disasters* 176, 180.

[36] *UNICEF's Humanitarian Principles*, July 2003 www.unicef.org/pathtraining/Documents/Session%204%20Humanitarian%20Principles/Participant%20Manual/4.2%20UNICEF%20Humanitarian%20Principles.doc.

humanitarian actors rather than their legal obligations. Considering the broad range of actors engaged in humanitarian activities during armed conflicts, displacement and disasters, and the multitude of binding and non-binding normative sources, it is therefore pertinent to consider how these various strands interlink and overlap, and any potential gaps in protection which may arise.

C. Humanitarian Principles: Humanity, Neutrality and Impartiality

Unlike more recent texts, the 1949 Geneva Conventions do not explicitly include operative articles on the humanitarian principles that underpin the provision of material assistance and protection activities to those in need. However, the requirement in the Conventions for relief to be distributed by neutral powers and impartial humanitarian bodies without distinction clearly established key humanitarian principles in international law.[37] Yet despite attempts by the League of Nations to codify international law relating to humanitarian responses to natural and human-made disasters in the 1920s,[38] it was not until the late 1970s that the legal, conceptual and operational similarities between the provision of international relief in times of war and in times of disaster were placed back on the UN agenda.[39] Relying on the 1977 ECOSOC Resolution on Measures to Expedite International Relief,[40] which called on the UN Disaster Relief Office (UNDRO) to 'promot[e] measures designed to remove obstacles and to expedite international relief assistance', the UN commenced work on a framework for humanitarian activities in disaster settings, commensurate to the framework established by the Geneva Conventions for relief in times of armed conflict.[41] Key to the plan was the inclusion of a set of humanitarian principles to ensure that assistance was provided in a manner that respected the intended beneficiaries, while simultaneously protecting and facilitating the work of humanitarian agencies and the affected state's local and national authorities.

[37] See, eg, Art 47 (Inviolability of rights), 59 (Collective relief) and 61 (Distribution), Geneva Convention IV Relative to the Protection of Civilian Persons in Times of War (adopted 12 August 1949, entered into force 21 October 1950) 75 UNTS 287 (GCIV).

[38] See Section II.B below.

[39] For two important academic examinations of the international structures for humanitarian assistance at this time, see: P MacAlister-Smith, *International Humanitarian Assistance: Disaster Relief Actions in International Law and Organization* (Martinus Nijhoff, 1985); R Kent, *Anatomy of Disaster Relief: The International Network in Action* (Pinter, 1987).

[40] *Measures to Expedite International Relief*, ECOSOC Res 2102 (LXIII) of 3 August 1977.

[41] R Kent, 'Reflecting upon a Decade of Disasters: The Evolving Response of the International Community' (Autumn 1983) 59(4) *International Affairs* 693. See also IFRC, *Law and Legal Issues in International Disaster Response: A Desk Study* (2007) 62.

Although the resultant 1982 UNITAR Model Rules for Disaster Relief Operations[42] and 1984 draft UN Convention on Expediting the Delivery of Emergency Assistance[43] were ultimately unsuccessful in codifying an international humanitarian law for disasters, they highlighted the need for a broader understanding of the scenarios, beyond armed conflicts, which should be viewed as humanitarian crises requiring international assistance. This period can therefore be seen as the modern starting point for a body of resolutions, guidelines and minimum standards aimed at improving the effectiveness and coordination of international humanitarian response operations in armed conflicts and disasters, and related population displacement.[44] Indeed, one can argue that these events foresaw the birth of 'International Disaster Law' as a distinct body of law in its own right, to complement the existing international law regimes covering armed conflicts and refugee protection. Following the failure of the 1984 draft UN Convention, and the new world order brought about with the end of the Cold War, a non-binding but no less influential attempt to gain international agreement on the principles underlying humanitarian activities took place in the UN General Assembly.

The resulting UNGA Resolution 46/182 of 1991 on 'Strengthening of the coordination of humanitarian emergency assistance of the United Nations' contained not just technical improvements for running UN humanitarian operations but a set of Guiding Principles for humanitarian activities in disasters and other emergencies such as mass displacement and refugee crises.[45] Mindful of the criticisms of NGOs at the purely technical approach of the draft 1984 Convention,[46] Resolution 46/182 elaborated a series of Guiding Principles covering the rationale and modalities for the provision of humanitarian assistance by UN agencies, while also revising and strengthening the UN system for disaster response coordination and funding of emergency appeals. The first three Guiding Principles state:

1. Humanitarian assistance is of cardinal importance for the victims of natural disasters and other emergencies.

[42] M el Baradei, *Model Rules for Disaster Relief Operations*, Policy and Efficacy Studies No 8, UN Institute for Training and Research (UNITAR), 1982.

[43] Draft Convention on Expediting the Delivery of Emergency Assistance, A/39/267/Add.2—E/1984/96/Add.2, 18 June 1984.

[44] For further discussion, see D Cubie, 'An Analysis of Soft Law Applicable to Humanitarian Assistance: Relative Normativity in Action?' (2011) 2 *Journal of International Humanitarian Legal Studies* 177, 191–200.

[45] *Strengthening of the Coordination of Humanitarian Emergency Assistance of the United Nations*, UNGA Res 46/182, 19 December 1991, Annex, Guiding Principle 2. See generally E Tsui, *Analysis of Normative Developments in Humanitarian Resolutions since the Adoption of 46/182*, independent review for UNOCHA (2009) http://saarc-sadkn.org/downloads/analysis.pdf.

[46] Y Beigbeder, *The Role and Status of International Humanitarian Volunteers and Organizations: The Right and Duty to Humanitarian Assistance* (Martinus Nijhoff, 1991) 375–77.

2. Humanitarian assistance must be provided in accordance with the principles of humanity, neutrality and impartiality.
3. The sovereignty, territorial integrity and national unity of States must be fully respected in accordance with the Charter of the United Nations. In this context, humanitarian assistance should be provided with the consent of the affected country and in principle on the basis of an appeal by the affected country.

Resolution 46/182 therefore presented a clear blueprint for understanding the conceptual and practical boundaries for the provision of humanitarian assistance. Yet its primary focus was on operational humanitarian responses by the UN and its specialised agencies, rather than enunciating the rights of individuals affected. Considering that well-established commentators such as Peter MacAlister-Smith had already highlighted the human rights implications of disasters, this was a conscious decision by states to avoid rights-based language in regard to humanitarian operations.[47] Nevertheless, the Guiding Principles represented an advancement of the international framework for humanitarian responses by recognising the need to balance fundamental principles of humanitarian action with practical operational rules, and by including measures covering the entire humanitarian cycle of pre-emergency preventative and risk reduction measures, emergency relief operations, post-emergency recovery and reconstruction, and follow-on developmental activities.[48] Reflecting concerns of states regarding potentially unregulated actions by other states and humanitarian agencies on their territory, state sovereignty was reaffirmed in the Guiding Principles by highlighting a state's primary responsibility to provide assistance to persons on their territory alongside the requirement for third parties to obtain consent from the affected country for their humanitarian activities.

Of key importance, the Resolution affirmed in unambiguous terms that humanitarian assistance must be provided in accordance with the principles of humanity, neutrality and impartiality. Although the Resolution did not elaborate these principles, the UN Office for the Co-ordination of Humanitarian Affairs (UNOCHA) has defined them as:

— ***Humanity:*** Human suffering must be addressed wherever it is found, with particular attention to the most vulnerable populations such as children, women, and the elderly. The dignity and rights of all victims must be respected and protected.
— ***Neutrality:*** Humanitarian actions must be provided without engaging in hostilities or taking sides in controversies of a political, religious or ideological nature.

[47] P MacAlister-Smith, 'Human Rights and Disaster Relief' (1980) 5 *Holdsworth Law Review* 173; MacAlister-Smith, above n 39, 63–69.

[48] For discussion of the concept of a cycle of protection, see ch 3, Section II.A.

— ***Impartiality:*** Humanitarian actions must be carried out on the basis of need alone, giving priority to the most urgent cases of distress and making no distinctions on the basis of nationality, race, gender, religious belief, class or political opinions.[49]

Of course, that is not to say that these humanitarian principles are uncontested.[50] A defining moment in the recent history of humanitarianism and humanitarian organisations occurred in 1971 when Bernard Kouchner left the Red Cross Movement following the Biafra conflict to form Médecins Sans Frontières (MSF). In the face of alleged genocide, Kouchner believed that by remaining neutral the ICRC was repeating its mistakes of the Second World War when it withheld information regarding the Nazi concentration camps.[51] MSF therefore developed the concept of 'active impartiality' whereby the organisation is impartial as regards people (so acts in a non-discriminatory manner) but is partial to their actions. In other words, MSF will speak out and publicly condemn actors they believe are breaching international humanitarian or human rights law.[52] The so-called 'French doctors' or '*sans Frontières* movement' remains a distinct group within humanitarian actors,[53] and highlights the multiplicity of approaches taken by different organisations who may be acting out of religious beliefs, human rights-based principles, or more traditional views of 'charity'.[54]

[49] See: *Guiding Principles for Public-Private Collaboration for Humanitarian Action*, prepared by the World Economic Forum and UNOCHA, December 2007, 1; *UNOCHA on Message: Humanitarian Principles*, April 2010 https://docs.unocha.org/sites/dms/Documents/OOM_HumPrinciple_English.pdf. For discussion of these principles from the Red Cross perspective, see ICRC, *The Fundamental Principles of the Red Cross and Red Crescent* (1996), Ref: 0513, 4–5.

[50] For critical analysis of the humanitarian principles, see generally: Slim, 'Relief Agencies', above n 3; N Leader, 'The Politics of Principle: The Principles of Humanitarian Action in Practice', Overseas Development Institute, Humanitarian Policy Group Report No. 2 (March 2000); Kennedy, *Dark Sides of Virtue*, above n 4; Barnett and Weiss, *Humanitarianism in Question* above n 1; S Collinson and S Elhawary, 'Humanitarian Space: A Review of Trends and Issues', Overseas Development Institute, Humanitarian Policy Group Report No. 32, April 2012.

[51] Rieff argues that the fact it was subsequently confirmed that no genocide took place in Biafra raised questions as to the wisdom of the stance taken by Kouchner and other NGOs such as Oxfam. Rieff, *Bed for the Night*, above n 8, 81–86.

[52] For discussion of various conceptions of impartiality, see Slim, 'Relief Agencies', above n 3, 348–49.

[53] As French Foreign Minister during the 2008 Cyclone Nargis disaster, Kouchner was one of the strongest proponents of the applicability of the Responsibility to Protect doctrine in natural disasters, arguing that governmental inaction could amount to a crime against humanity. See: J Wong, 'Reconstructing the Responsibility to Protect in the Wake of Cyclones and Separatism' (2009–2010) 84(2) *Tulane Law Review* 219, 221, 244–45; T Jackson, 'Bullets for Beans: Humanitarian Intervention and the Responsibility to Protect in Natural Disasters' (2010) 59 *Naval Law Review* 1, 2.

[54] For a description of the different traditions and approaches of humanitarian agencies, see Tong, 'Questionable Accountability', above n 35. For an historical account of the changing views of charity and humanitarianism, see Rieff, *Bed for the Night*, above n 8, 57–89.

Laura Hammond has argued that humanitarian aid workers are at risk of being targeted in insecure environments precisely because their projected image as neutral and impartial actors can be exploited by groups that wish to garner attention to their cause.[55] The attack on the UN compound in Baghdad which killed UN High Commissioner for Human Rights Sérgio Vieira de Mello in 2003,[56] or the more recent beheadings of Western journalists and humanitarian workers by the so-called Islamic State, tragically highlight the deliberate targeting of humanitarian staff which can occur when such actors are perceived as being partial. Indeed, the Aid Worker Security Database, which contains records of major incidences of violence against aid workers, documents over 3,900 incidents of serious violence against aid workers since 1997 including the deaths of 1,494 humanitarian personnel.[57]

Hammond argues that the principles of humanity, neutrality and impartiality can create a false sense of security for humanitarian aid workers in insecure environments, and proposes that transparency, accountability and responsiveness to local needs should supplement the overarching humanitarian principles. In a similar fashion, Mary Anderson has noted that while organisations may work on the basis of neutrality, the provision of humanitarian assistance is not a neutral activity. Anderson points out that humanitarian assistance can free up state resources such as food and medical supplies for military purposes, thereby prolonging conflicts. Alternatively, assistance can (intentionally or otherwise) benefit one group within a community to the detriment of others, for example male heads of household rather than females, or one religious or ethnic community over another.[58] Drawing on the Rwandese genocide and subsequent conflict in the former Zaire in the 1990s, Sarah Kenyon Lischer has argued that humanitarian aid in refugee crises can actually exacerbate conflicts by feeding militants, sustaining and protecting the militants' supporters, contributing to the war economy, and by providing legitimacy to combatants.[59] Lischer stresses that: 'Despite the desire for neutrality, it is virtually impossible for material assistance to have a neutral effect in a conflict situation.'[60] The potential risk that humanitarian actors unintentionally become forces of destruction, rather than salvation, is therefore clear.

[55] L Hammond, 'The Power of Holding Humanitarianism Hostage and the Myth of Protective Principles', in Barnett and Weiss, *Humanitarianism in Question*, above n 1, 177.

[56] See generally S Power, *Chasing the Flame: Sergio Vieira de Mello and the Fight to Save the World* (Allen Lane, 2008).

[57] The Aid Worker Security Database https://aidworkersecurity.org/incidents.

[58] See M Anderson, *Do No Harm: How Aid Can Support Peace—or War* (Lynne Rienner Publishers, 1999) 37–54.

[59] SK Lischer, 'Collateral Damage: Humanitarian Assistance as a Cause of Conflict' (Summer 2003) 28(1) *International Security* 79, 82.

[60] ibid, 109.

Nevertheless, the applicability of fundamental humanitarian principles in armed conflicts and disasters, as confirmed by Resolution 46/182, has traditionally been widely accepted in both law and practice. The International Court of Justice (ICJ) noted in the Nicaragua case that '[t]here can be no doubt that the provision of strictly humanitarian aid to persons or forces in another country … cannot be regarded as unlawful intervention, or as in any other way contrary to international law'.[61] The Court proceeded to recall that if the provision of humanitarian assistance is to escape condemnation as internal intervention in another state, it must be limited to 'the purposes hallowed in the practice of the Red Cross, namely "to prevent and alleviate human suffering", and "to protect life and health and to ensure respect for the human being"'. Above all, humanitarian assistance must be given without discrimination to all in need.[62] Humanitarian agencies have likewise stressed a firm commitment to these humanitarian principles, with the influential, albeit non-binding, *Sphere Handbook*'s Humanitarian Charter reaffirming the humanitarian imperative and requirement to act in accordance with the principles of humanity and impartiality. The Charter notes: '[b]y this we mean … that all possible steps should be taken to prevent or alleviate human suffering arising out of conflict or calamity, and that civilians so affected have a right to protection and assistance.'[63] At a regional level, the African Union's 2009 Convention for the Protection and Assistance of Internally Displaced Persons in Africa created binding obligations on signatory states to 'respect and ensure respect for the principles of humanity and human dignity of internally displaced persons'.[64] The Convention creates both horizontal obligations between signatory parties for co-operation in protecting and assisting IDPs, as well as vertical obligations between the state and displaced individuals on their territory.[65]

Likewise, following an extensive examination of the legal implications of humanitarian principles,[66] the International Law Commission (ILC) draft articles on the protection of persons in the event of disasters

[61] Military and Paramilitary Activities in and against Nicaragua (*Nicaragua v United States of America*), Merits, Judgment of 27 June 1986, ICJ Reports 1986, 14, para 242.

[62] ibid, para 243.

[63] *Sphere Handbook*, above n 25, 16.

[64] Art 3(1)(c), African Union, *Convention for the Protection and Assistance of Internally Displaced Persons in Africa* ('Kampala Convention') (adopted 22 October 2009, entered into force 6 December 2012).

[65] See generally: S Ojeda, 'The Kampala Convention on Internally Displaced Persons: Some International Humanitarian Law Aspects' (2010) 29(3) *Refugee Survey Quarterly* 58; F Giustiniani, 'New Hopes and Challenges for the Protection of IDPs in Africa: The Kampala Convention for the Protection and Assistance of Internally Displaced Persons in Africa' (2010–2011) 39(2) *Denver Journal of International Law and Policy* 347.

[66] E Valencia-Ospina, *Third Report on the Protection of Persons in the Event of Disasters* (31 March 2010) A/CN.4/629, paras 14–62.

explicitly include the principles of humanity, neutrality and impartiality, with the Commission noting that these are 'core principles recognised as foundational to humanitarian assistance'.[67] Although the ILC did not find it necessary to determine whether they were currently part of general international law, the Commentaries stress that '[t]he principle of humanity stands as the cornerstone of the protection of persons in international law'.[68] Furthermore, the Commission highlighted that humanity is an element of both international humanitarian law and international human rights law, while also informing the development of international disaster laws. Considering the ILC's role in the progressive development of international law, one can argue that the Commission's reaffirmation of the fundamental status of these humanitarian principles may promote their crystallisation as general rules of customary international law.[69]

Like the ICJ, the ILC was explicitly influenced by the role that humanity plays as the foundation for actions undertaken by the Red Cross Movement to alleviate suffering. Indeed, as argued by the ICRC, the principle of humanity is neither too vague nor general to form the basis of the Red Cross Movement's work as 'the words used …—to prevent, to alleviate, to protect, to ensure respect—require very concrete efforts'.[70] The concrete nature of the principle of humanity is evidenced by the existence of the international offence of crimes against humanity.[71] Reflecting revulsion at the atrocities committed against civilians during the Second World War, and the limitation of war crimes to actions that specifically took place in the context of armed conflicts, the need for an additional basis of individual criminal responsibility was clear.[72] Drawing on the older tradition of the 'law of humanity' during war, the original iteration of crimes against humanity in the Nuremberg Charter of the International Military Tribunal contained an express link to events taking place during war.[73] This link was retained in the Statute of the International Criminal Tribunal for the

[67] For the final text of the preamble, draft articles and commentaries adopted by the ILC, see Official Records of the General Assembly, Seventy-first Session, *Supplement No 10* (A/71/10), Chapter IV: Protection of Persons in the Event of Disasters (2016).

[68] For text of the Commentary to draft Art 6, see ibid, p 33.

[69] See generally: R Jennings, 'Recent Developments in the International Law Commission: Its Relation to the Sources of International Law' (1964) 13 *International and Comparative Law Quarterly* 385; A Lowe, 'Do General Rules of International Law Exist?' (1983) 9 *Review of International Studies* 207. For discussion of the ILC draft articles, see ch 8, Section III.A.

[70] ICRC, *Fundamental Principles*, above n 49, 3. For discussion of the universality of the concept of humanity, see R Coupland, 'Humanity: What is it and How does it Influence International Law?' (December 2001) 83(844) *International Review of the Red Cross* 969.

[71] Art 7 Rome Statute of the International Criminal Court (adopted 17 July 1998, entered into force 1 July 2002) 2187 UNTS 3.

[72] MC Bassiouni, *Crimes Against Humanity: Historical Evolution and Contemporary Application* (Cambridge University Press, 2011) 111–12.

[73] ibid, 96–97.

former Yugoslavia, albeit modified to recognise crimes against humanity in both international and non-international armed conflicts.[74] However, the Statute of the International Criminal Tribunal for Rwanda removed the express nexus to events occurring during armed conflicts, effectively redefining crimes against humanity as specified acts committed 'as part of a widespread or systematic attack against any civilian population on national, political, ethnic, racial or religious grounds'.[75] As discussed further in chapter seven, crimes against humanity (whether committed in times of war or peace) now form a central plank of the Rome Statute of the International Criminal Court.[76] Having discussed the principles of humanity, neutrality and impartiality that motivate humanitarian actors in their work, the following section analyses the concept of humanitarian action itself.

II. THE CONCEPT OF HUMANITARIAN ACTION

> The rise of global humanitarian action is one of humanity's greatest moral achievements. Today our goal is a world where every woman, man and child in need can receive … assistance and protection from the impacts of disaster, conflict, displacement, hunger or disease. This world is now within our grasp. Together we can make this vision a reality.
>
> Ban Ki-moon, 2016[77]

Terminology within the sphere of humanitarian operations often serves to confuse, rather than clarify, the specific obligations that exist or activities to be undertaken. The divergent inter-disciplinary understandings of what 'humanitarianism' means, as well as the multitude of state and non-state actors who engage in humanitarian activities, results in a veritable Tower of Babel. From the perspective of a lawyer, the lack of precision over terminology can be frustrating. Moreover, a perception may emerge that a *faux* consensus exists—for example, regarding the need to undertake 'protection activities' without a clear understanding of what such activities may entail. Even within the legal sphere, a range of terms and definitions (in both legal instruments and non-binding policy and guidance

[74] Art 5, UNSC, Statute of the International Criminal Tribunal for the Former Yugoslavia (as amended), 25 May 1993.

[75] Art 3, UNSC, Statute of the International Criminal Tribunal for Rwanda (as amended), 8 November 1994.

[76] See generally R Clark, 'History of Efforts to Codify Crimes Against Humanity: From the Charter of Nuremberg to the Statute of Rome' in LN Sadat (ed), *Forging a Convention for Crimes Against Humanity* (Cambridge University Press, 2011).

[77] UNSG, 'Strengths of All Humanitarian Actors Must Be Utilized, Secretary-General Says, at Norway Forum on Role of Civil Society', Press Release, SG/SM/16912-IHA/1371 (6 July 2015).

documents) have been advanced addressing the inter-related concepts of 'humanitarian assistance' and 'the protection of persons'. Therefore, it is beneficial to examine some of the sources of these definitions and understandings at this stage, in advance of more detailed discussion of the concept of protection in chapter three.

A. Defining 'Humanitarian Assistance'

Traditionally, 'humanitarian assistance' was viewed primarily as emergency life-saving material supplies, and was couched in the interchangeable terminology of charity, aid, relief, assistance or support. UNGA Resolution 46/182 epitomised such an approach by calling on states to facilitate the work of humanitarian agencies, in particular regarding the supply of food, medicine, shelter and healthcare.[78] Geneva Convention IV on the protection of civilians[79] and Additional Protocols I[80] and II[81] likewise provide a range of binding obligations on states to provide material assistance to certain categories of people not taking a direct part in hostilities during armed conflicts. However, with the increasing recognition of the different stages of humanitarian crises (namely the need for pre-, during, and post-emergency assistance), alongside an expanded understanding of the role of humanitarian agencies, a broader conception of 'humanitarian action' has gained traction.[82] Although detailed technical guidance is provided by documents such as the *Sphere Handbook*'s Minimum Standards in Humanitarian Response,[83] there is no universal legal definition of either humanitarian assistance or humanitarian action. Considering the variety of scenarios across the world which may engender a humanitarian crisis, it is important not to be overly prescriptive. Indeed, Hugo Slim has attacked the commodification of humanitarianism and its subsequent reduction to basic packages of material help as a 'serious heresy which undermines wider humanitarian values'.[84] Lawyers often

[78] UNGA, Res 46/182, above n 45, Annex, Principle 6.

[79] Geneva Convention IV, above n 37.

[80] Protocol Additional to the Geneva Conventions of 12 August 1949, and relating to the Protection of Victims of International Armed Conflicts (adopted 8 June 1977, entered into force 7 December 1978) 1125 UNTS 3 (API).

[81] Protocol II Additional to the Geneva Conventions of 12 August 1949 and relating to the Protection of Victims of Non-International Armed Conflicts (adopted 8 June 1977, entered into force 7 December 1978) 1125 UNTS 609 (APII).

[82] Although it should be noted that the phrase 'humanitarian assistance' is still commonly used in official documents, by the media and to a lesser extent within humanitarian organisations.

[83] *Sphere Handbook*, above n 25. The Minimum Standards contain sector-specific indicators covering: water supply and sanitation; food security and nutrition; shelter and non-food items; and health.

[84] Slim, 'Relief Agencies', above n 3, 345.

search for legal definitions as a means of pinning down specific rights and obligations. Conversely, practitioners may seek to maintain a broad understanding of what constitutes 'humanitarian action' (whether they use this phrase or not) to ensure flexibility in their response, taking into consideration cultural or regional specificities for the appropriate protection and assistance activities to be undertaken.

Reflecting the competing requirements of certainty and flexibility, a variety of legal definitions and policy approaches to humanitarian action and assistance can be identified. In the Nicaragua case, the ICJ examined the principles of humanitarian assistance in the context of sovereignty and non-intervention, but did not examine its substantive content beyond dryly noting the vague and circular definition contained in US legislation, namely: '"humanitarian assistance" means the provision of food, clothing, medicine, and other humanitarian assistance, and it does not include the provision of weapons, weapons systems, ammunition, or other equipment, vehicles, or material which can be used to inflict serious bodily harm or death.'[85] Two binding universal legal texts of specific relevance to humanitarian responses to disasters, namely the Tampere Convention on the Provision of Telecommunication Resources for Disaster Mitigation and Relief Operations and the Framework Convention on Civil Defence Assistance, likewise provide limited guidance in determining the limits of what constitutes humanitarian activities. The Tampere Convention does not define 'assistance' but clarifies that 'relief operations' encompass 'those activities designed to reduce loss of life, human suffering and damage to property and/or the environment caused by a disaster'.[86] Meanwhile, reflecting the specific aims and objectives of civil defence organisations,[87] the Framework Convention states:

> 'Assistance' means any action undertaken by the Civil Defence Service of a State for the benefit of another State, with the objective of preventing, or mitigating the consequences of disasters. This includes all duties assigned to the Civil Defence Service of the Parties and accepted by the Beneficiary Parties, potentially with the assistance of any other partner.[88]

[85] *Nicaragua v USA*, above n 61, para 97.

[86] Art 1(12), *Tampere Convention on the Provision of Telecommunication Resources for Disaster Mitigation and Relief Operations* (adopted 18 June 1998, entered into force 8 January 2005) 2296 UNTS 5.

[87] As set out in Art 61(a) API: '"Civil defence" means the performance of … humanitarian tasks intended to protect the civilian population against the dangers, and to help it to recover from the immediate effects, of hostilities or disasters and also to provide the conditions necessary for its survival.' Civil defence organisations are generally directly or indirectly affiliated with national governmental structures.

[88] Art 1(d), *Framework Convention on Civil Defence Assistance, International Civil Defence Association* (adopted 22 May 2000, entered into force 23 September 2001) 2172 UNTS 213.

The European Consensus on Humanitarian Aid[89] focuses on the principles of Good Humanitarian Donorship, including coordination and accountability, rather than providing a definition of 'aid'. In a similar vein, the current text of the ILC draft articles on the protection of persons in the event of disasters defines 'international cooperation' as including: 'humanitarian assistance, coordination of international relief actions and communications, and making available relief personnel, equipment and goods, and scientific, medical and technical resources'.[90] Meanwhile, the International Institute of Humanitarian Law's non-binding Guiding Principles on a Right to Humanitarian Assistance provide a more expansive definition:

> Humanitarian assistance may consist of any material indispensable to the survival of victims, such as foodstuffs, water, medication, medical supplies and equipment, minimum shelter, clothing; of services, such as medical services, tracing services, religious and spiritual assistance, as well as civil defence, in conformity with the tasks defined in international humanitarian law.[91]

In a similar manner, as a restatement of international law, the UN Guiding Principles on Internal Displacement enumerate the basic minimum that competent authorities must provide to internally displaced persons as: a) essential food and potable water; b) basic shelter and housing; c) appropriate clothing; and d) essential medical services and sanitation.[92] Finally, the 2003 Bruges Resolution of the Institute of International Law defines humanitarian assistance as: 'all acts, activities and the human and material resources for the provision of goods and services of an exclusively humanitarian character, indispensable for the survival and fulfilment of the essential needs of victims.'[93]

Although such definitions provide guidance on the types of material assistance and services during armed conflicts, displacement and disasters that should be considered as humanitarian, the expanding concept of humanitarian action and increased awareness of the inter-connections between 'humanitarian' activities and longer-term developmental needs

[89] Joint Statement by the Council and the Representatives of the Governments of the Member States meeting within the Council, the European Parliament and the European Commission, *The European Consensus on Humanitarian Aid*, OJ C25, 30 January 2008, 1. For analysis, see: Caritas Europa, *Bridging the Gap Between Policy and Practice: The European Consensus on Humanitarian Aid and Humanitarian Principles* (October 2011).

[90] For the current text of draft Art 8, see Official Records of the General Assembly, A/71/10, above n 67.

[91] *Guiding Principles on the Right to Humanitarian Assistance*, International Institute of Humanitarian Law (IIHL), San Remo, Italy, April 1993, Principle 9.

[92] UN Commission on Human Rights, *The Guiding Principles on Internal Displacement* (1998) E/CN.4/1998/53/Add.2, Principle 18(2).

[93] Art I(1) Resolution on Humanitarian Assistance, Institute of International Law, Bruges Session (September 2003).

means that humanitarian agencies often stress a broad definition of 'humanitarian assistance' encompassing both pre-emergency risk reduction and preventative measures, and post-emergency recovery and reconstruction.[94] Rather than using a temporal distinction as to the types of activities encompassed by humanitarian assistance, UNOCHA focuses on the intended beneficiaries of assistance, noting that 'assistance may be divided into three categories—direct assistance, indirect assistance and infrastructure support—which have diminishing degrees of contact with the affected population'.[95] Direct assistance covers the actual distribution of goods and services; while indirect assistance covers support activities such as the transportation of supplies and personnel. Finally, infrastructure support covers activities such as road repairs or power generation which facilitate humanitarian activities but also benefit the broader population.[96]

Therefore, from an operational perspective, both governmental and non-governmental humanitarian agencies use the concept of 'humanitarian action' to encompass a broad range of activities at all stages of emergency prevention, mitigation and response, not simply material assistance but all actions taken to protect and respect people in humanitarian crises. The Guidelines on Good Humanitarian Donorship developed by major donor countries and the UN defines the objectives of humanitarian action as: 'to save lives, alleviate suffering and maintain human dignity during and in the aftermath of man-made crises and natural disasters, as well as to prevent and strengthen preparedness for the occurrence of such situations.'[97] The Guidelines highlight that humanitarian action includes: 'the protection of civilians and those no longer taking part in hostilities, and the provision of food, water and sanitation, shelter, health services and other items of assistance, undertaken for the benefit of affected people and to facilitate the return to normal lives and livelihoods.'[98]

[94] As noted in the 2010 *HAP Standard in Accountability and Quality Management*: 'The work of many organisations is not limited to providing humanitarian relief, but includes all types of assistance to people affected by or prone to disasters, conflict, poverty or other crises. The dividing line between humanitarian and development assistance is fluid. For example, activities such as disaster risk reduction include both types of assistance and, over time, an organisation may provide both disaster relief and development aid to the same group of people', 2.

[95] UNOCHA, *Glossary of Humanitarian Terms in relation to the Protection of Civilians in Armed Conflict*, UN Office for the Coordination of Humanitarian Affairs, Policy Development and Studies Branch (2003) 13.

[96] See also HRC, *Final research-based report of the Human Rights Council Advisory Committee on best practices and main challenges in the promotion and protection of human rights in post-disaster and post-conflict situations*, 28th Session of the HRC (10 February 2015) A/HRC/28/76, para 25.

[97] Art 1, *Principles and Good Practice of Humanitarian Donorship*, as endorsed in Stockholm, 17 June 2003 at the International Meeting on Good Humanitarian Donorship.

[98] ibid, Art 3.

B. The Protection of Persons

Alongside the traditional view of humanitarian assistance as packages of material provisions in the form of food, medical care and shelter, the 'protection of persons' plays a fundamental role in several inter-related branches of international law: including the protection of refugees, human rights protection, and the concept of protected groups in the law of armed conflict.[99] The ICRC and the UN Inter-Agency Standing Committee's joint definition of 'protection' is: '[A]ll activities aimed at ensuring full respect for the rights of the individual in accordance with the letter and the spirit of the relevant bodies of law, i.e. human rights law, international humanitarian law, and refugee law';[100] and it is no coincidence that the current work of the International Law Commission is entitled the 'protection of persons in the event of disasters'. The Swedish government's Humanitarian Aid Policy provides an excellent example of the distinctions and interconnections between humanitarian protection and material assistance activities:

> Humanitarian aid is provided in two closely related forms: material aid and protection. Material aid may be given above all in the form of food, nutritional supplements, shelter, water, sanitary facilities, healthcare and other health services, and in some cases education, agricultural support and other not immediately lifesaving measures. Protection includes measures designed to ensure respect for the rights of people in need, in particular the right to physical safety and dignity. Related measures include calling attention to the obligations of armed groups, registration of the status of refugees or internally displaced persons and education about rights and obligations under international law. In many cases, individual humanitarian actions comprise both material aid and protection, since material aid protects the rights of vulnerable persons and protective measures improve the individual's chances of receiving material aid. The crucial criterion for humanitarian action is the individual's need of material aid or protection, or both.[101]

The Swiss government has likewise stressed the interconnections between material assistance and the protection of persons, arguing that: 'Shortage or lack of essentials such as food, water or healthcare is often closely linked to a lack of protection and fulfilment of corresponding human rights. Therefore, humanitarian assistance cannot be regarded exclusively as an action to provide relief to lessen the needs of a civilian population,

[99] As discussed in ch 3, Elizabeth Ferris has developed a typology of protection activities covering physical protection, humanitarian protection and human rights protection. See E Ferris, *The Politics of Protection: The Limits of Humanitarian Action* (Brookings Institution Press, 2011) 278.

[100] S Giossi Caverzasio, *Strengthening Protection in War: a Search for Professional Standards*, ICRC (2001) 19. For discussion, see ch 3, Section I.A.i.

[101] Swedish Ministry of Foreign Affairs, *Government Humanitarian Aid Policy*, above n 28, 6.

but also to contribute to the protection and fulfilment of socio-economic human rights.'[102] This dual approach of protection and assistance reflects the binding legal provisions of the 1989 Convention on the Rights of the Child, which provides that refugee children shall 'receive appropriate protection and humanitarian assistance'.[103] Meanwhile, at a regional level, the African Union's 2009 Kampala Convention created binding obligations on State Parties to provide both protection and material assistance to internally displaced persons.[104] Drawing on the Swedish government's approach, the twin components of humanitarian action can be envisaged as follows:

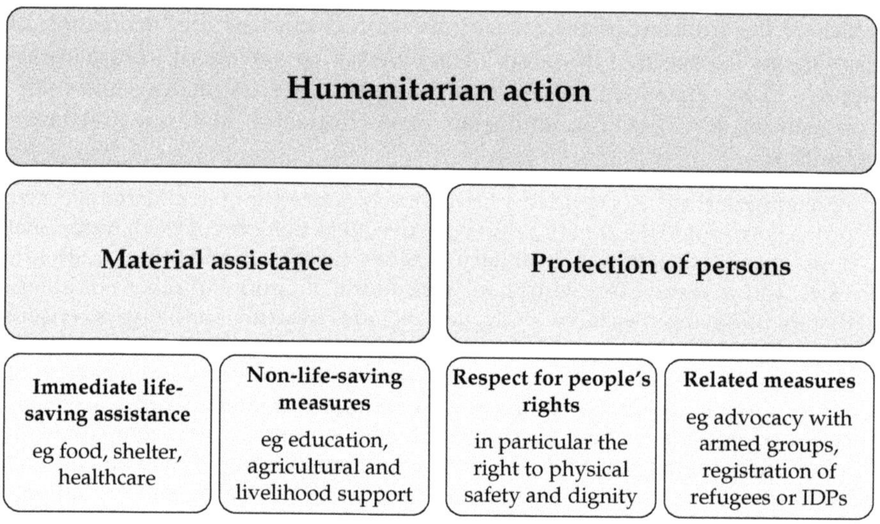

Figure 1.1: Twin components of humanitarian action

While it is always necessary to remain cognisant of the specific cultural and religious wishes and requirements of an affected community, one can generally identify the basic types of material assistance required in a humanitarian crisis (that is, food, water, sanitation, healthcare, shelter etc). However, the exact contours of the concept of protection remain insufficiently defined. A broad understanding of 'protection' can encompass activities as diverse as registering voters to building latrines in a displaced

[102] Swiss Federal Department of Foreign Affairs, *Humanitarian Access in Situations of Armed Conflict: Handbook on the International Normative Framework* 2nd edn, December 2014, 40.

[103] Convention on the Rights of the Child (adopted 20 November 1989, entered into force 2 September 1990) 1577 UTS 3 (CRC)

[104] Art 2(b) Kampala Convention, above n 64.

persons camp.[105] Yet if all rights-based activities fall under the rubric of 'protection' (for example, providing food fulfils an individual's right to food), does this render the concept meaningless from a legal or operational perspective? This question will be addressed in greater detail in chapter three.

C. Hazards, Vulnerability and Resilience

Before one can determine what specific humanitarian action to undertake in a given case, one also needs to understand the concepts of 'hazard', 'vulnerability' and 'resilience'. As with humanitarianism and protection, it is important to recognise that these key concepts are understood differently across disciplines and specialities within academia, not to mention the differential approaches taken by governmental or non-governmental stakeholders in conflicts, displacement or disasters. For example, the Overseas Development Institute has highlighted the fundamental difference in the meaning of 'resilience' when discussing natural ecosystems or human communities;[106] while Terry Cannon has argued that the terms 'vulnerability', 'resilience' and 'community' are widely misunderstood, which can result in differential perceptions of risk.[107] These differences reflect the multitude of actors engaged in analysing the root causes and required responses to events which precipitate large-scale human suffering. As befitting a book focused on international law, policy and practice, I intend to rely on the definitions and understandings provided in texts developed in inter-governmental fora through global transnational normative processes. Although the following texts do not have binding legal force, such non-binding norms can exert considerable authority in their own right, and consequently influence the actions of states and other humanitarian actors.[108] The Hyogo Framework for Action on disaster risk reduction (2005–2015) defined a 'hazard' as:

> A potentially damaging physical event, phenomenon or human activity that may cause the loss of life or injury, property damage, social and economic disruption or environmental degradation. Hazards can include latent conditions

[105] E Ferris and C Stark, 'Incorporating Protection into Humanitarian Action: Approaches and Limits', paper presented at IFI-UNRWA international conference, American University of Beirut, Lebanon, 8 October 2010, 16.

[106] S Levine et al, *The Relevance of 'Resilience'?*, Overseas Development Institute, Humanitarian Policy Group, Policy Brief 49, September 2012.

[107] T Cannon, *Reducing People's Vulnerability to Natural Hazards: Communities and Resilience*, United Nations University Research Paper No. 2008/34 (April 2008).

[108] For further discussion, see ch 2, Section II.A.

that may represent future threats and can have different origins: natural (geological, hydro-meteorological and biological) or induced by human processes (environmental degradation and technological hazards).[109]

'Vulnerability', meanwhile, is defined as: 'The conditions determined by physical, social, economic and environmental factors or processes, which increase the susceptibility of a community to the impact of hazards.'[110] In other words, the impact of a particular natural or human hazard will be magnified by any existing vulnerabilities of individuals, groups or communities. Both these definitions were reaffirmed in the Sendai Framework for Disaster Risk Reduction (2015–2030),[111] thereby providing additional authority to these definitions. While 'resilience' is not defined in either the Hyogo or Sendai Frameworks, the UN has defined it as:

> The ability of a system, community or society exposed to hazards to resist, absorb, accommodate to and recover from the effects of a hazard in a timely and efficient manner, including through the preservation and restoration of its essential basic structures and functions.[112]

It follows that the impact of a particular hazard, which may be exacerbated by existing vulnerabilities, can nevertheless be mitigated by the resilience factors existing within an individual, group and/or community. So although these definitions were elaborated within the context of the UN mechanisms for disaster risk reduction, the concepts of hazard, vulnerability and resilience mirror the challenges arising from both natural and human hazards, including the effects of armed conflict. Specific vulnerabilities, for example a child at risk of forcible recruitment into an armed group, can be off-set by resilience measures arising from the local population themselves, such as strong family and community bonds, or externally such as through specific governmental or NGO programmes

[109] UNISDR, *Hyogo Framework for Action 2005–2015: Building the Resilience of Nations and Communities to Disasters*, as adopted at the World Conference on Disaster Reduction, 18–22 January 2005, Kobe, Hyogo, Japan (A/CONF.206/6) para 1, fn 2 (the Hyogo Framework). For an analysis of the process that led to the creation of the Hyogo Framework and its soft law status, see L Corredig, 'Effectiveness and Accountability of Disaster Risk Reduction Practices: An Analysis through the Lens of IN–LAW' in A Berman et al (eds), *Informal International Lawmaking: Case Studies* (Torkel Opsahl Academic Epublisher, 2012).

[110] *Hyogo Framework*, ibid, para 1, fn 1.

[111] UNISDR, *Sendai Framework for Disaster Risk Reduction 2015–2030*, as adopted at the World Conference on Disaster Risk Reduction, 14–18 March 2015, Sendai, Miyagi, Japan (A/CONF.224/CRP.1) (the Sendai Framework).

[112] UNISDR, '2009 UNISDR Terminology on Disaster Risk Reduction', May 2009 www.unisdr.org/we/inform/terminology. For analysis of differential understandings of 'resilience' across social and ecological sciences, see L Olsson et al, 'Why Resilience is Unappealing to Social Science: Theoretical and Empirical Investigations of the Scientific Use of Resilience' (May 2015) 1(4) *Science Advances*.

targeting at-risk children to remain at school.[113] Accepting the differential disciplinary understandings of these terms, one must therefore consider how law and legal frameworks can assist in identifying potential hazards, minimising existing vulnerabilities, and strengthening resilience capacity.

III. THE EVOLUTION OF LEGAL HUMANITARIAN OBLIGATIONS

A. Humanitarian Responses in Armed Conflicts

Attempts to regulate the commencement and conduct of armed hostilities between states and other armed groups has a long pedigree, but gained urgency in the second half of the nineteenth century resulting from the increased mechanisation of war and escalating suffering both on and off the battlefield. It is not possible to undertake a detailed review of the historical development of international humanitarian law in this book.[114] Suffice to say that from the establishment of the Red Cross Movement in 1863, to the support provided to civilians by the Commission for Relief in Belgium during the First World War and the UN Relief and Rehabilitation Administration (UNRRA) during the Second World War, a range of important initiatives for the codification and coordination of international humanitarian responses had already taken place before the formal establishment of the United Nations in 1945 and conclusion of the four Geneva Conventions in 1949.[115]

Since its inception, the modern law of armed conflict (or international humanitarian law) has involved a fundamental balancing of military necessity with humanitarian considerations.[116] However, the massive shocks of the First and Second World Wars prompted major changes to the international political and legal structures for such humanitarian responses—moving from a laissez-faire and private philanthropic approach to a more coordinated and interventionist stance. The changing nature of warfare also changed the victims of war. While civilians and the local population had always suffered during war, the rate of civilian casualties rose

113 For application of these concepts across disciplines, see F Thomalla et al, 'Reducing Hazard Vulnerability: Towards a Common Approach between Disaster Risk Reduction and Climate Adaptation' (2006) 30(1) *Disasters* 39.

114 For a fascinating biographical account of five leading humanitarians, see B Cabanes, *The Great War and the Origins of Humanitarianism 1918–1924* (Cambridge University Press, 2014).

115 MacAlister-Smith, *International Humanitarian Assistance*, above n 39), 10–14.

116 Y Dinstein, *The Conduct of Hostilities under the Law of International Armed Conflict* 2nd edn (Cambridge University Press, 2010) 4–6. For Professor Dinstein's argument regarding the semantic differences between the 'law of international armed conflict' and 'international humanitarian law', see 18–19.

exponentially—from 5–15 per cent of total fatalities in the First World War to over 50 per cent in the Second World War.[117] The Holocaust and civilian death and destruction arising from the Second World War led directly to the establishment of many key tenets of modern international human rights law and the law of armed conflict. A second phase of deep soul-searching by states, individuals and humanitarian actors occurred in the early 1990s as the utopic vision of a new world order following the end of the Cold War was promptly crushed by the failures of protection in Somalia, the former Yugoslavia and Rwanda. These failures fuelled a determination to develop new international legal instruments and mechanisms.

Significantly, UNGA Resolution 46/182 of 1991[118] elaborated both guiding principles and operational structures for international humanitarian assistance, while highlighting the affected state's primary responsibility.[119] The central role of the UN and its specialised agencies was secured via the establishment of the Department of Humanitarian Affairs, with an Emergency Relief Coordinator designated at the level of UN Under-Secretary-General. To improve co-operation and coordination between humanitarian agencies, an Inter-Agency Standing Committee (IASC) was established, comprising UN agencies, the international Red Cross Movement, the International Organization for Migration and other relevant NGOs.[120] In an attempt to promote consistent and predicable funding streams, Resolution 46/182 provided improved funding mechanisms through the establishment of the Central Emergency Revolving Fund[121] and Consolidated Appeals Progress. Alongside such operational and structural innovations, international law has also advanced the legal basis for the regulation of armed conflicts, from the 1949 Geneva Conventions and their three Additional Protocols, to multilateral treaties covering specific types of weapons and tactics, such as anti-personnel mines and cluster munitions.

As the primary mechanism for the coordination of UN and non-UN humanitarian actors, it is pertinent to consider the IASC's definition of a 'complex emergency', which was elaborated following the horrors of the Rwandan genocide, namely:

> a humanitarian crisis in a country, region or society where there is total or considerable breakdown of authority resulting from internal or external conflict and which requires an international response that goes beyond the mandate or capacity of any single and/or ongoing UN country programme.[122]

[117] Swedish Ministry of Foreign Affairs, *Humanitarian Aid Policy*, above n 28, 7.
[118] UNGA Res 46/182, above n 45.
[119] Tsui, *Analysis of Normative Developments*, above n 45.
[120] For more information, see http://interagencystandingcommittee.org/iasc.
[121] The CERF was strengthened and renamed the Central Emergency Response Fund in August 2006.
[122] IASC, 10th meeting, 9 December 1994. See also IASC, *Civil–Military Relationship in Complex Emergencies: An IASC Reference Paper*, 28 June 2004, Part 1C.

This definition highlights the breakdown of authority which provides the justification for international action, as opposed to simply domestic actions by the state concerned. Likewise, it aims to keep the UN structures centre stage of this international response. UNOCHA has further elaborated that complex emergencies are typically characterised by 'extensive violence and loss of life, massive displacements of people, widespread damage to societies and economies, need for large-scale, multi-faceted humanitarian assistance, hindrance or prevention of humanitarian assistance by political and military constraints and significant security risks for humanitarian relief workers in some areas'.[123] Faced with such potentially overwhelming needs and challenges, the requirement for clearly articulated standards and structures for both states and humanitarian actors is apparent.

B. Codification of International Disaster Laws

Despite the long appreciation of the potential legal ramifications of major disasters, the concept of 'disaster law' received scant analysis during the nineteenth and twentieth centuries. Nonetheless, while the modern law of armed conflict stems from the 1864 Geneva Convention for the Amelioration of the Conditions of the Wounded in Armies in the Field, the regulation of humanitarian responses to disasters can also be traced to this era.[124] The founder of the Red Cross Movement, Henri Dunant, advocated an active role for national Red Cross Societies in both times of war and peace,[125] as reflected in an early resolution of the Red Cross Movement:

> To provide assistance and relief in disasters which may afflict peoples during peacetime is a condition of the vigorous development of [national Red Cross] Societies, and a useful preparation for their wartime work. Relief Societies should therefore, in peacetime, devote themselves to humanitarian work corresponding to their wartime duties, namely ... to giving relief in case of public calamity which, like war, demands immediate and organised assistance.[126]

[123] UNOCHA Financial Tracking Service, *Glossary of Humanitarian Terms* https://fts.unocha.org/pageloader.aspx?page=AboutFTS-definitions.

[124] For discussion of the changing role of the ICRC, see D Palmieri, 'An Institution Standing the Test of Time? A Review of 150 Years of the History of the International Committee of the Red Cross' (Spring 2013) 95(889) *International Review of the Red Cross* 1.

[125] In 1862 Dunant wrote: 'These [national] Societies could also render great services, by their permanent existence, in times of epidemics, or of disasters such as floods, fires or other natural catastrophes.' Quoted in IFRC, *90 Years of Improving the Lives of the Most Vulnerable* (2009) 3.

[126] Resolution 3, 2nd International Red Cross Conference, Berlin, 1869, quoted in M Hoffman, 'What is the Scope of International Disaster Response Law' in IFRC, *International Disaster Response Laws, Principles and Practice: Reflections, Prospects and Challenges* (2003) 13, fn 1.

Acknowledgement of the need to codify international law concerning the provision of relief to people caught up in peacetime calamities can be traced more specifically to 1908 and the powerful earthquake which hit the Italian province of Messina causing tens of thousands of deaths.[127] The President of the Italian Red Cross, Senator Giovanni Ciraolo, developed plans to establish an international mechanism of disaster insurance and mutual assistance for victims of natural disasters, but this initiative was overtaken by the outbreak of the First World War. In 1921 Senator Ciraolo reintroduced the proposal at the Tenth International Conference of the Red Cross Movement, resulting in a recommendation to the signatories of the 1864 Geneva Convention for a treaty extending the peacetime activities of the Red Cross, in particular during natural disasters. The proposal was subsequently transferred into the League of Nations system, ultimately leading to the conclusion of the 1927 Convention Establishing an International Relief Union.[128] Notwithstanding bitter divisions over the project within the Red Cross Movement and between states,[129] Senator Ciraolo's proposal was exceptional in many ways, not least because the proposed framework represented one of the first attempts to identify individuals as subjects in international law. By focusing on victims of disasters, rather than simply state relationships, it represented an attempt to codify a state's responsibilities towards its own citizens in disasters.[130] It was therefore one of the first international legal instruments to highlight the vertical obligations between a state and its citizens, not just the horizontal obligations between states.[131] However, after six years of political manoeuvres and a diplomatic conference attended by representatives of 43 states, the end result was not so revolutionary.

[127] For an illuminating comparison of the American response to the 1906 San Francisco earthquake and the Italian response to the 1908 Messina earthquake, see: Hutchinson, 'The Ciraolo Project', above n 16, 10–14.

[128] *Convention Establishing an International Relief Union* (adopted 12 July 1927, entered into force 27 December 1932) 135 LNTS 247. See generally: P MacAlister-Smith, 'The International Relief Union: Reflections on the Convention Establishing an International Relief Union of July 12, 1927' (1986) 54 *Tijdschrift voor Rechtsgeschiedenis* 363; J Hutchinson, 'Disasters and the International Order II: The International Relief Union' (June 2001) 23(2) *International History Review* 253.

[129] For background and analysis of the political manoeuvring and infighting within the Red Cross Movement resulting from the proposal, see Hutchinson, 'The Ciraolo Project', above n 16, 10–14.

[130] ibid, 25. Even the law of armed conflict at that time was primarily focused on ameliorating the suffering of soldiers resulting from their service for the state. See: S Wills, 'The Legal Characterization of the Armed Conflicts in Afghanistan and Iraq: Implications for Protection' (2011) 58(2) *Netherlands International Law Review* 173, 180.

[131] For a historical review of the vertical and horizontal obligations of states regarding public health and infectious diseases, see D Fidler, 'Emerging Trends in International Law Concerning Global Infectious Disease Control' (2003) 9(3) *Emerging Infectious Diseases* 285.

The 1927 Convention contained both the overarching aims and principles of the newly established International Relief Union (IRU), as well as the IRU's Statute detailing its organisation and functions. The IRU's four objectives were: a) in the event of a disaster to furnish to the suffering population first aid and to assemble funds, resources and assistance of all kinds; b) to coordinate efforts made by relief organisations; c) to encourage the study of preventive measures against disasters; and d) to induce all peoples to render mutual international assistance. In other words, the IRU was intended to be an operative relief agency in certain disasters, whereby it would provide direct assistance to those in need. It would also act as a coordination body, both for the delivery of relief assistance and the scientific study and understanding of prevention methods. Finally, the IRU was also expected to act as a fundraising organisation encouraging international cooperation in disasters. Despite these broad objectives, the IRU only twice engaged in relief operations between 1932 and 1967 when it was formally wound down. A suggestion from the British government, supported by the IRU Executive Committee, to provide relief during the Spanish Civil War provoked controversy as an attempt to blur the lines between armed conflicts and disasters, and so was ultimately rejected.[132]

However, providing a focal point to advance and systemise knowledge and understanding of disasters may have been the greatest achievement of the IRU, even if its ambitious aims of international regulation and operational activities were not realistic at the time. John Hutchinson has argued that the IRU's failure was inevitable due to the intransigence of certain states and conflicts within the Red Cross Movement, as reflected in the text of the 1927 Convention.[133] Nevertheless, by recognising the importance of international co-operation, mutual assistance and coordination in response to large-scale disasters, the IRU provided the foundation for future approaches towards both disaster response and international regulation. Key topics of contemporary importance the IRU attempted to address include: focusing on individuals, while recognising the role of the affected state; statements of humanitarian principles alongside technical and operational rules; the role and involvement of NGOs; and the importance of understanding the causes and impacts of disasters and implementing disaster risk reduction and prevention measures.

In contrast to the IRU, the success of the UN Relief and Rehabilitation Administration (UNRRA) during the Second World War in ensuring effective delivery of life-saving supplies to civilian populations provided a key model for the emerging United Nations system. UNICEF, the UN

[132] Hutchinson, 'The IRU', above n 128, 292–95. Tensions within the Red Cross Movement also came to the fore, since the ICRC was already active in Spain, and did not want the IRU or League of Red Cross Societies to duplicate their efforts.

[133] Hutchinson, 'The IRU', above n 128, 295–98.

Children's Fund, received residual funds of US$34 million from UNRRA at the end of the War, while the Food and Agriculture Organisation and World Health Organisation inherited the functional responsibilities of UNRRA in their respective domains.[134] Like the IRU before it, UNRRA had highlighted the importance of international co-operation to facilitate the mobilisation of resources to alleviate suffering of civilian populations. Yet while the establishment of the UN and its specialised agencies provided specific outlets for global issues and vulnerable groups such as refugees (UNHCR), children (UNICEF), and health (WHO), attempts to revive the IRU in the late 1940s and 1950s were unsuccessful.[135] Furthermore, despite the extensive codification of international law at the end of the Second World War in areas of immediate pressing concern, namely armed conflict, refugee protection and human rights, the international community did not attempt to reconstruct a binding international legal framework regarding peacetime natural and human-made disasters.

C. Similarities and Differences between Armed Conflicts and Disasters

The divergent legal histories of attempts to minimise the suffering arising from armed conflict and disasters highlight some of the fundamental differences between the factual situations of natural or human-made disasters and armed conflicts.[136] In general, a natural or human-made disaster will comprise one key event or series of linked events—as in the Japanese Tōhoku earthquake of March 2011, where a powerful earthquake and tsunami created a radiological emergency at the Fukushima nuclear power plant.[137] Accordingly, there is generally an identifiable start point to the disaster and while recovery and rehabilitation may take years, the immediate emergency response phase of the operation (and therefore need for humanitarian support as opposed to longer-term rehabilitation and developmental co-operation) normally only spans a period of weeks or months after the key event.[138] However, in armed conflicts the humanitarian needs of the population may continue for years, depending on the resolution or

[134] MacAlister-Smith, *International Humanitarian Assistance*, above n 39, 10–14.

[135] MacAlister-Smith, 'The IRU', above n 128, 371–72.

[136] For discussion, see IFRC, *Desk Study*, above n 41, 156–57.

[137] See D Farber, 'Legal Scholarship, The Disaster Cycle, and the Fukushima Accident' (2012) 23(1) *Duke Environmental Law and Policy Forum* 1.

[138] Slow-onset disasters, such as famines, may have a less identifiable start point but national and international humanitarian responses to such disasters generally follow the same trajectory of emergency relief operations followed by longer-term recovery, rehabilitation and developmental actions.

otherwise of the conflict. One only needs to think of the on-going need for humanitarian protection and assistance in places such as Syria, Palestine, Iraq and Afghanistan to realise the difficulty in viewing humanitarian action as a short-term measure in complex armed conflicts. As noted in the *Sphere Handbook*: 'the period of humanitarian response ... cover[s] activities which meet the urgent survival needs of disaster-affected populations. This phase can range from a few days or weeks to many months and even years, particularly in contexts involving protracted insecurity and displacement. It is, therefore, impossible to assign a particular timeframe to the usefulness of the Sphere standards.'[139]

Yet both armed conflicts and disasters can lead to large-scale population movements, either internally within the borders of an affected state, or across an international border. Likewise, extensive human rights violations directed against particular groups of society, without reaching the threshold of armed conflict, can result in a humanitarian crisis and need for international protection and assistance. While such forced population displacements may have an identifiable start point, and those affected may need immediate emergency assistance, as with armed conflicts the continuing need for basic necessities and protection services can continue for a long period. For example, the 86,000 Bhutanese refugees who fled to Nepal in the early 1990s initially required emergency shelter, medical care, food and registration services in newly established refugee camps. Following a series of drawn-out and ultimately unsuccessful negotiations on return between the Nepalese and Bhutanese governments, an extensive third country resettlement programme was commenced in 2007.[140] Nevertheless, over 20 years after their initial flight from Bhutan nearly 20,000 refugees remain in camps Nepal receiving on-going protection and assistance from the international community.[141]

Reflecting the inherent vulnerabilities, capacities and resilience of particular groups and communities, Jose-Miguel Albala-Bertrand has noted that a natural disaster primarily constitutes an interaction between a natural event and a social system, while an armed conflict constitutes an interaction between a social event and a social system.[142] Indeed, there is no such thing as a 'natural' disaster—although geological or hydrometeorological hazards such as hurricanes and landslides may pose a real threat to individuals and communities, the impact of such events is

[139] *Sphere Handbook*, above n 25, 9.

[140] DD Shrestha, 'Resettlement of Bhutanese Refugees Surpasses 100,000 Mark,' *UNHCR Press Release*, 19 November 2015 www.unhcr.org/564dded46.html.

[141] For discussion of sexual and gender-based violence in the Bhutanese refugee camps, see ch 9, Section II.A.i.

[142] J-M Albala-Bertrand, 'Responses to Complex Humanitarian Emergencies and Natural Disasters: An Analytical Comparison' (2000) 21(2) *Third World Quarterly* 215, 215.

determined by social factors such as building codes, early warning systems and response mechanisms. Likewise, while a long-running conflict may be resolved militarily (as in the final push to defeat the Tamil Tigers in Sri Lanka in 2009), in the majority of cases it is only through a combination of political, diplomatic and military action that a conflict will come to a sustainable conclusion. In other words, politics plays a fundamental role in not just creating the root causes of a humanitarian crisis, but also its resolution. Yet politics can also cause the prolongation of humanitarian assistance. Using the example of Palestinian refugees, Dale Jamieson has noted: 'rather than providing temporary life-saving aid, humanitarian assistance has become the de facto policy of a world that is unwilling to take decisive action to address the underlying causes of global poverty.'[143] So the establishment of effective laws, policies and practices at the national, regional and international levels to promote durable solutions are of particular significance. Actions are therefore required to both reduce potential causes of a humanitarian crisis (for example through disaster risk reduction measures, peaceful dispute settlement mechanisms or international dialogue), and to support holistic humanitarian responses when a crisis does emerge. Such responses may range from governmental action to identify safe areas for those displaced, to clearly promulgated laws on the entry and coordination of international humanitarian personnel, food, medicine and other materials and services.

There are important differences in the humanitarian challenges faced in conflicts, forced displacement and disasters, and therefore the responses required. Sudden-onset disasters such as earthquakes and tsunamis raise immediate questions of search and rescue,[144] and challenges of physical access due to the destruction of major infrastructure such as roads, bridges and airports. Slow-onset disasters such as drought-induced famine present distinct challenges, such as identifying the needs of people over an extensive area or attempting to resist deliberate policies which prolong or exacerbate the famine conditions.[145] Meanwhile, there are fundamental distinctions between an international conflict involving the professional armed forces of two or more states, and a non-international armed conflict involving non-state armed groups whose members may have little or no training in the laws of war, the role of the ICRC or the use of starvation as

[143] D Jamieson, 'Duties to the Distant: Aid, Assistance, and Intervention in the Developing World' (2005) 9(1/2) *The Journal of Ethics* 151, 157.

[144] See, eg, *Strengthening the Effectiveness and Coordination of International Urban Search and Rescue Assistance*, UNGA Resolution 57/150 (27 February 2003).

[145] Like other so-called natural disasters, the 'natural' origin of famines is fiercely contested. See D Marcus, 'Famine Crimes in International Law' (April 2003) 97(2) *American Journal of International Law* 245.

a method of warfare.[146] Finally, forced displacement resulting from disasters or conflict can either lead to cross-border population flows, or internal displacement within a country. In some circumstances those displaced will end up in identifiable camps or settlements, while others may be broadly dispersed across rural or urban settings thereby posing additional challenges to provide effective protection activities and material assistance.

Despite these differences, there are also important similarities in the rationale for providing protection and assistance in all these settings, and the practical and operational challenges in so doing. As discussed in the following chapter, international law recognises that a primary motivation behind all responses to massive human suffering arising from conflict, displacement and disasters are the principles of humanity and respect for human dignity. These principles apply in all humanitarian crises, and form the bedrock of most actions taken to assist those in need. As noted by Gabriella Venturini, the laws of armed conflict and disasters should be viewed as complementary as they share the same aim—'the protection of the human person in situations of danger and suffering'.[147] Moreover, it is not unusual for humanitarian actors to simultaneously navigate both peacetime and conflict-related humanitarian needs—whether it is different branches of a global organisation such as the UN or the International Red Cross Movement; donor governments that provide financial and technical support for humanitarian actions; or NGOs that operate across the boundaries of prevention, relief, rehabilitation and development.[148] As noted by Peter MacAlister-Smith over 30 years ago: 'Post-impact problems in relief management such as evacuation, emergency feeding, temporary shelter and disease control exist in a similar manner in both armed conflict and other disaster situations.'[149]

The need for humanitarian agencies to engage in multi-dimensional activities was starkly highlighted by the 2004 Indian Ocean Tsunami, which severely affected regions in both Aceh Province in Indonesia and north-east Sri Lanka that were actively engaged in armed conflicts. Likewise, armed conflict existed in northern Pakistan during the 2010 floods, while the 2010 Haiti earthquake struck areas where post-conflict capacity building and reconstruction activities were ongoing. Such complex scenarios did not prevent humanitarian actors responding to the needs of the affected populations, many of whom were displaced from their homes as a result of the crises. Nonetheless, there is an evident need for increased

[146] D Forsythe, 'The International Committee of the Red Cross and Humanitarian Assistance—A Policy Analysis' (October 1996) 36(314) *International Review of the Red Cross* 512, 513.

[147] G Venturini, 'Disasters and Armed Conflict' in A de Guttry, M Gestri and G Venturini, *International Disaster Response Law* (TMC Asser Press, 2012) 251, 264.

[148] See *HAP Standard in Accountability and Quality Management*, above n 94.

[149] MacAlister-Smith, *International Humanitarian Assistance*, above n 39, 34.

understanding of the coherence between existing bodies of international law regulating such responses. Philip Jessup advanced the concept of transnational law in the 1950s as a response to the blurring of boundaries between previously distinct bodies of international law.[150] Recognition of the similarities and differences in the factual situation on the ground and the legal frameworks regulating humanitarian actions therefore forms the heart of the *acquis humanitaire*, as will be examined in more depth in the following chapter.

[150] C Tietje, A Brouder and K Nowrot (eds), 'Philip C Jessup's *Transnational Law* Revisited on the Occasion of the 50th Anniversary of its Publication', Essays in Transnational Economic Law, No 50, February 2006, Transnational Economic Law Research Center, Martin Luther University.

2

Defining the Acquis Humanitaire

I. THE CONCEPT OF AN EMERGING *ACQUIS HUMANITAIRE*

EVERY FEW YEARS, the naturally occurring El Niño cycle affects global weather patterns. The El Niño-Southern Oscillation cycle describes the fluctuations in temperature of the east-central Equatorial Pacific Ocean and surrounding atmosphere.[1] The effects are not just felt in the Pacific, but radiate out globally as warm water around Indonesia spreads back towards the Americas triggering a series of chain reactions within the global oceans.[2] Of particular concern is whether global climate change is negatively influencing the frequency and severity of the El Niño cycle. From a humanitarian perspective, large temperature fluctuations arising from a particularly strong El Niño event (often called a 'super El Niño', which occurs every 10–20 years) leads to greater levels of rainfall, drought and severe storms.[3] The diversity of humanitarian risks arising from El Niño events, particularly super El Niño events, was reflected in the global weather patterns over winter 2015 and spring 2016. In April 2016, the UN Under-Secretary-General and Emergency Relief Coordinator, Stephen O'Brien, highlighted the human impact through a global call for action.[4] O'Brien stressed that 60 million people around the world were facing food insecurity as a result of the 2015–16 El Niño, including 32 million people in Sub-Saharan Africa, while in Haiti over 50 per cent of the national crops had been lost as a result of drought.[5] Eight countries across Central America, Africa and the Pacific declared a national state of emergency resulting from the El Niño effects, while the Southern African Development Community declared a regional drought disaster in March 2016.

[1] National Oceanic and Atmospheric Administration (NOAA), *What are El Niño and La Niña?* http://oceanservice.noaa.gov/facts/ninonina.html.

[2] F Pearce, *El Niño and Climate Change: Wild Weather May Get Wilder*, Yale Environment 360, Yale School of Forestry and Environmental Studies, http://e360.yale.edu/feature/el_nino_and_climate_change_wild_weather_may_get_wilder/2960.

[3] The last two super El Niño events were in 1982–83 and 1997–98, ibid.

[4] UNOCHA, *Global Call for Support and Action: Responding to El Niño*, S O'Brien, 26 April 2016.

[5] UNOCHA, *El Niño: Overview of Impact, Projected Humanitarian Needs and Response*, 13 April 2016.

Responding to such diverse and widespread humanitarian needs poses challenges for both national authorities and international organisations.

Therefore, following the preceding overview of the concepts of humanitarianism, humanitarian action and legal obligations to protect and assist people caught up in complex emergencies, this chapter introduces the concept of an *acquis humanitaire*, as a body of laws, policies and practices relating to the protection of persons in humanitarian crises. First, the constituent parts of the *acquis humanitaire*, namely its prime objective, conceptual basis and accountability mechanisms, as well as its substantive sources will be examined. The chapter then continues with an in-depth discussion of the conceptual underpinnings of humanity and human dignity, and how to demarcate the boundaries of the *acquis humanitaire.* Daniel Farber et al have described disaster laws as 'the best portfolio of legal rules to deal with catastrophic risks—a portfolio that includes mitigation, emergency response, compensation and insurance, and rebuilding strategies'.[6] Likewise, the *acquis humanitaire* is intended to provide a conceptual framework for grouping together a portfolio of specific legal and non-legal sources that influence state and humanitarian actors. As explained below, the concept is premised on a broad tent approach in recognition of the divergent, but equally applicable, operational modalities for promoting the international legal protection of persons in humanitarian crises. As such, the *acquis humanitaire* recognises both needs-based and rights-based approaches to humanitarian action, and draws from binding and non-binding sources. In so doing, the concept should help clarify for practitioners and academics the existing *lex lata,* and associated legal obligations of states and other humanitarian actors, while simultaneously providing space for discussion of *lex ferenda* and the normative development of legal protection.

Reflecting the similarities and differences between the factual and legal situation of persons caught up in conflicts, displacement and disasters,[7] the aim of elaborating an *acquis humanitaire* is: a) to identify obligations for states, inter-governmental and non-governmental organisations relating to the protection of persons in humanitarian crises; and b) to draw together the specific binding and non-binding sources of international law, policy and practice which relate specifically to humanitarian action. The *acquis humanitaire* therefore is not intended to constitute a new body

[6] D Farber et al (eds), *Disaster Law and Policy* 2nd edn (Aspen, 2010) xxi. See also: J Chen, 'Modern Disaster Theory: Evaluating Disaster Law as a Portfolio of Legal Rules' (2011) 25 *Emory International Law Review* 1121.

[7] As noted by Frans Viljoen, 'ultimately, [international humanitarian law and international human rights law] serve the same goal: the protection of the dignity and humanity of everyone.' F Viljoen, 'Africa's Contribution to the Development of International Human Rights and Humanitarian Law' (2001) 1 *African Human Rights Law Journal* 18, 32.

of international law, or unjustifiably conflate different legal regimes. However, from the perspective of policy-makers, practitioners and academics, there are practical benefits to examining the coherence between legal obligations and non-binding norms which influence the actions of states and other humanitarian actors. By grouping potential sources of humanitarian obligations and influences under a broad conceptual framework, the *acquis humanitaire* can provide an opportunity to identify the overlaps and gaps in assistance and protection which may exist, and therefore presents an opportunity to expand our understanding and analysis of how best to promote the international legal protection of persons in humanitarian crises.

A. Core Components

i. Identifying the Constituent Parts

The concept of an 'acquis' comes originally from the institutional and legal framework established by the European Union (EU). First introduced in the Treaty on European Union,[8] the *acquis communautaire* is not specifically defined in EU law, although is held to be the body of common rights and obligations which bind together all the EU Member States.[9] The French word *'acquis'*, meaning 'accepted' or 'established',[10] has likewise been used by the Council of Europe to describe its normative activities in the fields of democracy, the rule of law and fundamental human rights and freedoms,[11] and is generally understood to comprise a body of laws, rules and regulations established within a particular institutional framework.[12] Notably, the ILC Special Rapporteur on the protection of persons in the event of disasters, Eduardo Valencia-Ospina, has acknowledged the existence of 'the *acquis* of the international law of disaster response'.[13] The

[8] Art 2 The Consolidated Version of the Treaty on European Union (TEU), OJ C340, 10 November 1997.

[9] As defined by the European Commission: 'Glossary', http://ec.europa.eu/justice/glossary/index_en.htm. See also A Magen, 'The *Acquis Communautaire* as an Instrument of EU External Influence' (2007) 9(3) *European Journal of Law Reform* 361.

[10] J-B Ormal-Grenon and N Pomier (eds), *Oxford Hachette French Dictionary* 3rd edn (Oxford University Press, 2001).

[11] Council of Europe, Resolution 1290 (2002): *Future of the Co-operation between European Institutions*, Assembly debate, 26 June 2002 (20th Sitting).

[12] For references to the GATT *acquis*, see WTO, *Japan—Taxes on Alcoholic Beverages*, Report of the Appellate Body (AB-1996-2) 14–15; and the UNCITRAL *acquis*, see A Markel, 'American, English and Japanese Warranty Law Compared: Should the US Reconsider her Article 95 Declaration to the CISG?' (Winter 2009) 21 *Pace International Law Review* 163, 200.

[13] E Valencia-Ospina, *Fourth Report on the Protection of Persons in the Event of Disasters* (11 May 2011) A/CN.4/643, para 97.

acquis humanitaire therefore refers to the established and emerging body of laws, policies and practices (including provisions of general and customary international law, plus relevant non-binding sources) which establish legal obligations and provide operational and normative guidance for state and non-state actors' preparations and responses to a variety of humanitarian challenges, including armed conflicts, forced displacement, and natural or human-made disasters.

To understand which laws, policies and practices potentially fall within this broad concept of an *acquis humanitaire*, it is useful to visualise three specific elements which are applicable to all rules and standards of humanitarian action within the *acquis humanitaire*. As set out in Figure 2.1 below, these constituent parts are: a) the prime objective; b) its conceptual basis; and c) the applicable accountability mechanisms.

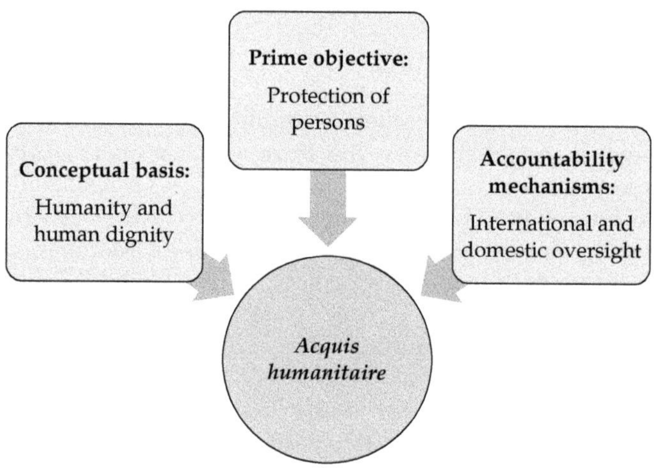

Figure 2.1: Constituent parts of the *acquis humanitaire*

To elaborate, the prime objective of humanitarian action is the protection of persons based on the concepts of humanity and human dignity as set out in international law, and which are practically supported by means of international, regional and domestic accountability mechanisms. Crucially, the differential obligations stemming from the unique factual and legal circumstances posed by armed conflicts and other humanitarian emergencies means that the normative content of these rules and standards will vary depending on the type of humanitarian crisis. In other words, to identify the applicable law and standards in armed conflicts for humanitarian activities to protect civilians and those *hors de combat*, one must first look to the provisions of the law of armed conflict; while for activities to protect and assist persons in forced displacement settings one must first look to refugee and displaced persons law, and so forth.[14] Nevertheless, certain cross-cutting binding and non-binding sources, such as the Convention on the Rights of the Child,[15] UNGA Resolution 46/182[16] or the *Sphere Handbook*,[17] may be applicable in all humanitarian crises. Moreover, the extent or lack of judicial and non-judicial accountability mechanisms at the international, regional or national level may vary depending on the type of humanitarian crisis. Separating the binding or non-binding nature of particular provisions, and identifying the existing *lex lata* from an anticipated *lex ferenda*, therefore takes on a particular importance for humanitarian actors. As a result, it is necessary to also identify the substantive sources of the *acquis humanitaire* and, as set out in Part II of this book, the normative content of established branches of international law relating specifically to the implementation of humanitarian protection and assistance.

ii. Determining the Substantive Sources

Considering the range of potential international, regional or domestic sources relating to humanitarian protection and assistance, it is instructive to consider whether these disparate laws, policies and practices can be classified as a distinct body of law. It is noticeable that the two foundational humanitarian concerns codified at the end of the Second World War, namely the laws of armed conflict and refugee protection, proceeded in parallel but without substantive crossover between the texts or regimes established.[18] Meanwhile, after the initial enthusiasm for the non-binding Universal Declaration of Human Rights in 1948, it was not until 1966 that the two binding International Covenants were finalised, by which time the Cold War had created stark ideological lines between civil and political, and economic, social and cultural rights.[19]

As a result, it is recognised that the phrase 'international humanitarian law' refers exclusively to the protection of specific groups of people

[14] For discussion of functional regimes in international law generally, see M Koskenniemi, 'The Fate of Public International Law: Between Technique and Politics' (2007) 70(1) *Modern Law Review* 1.

[15] Convention on the Rights of the Child (adopted 20 November 1989, entered into force 2 September 1990) 1577 UTS 3 (CRC).

[16] *Strengthening of the Coordination of Humanitarian Emergency Assistance of the United Nations*, UNGA Res 46/182 (19 December 1991).

[17] The Sphere Project, *Humanitarian Charter and Minimum Standards in Humanitarian Response* 3rd edn, April 2011.

[18] For example, the 1951 Refugee Convention regime was premised on national refugee status determination procedures and support mechanisms overseen by the UN, while the 1949 Geneva Conventions provided a key role for the non-governmental ICRC.

[19] See generally B Authers and H Charlesworth, 'The Crisis and the Quotidian in International Human Rights Law' (2013) 44 *Netherlands Yearbook of International Law* 19.

within international and non-international armed conflicts, rather than all 'humanitarian' crises. This misnomer prompted the International Federation of Red Cross and Red Crescent Societies (IFRC) to coin the phrase 'International Disaster Response Laws, Rules and Principles' or 'IDRL' in 2001, to describe the range of binding and non-binding sources of non-conflict humanitarian norms covering natural and human-made disasters that had built up in the intervening years.[20] The IFRC now simply refers to 'Disaster Law' to reflect the difficulty of separating the regulation of international disaster relief from domestic responses, and to move beyond emergency responses to include areas such as disaster risk reduction and regulatory barriers to post-disaster shelter.[21]

The *acquis humanitaire* therefore comprises aspects of the general and customary law of armed conflicts relating specifically to the provision of material assistance to and protection of civilian populations, but does not include the majority of rules relating to the conduct of hostilities in either international or non-international armed conflicts. However, reflecting the broader concept of humanitarian action (as opposed to humanitarian assistance in the traditional sense), the treatment of former combatants who have been placed *hors de combat* (that is as a result of wounds, sickness, shipwreck or prisoner of war status) can be considered to fall within the ambit of the *acquis humanitaire*.[22] Yet the increasing complexity and overlap between these different international laws and non-binding norms starkly highlights the challenge of identifying the applicable rights and obligations in any given humanitarian crisis.[23] As is increasingly recognised, focusing in isolation on separate branches of international law can obscure the multiple interactions that may occur for a particular individual in the midst of a complex emergency.[24]

[20] See generally: H Fischer, *International Disaster Response Law: A Preliminary Overview and Analysis of Existing Treaty Law*, IFRC (January 2003); IFRC, *International Disaster Response Laws, Principles and Practice: Reflections, Prospects and Challenges* (2003); IFRC, *Law and Legal Issues in International Disaster Response: A Desk Study* (2007).

[21] IFRC, *The IFRC's IDRL Programme is becoming the Disaster Law Programme* (2 February 2012), www.ifrc.org/PageFiles/53419/name%20change%20announcement_FINAL%20LATEST%2002.02.2012.pdf; IFRC, *Disaster Law Programme Annual Report 2015—Advance version* (16 February 2016).

[22] For discussion of applicable sources from the law of armed conflict see ch 6. For discussion of civilian detainees in the *Čelebići* and *Stakiç* cases before the International Criminal Tribunal for the former Yugoslavia, see ch 7, Section II.D.i.

[23] See R Stoffels, 'Legal Regulation of Humanitarian Assistance in Armed Conflict: Achievements and Gaps' (September 2004) 86(855) *International Review of the Red Cross* 515.

[24] See generally R Teitel, 'Humanity Law: A New Interpretative Lens on the International Sphere' (2008) 77 *Fordham Law Review* 667.

a. Mali: Complex Emergency and Complex Needs

Background: In January 2012, an armed conflict erupted in the north of Mali between the National Movement for the Liberation of Azawad (MNLA, comprising several different nomadic Tuareg groups), which sought to create an independent state of Azawad, and the central government of President Amadou Toumani Touré. The MNLA rapidly gained control of large parts of the north, in part through their collaboration with Islamic groups, including al-Qaeda in the Islamic Maghreb (AQIM), Ansar Dine and the Movement for Oneness and Jihad in West Africa (MUJWA).[25] Despite the resignation of President Touré following a military coup in March 2012, fighting continued both between the various armed groups in the north, and with the central government.

In the face of a large-scale humanitarian crisis, in December 2012 UNSC Resolution 2085 called for an African-led International Support Mission in Mali (AFISMA). However, events in early January 2013, including the advance of armed groups from the north and attacks near to the capital of Bamako, prompted the French government to unilaterally deploy Special Forces and other French military to support the government forces.[26] A peace agreement was initially signed with MNLA in September 2013, and a more comprehensive ceasefire agreement was concluded in February 2015 resulting in the June 2015 Agreement for Peace and Reconciliation. However, the humanitarian situation remains challenging and on-going armed attacks have continued, including an attack on the Radisson Blu Hotel in Bamako in November 2015, which killed 20 people.[27]

Humanitarian impact: The conflict resulted in the internal and cross-border displacement of over 700,000 people, of whom nearly 200,000 remained displaced as of April 2016. A total of 2.5 million people were in need of humanitarian assistance in the form of food, water, health care, education, protection and livelihood opportunities.[28] Widespread breaches of international humanitarian and human rights law were committed by all parties during the 2012–15 conflict, including the torture, ill-treatment and detention of civilians, and destruction of cultural heritage in Timbuktu.[29] The Government of Mali referred the situation to the

[25] DE Stigall, 'The French Military Intervention in Mali, Counter-terrorism, and the Law of Armed Conflict' (2015) 223(1) *Military Law Review* 1, 5–9.

[26] F Heisbourg, 'A Surprising Little War: First Lessons of Mali' (2013) 55(2) *Survival* 7.

[27] UNOCHA, *Mali Humanitarian Brief: A Rare Possibility to Avoid a Protracted Crisis*, April 2016.

[28] ibid.

[29] International Coalition for the Responsibility to Protect, *Crisis in Mali* www.responsibilitytoprotect.org/index.php/crises/crisis-in-mali#III._2012_Conflicts.

International Criminal Court (ICC) in July 2012, resulting in criminal prosecutions and the first guilty plea before the ICC in August 2016.[30] Humanitarian activities continue to be hampered by on-going insecurity and threats to the safety of humanitarian staff from non-state armed groups. Equally seriously, donor countries had only provided 10 per cent of the $354 million required for humanitarian activities in 2016.[31] Meanwhile, the vulnerability of those affected has been exacerbated by natural hazards such as floods, droughts and epidemics, as well as the chronic poverty and under-development of the country as a whole.

Legal framework: The Government of Mali is a signatory to all the relevant international legal conventions, including the 1949 Geneva Conventions and 1977 Additional Protocol II, the Rome Statute of the ICC, the 1951 Refugee Convention, the International Covenants on Civil and Political, and Economic, Social and Cultural Rights, as well as the African Union's 2009 Kampala Convention for the Protection and Assistance of Internally Displaced Persons in Africa. Moreover, in December 2015, the Malian government committed to 'strengthening the country's normative framework by developing national legislation on displacement in accordance with its obligations under the Convention.'[32]

However, the protection needs for persons caught up in an internal armed conflict exacerbated by natural hazards and large-scale displacement, such as in Mali, are complex and ultimately their fulfilment is dependent on parties to the conflict allowing humanitarian access so that protection activities and material assistance can be provided. In such situations, humanitarian actors are required to negotiate access based on a combination of binding and non-binding norms. As noted by David Forsythe:

> Particularly large-scale relief requires the cooperation of those with the guns on the ground, whatever diplomats and lawyers might say about a right to humanitarian assistance. The only alternative to negotiated cooperation is to overwhelm with military force, which is not a viable option in most situations owing to lack of political will, as well as moral opposition, by important parts of the international community.[33]

[30] *The Prosecutor v Ahmad Al Faqi Al Mahdi*, ICC-01/12-01/15. See also ICC, *Al Mahdi Case: Accused Makes an Admission of Guilt at Trial Opening*, Press Release, 22 August 2016.

[31] UNOCHA, *Mali Humanitarian Brief*, above n 27, 4.

[32] Internal Displacement Monitoring Centre, *Kampala Convention: From Ratification to Domestication and Operationalisation*, Workshop Report, Addis Ababa, Ethiopia, 30 November—2 December 2015, p 8.

[33] D Forsythe, 'International Humanitarian Assistance: The Role of the Red Cross' (1996–1997) 3 *Buffalo Journal of International Law* 235, 239.

In recognition of the challenges of humanitarian access for agencies on the ground, in the past couple of decades the coherence (and divergences) between IHL and refugee law,[34] or IHL and human rights law,[35] have been examined. There has also been an increased focus on understanding the linkages between these established branches of international law and contemporary challenges, such as the increasing incidence of internal displacement and greater societal vulnerability to natural and human-made disasters.[36] A significant example is the Nansen Initiative commenced by the Norwegian and Swiss governments in 2012 to examine the protection gap for people displaced across borders as a result of disasters and the effects of climate change.[37] Led by the former Representative of the UN Secretary-General on the Human Rights of Internally Displaced Persons, Walter Kälin, this governmental initiative explored the connections between refugees, forced displacement, disasters and climate change through research, case studies and policy papers.[38] Following a series of regional consultations, a 'Protection Agenda' was finalised at a global intergovernmental conference in Geneva in October 2015 to build consensus on the policy and legal implications of such cross-border displacement.[39]

This expanding and evolving web of laws, policies and practices relating to protection and assistance for persons in humanitarian crises provides an opportunity to re-evaluate the motivations and objectives underlying applicable provisions of these different branches of international law. By

[34] See R Brett and E Lester, 'Refugee Law and International Humanitarian Law: Parallels, Lessons and Looking Ahead' (September 2001) 83(843) *International Review of the Red Cross* 713; S Jaquemet, 'The Cross-Fertilization of International Humanitarian Law and International Refugee Law' (September 2001) 83(843) *International Review of the Red Cross* 651.

[35] See T Meron, 'On the Inadequate Reach of Humanitarian and Human Rights Law and the Need for a New Instrument' (July 1983) 77(3) *American Journal of International Law* 589; R Barber, 'Facilitating Humanitarian Assistance in International Humanitarian and Human Rights Law' (June 2009) 91(855) *International Review of the Red Cross* 371.

[36] See D Fisher, 'Domestic Regulation of International Humanitarian Relief in Disasters and Armed Conflict: A Comparative Analysis' (June 2007) 89(866) *International Review of the Red Cross* 345. See also G Venturini, 'International Disaster Response Law in Relation to Other Branches of International Law' in A de Guttry, M Gestri and G Venturini (eds), *International Disaster Response Law* (Springer Press, 2012) 45–64; plus specific chapters on the relationship between disasters and armed conflicts (ch 11), various aspects of human rights law (chs 14–17), and international criminal law (ch 18) in the same volume.

[37] For further discussion of the Nansen Initiative, see ch 9, Section II.C.

[38] See W Kälin and N Schrepfer, *Protecting People Crossing Borders in the Context of Climate Change: Normative Gaps and Possible Approaches*, UNHCR Division of International Protection (February 2012); J McAdam, *Climate Change Displacement and International Law: Complementary Protection Standards*, UNHCR Division of International Protection (May 2011). See also: R Cohen and M Bradley, 'Disasters and Displacement: Gaps in Protection' (2010) 1 *Journal of International Humanitarian Legal Studies* 95.

[39] The Nansen Initiative, *Global Consultation Conference Report* (Geneva, 12–13 October 2015).

drawing together divergent sources of direct relevance to humanitarian action (including the acknowledged coherence, overlaps and gaps between traditionally distinct aspects of international law) an *acquis humanitaire* can be discerned. Figure 2.2 below sets out the principal branches of international law that directly contribute to the protection and assistance of persons in humanitarian crises (without reflecting specific areas of overlap). However, it should also be noted that while these five identified bodies of law provide key sources of the *acquis humanitaire*, other existing and emerging branches also exist and transect the *acquis humanitaire*. For example, Lawrence Gostin has proposed the concept of a global health law based on the basic human right to live a healthy life. In particular, Gostin calls for genuine global solidarity (not just foreign assistance) to tackle both international concerns such as the threat of pandemic diseases, such as Ebola and flu pandemics, and challenges for domestic healthcare systems such as mental health, tobacco control and AIDS.[40]

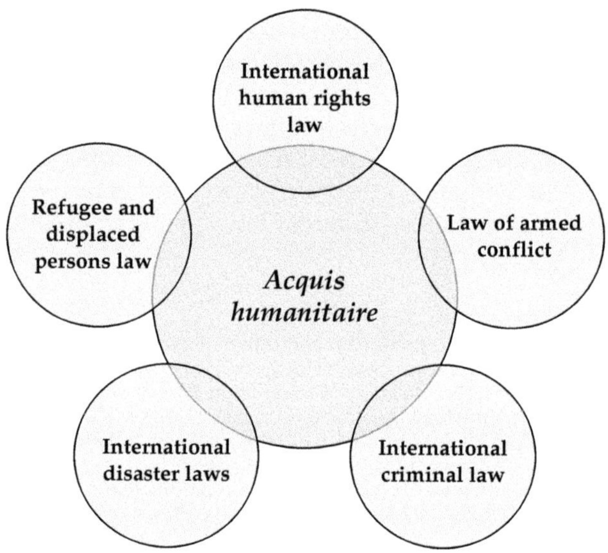

Figure 2.2: Sources of the *acquis humanitaire*

From the perspective of both state practice and international law, the UN General Assembly has provided a consistent focus on humanitarian assistance for over 40 years, highlighting the importance governments place

[40] L Gostin, *Global Health Law* (Harvard University Press, 2014). See in particular 'Health and Human Rights' (ch 8).

on the effective delivery of aid.[41] Moreover, general international law contains express rules for humanitarian activities, with specialised multilateral treaties elaborating obligations and mechanisms of direct relevance for humanitarian response operations, including those in the Tampere Convention on the Provision of Telecommunication Resources for Disaster Mitigation and Relief Operations[42] and the Framework Convention on Civil Defence Assistance.[43] Other multilateral conventions, such as the UN Convention on Facilitation of International Maritime Traffic,[44] include subsidiary provisions relating to emergency responses without a primary aim of regulating international humanitarian activities per se. Further multilateral conventions regulate specific types of human-made disasters, such as the UN Convention on Assistance in the Case of Nuclear Accident or Radiological Emergency[45] drawn up following the Chernobyl disaster. Finally, under customary international law civilians in times of armed conflict are entitled to specific humanitarian support,[46] and the potential emergence of provisions in customary international law relating to disasters has been identified but remains insufficiently analysed to date.[47]

Moreover, the fundamental importance of non-governmental sources in international law making have long been recognised,[48] so the *acquis humanitaire* incorporates a wide range of non-binding texts developed by

[41] See, eg, the series of General Assembly resolutions on humanitarian issues entitled: *Strengthening of the Coordination of Humanitarian Emergency Assistance of the United Nations*, most recently UNGA Res 70/106 (10 December 2015); *Safety and Security of Humanitarian Personnel and Protection of United Nations Personnel*, most recently UNGA Res 70/104 (10 December 2015); *International Cooperation on Humanitarian Assistance in the Field of Natural Disasters, from Relief to Development*, most recently UNGA Res 70/107 (10 December 2015). For discussion, see A Katoch, 'International Natural Disaster Response and the United Nations' in IFRC, *International Disaster Response Laws, Principles and Practice: Reflections, Prospects and Challenges* (2003).

[42] Tampere Convention on the Provision of Telecommunication Resources for Disaster Mitigation and Relief Operations (adopted 18 June 1998, entered into force 8 January 2005) 2296 UNTS 5.

[43] Framework Convention on Civil Defence Assistance, International Civil Defence Association (adopted 22 May 2000, entered into force 23 September 2001) 2172 UNTS 213.

[44] UN Convention on Facilitation of International Maritime Traffic (adopted 9 April 1965, entered into force 5 March 1967) 591 UNTS 265.

[45] UN Convention on Assistance in the Case of Nuclear Accident or Radiological Emergency (adopted 26 September 1986, entered into force 26 February 1987) 1457 UNTS 133.

[46] JM Henckaerts, 'Customary International Humanitarian Law: Taking Stock of the ICRC Study' (2010) 78 *Nordic Journal of International Law* 435. See also Section II.B below.

[47] See M Hoffman, 'What is the Scope of International Disaster Response Law?' in IFRC, *International Disaster Response Laws*, above n 20, 16; IFRC, *Desk Study*, above n 20, 21–22; E Valencia-Ospina, *Preliminary Report on the Protection of Persons in the Event of Disasters* (8 May 2008) A/CN.4/598, para 42.

[48] M Reimann, 'From the Law of Nations to Transnational Law: Why We Need a New Basic Course for the International Curriculum' (2003–2004) 22 *Penn State International Law Review* 397, 403–04.

inter-governmental and non-governmental humanitarian actors.[49] Relevant sources include the influential 1994 Code of Conduct for the International Red Cross and Red Crescent Movement and NGOs in Disaster Relief which elaborated the humanitarian imperative to alleviate human suffering without discrimination wherever it may be.[50] Despite its title stating it is for 'Disaster Relief', the RCRC Code of Conduct is intended to apply in both situations of armed conflicts and natural or human-made disasters.[51] Subsequent Red Cross guidance for governments in respect of their national legislation for disaster-preparedness and response includes the IDRL Guidelines[52] and the Model Act and Model Emergency Decree for the Facilitation and Regulation of International Disaster Relief and Initial Recovery Assistance.[53] Other influential non-binding texts for state and non-state responses to various types of humanitarian crises include the *Sphere Handbook*,[54] IASC operational guidelines on the protection of persons in natural disasters,[55] UN Guiding Principles on Internal Displacement,[56] and the Guiding Principles of UNGA Resolution 46/182.[57]

In addition to promoting a systematic framework for understanding evolving legal obligations by identifying positive rights and duties applicable in humanitarian crises, such binding and non-binding sources of the *acquis humanitaire* also provide practical and operational guidance to humanitarian agencies. Perhaps even more pertinently, non-binding texts can significantly influence funding decisions. As noted in the context of the Sendai Framework for disaster risk reduction, 'conventions and frameworks at this scale tend to guide the flow of funding and project

[49] See generally D Cubie, 'An Analysis of Soft Law Applicable to Humanitarian Assistance: Relative Normativity in Action?' (2011) 2 *Journal of International Humanitarian Legal Studies* 177.

[50] Hereinafter 'the RCRC Code of Conduct'. For discussion, see D Hilhorst, 'A Living Document? The Code of Conduct of the Red Cross and Red Crescent Movement and NGOs in Disaster Relief', research paper for conference *Ten Years Code of Conduct: Principles in Practice*, Disaster Studies Wageningen University, 2004.

[51] For analysis by one of its principal authors, see P Walker, 'Cracking the Code: The Genesis, Use and Future of the Code of Conduct' (2005) 29(4) *Disasters* 323.

[52] IFRC, *Introduction to the Guidelines for the Domestic Facilitation and Regulation of International Disaster Relief and Initial Recovery Assistance* (2008) (the IDRL Guidelines). For discussion, see ch 8, Section III.C.i.

[53] For discussion, see ch 8, Section III.C.ii.

[54] *Sphere Handbook*, above n 17.

[55] IASC, *Operational Guidelines on the Protection of Persons in Situations of Natural Disasters*, Brookings-Bern Project on Internal Displacement (January 2011). These Operational Guidelines provide practical advice to humanitarian agencies for implementation of rights-based approaches.

[56] UN Commission on Human Rights, *The Guiding Principles on Internal Displacement* (1998) E/CN.4/1998/53/Add.2. For discussion, see ch 9, Section II.B.

[57] UNGA, *Res 46/182*, above n 16.

implementation for a considerable period (often a decade or more)'.[58] Understandably, such funding decisions can have a direct impact on state practice and other humanitarian actors. Yet considering the wide divergence of cultural, religious and ideological backgrounds of the multitude of humanitarian actors likely to respond to a major humanitarian crisis, can one identify a fundamental or underlying basis for the proposed *acquis humanitaire*?

B. Conceptual Underpinnings: Humanity and Human Dignity

The conceptual basis of the *acquis humanitaire* is founded equally on the principle of humanity ('the cornerstone of the protection of persons in international law') and the concept of human dignity ('the primary aim of humanitarian activity, regardless of the context or actor'). As set out below, the rationale for identifying these as the conceptual underpinnings for the normative content of the *acquis humanitaire* reflects on-going transnational interactions between and interpretations by key actors, including the International Law Commission (ILC), UN Secretary-General, the World Humanitarian Summit, academic commentators and humanitarian practitioners.

i. Humanity

> In the doctrine of the Red Cross, the principle of humanity, from which all the other principles flow, obviously has to stand in first place.
>
> Jean Pictet, 1979[59]

Despite the ILC's reluctance to pronounce whether or not the humanitarian principles of humanity, neutrality and impartiality have become part of general international law, the ILC has noted that they are 'core principles recognised as foundational to humanitarian assistance'.[60] As discussed in chapter one,[61] these humanitarian principles have received widespread support in a range of international legal contexts such as UNGA Resolution 46/182 and the ICRC Customary International Humanitarian Law

[58] A Tozier de la Poterie and M-A Baudoin, 'From Yokohama to Sendai: Approaches to Participation in International Disaster Risk Reduction Frameworks' (June 2015) 6(2) *International Journal of Disaster Risk Science* 128, 129.

[59] J Pictet, 'The Fundamental Principles of the Red Cross: Commentary' (May–June 1979) 210 *International Review of the Red Cross* 130, 144.

[60] For the final text of the preamble, draft articles and commentaries adopted by the ILC, see Official Records of the General Assembly, Seventy-first Session, *Supplement No 10* (A/71/10), Chapter IV: Protection of Persons in the Event of Disasters (2016).

[61] See ch 1, Section I.C.

project,[62] as well as non-binding normative texts such as the RCRC Code of Conduct and the *Sphere Handbook*, thereby highlighting a broad consensus between both state and non-state actors as to their normative and operational applicability. However, despite the recognised applicability and importance of the core humanitarian principles as operative standards, the extent of their acceptance in state practice as legal obligations has been contested. In the 1980s, Theodor Meron noted the tendency of international judicial bodies 'to assume that noble humanitarian principles that deserve recognition as the positive law of the international community have in fact been recognised as such by states'.[63] Likewise, Hugo Slim has argued that despite the importance of altruism to human nature, it is usually in 'fierce competition with human traits which tend towards inhumanity, like fear, oppression, self-determination, enmity, hatred, aggression and violence'.[64]

Yet the International Law Commission has singled out the principle of humanity as 'the cornerstone of the protection of persons in international law' due to its recognition in various branches of international law.[65] As far back as 1758, Emer de Vattel advanced a natural law duty to provide humanitarian assistance, noting that 'To give assistance in such extreme necessity is so essentially conformable to humanity, that the duty is seldom neglected by any nation that has received the slightest polish of civilization'.[66] States have likewise accepted hard obligations based on the principle of humanity, with the 1899 Convention with respect to the Laws of War on Land codifying a general protection for non-combatants on the basis of 'the laws of humanity and the requirement of the public conscience'.[67] Fifty years later, in the Corfu Channel case, the International Court of Justice affirmed that elementary considerations of humanity were well-recognised principles of the international legal order 'even more exacting in peace than in war'.[68] Such an approach was reflected in the definition of 'crimes against humanity' in the 1998 Rome Statute of the International Criminal Court (ICC), which criminalises actions undertaken as part of a 'widespread or systematic attack directed against

[62] See Section II.B below.

[63] T Meron, 'The Geneva Conventions as Customary Law' (1987) 81 *American Journal of International Law* 348, 361.

[64] H Slim, 'Relief Agencies and Moral Standing in War: Principles of Humanity, Neutrality, Impartiality and Solidarity' (November 1997) 7(4) *Development in Practice* 342, 346.

[65] *Commentary to draft article 7*, A/69/10, above n 60, 103.

[66] E de Vattel, *The Law of Nations or the Principles of Natural Law Applied to the Conduct and to the Affairs of Nations and of Sovereigns*, 1758, Books I–IV, vol iii, 114.

[67] Convention with respect to the Laws and Customs of War on Land (Hague II) (adopted 29 July 1899, entered into force 4 September 1900) 32 Stat 1803, Treaty Series 403.

[68] Corfu Channel (*United Kingdom of Great Britain and Northern Ireland v Albania*), Merits, Judgment, ICJ Reports 1949, 4, 22.

any civilian population'.[69] More recently, Wilson and Brown noted that 'human rights and humanitarian law share a view of humanity as a unified legal community when crimes are committed that offend not only a nation or country, but the entire human race'.[70]

Drawing on such sources, Ruti Teitel has advanced the concept of a modern 'humanity's law', which she describes as a body of law encompassing the laws of war, international human rights law and international criminal justice that 'legal and political actors employ … as they confront the challenges of conflict and insecurity'.[71] While not proposing the formal merger of these three branches of law, Teitel describes the humanity law framework as one which 'reconceives security in terms of the protection and preservation of persons and peoples'.[72] Yet there remains disagreement on the legal impact of the principle of humanity. As argued by Greece in debates on the ILC draft articles on the protection of persons in the event of disasters, although the principle of humanity may constitute a 'motivating factor and an overarching idea in all disaster-response operations, [it] was scarcely measurable in legal terms'.[73] Moreover, Theodor Meron, writing in 2000, regretfully noted the sharp contrast between the developing normative framework of 'humanization' and the 'harsh, often barbaric reality of the battlefield'.[74]

Nevertheless, the normative importance of humanity as a humanitarian principle continues to be of direct relevance to all branches of humanitarian action, as evidenced in the preparations for the World Humanitarian Summit in May 2016. The UN Secretary-General's advance report was entitled An Agenda for Humanity, and identified five core responsibilities of the international community, including the need to uphold the norms that safeguard humanity (particularly in the context of armed conflicts) and to invest in humanity (in particular reducing risk to known natural and human-made hazards).[75]

[69] Art 7(1) Rome Statute of the International Criminal Court (adopted 17 July 1998, entered into force 1 July 2002) 2187 UNTS 3.

[70] 'Introduction' in RA Wilson and RD Brown (eds), *Humanitarianism and Suffering: The Mobilization of Empathy* (Cambridge University Press, 2009) 5.

[71] R Teitel, *Humanity's Law* (Oxford University Press, 2011) 4, 6. See also: R Teitel, 'Humanity's Law: Rule of Law for the New Global Politics' (2002) 35(2) *Cornell International Law Journal* 355; Teitel, 'Humanity Law', above n 24. For analysis of Teitel's concept of humanity law, see G Hankel, 'Book Review: Humanity's Law' (2012) 23(2) *European Journal of International Law* 583.

[72] Teitel, *Humanity's Law*, above n 71, 13.

[73] *Summary of 22nd UNGA Sixth Committee Meeting 2010* (1 December 2010) A/C.6/65/SR.22, para 50.

[74] T Meron, 'The Humanization of Humanitarian Law' (2000) 94 *American Journal of International Law* 239, 276.

[75] World Humanitarian Summit secretariat, *Agenda for Humanity: Annex to the Report of the Secretary-General for the World Humanitarian Summit*, advance unedited version (New York, United Nations, 2016), 4, 11.

ii. Human Dignity

In addition to the prominent role in international law played by the principle of humanity, the concept of human dignity forms a core rationale behind international human rights law. As affirmed in very first clause of the Preamble to the Universal Declaration of Human Rights: 'Recognition of the inherent dignity and of the equal and inalienable rights of all members of the human family is the foundation of freedom, justice and peace in the world.'[76] Likewise, the first article of the EU's Charter of Fundamental Rights proclaims that: 'Human dignity is inviolable. It must be respected and protected.'[77] Therefore, drawing inspiration from this fundamental tenet of international human rights law, the current text of the ILC draft articles uniquely include an operative article which affirms, in hortatory language, that: 'The inherent dignity of the human person shall be respected and protected in the event of disasters.'[78] Christopher McCrudden has argued that although the concept of human dignity may be interpreted differently in domestic adjudication systems, it provides an important method for interpreting human rights.[79] In particular, McCrudden identifies the basic minimum content of human dignity across religious, cultural and judicial spectrums, and argues that the core of human dignity contains three key elements:

1. Every human being possesses an intrinsic worth, merely by being human;
2. This intrinsic worth should be recognised and respected by others; and
3. The intrinsic worth of the individual requires that the state should be seen to exist for the sake of the individual human being, and not vice versa.[80]

Despite the differential interpretation within domestic judicial interpretations of the concept of human dignity, the existence of a 'minimum core'

[76] Preamble, *Universal Declaration of Human Rights* (adopted 10 December 1948) UNGA Res 217 A(III) (hereinafter 'UDHR').

[77] Art 1 Charter of Fundamental Rights of the European Union, Official Journal of the European Union C 326/391 (26.10.2012). Indeed, the entire first section of the Charter is entitled 'Dignity'.

[78] Draft Art 4, Official Records of the General Assembly, A/71/10, above n 60, p 14.

[79] As noted by McCrudden, many judicial decisions based on human dignity view the concept not as a synonym for human rights but rather as 'expressing a value unique to itself, on which human rights are built'. C McCrudden, 'Human Dignity and Judicial Interpretation of Human Rights' (2008) 19(4) *European Journal of International Law* 655, 680–81. For discussion of human dignity in humanitarian and human rights instruments, see 667–71.

[80] ibid, 679–80. There is a growing body of literature on the concept of human dignity in both domestic and international law; see generally: S Hennette-Vauchez, 'A Human *Dignitas*? Remnants of the Ancient Legal Concept in Contemporary Dignity Jurisprudence' (2011) 9(1) *International Journal of Constitutional Law* 32; C O'Mahony, 'There Is No Such Thing as a Right to Dignity' (2012) 10(2) *International Journal of Constitutional Law* 551. For a detailed jurisprudential examination of human dignity, see P Capps, *Human Dignity and the Foundations of International Law* (Hart Publishing, 2010).

relating to the intrinsic worth of each individual ties directly into the motivation and foundations of humanitarian action: namely, assisting people in times of extreme distress to ensure that a certain minimum of protection and respect is accorded to them despite the challenging circumstances they find themselves in.[81] Therefore, by recognising human dignity as the core principle that informs and underpins international human rights law, the ILC draft articles authoritatively connect humanitarian action with human rights.[82] Indeed, the synthesis report of global consultations for the 2016 World Humanitarian Summit noted that: 'People's safety and dignity must be considered the primary aim of humanitarian activity, regardless of context or actor.'[83] Such an approach acknowledges the coherence between humanitarian law, disaster law and human rights law, and the similarities in the underlying motivations for the establishment of international rules regulating humanitarian and human rights protection. Likewise, recognition of the role of the state in providing a minimum level of protection (either directly or through external assistance) reflects the need for accountability mechanisms to ensure compliance. As the International Criminal Tribunal for the Former Yugoslavia forcefully noted in the Furundzija case:

> The essence of the whole corpus of international humanitarian law as well as human rights law lies in the protection of the human dignity of every person, whatever his or her gender. The general principle of respect for human dignity is the basic underpinning and indeed the very raison d'être of international humanitarian law and human rights law; indeed in modern times it has become of such paramount importance as to permeate the whole body of international law. This principle is intended to shield human beings from outrages upon their personal dignity, whether such outrages are carried out by unlawfully attacking the body or by humiliating and debasing the honour, the self-respect or the mental well-being of a person.[84]

It should, however, be recognised that there is an inherent flexibility of interpretation, judicially or otherwise, in the principles of humanity and human dignity—not least as they can be understood from a moral or

[81] For discussion of the minimum core set out by McCrudden, see P Carozza, 'Human Dignity and Judicial Interpretation of Human Rights: A Reply' (2008) 19(5) *European Journal of International Law* 931, 936–37. For a contrary (anthropological) view that human dignity has an important role to play as an abstract concept in humanitarianism, but not as an operative goal, see R Nockerts and P Van Arsdale, 'A Theory of Obligation' (May 2008) *Journal of Humanitarian Assistance*.

[82] Draft Art 5 states: 'Persons affected by disasters are entitled to the respect for and protection of their human rights in accordance with international law.' See Official Records of the General Assembly, A/71/10, above n 60, p 15.

[83] World Humanitarian Summit secretariat, *Restoring Humanity: Synthesis of the Consultation Process for the World Humanitarian Summit* (New York, United Nations, 2015) 23.

[84] *Prosecutor v Furundzija*, Judgment (1T-95-17/1-T) 10 December 1998, para 183.

ethical perspective, as well as legally. Nevertheless, the commonality of the principles of humanity and human dignity across different types of emergency situations and different branches of international law supports the argument that general international law should now recognise the role and importance played by these principles in the planning and delivery of humanitarian action.

iii. Human Rights Conditionality

While there may be a general commonality of motivation, this is not to say that humanitarianism and human rights are synonymous.[85] Traditional humanitarians in the nineteenth century may have worked to abolish slavery or improve the living conditions of the urban poor, but generally did not view the recipients of their charity as rights-bearing individuals.[86] Such differences remain today, as evidenced by the debate between the more politically active rights-based approaches to humanitarianism and more traditional needs-based approaches.[87] The more muscular 'new' humanitarianism, exemplified by organisations such as MSF which apply political conditionality to the delivery of services, can be contrasted with more 'traditional' humanitarian organisations which argue that the withholding of aid due to the human rights record of the affected state can create classes of deserving and undeserving victims.[88] In rejecting the politicisation of aid represented by new humanitarianism, Fiona Fox of CAFOD has argued that human rights conditionality has produced a moral hierarchy of victims. Citing the limited support provided to the Serbian population during the Kosovo bombing in 1999, Fox notes that despite obvious need across the country, the EU only offered fuel to those town councils which had opposed President Slobodan Milošević.[89] So while most humanitarian agencies aim to work in an impartial (or non-discriminatory) manner, there is less consensus on the principle of neutrality. Indeed, the debate about the role of 'neutrality' in humanitarian action, and the contentious question of military humanitarian interventions, reflects deeper divisions between humanitarian agencies over rights-based and needs-based

[85] Nockerts and Van Arsdale, 'Theory of Obligation', above n 81.

[86] 'Introduction', Wilson and Brown (eds), *Humanitarianism and Suffering*, above n 70, 11.

[87] For discussion, see ch 3, Section II.

[88] For discussion of 'new humanitarianism', see C Allan and T O'Donnell, 'An Offer You Cannot Refuse? Natural Disasters, the Politics of Aid Refusal and Potential Legal Implications' (2013) 5(1) *Amsterdam Law Forum* 36, 59–62; A Orford, 'Muscular Humanitarianism: Reading the Narratives of the New Interventionism' (1999) 10 *European Journal of International Law* 679.

[89] F Fox, 'New Humanitarianism: Does It Provide a Moral Banner for the 21st Century?' (2001) 25(4) *Disasters* 275, 282.

approaches to humanitarian action. In addition, by highlighting the differences between armed conflicts and disasters, ILC member Ali Mohsen Fetais Al-Marri has argued that the principle of neutrality was inappropriate for the topic of protection of persons in the event of disasters, as it pertained exclusively to the sphere of armed conflicts.[90] Denise Plattner from the ICRC has similarly noted that, apart from in the context of international humanitarian law, 'scrutiny of other branches of international law in the light of the concept of neutrality seems inappropriate and likely to lead to misunderstandings.'[91]

Therefore, recognising the operational and ethical/moral debates regarding the concept of humanitarianism, and the principles of impartiality and neutrality in times of armed conflict,[92] I propose that the overarching principles of humanity and human dignity should be considered as the essential conceptual underpinning for the laws, policies and practices of humanitarian action contained within the *acquis humanitaire*. This is not to underestimate the importance of other humanitarian and human rights principles, such as independence, impartiality or non-discrimination. On the contrary, as will be explained below, the *acquis humanitaire* is conceived as a broad tent to include diverse operational and academic understandings of existing and emerging normative standards, while recognising that a conceptual framework for humanitarian preparations and responses does exist and has received legal force in certain circumstances. For example, the AU Kampala Convention for the Protection and Assistance of Internally Displaced Persons in Africa places a legal obligation on all state parties to '[r]espect and ensure respect for the principles of humanity and human dignity of internally displaced persons'.[93]

In particular, these two fundamental concepts cross-sect different branches of international law, thereby highlighting the coherence between the various sources of the *acquis humanitaire*. By identifying these two concepts as foundational to the *acquis humanitaire*, the underlying rationale and motivation for humanitarian rules and practice in armed conflicts, displacement and disasters are acknowledged, without limiting the content or status of norms within the *acquis humanitaire*. This provides leeway for developing the required minimum core of domestic protection in recognition of the potentially differential interpretations the concepts may have at

[90] *Provisional Summary Record of 3104th ILC Meeting*, A/CN.4/SR.3104, 7 February 2012, Mr Al-Marri, 10.

[91] D Plattner, 'ICRC Neutrality and Neutrality in Humanitarian Assistance' (1996) 36 (311) *International Review of the Red Cross* 161, 171.

[92] See Slim, 'Relief Agencies', above n 64, 346–48.

[93] Art 3(1)(c) African Union Convention for the Protection and Assistance of Internally Displaced Persons in Africa ('Kampala Convention') (adopted 22 October 2009, entered into force 6 December 2012).

the national or regional levels, alongside effective accountability mechanisms to monitor their application in practice. Furthermore, it reflects the reality of the overlapping work undertaken by many humanitarian actors in conflict, displacement and disaster settings (and the potential difficulty of determining clear divisions between such settings),[94] while recognising their divergent operational modalities to issues such as neutrality.

C. Demarcating the *Acquis Humanitaire*

Although one cannot situate the evolving body of humanitarian norms within a single institutional framework, in contrast to the EU's *acquis communautaire*, it is possible to identify a variety of framework documents that establish specialised institutional regimes for component parts of the *acquis humanitaire*. For example, the 1998 ICC Rome Statute provides the key foundation for establishing individual criminal responsibility for internationally accepted crimes—including the deliberate targeting of humanitarian personnel and the wilful denial of humanitarian assistance—as well as international judicial structures for the prosecution of such offences. Similarly, the 1949 Geneva Conventions and 1977 Additional Protocols provide the overarching framework for the legal obligations of states and combatants in times of war, including requirements to provide protection and assistance to civilians, while also reaffirming the institutional mandates of the ICRC and national relief societies. Meanwhile, the 1951 Refugee Convention and 1967 Protocol provide the legal basis for the protection of persons fleeing specific forms of persecution across international borders, and the non-binding UN Guiding Principles on Internal Displacement offer concrete and authoritative guidance on protection and assistance for non-international forced population movements. The absence of an internationally binding legal text for humanitarian responses to disasters reflects the inherently dynamic and evolving nature of the *acquis humanitaire*. One can envisage that the ILC draft articles for the protection of persons in the event of disasters may in time become the institutional and overarching framework for humanitarian actions relating to major natural and human-made disasters. Indeed, there is already support within the ILC and from states for the draft articles to be concluded as a Framework Convention.[95] Such a framework

[94] For discussion of the difficulties in identifying the root causes of population movements, see E Ferris, 'Climate Change and Internal Displacement: A Contribution to the Discussion', Brookings-Bern Project on Internal Displacement, February 2011.

[95] At the conclusion of the second reading of the draft articles in August 2016, the ILC formally recommended that the General Assembly should elaborate a convention on the

would then be read in conjunction with inter-governmental non-binding texts such as the Sendai Framework for Disaster Risk Reduction[96] and non-governmental documents such as the IFRC IDRL Guidelines.[97] Nevertheless, as noted by Verdirame in his analysis of the international law of humanitarian assistance back in 2001: 'there is a degree of conceptual fluidity with notions, categories, and principles moving across these legal regimes [IHL, refugee law and human rights law], often accompanied by a process of partial re-definition and contextual adaptation.'[98]

In another key difference from the EU's *acquis communautaire*, the proposed *acquis humanitaire* does not require states to incorporate all its provisions into their domestic law. Rather, the *acquis humanitaire* provides a mechanism to identify the sources that form the legal and policy framework of humanitarian actions in times of crisis. Despite the *acquis humanitaire* encompassing both highly developed systems of positive international law, such as the law of armed conflict and refugee protection, and evolving systems such as international criminal law and international disaster laws, the common themes of humanity and human dignity underpin these various sources. Moreover, by incorporating legal obligations to protect persons in humanitarian crises, in addition to technical regulations for the effective delivery of material assistance, the *acquis humanitaire* provides an inclusive framework for promoting and respecting the rights of individuals and groups, while simultaneously recognising the fundamental role played by operational standards and frameworks for efficient prevention and response activities.

The extent of political, academic and practitioner interest in the protection of persons in humanitarian crises indicates that the international community is currently engaged in a process of creating, strengthening and elaborating a broad body of laws and standards relating to humanitarian activities. Reflecting the on-going nature of these developments, interactions between multiple actors are stimulating a range of academic,

basis of the draft articles: Official Records of the General Assembly, A/71/10, above n 60, p 13. For the positions of various states, see: Official Records, Sixty-first session, *Supplement No 10* (A/61/10), Annex C, para 24; UNGA Sixth Committee's 22nd to 25th meetings in 2008 (A/C.6/63/SR.22—A/C.6/63/SR.25); and 20th to 22nd meetings in 2009 (A/C.6/64/SR.20—A/C.6/64/SR.22).

96 UNISDR, *Sendai Framework for Disaster Risk Reduction 2015–2030*, as adopted at the World Conference on Disaster Risk Reduction, 14–18 March 2015, Sendai, Miyagi, Japan (A/CONF.224/CRP.1). For discussion of this point, see R Connolly, E Flaux and A Wu, 'Working Paper on the ILC Draft Articles on the Protection of Persons in the Event of Disasters', Human Rights Centre, Queen's University Belfast, February 2016, 32–35.

97 IFRC, *IDRL Guidelines*, above n 52.

98 G Verdirame, 'Testing the Effectiveness of International Norms: The Provision of Humanitarian Assistance by the UN and Sexual Apartheid in Afghanistan' (2001) 23 *Human Rights Quarterly* 733, 746.

judicial, practitioner and state interpretations of the applicable humanitarian norms both internationally and at the domestic level. The resultant *acquis humanitaire* contains binding obligations from existing international law sources, including judicial decisions by international tribunals such as the International Court of Justice[99] and the European Court of Human Rights,[100] as well as authoritative non-binding norms for humanitarian action, such as the RCRC Code of Conduct. Taken together, the content and sources of these various authorities on prevention and response in conflict and non-conflict settings represent an emerging body of humanitarian laws, policies and practice.

This understanding of an *acquis humanitaire* draws from, but is not contiguous with, Ruti Teitel's elaboration of 'humanity's law' and connected global accountability mechanisms.[101] On the one hand, the *acquis humanitaire* addresses a broader set of concerns than Teitel's humanity's law, as it focuses on all situations of humanitarian crises, including peace-time natural and human-made disasters. Moreover, due to the operational nature of humanitarian action, more emphasis must be placed on non-binding norms developed by states and non-governmental actors, alongside positive domestic and international law. On the other hand, the content of *acquis humanitaire* is more narrowly focused, as the key aspect under consideration is the protection of persons and provision of material assistance by humanitarian actors, as opposed to questions of international peace, conflict and security per se. Identifying the sources and content of the *acquis humanitaire* highlights the disparate legal and normative influences on humanitarian actors in their operational programmes, while also providing an opportunity for legal analysis of these evolving influences. The *acquis humanitaire* therefore reflects many of the themes of Teitel's concept of humanity law by providing a detailed examination of the implementation of humanitarian action in times of armed conflict, forced displacement and major disasters. The *acquis humanitaire* can therefore be thought of as the conceptual basis and practical application of the 'law of humanitarian assistance', as a complement to Teitel's call to recognise the transformative emergence of a humanity law framework in international law and politics.

As explained in chapter four, the transnational legal process of multiple interactions leading to legal interpretations of emerging and existing humanitarian norms contained within this *acquis humanitaire* ultimately helps promote the internalisation of such norms into domestic legal and

[99] eg Military and Paramilitary Activities in and against Nicaragua (*Nicaragua v United States of America*), Merits, Judgment of 27 June 1986, ICJ Reports 1986, paras 242–43.

[100] For discussion of state responsibility to undertake preventative measures in ECtHR jurisprudence, see ch 5, Section II.C.i.

[101] Teitel, *Humanity's Law*, above n 71.

policy frameworks. As such, the *acquis humanitaire* is not intended as a constrictive description of purely positive law, but a dynamic reflection of the sources that influence state and humanitarian actors in their preparations for and responses to humanitarian crises. These sources may overlap in approach and content, but also reflect separate and distinct bodies of law and practice. So while the humanitarian motivations behind the law of armed conflict share many similarities with those of international criminal law or refugee law, in actual cases one must examine the specific humanitarian crisis to determine which binding or non-binding aspects of the *acquis humanitaire* may be applicable.

Following this introduction to the core components and conceptual underpinnings of the *acquis humanitaire*, it is necessary to examine the sources of its normative content. Considering the evolving nature of international law in general, and the normative content of the *acquis humanitaire* in particular, the following section will first examine international law-making processes which create binding and non-binding norms of relevance to humanitarian action, before examining the role of customary international law in the *acquis humanitaire*. The chapter will conclude with analysis of the opposing forces of fragmentation and cohesion between different branches of international law.

II. SOURCES OF THE *ACQUIS HUMANITAIRE*

A. Law, Non-Binding Norms and Non-Law

A strict legal positivist would argue that the inclusion of soft law sources within the *acquis humanitaire* represents an unnecessary and unhealthy blurring of the distinctions between 'law' and 'non-law'.[102] However, while 'soft law' does not create binding legal obligations on states, such non-binding norms can directly influence the actions of state and non-state actors.[103] In evolving areas of international law, such as the legal regulation of international humanitarian activities, clearly identifiable obligations are a necessary prerequisite to the codification, progressive development and domestic internalisation of international law. Nevertheless, the evolution of international humanitarian norms does not preclude non-binding sources exerting considerable authority in their own right, at times greater

[102] See P Weil, 'Towards Relative Normativity in International Law?' (1983) 77 *American Journal of International Law* 413; J Klabbers, 'The Redundancy of Soft Law' (1996) 65 *Nordic Journal of International Law* 167; J Klabbers, 'The Undesirability of Soft Law' (1998) 67 *Nordic Journal of International Law* 381.

[103] See M Finnemore, 'Are Legal Norms Distinctive?' (1999–2000) 32 *NYU Journal of International Law and Policy* 699.

than the authority wielded by binding international law.[104] Therefore, I use the term 'non-binding norms' to refer to the range of guidelines, recommendations and minimum standards relating to the protection of persons in humanitarian crises developed at operational, policy and political levels by states, humanitarian agencies and international organisations. This term is intended to reflect the strongly persuasive value one must place on certain documents,[105] which cannot be classified as internationally legally binding norms in themselves. Moreover, such non-binding norms should not be considered as enforceable from a judicial perspective, although they may engage other forms of accountability mechanisms.[106]

An example of the interplay between positive international law and non-binding policies and practices can be found in the Convention on the Rights of the Child, which requires state parties to 'undertake all appropriate legislative, administrative, and other measures for the implementation of the rights recognised in the present Convention'.[107] The Committee on the Rights of the Child has held that such general measures of implementation are intended to promote the full enjoyment of all rights through a series of policy and institutional approaches, including the establishment of governmental and independent coordinating and monitoring bodies, comprehensive data collection, awareness raising and training, and the development and implementation of appropriate policies, services and programmes.[108] Such an approach reflects the combination of legal and non-legal measures which are required to ensure effective accountability mechanisms. In short, 'non-binding norms' refer to authoritative norm-creating texts and practices which are not 'law' in the positivist sense but which may directly influence the actions of states, communities, combatants and humanitarian actors and therefore must be included within the *acquis humanitaire*.

i. Normative Hierarchies in International Law

As debates surrounding soft law exemplify, determining what constitutes 'law' at an international level is a complex task.[109] Prosper Weil argued

[104] For discussion of specific soft law sources, see Cubie, 'Analysis of Soft Law', above n 49.

[105] Steven Ratner has referred to soft law texts as 'tools of persuasion'. S Ratner, 'Does International Law Matter in Preventing Ethnic Conflict?' (2000) 32 *NYU Journal of International Law and Politics* 591, 695.

[106] For discussion of such accountability mechanisms, see ch 4, Section III.

[107] Art 4 CRC, above n 15.

[108] CRC, *General Comment No 5: General Measures of Implementation of the Convention on the Rights of the Child* (27 November 2003) CRC/GC/2003/5, para 9. As noted by the Committee, equivalent implementation provisions can be found in Art 2 ICCPR and Art 2 ICESCR, see para 5.

[109] See L Blutman, 'In the Trap of a Metaphor: International Soft Law' (2010) 59(3) *International and Comparative Law Quarterly* 605.

strongly against the concept of soft law, and coined the phrase 'relative normativity' in a pejorative sense to describe the blurring of the normative threshold between law and non-law in the international legal system.[110] By definition, such a blurring of the normative threshold entails the creation of a hierarchy of norms, whereby within the body of international law different legal obligations are ascribed a different legal weight. For example, it has been argued that the universal acceptance of the Geneva Conventions gives them a 'corresponding weight in international law'.[111] It is therefore generally accepted that a relative hierarchy exists within accepted international law ('hard law'), for example vis-à-vis *jus cogens* norms and obligations *erga omnes*[112] and in respect to the UN Charter.[113] However, as Dinah Shelton notes: 'while the concept [of *jus cogens*] is widely supported in the literature, sometimes to an abusive extent, state practice and judicial opinions have been slow to recognize or give legal effect to assertions of such norms.'[114] Furthermore, even if one accepts that a hierarchy exists between legally binding norms, there is still debate regarding the relative status of various international norms within such a hierarchy.[115]

Notwithstanding disputes regarding the existence or content of a hierarchy within international law, it is well recognised that resolutions and declarations by states, international organisations and other non-state actors can strongly influence state practice which, in turn, can lead to the creation of legally binding norms.[116] As a result, Jonathan Charney has argued for an expanded view of international law making, stressing

110 Weil, 'Relative Normativity', above n 102, 415.

111 A Wiebalck, 'International Humanitarian Law and the ICRC in the Republic of the Sudan' (2003) 36 *Comparative and International Law Journal of South Africa* 198, 205.

112 See: D Shelton, 'Normative Hierarchy in International Law' (2006) 100 *American Journal of International Law* 291; W Aceves, 'Relative Normativity: Challenging the Sovereignty Norm Through Human Rights Litigation' (2001–2002) 25 *Hastings International and Comparative Law Review* 261.

113 See Art 103 UN Charter: 'In the event of a conflict between the obligations of the Members of the United Nations under the present Charter and their obligations under any other international agreement, their obligations under the present Charter shall prevail.'

114 Shelton, 'Normative Hierarchy', above n 112, 292. Shelton further argues that, in practice, the real question is securing states' compliance with obligations they have already agreed to, such as in the UN Charter or Geneva Conventions, rather than imposing *jus cogens* obligations on dissenting states, 304–05.

115 See generally: T Meron, 'On a Hierarchy of International Human Rights' (1986) 80 *American Journal of International Law* 1; U Fastenrath, 'Relative Normativity in International Law' (1993) 4 *European Journal of International Law* 365; M Koskenniemi, 'Hierarchy in International Law: A Sketch' (1997) 8 *European Journal of International Law* 566.

116 As per Martha Finnemore: 'Moral norms with no legal status can have powerful effects on state behavior, as work on the suffrage, anti-slavery, anti-apartheid, and early human rights movements shows.' Finnemore, 'Are Legal Norms Distinctive?', above n 103, 702.

that pronouncements of multilateral forums play an important role in the process of international norm creation.[117] It follows that the outcomes of multilateral forums, such as declarations and resolutions, can advance and formalise international law. Norms can become part of international law through positive support within the international community as evidenced by decisions taken at international fora, followed by their publication in written form and notice being provided to the international legal system of the rule's existence.[118] Yet even such an expansion of the traditional positivist view of international law making still primarily refers to sources that emanate from the international legal system itself, such as UN General Assembly Resolutions, inter-governmental regional fora and specialised agencies of the international community. In an increasingly connected world with multiple transnational actors, it is hard to accept the traditional view of states as the sole creators of international law. As noted by Anne-Marie Slaughter:

> NGO's … face growing challenges to their accountability, to which they are responding by adopting codes of conduct on their own. These codes and norms may not seem like law at all. Yet scholars and practitioners seeking to predict actual behaviour must take them into account as empirical facts that guide action. Further … these bodies of rules may be templates for future law.[119]

This range of potential sources of international norms led Steven Ratner to note succinctly that 'softness and hardness come in degrees'.[120] Yet Martha Finnemore has questioned Ratner's conclusion that policy-makers are often unaware of or actively ignore the 'hardness' or 'softness' of international legal norms, arguing that a preliminary question must be asked: 'do legal norms … operate differently from any other kinds of norms in world politics?'[121] Finnemore notes that legal norms may be invested with authority due to a range of factors, including: a state's coercive powers; the fact that foreign policy-makers often have legal training so their professional experience influences the weight they place on legal norms; and cultural factors whereby 'the contemporary world is permeated by a culture that invests authority in impersonal rules, procedures, and legalities'. Ultimately, Finnemore argues that debate about hard and soft law is irrelevant if legal norms do not have distinctive effects over and above

[117] J Charney, 'Universal International Law' (1993) 87 *American Journal of International Law* 530, 544. For a more cynical take on the role of international institutions in the creation of international law, see U Baxi, 'Too Many, or Too Few, Human Rights?' (2001) 1 *Human Rights Law Review* 1.

[118] Charney, above n 117, 544–47.

[119] A-M Slaughter, 'A Liberal Theory of International Law' (April 2000) 94 *American Society of International Law Proceedings* 240, 243–44.

[120] Ratner, 'Does International Law Matter?', above n 105, 653.

[121] Finnemore, 'Are Legal Norms Distinctive?', above n 103, 701.

other forms of norms.[122] So despite moves to promote a more integrated understanding of norm creation and compliance between international lawyers and international relations scholars,[123] and areas of convergence between legal theories such as transnational legal process and international relations theories such as constructivism, there remains a conceptual gap between the weight placed on 'legal norms' and 'non-legal norms' between the two disciplines.[124]

Nevertheless, as some 'soft law' sources directly influence state practice, it follows that one must place greater weight on such sources. This suggests a hierarchy within non-law sources, in addition to the differentiation between law/non-law and the internal hierarchy within accepted international norms. For example, Walter Kälin has described the Guiding Principles on Internal Displacement as 'hard standards even if they are still not hard law'.[125] Jan Klabbers, meanwhile, identified the question faced by international lawyers as such:

> The problem with law ... is that descriptive things tend to take on normative meaning, or more accurately: descriptive categories sooner or later transform into normative categories ... [A]cademic international lawyers' ... training consists of transforming practice into norms; so it almost inevitably follows that whatever descriptions we come up with, tend to become normatively relevant.[126]

So arguably, international law faces an inflationary tendency whereby non-law becomes soft law, soft law becomes hard law, and certain customary and treaty norms become *jus cogens*.[127] This can be seen as a positive reflection of the progressive development of international law, if one accepts that there is a benefit of legal certainty for individuals and the international community resulting from the creation of binding international legal rules.[128] However, this can also mask the fact that non-binding

[122] ibid, 703–05.

[123] See: A-M Slaughter-Burley, 'International Law and International Relations Theory: A Dual Agenda' (1993) 87 *American Journal of International Law* 205; A-M Slaughter, A Tulumello and S Wood, 'International Law and International Relations Theory: A New Generation of Interdisciplinary Scholarship' (1998) 92 *American Journal of International Law* 367.

[124] For discussion of the legal effects of 'non-legal norms', see: A Nollkaemper, 'The Distinction Between Non-Legal and Legal Norms in International Affairs: an Analysis with Reference to International Policy for the Protection of the North Sea from Hazardous Substances' (1998) 13 *International Journal of Marine and Coastal Law* 353, 363–67.

[125] W Kälin, 'How Hard is Soft Law? The Guiding Principles on Internal Displacement and the Need for a Normative Framework', presentation at Roundtable Meeting, Ralph Bunche Institute for International Studies, 19 December 2001, 8.

[126] Klabbers, 'Undesirability of Soft Law', above n 102, 385.

[127] Shelton, 'Normative Hierarchy', above n 112, 322.

[128] As per Preamble, VCLT: '*Believing* that the codification and progressive development of the law of treaties ... will promote the purposes of the United Nations set forth in the Charter, namely, the maintenance of international peace and security, the development of friendly relations and the achievement of cooperation among nations.'

norms may be complied with by states and non-state actors on the basis of political, moral or technical considerations, and not on the basis of legal obligation.[129]

ii. International Law Making and Humanitarian Action

This distinction between legal obligations which demand compliance and compliance based on non-legal considerations complicates determining which rules or standards should be applied to humanitarian activities. For example, David Fisher has argued that a general right to humanitarian assistance exists through binding obligations upon states set out in international humanitarian law, human rights law, and refugee law, as well as soft law sources and consistent state and humanitarian organisation practice.[130] Indeed, a range of processes over the past 35 years have led to the conclusion of authoritative non-binding resolutions, guidelines and minimum standards by states, international organisations and NGOs which aim to improve the delivery of material assistance and the protection of persons in humanitarian crises. So one must consider the interplay and relative importance of humanitarian norms that states comply with for non-legal reasons, for example due to domestic or international politics, humanitarian values, international relations or self-interest, and legal obligations originating in international law.[131]

It may be that non-binding norms relating to humanitarian activities constitute an important *stage* in the process of elaborating binding international law,[132] as a means of supplementing existing legal obligations or interpreting existing policies and practices. Dinah Shelton has explained this function of soft law as: 'part of an increasingly complex international system with variations in forms of instruments, means, and standards of measurement that interact intensely and frequently, with the common purpose of regulating behavior within a rule-of-law framework.'[133] On this basis, non-binding norms relating to humanitarian action can be seen as a guide to decision making for state and non-state humanitarian actors in the absence of specific binding international rules. Yet if this is the case, how does one

[129] See Ratner, 'Does International Law Matter?', above n 105, in particular 620–23.

[130] D Fisher, 'The Right to Humanitarian Assistance' in W Kälin et al (eds), *Incorporating the Guiding Principles on Internal Displacement into Domestic Law: Issues and Challenges*, ASIL and Brookings-Bern Project on Internal Displacement, Studies in Transnational Legal Policy, No. 41 (2010), 48.

[131] For a detailed account of compliance theories in international law and international relations, see H Koh, 'Why do Nations Obey International Law?' (June 1997) 106(8) *Yale Law Journal* 2599.

[132] Weil, 'Relative Normativity', above n 102, 417.

[133] Shelton, 'Normative Hierarchy', above n 112, 320.

measure the weight to be placed on a particular non-binding norm? As noted by Jean-Marie Henckaerts, the ICRC's Customary IHL project is premised on the recognition that: 'resolutions are normally not binding in themselves and therefore the value accorded to any particular resolution depends on its content, its degree of acceptance and the consistency of State practice outside it.'[134] So should more weight be placed on the content of a particular document, or on the form and process of its adoption? Are there soft obligations that run parallel to soft law or can hard obligations be teased from soft law sources? By analysing key internationally authoritative texts, one can identify certain non-binding norms that play an essential role for effective humanitarian action, albeit on the basis that these norms do not carry the weight of international law. As a result, subject to the voluntary application of these norms by humanitarian actors, their enforceability vis-à-vis the intended beneficiaries remain limited. As David Kennedy has noted:

> International humanitarians all too often come to think of their tools—multilateral declarations, documents, institutional networks—as having a kind of inherent humanitarian potency. And the commitment to more global governance fuels enthusiasm to develop and test drive new techniques. This tendency to enchant our tools should make us wary—it often comes at a cost to analysis of the substantive results of their use.[135]

In examining gender-discriminatory practices undertaken by the UN in humanitarian assistance operations during the Taliban rule in Afghanistan, Guglielmo Verdirame has warned that 'the "softer than soft law" body of institutional practice can end up being more "effective" in determining behavior than "hard law" ... in spite of the hierarchical superiority and the avowed greater normative strength of the latter'.[136] Therefore, in recognition of the different processes of norm-creation, Joost Pauwelyn et al coined the phrase 'informal international law making', or 'IN-LAW', to reflect the emergence of new actors, or levels of actors, who may play an influential role in international law making.[137] A key focus of the IN-LAW approach is to examine the challenges for accountability mechanisms at the domestic and international levels that output, process and/or actor informality may occasion. As such, the definition of informal international law making applied by Pauwelyn et al is:

> Cross-border cooperation between public authorities, with or without the participation of private actors and/or international organisations, in a forum other

[134] Henckaerts, 'Customary IHL', above n 46, 444.

[135] D Kennedy, *The Dark Sides of Virtue: Reassessing International Humanitarianism* (Princeton University Press, 2004) 119.

[136] Verdirame, 'Effectiveness of International Norms', above n 98, 736.

[137] J Pauwelyn, 'Informal International Lawmaking: Framing the Concept and Research Questions' in J Pauwelyn, R Wessel and J Wouters (eds), *Informal International Lawmaking* (Oxford University Press, 2012).

> than a traditional international organisation (process informality), and/or as between actors other than traditional diplomatic actors (such as regulators or agencies) (actor informality) and/or which does not result in a formal treaty or other traditional source of international law (output informality).[138]

We will return to the processes of norm-creation and accountability mechanisms in chapter four. For now, it is useful to note the relevance of the informal international law-making approach to understanding some of the sources of the *acquis humanitaire*.[139] Owing to the extensive interactions between non-governmental actors (in addition to public authorities and international organisations) active in humanitarian crises, chapter four also considers Harold Koh's theory of transnational legal process in detail. A transnational approach helps explain the non-traditional, non-statist, dynamic and normative elements of the *acquis humanitaire*, and methods for the social, political and legal internalisation of international norms at the domestic level.[140]

B. Customary International Law and State Practice

In addition to international conventions and non-binding norms, the third source of potential international obligations for humanitarian actors is customary international law.[141] In the *North Sea Continental Shelf* cases, the International Court of Justice (ICJ) clearly stressed that to create new rules of customary international law actions by states must be carried out in such a way 'as to be evidence of a belief that this practice is rendered obligatory by the existence of a rule of law requiring it', and that the frequency or even habitual character of specific acts is not in itself enough to constitute *opinio juris*.[142] Harold Koh discussed this traditional view of international law when he argued: '[T]he concept of legal obligation (so-called *opinio juris sive necessitatis*) emerged as the keystone for distinguishing customary international law from voluntary practice to which states might conform, but which they felt legally free to disregard. The very concept of obligatory custom assumed that nations, by virtue

[138] ibid, 22.

[139] For discussion of the Hyogo Framework from the perspective of IN-LAW, see: L Corredig, 'Effectiveness and Accountability of Disaster Risk Reduction Practices: An Analysis through the Lens of IN-LAW' in A Berman et al (eds), *Informal International Lawmaking: Case Studies* (Torkel Opsahl Academic Epublisher, 2012).

[140] See, eg, H Koh, 'Transnational Legal Process' (1996) 75 *Nebraska Law Review* 181; Koh, 'Why do Nations Obey?', above n 131.

[141] Art 38(1) Statute of the International Court of Justice. See generally Meron, 'Geneva Conventions', above n 63.

[142] North Sea Continental Shelf (*Germany v Denmark; Germany v The Netherlands*) Judgment, ICJ Reports 1969, 3, para 77.

of their sovereign statehood, had de facto consented to compliance with customary practices out of a sense of legal obligation.'[143] It has even been argued that instant customary international law can be created, for example through a unanimously accepted General Assembly Resolution that explicitly adopts particular principles as international law.[144] This key focus on the role played by state practice in the creation of customary international law is exemplified by the EU Guidelines on Promoting Compliance with International Humanitarian Law which assert that: 'Customary international law is formed by the practice of states which they accept as binding upon them.'[145]

Yet non-governmental and other transnational actors also play an important role in norm creation, including customary international law.[146] In addition to the traditionally accepted concept of 'state practice', Verdirame has identified three types of practice relevant to the identification of norms for humanitarian operations, namely: practice of political organs of the UN; institutional practice of specialised agencies; and operational practice on the ground.[147] For example, UNHCR has consistently argued that the principle of *non-refoulement* (non-return to a place where an individual is at risk) constitutes a rule of customary international law which all states are required to respect.[148] Likewise, the ICRC has played a fundamental role in expanding our understanding of the customary international law obligations in times of armed conflict. Owing to the divergent extent of signature and ratification of key international humanitarian law instruments (not least Additional Protocols I and II), in 1995 the ICRC commenced an extensive research project into the customary rules applicable in armed conflict, in conjunction with the Lauterpacht Centre of the University of Cambridge and the British Red Cross.[149] As discussed in chapter six, key customary rules identified by the ICRC relating specifically

143 Koh, 'Why do Nations Obey?', above n 131, 2608.

144 See H Charlesworth, 'Customary International Law and the Nicaragua Case' (1984–1987) 11 *Australian Yearbook of International Law* 1, 11; and generally B Simma and P Alston, 'The Sources of Human Rights Law: Custom, *Jus Cogens* and General Principles' (1988–1989) 12 *Australian Yearbook of International Law* 82.

145 *EU Guidelines on Promoting Compliance with International Humanitarian Law (IHL)* [2005] OJ C327/04, para 7.

146 Reimann, 'Transnational Law', above n 48, 403–04.

147 Verdirame, 'Effectiveness of International Norms', above n 98, 736–37.

148 See, eg, UNHCR, *The Principle of Non-Refoulement as a Norm of Customary International Law: Response to the Questions Posed to UNHCR by the Federal Constitutional Court of the Federal Republic of Germany in Cases 2 BvR 1938/93, 2 BvR 1953/93, 2 BvR 1954/93*, 31 January 1994 www.refworld.org/docid/437b6db64.html. See also E Lauterpacht and D Bethlehem, 'The Scope and Content of the Principle of *Non-Refoulement*: Opinion' in E Feller, V Türk and F Nicholson (eds), *Refugee Protection in International Law* (Cambridge University Press, 2003), in particular 140–63.

149 JM Henckaerts and L Doswald-Beck, *Customary International Humanitarian Law: Rules* (Cambridge University Press, 2009). See also Henckaerts, 'Customary IHL', above n 46.

to humanitarian action include that humanitarian relief personnel must be respected and protected,[150] and that parties to either international or non-international armed conflicts must allow unimpeded passage for impartial humanitarian relief for civilians.[151] Reflecting the authoritative nature of the ICRC study, it has been argued that their work is 'something in between private scholarly codification and codification by states'.[152]

Conversely, there has been limited examination of the potential customary rules applicable in disaster scenarios. In 2000 the IFRC highlighted the possibility that the minimum standards set out in the *Sphere Handbook* might be a case study of customary international law in formation.[153] However, Michael Hoffman subsequently noted that: 'Research completed to date does not suggest the existence of a system of customary IDRL, whereas customary rules are a long-established component of IHL'.[154] Eduardo Valencia-Ospina likewise noted in his 2008 Preliminary Report that: 'The IFRC … recognises that research does not suggest the existence of a system of customary IDRL … [However] IFRC research might yet produce evidence warranting reconsideration of that point.'[155] Conversely, Boško Jakovljević has argued that the provision of humanitarian assistance following natural disasters is 'so intense, dense, widespread, and extensive, that it represents a solid body of State practice, required for the formation of a customary law rule'.[156] However, Jakovljević was discussing a specific customary rule for third states to provide humanitarian assistance in disasters, while Hoffman and Valencia-Ospina were considering the broader concept of a system of customary rules relating to all aspects of disaster prevention, mitigation and response.

While state practice and *opinio juris* provide the overarching means of identification of customary international law rules, in reality it can prove challenging to determine in advance of a dispute arising which activities are binding on all states. This is evidenced by the fact that the ICRC study, while widely cited, is not considered a definitive determination of the customary international law rules for armed conflicts.[157] Indeed, in

150 Henckaerts and Doswald-Beck, above n 149, Rule 31. See ch 6, Section I.B.

151 Henckaerts and Doswald-Beck, above n 149, Rule 55.

152 T Treves, 'Customary International Law' in R Wolfrum (ed), *The Max Planck Encyclopaedia of Public International Law* (Oxford University Press, 2008) www.mpepil.com.

153 IFRC, *World Disasters Report 2000* (2000) 153.

154 Hoffman, 'Scope of IDRL', above n 20, 16.

155 Valencia-Ospina, *Preliminary Report*, above n 47, para 42. See also IFRC, *Desk Study*, above n 20, 21–22.

156 B Jakovljević, 'Right to Humanitarian Action and State Sovereignty', Report of the IIHL Roundtable: Humanitarian Action and State Sovereignty (2000) 95, 96.

157 As noted by François Bugnion at the launch of the ICRC CIL study in 2005. See Chatham House, *The Law of Armed Conflict: Problems and Prospects*, Transcripts and summaries of presentations and discussions, 18–19 April 2005, 3.

2012 the ILC added the identification of customary international law onto its work programme with the aim of producing 'authoritative guidance for those called upon to identify customary international law, including national and international judges'.[158] Considering the importance of customary international law in determining the actions of state and non-state actors, it follows that the normative content of the *acquis humanitaire* must include rules of customary international law relating to the provision of material assistance and the protection of persons in humanitarian crises. Taking into consideration the challenges of identifying such rules, guidance must come from both judicial pronouncements and authoritative statements of customary rules of international law, such as from UNHCR and the ICRC, as well as emerging understandings of new customary rules—for example in disaster settings.

C. Fragmentation and Coherence between Distinct Bodies of Law

Just as the phrase 'international law' itself can be viewed as comprising a series of interlinked yet distinct bodies of law (such as diplomatic immunity, the law of the sea, and commercial arbitration), so too can the phrase '*acquis humanitaire*'. As described above, provisions from several existing or emerging branches of international law fall within the ambit of the *acquis humanitaire*.[159] Such an approach recognises international law as a 'dense web of overlapping and detailed prescriptions' addressing diverse topics,[160] and has been expressly adopted by the UN Human Rights Council (HRC). In research examining the human rights implications of post-disaster and post-conflict situations, the HRC noted the similarity of the threats to health, safety, security and well-being of individuals in both disaster and conflict settings, and urged a holistic approach towards different branches of international law to ensure the effective protection of all human rights.[161] In a similar fashion, one of Philip Jessup's objectives in developing the concept of 'transnational law' was to challenge the traditional view of international law that ignored the connections between

158 UN, *Report of the International Law Commission*, Sixty-third session (2011) A/66/10, Annex A, para 4, 305.

159 For a similar approach in the context of the right to food, see L Cotula and M Vidar, *The Right to Adequate Food in Emergencies* (2002) FAO Legislative Study 77, 3.

160 See B Simma and D Pulkowski, 'Of Planets and the Universe: Self-contained Regimes in International Law' (2006) 17(3) *European Journal of International Law* 483, 483.

161 HRC, *Final Research-based Report of the Human Rights Council Advisory Committee on best practices and main challenges in the promotion and protection of human rights in post-disaster and post-conflict situations*, 28th Session of the HRC (10 February 2015) A/HRC/28/76, para 6.

its different branches.[162] In particular, Jessup was keen to highlight the blurring of the boundaries between international and national law, and public and private law.[163] One can argue that Jessup was returning to the more expansive description of the 'law of nations' provided by William Blackstone in the eighteenth century encompassing multiple actors, compared to Jeremy Bentham's more state-orientated understanding of 'international law' from the nineteenth century.[164]

Yet despite their similarities, the different bodies of law, policy and practice that make up the *acquis humanitaire* remain distinct. Using the language and imagery of François Hampson, international law is one train with many carriages, as opposed to several different trains.[165] For example, there are key differences in the enforcement mechanisms between international criminal law and international human rights law. The Rome Statute of the ICC creates individual criminal responsibility for specified actions, including the use of starvation as a method of warfare or deliberate attacks on humanitarian workers. States may either pursue cases within their domestic legal systems (for example through a court martial process for members of the armed forces or domestic criminal courts for civilians), through the establishment of hybrid domestic-international tribunals (as in Cambodia and Lebanon),[166] or alternatively the ICC may be empowered to pursue cases directly thereby engaging obligations of support from all state parties to the ICC. Yet the ICC is not simply the enforcement mechanism for breaches of the law of armed conflict. Domestic courts may be empowered to hear cases involving international crimes such as genocide or war crimes, while military forces may have internal accountability mechanisms or sanctions procedures.

Refugee law, meanwhile, is premised on national refugee status determination procedures, the exact composition of which each signatory state to the 1951 Refugee Convention is entitled to determine. However, as guardian of the Refugee Convention, UNHCR is entitled to provide non-binding normative guidance to states in the development and application of their

[162] C Oliver, 'Philip C Jessup's Continuing Contribution to International Law' (November 1962) 62(7) *Columbia Law Review* 1132, 1134–35.

[163] For a general overview, see Reimann, 'Transnational Law', above n 48.

[164] MW Janis, 'Jeremy Bentham and the Fashioning of "International Law"' (1984) 78 *American Journal of International Law* 405, 416.

[165] F Hampson, 'Other Areas of Customary Law in Relation to the Study' in E Wilmshurst and S Breau, *Perspectives on the ICRC Study on Customary International Humanitarian Law* (Cambridge University Press, 2007) 55–56. Hampson nevertheless notes there is considerable overlap, and therefore no rigid barriers, between different areas of international law, 56.

[166] See, eg, R Killean, 'Procedural Justice in International Criminal Courts: Assessing Victims' Perceptions of Justice at the Extraordinary Chambers in the Courts of Cambodia' (2016) 16(1) *International Criminal Law Review* 1.

refugee status determination regimes.[167] Conversely, international disaster laws at present do not have a clear overarching international legal framework and so lack even the guidance of whether compliance should be enforced via some international or regional tribunal or agency, or at the domestic level. Despite various UN human rights bodies and the European Court of Human Rights examining aspects of the human rights implications of disasters,[168] there remains a greater level of reliance on non-binding norms of humanitarian action to understand the potential content and limitations of the evolving field of 'international disaster laws'.

This understanding of the *acquis humanitaire* mirrors debates surrounding the fundamental nature of general international law and the inherent risk of fragmentation and potential existence of self-contained regimes arising from the increasing specialisation of particular branches of international law. Martti Koskenniemi and Päivi Leino have highlighted some of the challenges to general international law principles arising from the proliferation of fora for adjudication of international criminal law cases.[169] For example, the International Criminal Tribunal for the Former Yugoslavia interpreted the concept of state responsibility and effective control of non-state armed groups in the *Tadić* case[170] in a different manner from the ICJ in the *Nicaragua* case.[171] Koskenniemi and Leino argue that the threat to general principles of international law from forum proliferation and fragmentation of international law arises less from self-contained regimes than from semi-autonomous ones. They note that the core of the problem is perhaps 'not so much in the emergence of new sub-systems but in the use of general law by new bodies representing interests or views that are not identical with those represented in old ones'.[172] The potential for divergent interpretations by different courts, tribunals, or other adjudicatory bodies regarding the normative content of the *acquis humanitaire* must therefore be recognised. Indeed, the fragmentation of international law into functional regimes represents a serious threat to the concept of universalism, whether for human rights norms or general principles of international

[167] As noted by UNHCR, the rationale behind the 'good offices' role of UNHCR is that 'strengthened supervision by an international organization is indispensable for a predictable framework of international cooperation and to ensure the proper functioning of such a system'. UNHCR, *Note on the Mandate of the High Commissioner for Refugees and his Office* (October 2013) Division of International Protection, 6.

[168] See D Cubie and M Hesselman, 'Accountability for the Human Rights Implications of Natural Disasters: A Proposal for Systemic International Oversight' (2015) 33(1) *Netherlands Quarterly of Human Rights* 9.

[169] M Koskenniemi and P Leino, 'Fragmentation of International Law? Postmodern Anxieties' (2002) 15 *Leiden Journal of International Law* 553, 562–67.

[170] *The Prosecutor v Duško Tadić*, Appeals Judgment (IT-94-1-A) 15 July 1999.

[171] *Nicaragua v USA*, above n 99, 14.

[172] Koskenniemi and Leino, 'Fragmentation', above n 169, 561.

law.[173] As noted by Joost Pauwelyn: 'What must be avoided ... is this fragmentation leading to self-contained islands of international law, de-linked from other branches of international law'.[174]

As noted previously, the concept of an *acquis humanitaire* is not intended to be a prescriptive model of international law, or introduce new adjudicatory bodies. Neither should it be considered a 'special law'. Rather, it should be viewed as a means of highlighting specific aspects of existing branches of international law that aim to provide protection and assistance to persons in humanitarian crises. As Koskenniemi has argued: '[t]he point of the emergence of something like "international criminal law" or "international human rights law" (or any other special law) is precisely to institutionalise the new priorities carried within such fields.'[175] Pauwelyn meanwhile has discussed the need to bridge the fragmentation and unity of international law by 'connecting the different islands or branches of international law while at the same time respecting the need for specialization and the diversity between states'.[176] On this basis, the rationale for drawing together such laws, policies and practices of humanitarian action from different 'islands' of international law is the underlying motivation (or source of cohesion) behind such actions, namely the principles of humanity and human dignity in crises. Reflecting the range of factual scenarios that can give rise to large-scale human suffering, and therefore the applicable binding and non-binding norms of humanitarian action, one can argue that different interpretations are a crucial component of the process of developing and understanding the rights and obligations of various actors in humanitarian crises.[177] While there is a clear benefit to ensuring legal certainty for states and individuals, and coherence between different branches of international law, the multi-disciplinary and transnational nature of humanitarian action entails on-going multi-faceted dialogue between those directly affected, and those who aim to provide support and assistance. Such interactions may well lead to different interpretations of the applicable humanitarian norms, but this should be seen as a positive means of developing our understanding of the binding and non-binding normative content of the *acquis humanitaire*. The following chapter therefore examines in detail some of the different interpretations within international law and practice to the core concept of the protection of persons.

[173] Koskenniemi, 'Fate of Public International Law', above n 14.

[174] J Pauwelyn, 'Bridging Fragmentation and Unity: International Law as a Universe of Inter-connected Islands' (2003–2004) 25 *Michigan Journal of International Law* 903, 904.

[175] Koskenniemi, 'Fate of Public International Law', above n 14, 5.

[176] Pauwelyn, 'Bridging Fragmentation', above n 174, 905.

[177] For discussion of the transnational legal process method of interactions, interpretations and internalisation of international norms at the domestic level, see ch 4, Section III.

3

Protection of Persons in Humanitarian Crises

I. EXPLORING THE CONCEPT OF PROTECTION

> Protection defies neat labelling because it is at the same time the goal underlying the whole humanitarian response (the reason for humanitarian action), an approach or lens on the humanitarian response (a way of understanding all dimensions of humanitarian endeavour), and a more narrowly defined family of activities that aim to prevent and mitigate threats to vulnerable persons.
>
> Study on Protection Funding in Complex Humanitarian Emergencies, 2013[1]

THE MODEL OF humanitarian action set out in chapter one highlighted the interconnected twin components of the protection of persons and material assistance that arise from the humanitarian imperative to prevent and alleviate suffering wherever it may occur. Foundational to this are the principles of humanity and human dignity, which act as the conceptual underpinning for actions taken before, during and after a humanitarian crisis. However, while one can generally identify the basic types of material assistance required in a humanitarian crisis, the exact contours of the concept of protection remain insufficiently defined. As noted by Elizabeth Ferris, 'The lack of a clear definition of a concept that has become so central to so many organizations is striking.'[2] This is particularly true when trying to identify the legal obligations of protection owed by various actors. From an operational perspective, rather than identifying specific protection activities, the Sphere Humanitarian Charter sets out four 'Protection Principles' as a means of encouraging humanitarian actors to address the safety, dignity and rights of people affected

[1] J Murray and J Landry, *Placing Protection at the Centre of Humanitarian Action: Study on Protection Funding in Complex Humanitarian Emergencies* (17 September 2013), Independent study commissioned by the Global Protection Cluster, 4.

[2] E Ferris, *The Politics of Protection: The Limits of Humanitarian Action* (Brookings Institution Press, 2011) 274.

by disasters or armed conflicts.[3] Yet a wide variety of activities can be encompassed within the heading of 'protection', resulting in divergent understandings of what the 'protection of persons' actually means in a humanitarian crisis.

In particular, one needs to separate out the specific legal obligations of identifiable duty-bearers to protect individuals and communities, from the broader understanding of 'protection' as any action taken to promote the safety, dignity and rights of those caught up in humanitarian crises. Judith Soussan of MSF has argued that protection in the law of armed conflict comprises two elements. The first are prohibitions, such as prohibitions against attacks on protected persons or the taking of hostages; while the second are positive measures, such as the provision of neutral zones, the evacuation of besieged areas or the provision of humanitarian assistance. Soussan concludes that '"legal" protection is a broad framework in which relief is just one right among others'.[4] Drawing on the Inter-Agency Standing Committee's tripartite model of protection as an objective, a legal responsibility and an activity,[5] this chapter will critically analyse the prime objective of humanitarian action, namely the protection of persons in humanitarian crises. In particular, the chapter first examines what protection means in an international legal context, and the differences between rights-based and needs-based approaches to humanitarian action. It continues by examining the existing international protection infrastructure and the operationalisation of protection strategies by humanitarian agencies.

The second half of the chapter examines Walter Kälin's description of the cycle of protection activities required at all stages of a humanitarian crisis, drawing on Elizabeth Ferris's categorisation of physical protection, humanitarian protection and human rights protection.[6] The chapter concludes by proposing a method for the practical amalgamation of rights-based and needs-based approaches to humanitarian activities. In particular, the chapter argues for a separation between proactive human rights advocacy approaches which aim to tackle the substantive content of human rights law, and the application of human rights principles, namely empowerment, participation, non-discrimination and accountability, to all humanitarian programming. Such a rights-based approach to humanitarian action is premised on a more limited understanding of the types

[3] The Sphere Project, *Humanitarian Charter and Minimum Standards in Humanitarian Response* 3rd edn, April 2011, 29.

[4] J Soussan, *MSF and Protection: Pending or Closed? Discourse and Practice Surrounding the 'Protection of Civilians'* (July 2008) CRASH/Fondation-Médecins Sans Frontières, 8.

[5] IASC, *Handbook on the Protection of Internally Displaced Persons*, Global Protection Cluster Working Group (2010) 7.

[6] Ferris, *Politics of Protection*, above n 2, 278.

of activities which should be classified as promoting the legal protection of persons in humanitarian crises; while simultaneously recognising the divergent operational approaches of different humanitarian organisations, and the necessary division of labour between humanitarian and human rights actors.

A. Protection in International Law

i. ICRC-IASC Definition of 'Protection'

The modern concept of 'protection' as a legal obligation came into prominence at the end of the Second World War, in particular through the 1949 Geneva Conventions, which identified specific groups as 'protected persons', namely prisoners of war, the wounded, sick and shipwrecked, and civilians.[7] Moreover, all four Geneva Conventions specifically highlighted the ICRC's role in conducting humanitarian activities and relief for such protected persons.[8] Parallel to the 1949 Geneva Conventions, international refugee law was fundamental in enshrining 'protection' into international law,[9] through the obligation in the 1951 Refugee Convention for the international community to protect individuals fleeing persecution on one of five enumerated grounds if their own state was unable or unwilling to provide protection and they had crossed an international border.[10] Owing to the binding nature of these conventions, they also firmly established the need for domestic and international protection mechanisms, in other words institutions and activities to ensure respect for the rights of those facing persecution or the effects of conflict.[11]

These innovations in the law of armed conflict and refugee law directly fed into the emerging body of international human rights law focused

[7] 'Diplomatic protection' has been a key feature of international law and relations for centuries, and the 'protection of (religious) minorities' motivated early legal obligations towards persons who were stateless or refugees. See generally B Cabanes, *The Great War and the Origins of Humanitarianism 1918–1924* (Cambridge University Press, 2014) 133–88. Other forms of protection not relating directly to individuals' safety and security in crises, such as environmental protection, are beyond the scope of this book.

[8] Art 9/9/9/10 Geneva Conventions.

[9] See G Jaeger, 'On the History of the International Protection of Refugees' (September 2001) 83(843) *International Review of the Red Cross* 727.

[10] Convention relating to the Status of Refugees (adopted 28 July 1951, entered into force 22 April 1954) 189 UNTS 137 ('the 1951 Refugee Convention'). The temporal and geographic restrictions relating to the Second World War in Europe were removed via the Protocol relating to the Status of Refugees (adopted 31 January 1967, entered into force 4 October 1967) 606 UNTS 267.

[11] For analysis of the different protection roles of the ICRC and UNHCR, see D Forsythe, 'Humanitarian Protection: The International Committee of the Red Cross and the United Nations High Commissioner for Refugees' (September 2001) 83(843) *International Review of the Red Cross* 675.

on domestic protection mechanisms, which recognised individuals as rights-holders with claims against their national authorities. The legal concept of protection therefore derives considerable additional legitimacy from a state's vertical obligations towards individuals to respect, protect and fulfil international human rights law without discrimination.[12] However, despite the original close linkage in time and objectives connecting the 1948 Universal Declaration of Human Rights, 1949 Geneva Conventions and 1951 Refugee Convention, these different branches of international law developed on divergent paths over the next 60 years. As a result, it is not possible (or indeed warranted) to talk about a unified 'law of protection'. Despite Judge Tanaka arguing as early as 1966 that 'surely the law concerning the protection of human rights may be considered to belong to the *jus cogens*',[13] more than 20 years later in the context of refugee law, Goodwin-Gill noted that 'the word "protection" has become something of a term of art, obscuring the scope of an activity that ought to be fundamentally clear'.[14] Therefore, in an attempt to address this lack of precision on what constituted 'protection', between 1996 and 2000 the ICRC convened a series of inter-agency workshops to strengthen the professional standards of protection activities.[15] These workshops resulted in an expansive definition of 'protection', subsequently endorsed by the Inter-Agency Standing Committee (IASC), as:

> [A]ll activities aimed at ensuring full respect for the rights of the individual in accordance with the letter and the spirit of the relevant bodies of law, ie human rights law, international humanitarian law, and refugee law. Human rights and humanitarian organisations must conduct these activities in an impartial manner (not on the basis of race, national or ethnic origin, language or gender).[16]

While providing a highly authoritative statement of the coherence between different branches of international law in the context of humanitarian crises, this is neither a legally binding definition of protection nor a definition of the legal obligations of specific actors in regard to protection (notwithstanding its invocation of international law). So despite providing some clarity on the types of activities which may fall under the rubric of 'protection', the definition is also open to extensive interpretation.

[12] See IASC, *Operational Guidelines on the Protection of Persons in Situations of Natural Disasters*, Brookings-Bern Project on Internal Displacement (January 2011) 5.

[13] South West Africa (*Ethiopia v S Africa; Liberia v S Africa*), Second Phase, Judgment, ICJ Reports 1966, 6 (J Tanaka, diss op) 298.

[14] G Goodwin-Gill, 'The Language of Protection' (1989) 1 *International Journal of Refugee Law* 6, 6.

[15] ICRC, *Professional Standards for Protection Work Carried out by Humanitarian and Human Rights Actors in Armed Conflict and Other Situations of Violence* 2nd edn, February 2013, 12.

[16] S Giossi Caverzasio (ed), *Strengthening Protection in War: A Search for Professional Standards: Summary of Discussions among Human Rights and Humanitarian Organizations*, Workshops at the ICRC, 1996–2000, ICRC, (2001) 19.

For example, the Protection Agenda of the inter-governmental Nansen Initiative on disaster-induced cross-border displacement[17] expressly invokes the ICRC-IASC definition, stating: 'This agenda uses "protection" to refer to any positive action, *whether or not based on legal obligations*, undertaken by States on behalf of disaster displaced persons or persons at risk of being displaced.'[18] Elizabeth Ferris has noted a particular risk that this 'maximalist' approach to protection engenders: 'The vast array of humanitarian activities now labelled as protection contributes to an illusion that the international community is making great progress in protecting people. Sadly, it also creates expectations within affected communities that humanitarians simply cannot meet.'[19]

Reflecting the evolving nature of international law and humanitarian crises, it may be opportune to revisit this ICRC-IASC definition. Over the past 15 years there has been an explosion of interest in the legal implications of natural and human-made disasters, and notably the ILC entitled its work on international disaster law 'the protection of persons in the event of disasters'.[20] Likewise, we have seen major developments in international criminal law (not least the establishment of the International Criminal Court), and although many aspects of international criminal law specifically relate to violations of the law of armed conflict, not all crimes in the Rome Statute are exclusively applicable in times of armed conflict.[21] Crimes against humanity may be committed in the general context of widespread or systematic attacks on a civilian population;[22] while the crime of genocide is predicated on the specific intent to partially or completely destroy a national, ethnic, racial or religious group (known as a 'protected group'), which may occur both within and outwith times of armed conflict.[23] It should also be noted that while internally displaced persons and persons displaced across borders as a result of disasters or climate change do not benefit from a universal binding convention comparable to the 1951 Refugee Convention, the non-binding UN Guiding Principles on Internal Displacement have provided a key source of inspiration for both national and regional laws. Therefore, in the context of the ICRC-IASC

[17] See ch 9, Section II.C.

[18] Nansen Initiative, *Agenda for the Protection of Cross-border Displaced Persons in the Context of Disasters and Climate Change* (December 2015) 7 [emphasis added].

[19] Ferris, *Politics of Protection*, above n 2, 275.

[20] E Valencia-Ospina, *Preliminary Report on the Protection of Persons in the Event of Disasters* (8 May 2008) A/CN.4/598, paras 14–20.

[21] For detailed analysis of the elements of international crimes, see G Boas, JL Bischoff and NL Reid, *Elements of Crimes under International Law*, International Criminal Law Practitioner Library Series, Vol II (Cambridge University Press, 2008).

[22] Art 7 Rome Statute of the International Criminal Court (adopted 17 July 1998, entered into force 1 July 2002) 2187 UNTS.

[23] Boas et al, *Elements of Crimes*, above n 21, 168–76.

definition, the phrase 'refugee law' should be understood to include legal obligations relating equally to persons who have crossed an international border and those forcibly displaced within the borders of their country of origin or residence.

The modification required in the ICRC-IASC definition to encompass the evolving nature of international law and global humanitarian challenges may be as simple as changing the 'ie' to 'eg', alongside commentary on the applicability of relevant international criminal, displacement and disaster laws. This would expand our understanding of 'protection' in humanitarian crises by including a broader range of international law sources. However, we need to be careful how such a definition is used, as one can view protection from both a legal and non-legal perspective. Elizabeth Ferris has warned of the dangers of adopting a maximalist perspective as 'it stretches the concept of protection so far that it incorporates almost all humanitarian and development work and risks becoming meaningless'.[24] Ferris highlights that such an approach includes many activities which should simply be seen as 'good programming', rather than 'protection activities'. Just as the concept of 'human rights' has a specific legal meaning and content (which is often far more limited than the broad use that the term is given outside the legal context), so does the concept of protection. Indeed, the concept of protection can mistakenly be conflated with human rights—as discussed in Section I.A.iii below, it is important to differentiate between humanitarian protection and human rights protection.

The international legal protection of persons relies primarily upon identifiable legal obligations in binding international, regional or domestic law. Lawyers are well used to adapting existing principles and instruments to reflect emerging or novel situations, such as the obligations of non-state armed groups in internal armed conflicts, responding to cross-border displacement arising from climate change, or the human rights implications of natural or human-made disasters. It follows that the protection of persons in humanitarian crises will have a different meaning and content when viewed from a legal, institutional or operational perspective. The *acquis humanitaire* set out in this book aims to identify legal obligations of state and non-state actors to provide material assistance or protection activities, in particular those arising from general international law. However, considering the broad usage of the terms 'protection' and 'human rights', and the acknowledged interconnections between them, it is important to review the operational approaches of humanitarian actors—in particular, the differences between rights-based and needs-based approaches to humanitarian crises.

[24] Ferris, *Politics of Protection*, above n 2, 275.

ii. Distinguishing Rights-based and Needs-based Approaches

As explained by the UN Population Fund (UNFPA), most UN development agencies pursued a needs-based approach to programme activities until the late 1990s.[25] In other words, their traditional approach was to identify the basic requirements of beneficiaries and then either support initiatives to improve service delivery or undertake advocacy for their fulfilment. The subsequent move towards a rights-based approach by UN agencies reflected a broader shift in academic and practitioner analysis regarding the importance of addressing the root causes of poverty, vulnerability and risk through the application of human rights principles. The UNFPA defines a rights-based approach as one which: 'seeks to reinforce the capacities of duty-bearers (usually governments) to respect, protect and guarantee … rights. It aims to address development complexities holistically, taking into consideration the connections between individuals and the systems of power or influence. And it endeavours to create dynamics of accountability.'[26] The difference for operational programming that a rights-based approach entails over a needs-based one was highlighted in a 2003 UNICEF report, which notes: 'the basic needs approach does not imply the existence of a duty-bearer. When demands for meeting needs have no "object", nobody has a clear-cut duty to meet needs, and rights are vulnerable to on-going violation.'[27] For example, a needs-based approach may state that a vaccination programme has met the needs of 80 per cent of children in a locality; but a rights-based approach would highlight that the right to health of the remaining 20 per cent may be violated. As a result:

> the idea of 'low cost-high impact' projects (covering a large number of 'beneficiaries' at a low per-person cost) has often been regarded as a good principle. Such a utilitarian approach may sometimes have to be rejected … Addressing certain gross violations of a few children's rights might receive priority over addressing less severe violations of a larger number of children's rights in a human rights approach.[28]

While the shift towards a rights-based approach to programming originated in the field of international development, the implementation of rights-based approaches to humanitarian action has been similarly

[25] UN Population Fund, *The Human Rights-Based Approach*, www.unfpa.org/human-rights-based-approach.

[26] ibid.

[27] U Jonsson, *A Human Rights Approach to Development Programming*, Nairobi: UNICEF Eastern and Southern Africa Regional Office, 2003, 20.

[28] ibid, 21, 25. See also H Slim, 'Claiming a Humanitarian Imperative: NGOs and the Cultivation of Humanitarian Duty', paper presented at the Seventh Annual Conference of Webster University on Humanitarian Values for the Twenty-First Century, Geneva, 21–22 February 2002.

prevalent.[29] However, there is a wide variety of interpretations of what a 'rights-based' approach entails, and the attendant difference in methodologies and practices between multilateral and non-governmental organisations.[30] Indeed, Stephen Marks has identified at least seven different approaches through which human rights thinking is applied to development.[31] While recognising the generalisations inherent in summarising multiple approaches to programming, CARE Denmark produced a useful overview of the different perspectives inherent in needs-based and rights-based approaches:[32]

Table 3.1: Needs-based and rights-based approaches to programming

Needs-based approaches	Rights-based approaches
Vulnerability viewed as a symptom of poverty	Vulnerability viewed as a structural issue and an underlying cause of poverty
Focus on poverty reduction or alleviation	Focus on poverty eradication and social justice
Programme interventions rarely take account of power and even if it is recognised, no remedial action is taken	Programme interventions specifically acknowledge power and its unequal distribution, and seek ways to redress the balance, or level the 'playing field'
Poor are seen as victims, who are there to be helped and to accept assistance as and when it is provided	Supports the transformation of the poor person from a passive receiver to one participating in decision making and asserting rights
Activities focus on technical solutions/innovations to address poverty (eg new agricultural practices)	In addition to technical solutions/innovations, activities focus on helping the poor to claim their rights through supporting legal literacy

(*continued*)

[29] There is extensive literature on rights-based approaches to international development, although less so on their application in humanitarian crises. See, eg, P Gready, 'Rights-based Approaches to Development: What's the Added Value?' (2008) 18(6) *Development in Practice* 735; S Kindornay, J Ron and C Carpenter, 'Rights-Based Approaches to Development: Implications for NGOs' (2012) 34(2) *Human Rights Quarterly* 472.

[30] A Cornwall and C Nyamu-Musembi, 'Putting the "Rights-Based Approach" to Development into Perspective' (2004) 25(8) *Third World Quarterly* 1415, 1425–30.

[31] S Marks, *The Human Rights Framework for Development: Seven Approaches* (François-Xavier Bagnoud Center for Health and Human Rights, Working Paper, 2003).

[32] CARE Denmark, *Rights-Based Approach Guidelines* (Draft—April 2009) 3. CARE Denmark has stated: 'We will use a rights-based approach to empower poor people as citizens and rights holders, strengthen their ability to organise in civil society organisations in order to influence decision makers and duty bearers to respect, protect and fulfil their rights.' CARE Denmark, *Programme Policy*, April 2013, 4–5.

Table 3.1: (*Continued*)

Needs-based approaches	Rights-based approaches
Gender: focus tends to be on addressing the symptoms of discrimination (eg encouraging attendance at meetings) but not supporting meaningful participation	Gender: Focus tends to be on challenging discrimination and social, cultural and institutional norms related to exclusion
Partner selection driven by track record in service delivery	Partner selection driven by a commitment to rights and empowerment
Monitoring measures success in the form of tangible outputs (farmers trained, new agricultural practices adopted etc)	Monitoring measures success in the form of process indicators (empowerment, increased rights and greater accountability)
Accountability flows from the implementing agency to the funding agency	New lines of accountability are explored, such as to government and to target group, and links between these two

Within the field of humanitarianism, there has been a blurring of the distinctions between needs-based and rights-based approaches. One should not forget that the International Red Cross Movement had already been in existence for 85 years before the Universal Declaration of Human Rights was concluded in 1948.[33] One of the fundamental guiding principles of the International Red Cross Movement is the concept of impartiality. According to the Red Cross, this means that they identify those who require help 'based on need, and the order in which available aid is shared out must correspond to the urgency of the distress it is intended to relieve'.[34] This reflects the concept of triage in medical settings, whereby those in most urgent need of medical attention should receive it first. Despite its original self-acknowledged reluctance to utilise human rights language,[35] it is now generally recognised that the Red Cross engages in programmes and advocacy not just in accordance with the law of armed conflict but also with international human rights law.[36]

[33] For discussion of the UDHR and the 1949 Geneva Conventions by the Vice-President of the ICRC, see F Siordet, 'The Red Cross and Human Rights' (March 1968) 8(84) *International Review of the Red Cross* 118. Of note, Siordet states 'Humanitarian law has two distinct but complementary branches: human rights and the law of war', 119.

[34] IFRC, *Impartiality*, www.ifrc.org/en/who-we-are/vision-and-mission/the-seven-fundamental-principles/impartiality.

[35] As noted by Jacques Moreillion: '[A]lthough the Red Cross movement has always been motivated by concern that certain fundamental human rights should be respected, human rights as such have only been a marginal consideration—at least until now.' J Moreillion, 'The Fundamental Principles of the Red Cross, Peace and Human Rights' (July–August 1980) 217 *International Review of the Red Cross* 171, 171.

[36] D Forsythe, 'Human Rights and the International Committee of the Red Cross' (1990) 12(2) *Human Rights Quarterly* 265.

Likewise, despite Médecins Sans Frontières' (MSF) self-acknowledged status as an outspoken organisation that bears witness or *témoignage* as a means of publicising abuses and intolerable situations, MSF's approach to offering assistance to people is 'based on need and irrespective of race, religion, gender or political affiliation. We give priority to those in the most serious and immediate danger.'[37] Such a blended approach can also be seen in the strategy of CARE International,[38] which comprises three strands: a) humanitarian action; b) promoting lasting change and innovative solutions; and c) multiplying impact. In humanitarian emergencies, CARE will respond 'to save lives, with special attention to the needs of women, girls and the most marginalised'. Concurrently, CARE notes that: 'Together with our partners we use the evidence, learning and innovation from our humanitarian action and long-term development programmes to influence broader social change, at significant scale.'[39]

The International Law Commission has acknowledged the debate within the humanitarian community regarding rights-based and needs-based approaches.[40] However, the Commission's position is that the two approaches are not necessarily mutually exclusive, and are best viewed as being complementary.[41] The ILC has therefore recognised the complex reality of humanitarian operations, whereby a broad range of different organisations provide protection and assistance, for a variety of express or implied motivations. While some actors may undertake an overtly rights-based approach, the distinctions on the ground are generally less clear-cut than on paper or in academic commentary. The organisational hierarchy, or field staff, may not have a clear idea of the differences between needs-based and rights-based approaches, plus the exigencies of the situation may require action to be undertaken. As noted by ALNAP: 'The balance between getting the job done, getting it done well, and getting the principles right is often skewed by urgency.'[42] Moreover, following

[37] MSF, *Charter and Principles* www.msf.org/about-msf/msf-charter-and-principles. For analysis of MSF's approach, see Soussan, *MSF and Protection*, above n 4.

[38] CARE International is a global confederation of 14 National Members and one Affiliate Member with the common goal of fighting global poverty. Each CARE Member is an autonomous NGO and implements programmes, advocacy, fundraising and communications activities in its own country and in developing countries where CARE has programmes. See www.care-international.org/about-us/global-network.

[39] CARE International, *Working for Poverty Reduction and Social Justice: The CARE 2020 Program Strategy*, August 2014, 3–4.

[40] For the final text of the commentaries to draft Art 2, see Official Records of the General Assembly, Seventy-first Session, *Supplement No 10* (A/71/10), Chapter IV: Protection of Persons in the Event of Disasters (2016), pp 20–21.

[41] ibid.

[42] D Brown, A Donini and P Knox Clarke, *Engagement of Crisis-affected People in Humanitarian Action*, Background Paper, ALNAP 29th Annual Meeting, 11–12 March 2014, Addis Ababa, 19.

empirical research, the Brookings-Bern Project on Internal Displacement found that in the midst of conflicts and natural disasters it can be difficult, if not impossible, to identify appropriate people to engage with, noting that: 'The effects of displacement may include social fragmentation, psychological distress, and/or physical wounds, which may leave IDPs unable to participate or uninterested in engagement.'[43] Ensuring that those most affected by humanitarian crises are consulted and participate in the actions taken to assist them therefore entails both operational and conceptual challenges.[44]

Yet such challenges are not insurmountable. A rights-based approach to programming should therefore recognise the difference between an obligation of conduct and an obligation of result. In the midst of a complex emergency, it may not be possible for a particular organisation to guarantee the full range of rights due to resource constraints, the denial of humanitarian access by government officials or non-state armed groups, or a lack of specific expertise within the organisation in question. However, as explained in Section II.B below, a rights-based approach to humanitarian action requires the incorporation of human rights principles into all programme decision making. Nevertheless, one has to be careful not to conflate humanitarian and human rights activities so it is important to recognise the differences between humanitarian protection and human rights protection.

iii. Distinguishing Humanitarian Protection from Human Rights Protection

Despite the different branches of international law set out in the ICRC-IASC definition of protection each elaborating rights for particular protected groups (such as civilians, prisoners of war or refugees), this does not mean that the law of armed conflict or refugee law are simply subsets of human rights law. Yet the inclusion of international human rights law within the definition has led to interpretations which incorporate the transformative and societal change objectives of human rights law into all protection activities. Hugo Slim and Andrew Bonwick have argued that protection is something that 'people struggle for and achieve within a given situation, or secure more widely in the politics of their own

[43] Brookings-Bern Project on Internal Displacement, *Moving Beyond Rhetoric: Consultation and Participation with Populations Displaced by Conflict or Natural Disasters* (October 2008), 47.

[44] Brown, Donini and Knox Clarke, *Engagement of Crisis-affected People*, above n 42, 19–24. For a series of case examples of community engagement in protection, see *Humanitarian Exchange* (2010) 46, in particular Y Ageng'o, N dos Reis da Costa and L Searle, 'Community Perceptions of "Protection" in Kenya and Timor-Leste'; H Nic an Rí and C Brady, 'Protection Through Partnership: Lessons Learnt from Pakistan's Displacement Crisis'; A South, M Perhult and N Carstensen, 'Self-protection and Survival in South-east Burma'.

society'.[45] Slim and Bonwick stress that protection is not just a legalistic conversation between states and other humanitarian actors, but is a fundamental aspiration of local communities. Their 'rights-based approach to protection'[46] is broader than simply 'legal protection' and encompasses actions undertaken by local communities or humanitarian actors despite a lack of binding domestic or international legal obligations to do so. For example, the affected population may self-organise to ensure continuity of education and schooling for children caught up in a long-running armed conflict. Likewise, NGOs may decide to engage in specific types of protection work, such as awareness raising on sexual and gender-based violence in refugee camps, without having a legal responsibility to undertake such activities. This reflects the increasingly important role played by human rights law (and rights-discourse more generally) in influencing the policies and practice of states, communities and humanitarian actors.

However, as Elizabeth Ferris has convincingly argued, the legal obligations of specified state and non-state actors to provide humanitarian protection must not be conflated with human rights protection or confused with physical protection.[47] Ferris defines 'humanitarian protection' as access to life-saving assistance,[48] while 'human rights protection' encompasses the full enjoyment of a broad range of rights. Drawing on this distinction, rather than focusing on a 'rights-based approach to protection' (which risks obscuring the distinct nature of different types of protection), a more appropriate terminology is a 'rights-based approach to humanitarian action'. As set out in chapter one, a multitude of actions are required in a humanitarian crisis, spanning the provision of material assistance to dedicated protection activities. Likewise, affected populations may be in need of different types of protection: physical, humanitarian and/or human rights. A rights-based approach to humanitarian action encompasses these various strands while recognising the divergent mandates, legal responsibilities and operational approaches of different humanitarian actors. It is extremely unlikely that any one state or humanitarian actor will be able to fulfil all urgent needs in the midst of a major humanitarian crisis. Therefore, one must consider who has a legal responsibility to undertake particular activities, and how can an effective division of labour be achieved to ensure that all the needs and rights of the affected population are met?

[45] H Slim and A Bonwick, *Protection: An ALNAP Guide for Humanitarian Agencies* (August 2005) Overseas Development Institute, 32.

[46] ibid, 33.

[47] Ferris, *Politics of Protection*, above n 2, 279. For further discussion of Ferris's three-part typology of protection, see Section II.A below.

[48] David Forsythe has likewise argued that material assistance is part and parcel of humanitarian protection. See Forsythe, 'Humanitarian Protection', above n 11, 681.

As will be examined further in the following sections, a rights-based approach to humanitarian action requires all those involved in preparation and response to respect the wishes of the local community in their activities.[49] This can be seen as a procedural requirement. Additionally, certain duty-bearers will have a legal obligation to respect, protect and fulfil specific rights, while other actors may choose to undertake human rights-based activities and advocacy. These can be seen as actions to address the substantive content of human rights law. As noted by UNICEF in the context of international development: 'A human rights approach to programming suggests an ethical dimension both to what should be done (desired outcome) and how it should be done (process).'[50] Therefore, building on concepts first elaborated in the context of international development programmes, one can identify four principles for such a rights-based approach to humanitarian action, namely:

1. Empowerment of rights-holders
2. Participation in decision-making processes
3. Non-discrimination and prioritisation of vulnerable groups
4. Accountability of duty-bearers to rights-holders[51]

However, it is important to note that, as with 'humanitarianism' and 'protection', there is not just one rights-based approach.[52] Different organisations may apply diverse approaches in distinct contexts—for example, some actors may focus specifically on the provision of a particular type of material assistance, such as the dedicated water and sanitation services of WaterAid. Alternatively, large international organisations such as Oxfam may provide a broad suite of material assistance and protection activities; while others may prioritise a potentially vulnerable group, such as Save the Children. Moreover, the challenges posed by an armed conflict may differ greatly from those in the aftermath of a major earthquake, and therefore the types of activities which can be conducted. Nonetheless, at

[49] As stressed by the IASC: 'In all undertakings, primary consideration will be given to our accountability to affected populations, to identify, understand and support their own protection measures. Different segments of affected populations need to be meaningfully engaged in all decisions and actions that have a direct impact on their well-being. A commitment to support national and local civil society in their important role to enhance the protection of persons affected and at risk is central to this endeavour.' IASC, *The Centrality of Protection in Humanitarian Action: Statement by the Inter-Agency Standing Committee (IASC) Principals* (17 December 2013).

[50] Jonsson, *Human Rights Approach*, above n 27, 20–21.

[51] Adapted from: International Human Rights Network, *Core Principles* www.ihrnetwork.org/what-are-hr-based-approaches_189.htm; and *Towards Freedom from Fear and Want: Human Rights in the Post-2015 Agenda*, Thematic Think Piece, Office of the High Commissioner for Human Rights, May 2012, produced for the UN System Task Team on the Post-2015 UN Development Agenda, 4.

[52] ibid. See also Cornwall and Nyamu-Musembi, 'Rights-Based Approach', above n 30.

the core of all rights-based approaches is the application of human rights principles—as noted by the former UN Special Rapporteur on the Right to Food, Olivier De Schutter: 'a human rights approach turns what has been a bilateral relationship between donor and partner, into a triangular relationship, in which the ultimate beneficiaries of these policies play an active role.'[53] In other words, a rights-based approach to humanitarian action requires a conceptual shift from viewing humanitarian assistance as top-down charity, to a collaborative process between the affected state, affected communities and external humanitarian agencies. Such collaborative processes need to be planned and implemented, so we will now examine the organisational mandates and international coordination mechanisms that underpin protection activities.

B. Protection Infrastructure

i. Organisational Protection Mandates

Many NGOs adopt a rights-based approach and engage in protection activities, irrespective of whether or not they have a legal obligation to do so. However, certain international organisations have an express legal mandate to provide a specific type of protection. For example, UNHCR has a mandate to provide international protection to refugees, asylum seekers and certain groups of internally displaced persons, and to seek permanent solutions from governments and private organisations to facilitate the voluntary return or integration of refugees into their new communities.[54] UNICEF's original mandate, confirmed just two weeks after UNHCR's Statute was agreed in December 1950, directs it to advocate for the protection of children's rights, to help meet their basic needs and to expand their opportunities to reach their full potential.[55] The Office of the High Commissioner for Human Rights (OHCHR) meanwhile has a broad mandate to promote and protect all human rights for all people, through the provision of technical expertise and capacity development, assisting

[53] HRC, *Promotion and Protection of All Human Rights, Civil, Political, Economic, Social and Cultural Rights, including the Right to Development: Report of the Special Rapporteur on the Right to Food, Mr Olivier De Schutter* (11 February 2009) A/HRC/10/5, 1.

[54] Art 1 Statute of the Office of the United Nations High Commissioner for Refugees, as adopted by UNGA Res 428(V) (14 December 1950). The specific situation of Palestinian refugees is covered by the UN Relief Works Agency for Palestine (UNRWA), which provides assistance, but not formal protection, to Palestinians. See also Ferris, *Politics of Protection*, above n 2, 33–39.

[55] For the original UNGA mandates for UNICEF, see: *Continuing Needs of Children: United Nations International Children's Emergency Fund*, UNGA Res 417(V) (1 December 1950); *United Nations Children's Fund (UNICEF)*, UNGA Res 802(VIII) (6 October 1953).

governments to fulfil their obligations, supporting individuals claim their rights, and objectively speaking out on human rights violations.[56]

Outwith the UN system, the ICRC has a unique legal position as a hybrid inter-governmental/non-governmental organisation, and is formally classified as a private association formed under the Swiss Civil Code.[57] The ICRC's promotion of the codification of the laws of war, as well as active involvement in the drafting process, provided a strong rationale for legally acknowledging ICRC's activities in the 1949 Geneva Conventions. As the custodian of IHL, ICRC was therefore empowered to protect the lives and dignity of victims of international and non-international armed conflicts and other situations of violence, as well as to provide them with assistance via the Geneva Conventions.[58] In addition to these specific protection mandates, and reflecting the centrality of human rights within the UN Charter and the UN as a whole, all UN and partner agencies have a general responsibility to integrate human rights into their activities and to approach their work with due regard to protection issues, drawing on the support of the Office for the High Commissioner for Human Rights (OHCHR).[59]

The explicit mandates of UNHCR, UNICEF, OHCHR and ICRC provide a legal basis for action by these organisations in protection work. Yet it is well recognised that the primary responsibility for the protection of persons within their territory falls on national authorities, and that local communities are often the first (or indeed only) to respond in the immediate aftermath of disasters and armed conflicts.[60] Research conducted in Indonesia following the 2004 Indian Ocean Tsunami found that 91 per cent of the immediate rescue services were provided by private individuals (not affiliated with any aid group or government), and that the vast majority of aid provided in the first 48 hours was provided by private individuals and the local community.[61] It is only if a state is unable or unwilling to provide the necessary protection to victims of humanitarian crises that domestic

[56] *High Commissioner for the Promotion and Protection of all Human Rights*, UNGA Res 48/141 (20 December 1993). See also Office for the High Commissioner for Human Rights, *Annual Report 2015* (May 2016) 41.

[57] G Rona, 'The ICRC's Status: In a Class of its Own', 17 February 2004, www.icrc.org/eng/resources/documents/misc/5w9fjy.htm.

[58] See 'ICRC Protection Policy' (September 2008) 90(871) *International Review of the Red Cross* 751.

[59] *Renewing the United Nations: A Programme for Reform, Report of the Secretary-General to the United Nations General Assembly* (14 July 1997) A/51/950.

[60] For discussion of the role of local communities, see Ferris, *Politics of Protection*, above n 2, 63–66.

[61] Fritz Institute, *Recipient Perceptions of Aid Effectiveness: Rescue, Relief and Rehabilitation in Tsunami Affected Indonesia, India and Sri Lanka* (2005) 3. See also J Telford and J Cosgrave, *Joint Evaluation of the International Response to the Indian Ocean Tsunami: Synthesis Report*, Tsunami Evaluation Coalition (July 2006) 42–45.

action should be supplemented by the international community of donor states, the UN and humanitarian organisations. However, this is where the twin aspects of humanitarian action can come into conflict. The distribution of packages of material assistance in a non-discriminatory manner is generally less contentious than rights-based activities for the protection of persons.[62] While the clearly defined international protection mandates of a select group of international organisations is generally acknowledged (even if in practice their mandates can be difficult to implement on the ground), the debate between needs-based approaches, which aim to simply secure and deliver additional resources to particular groups, and more explicitly political and transformative rights-based approaches remains.[63]

Through a historical analysis of humanitarianism, Michael Barnett has argued that the massive failures in humanitarian protection that occurred in Somalia, Yugoslavia and Rwanda during the 1990s led many humanitarian agencies to examine the domestic political causes of suffering. This led NGOs such as CARE International, Catholic Relief Services and World Vision to move from a technocratic (needs-based) approach to a more explicitly rights-based approach to their humanitarian activities. This entailed an organisational policy transformation towards effecting societal change beyond simply the delivery of aid.[64] Conversely, even in the face of fierce criticism, the ICRC has stuck to the principles of impartiality and neutrality as a means of safeguarding its position as a 'neutral humanitarian intermediary'.[65] The ICRC would argue that espousing a 'traditional' or 'pure' humanitarian approach based on saving lives at risk rather than social transformation ensures access to victims on all sides of a conflict.[66]

Yet the distance between the 'traditional' and 'societal change' models of humanitarianism is not necessarily so great. Even the ICRC proactively advocates for protected persons, such as prisoners of war or the wounded and sick, as per the Geneva Conventions, and the ICRC's right of initiative is formalised in Article 5 of the Statutes of the Red Cross and Red Crescent

[62] Although in some cases the imposition of suffering on specific parts of the civilian population, eg through the denial of food and other material support, may be a deliberate political strategy to weaken members of an opposing group. H Slim and D Mancini-Griffoli, *Interpreting Violence: Anti-Civilian Thinking and Practice and How to Argue Against it More Effectively*, Centre for Humanitarian Dialogue (2007).

[63] See Cornwall and Nyamu-Musembi, 'Rights-Based Approach', above n 30, 1417.

[64] M Barnett, *Empire of Humanity: A History of Humanitarianism* (Cornell University Press, 2011) 196–212.

[65] F Fox, 'New Humanitarianism: Does It Provide a Moral Banner for the 21st Century?' (2001) 25(4) *Disasters* 275, 277.

[66] 'Humanitarian Assistance in Armed Conflict Conference of the Luxemburg Group, 24–25 May 2004, Graduate Institute of International Studies, Geneva' (2004) 86(856) *International Review of the Red Cross* 879, 903.

Movement.[67] As Barnett and Weiss have eloquently observed: 'Lurking behind their seemingly reformist impulses, at times, beats the heart of a radical.'[68] The main difference therefore lies more in the manner in which such proactive advocacy stances are taken—for example by naming and shaming through the media, or behind closed doors to state officials.[69] David Forsythe has noted that both the ICRC and UNHCR's approach to 'non-political' humanitarian protection should be understood in the sense that: '[t]he agencies are not motivated to affect interests and values other than the social well-being of persons falling within their mandates. They are not motivated to advance the strategic and/or partisan goals of public authorities.'[70] Nevertheless, these different approaches reflect the on-going debate about not just the conceptual heart of 'humanitarianism', but also the operational implications of different organisations' mandates. This raises the question whether a humanitarian organisation should act like a human rights organisation, or vice versa?

Marc DuBois from MSF has argued that not only does the use of the word 'protection' convey an unrealistic impression of the type of safety and security that humanitarian agencies can provide, it has also blurred the lines between humanitarian and human rights activities.[71] Providing education for girls in areas controlled by the Taliban or the so-called Islamic State is a contentious issue and potentially dangerous for both children and humanitarian workers—as evidenced by the attempted murder of youth activist and Nobel Peace Prize recipient Malala Yousafzai in the Swat Valley of Pakistan in October 2012.[72] Yet from a human rights-based perspective all children, even in humanitarian crises, are entitled to education as a right. DuBois argues against conflating humanitarian and human rights activities, noting that a human rights-based approach can recast any activity as 'protection'. For example, distributing sacks of corn can be viewed as protecting people's right to food, which may result in an over-reliance on monitoring and advocacy at the expense of the actual delivery of aid.[73] The potential challenges that arise from these divergent approaches and perspectives have multiplied in recent years, fuelled by the expansion in the number of humanitarian actors, and changing

[67] As noted by Jelena Pejic (ICRC), quoted in ibid, 900.

[68] M Barnett and T Weiss, *Humanitarianism Contested: Where Angels Fear to Tread* (Routledge, 2011) 107.

[69] D Chandler, 'The Road to Military Humanitarianism: How the Human Rights NGOs Shaped a New Humanitarian Agenda' (2001) 23(3) *Human Rights Quarterly* 678.

[70] Forsythe, 'Humanitarian Protection', above n 11, 679.

[71] M DuBois, 'Protection: Fig-Leaves and Other Delusions' (March 2010) 46 *Humanitarian Exchange* 2. This special edition of *Humanitarian Exchange* focused specifically on protection from the perspective of humanitarian actors and local and affected communities.

[72] See www.nobelprize.org/nobel_prizes/peace/laureates/2014/yousafzai-bio.html.

[73] DuBois, 'Protection', above n 71, 3.

perceptions regarding the impartiality and neutrality of humanitarian organisations. Therefore, before examining how protection principles can be operationalised by humanitarian agencies, it is useful to briefly examine existing international coordination mechanisms.

ii. Coordination of International Protection Activities

The expansion of the overall size and number of inter-governmental and non-governmental humanitarian organisations, along with their increased professionalism, should generally be welcomed.[74] However, as far back as 1987, a senior US government official warned that humanitarian responses in complex emergencies were 'pluralism run riot'.[75] The past 30 years have only served to highlight the challenges that the international humanitarian system as a whole, and individual actors within it, face in living up to the humanitarian imperative to prevent and alleviate human suffering wherever it may be found. Although UNGA Resolution 46/182[76] played a key role in advancing the international framework for humanitarian action, the subsequent complex emergencies in Somalia, Yugoslavia and Rwanda far outweighed the UN's ability to provide effective humanitarian coordination. This served to highlight the continuing reliance on the concept of state sovereignty in determining how the international community responded to humanitarian crises. Consequently, following the UN reform process in 1997, the Department of Humanitarian Affairs was merged with other UN bodies to create the Office for the Co-ordination of Humanitarian Affairs (UNOCHA) with a mandate to coordinate humanitarian responses, policy development and humanitarian advocacy.[77]

Meanwhile, the extent of devastation across 13 countries resulting from the 2004 Indian Ocean Tsunami starkly highlighted both the strengths and shortcomings of international humanitarian responses to massive natural disasters. The unprecedented geographic reach of the tsunami, as well as the degree of destruction in areas such as Aceh Province in Indonesia and eastern Sri Lanka which were already in the grip of internal armed conflicts, severely stretched the emergency response capacities of most

[74] For discussion of the professionalisation of humanitarian organisations following the First World War, see Cabanes, *Origins of Humanitarianism*, above n 7, 189–247.

[75] Victor Palmieri, former US Assistant Secretary of State, quoted in R Kent, *Anatomy of Disaster Relief: The International Network in Action* (Pinter, London, 1987) 173.

[76] *Strengthening of the Coordination of Humanitarian Emergency Assistance of the United Nations, UNGA Res 46/182* (19 December 1991) A/RES/46/182.

[77] E Tsui, *Analysis of Normative Developments in Humanitarian Resolutions since the Adoption of 46/182*, independent review for UNOCHA (2009) 7–12.

humanitarian agencies.[78] This prompted Jan Egeland, then UN Emergency Relief Co-ordinator, to commission an independent review of the global humanitarian system. The Humanitarian Response Review (HRR) commenced in February 2005 to determine: 'the preparedness of international humanitarian organizations to predict crises, prevent them, mitigate their impact on vulnerable populations and respond effectively to their needs.'[79] The key innovation arising from the HRR was the 'cluster approach', whereby UN and non-UN humanitarian agencies came together in sectoral clusters (such as Protection, Food Security, and Health) under a designated lead agency to plan and coordinate operational responses in specific humanitarian crises. Under the direction of the UN Humanitarian and Emergency Relief Co-ordinator, 11 clusters coordinated by identified lead agencies have since been established.[80] These clusters cover the pre-emergency stages of prevention, mitigation and preparedness, and the post-emergency stages of response, recovery and rehabilitation in the sectors shown in Figure 3.1 below.

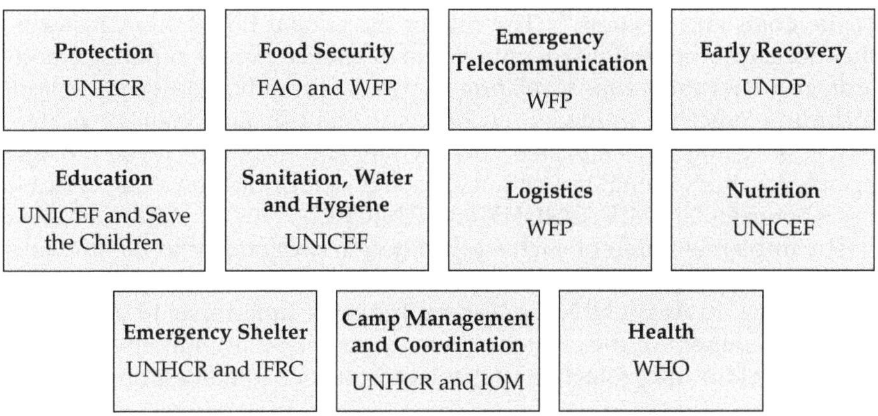

Figure 3.1: UN cluster system and designated lead agencies

The initial implementation of the cluster approach following the Pakistan earthquake of October 2005 did not provide a promising start for the

[78] See generally: J Telford and J Cosgrave, 'The International Humanitarian System and the 2004 Indian Ocean Earthquake and Tsunamis' (2007) 31(1) *Disasters* 1; D Fidler, 'Disaster Relief and Governance after the Indian Ocean Tsunami: What Role for International Law?' (2005) 6 *Melbourne Journal of International Law* 458; J Telford, 'Disaster Recovery: an International Humanitarian Challenge?' in P Daly et al (eds), *From the Ground Up: Perspectives on Post-Tsunami and Post-Conflict Aceh* (Institute of Southeast Asian Studies, 2012).

[79] UNOCHA, *Humanitarian Response Review*, August 2005, 8.

[80] For details on the various Clusters, see UNOCHA, *Cluster Coordination* www.unocha.org/what-we-do/coordination-tools/cluster-coordination.

new system. While the Indian Ocean Tsunami emphasised the need for improved coordination between humanitarian actors, the roll-out of the cluster approach was marked by confusion over roles, and limited information sharing or involvement of local actors.[81] However, as the international humanitarian community has gained experience of operating within the cluster approach, and following increased coordination between UNOCHA and the IASC, the cluster approach now represents the primary operational mechanism for inter-agency coordination and cooperation in international humanitarian responses. The cluster system works through the designation of a Global Cluster Lead agency for each sector, along with an identified National Cluster Lead agency that reflects the specifics of the country concerned and the agencies working in that country.

UNHCR acts as the Lead Agency for the Global Protection Cluster, which has specific responsibility for coordination of protection activities to ensure that: 'All people affected or threatened by a humanitarian crisis have their rights fully respected in accordance with international law and their protection assured by relevant and timely actions through all phases of the crisis and beyond.'[82] The role of the Global Protection Cluster is, therefore, to support field operations via the development of policy, standards and operational tools relating to protection in humanitarian action, including practical guidance on how to establish and manage protection coordination mechanisms. Meanwhile, at the country level, the lead agency for the National Protection Cluster is determined on a case-by-case basis between UNHCR, OHCHR and UNICEF.[83]

The implementation of such a coordination mechanism in the immediate aftermath of a major disaster or in the midst of an armed conflict can be challenging. In April 2015, the Nansen Initiative noted that 10 years after the establishment of the cluster system, institutional accountability at the global level for the protection of displaced persons remained unclear, and

[81] ActionAid International, *The Evolving UN Cluster Approach in the Aftermath of the Pakistan Earthquake: An NGO Perspective*, April 2006. See also A. Stoddard et al, *Cluster Approach Evaluation*, November 2007 (independent report commissioned by UNOCHA); J Steets et al, *Cluster Approach Evaluation 2: Synthesis Report*, April 2010 (independent report commissioned by the IASC).

[82] Global Protection Cluster, *Our Vision*, www.globalprotectioncluster.org/en/about-us/who-we-are.html.

[83] For the dedicated website for the Global Protection Cluster, see www.globalprotectioncluster.org. For discussion of UNHCR's role as the Lead Agency for both the Global and various National Protection Clusters, see B Deschamp et al, *Earth, Wind and Fire: A Review of UNHCR's Role in Recent Natural Disasters*, UNHCR Policy Development and Evaluation Service (June 2010).

at the operational level organisations and agencies were often 'unaware of or insufficiently trained on available tools and how to base their actions on a rights-based approach'.[84] Moreover, Elizabeth Ferris has highlighted that the establishment of parallel structures by international humanitarian agencies can undermine the role of local and national governments, despite the best intentions of the international actors.[85] It follows that humanitarian agencies need to work more closely with national authorities and local organisations and communities. As will be elaborated in Section II below, a rights-based approach to humanitarian programming does not require a 'name and shame' or judicial approach to human rights violations (which could lead to suspicion and non-co-operation with local and national authorities), but should be based on fundamental human rights principles such as participation and accountability for all actors. As the end objective of several branches of international law and associated humanitarian infrastructure is the protection of persons, we now turn to see how 'protection' has been operationalised by states and humanitarian actors.

C. Operationalising Protection

i. International Standards and Guidelines on Protection

An independent study commissioned by the Global Protection Cluster on protection funding in complex emergencies found that 'protection' is hard to explain to the public, politicians and funders. This stems, in part, from the fact that many protection activities are less visible, photogenic or seemingly media-worthy than the material assistance components of humanitarian action, such as the provision of food and shelter.[86] Registering children to prevent family separation or trafficking in persons is fundamental to the protection of persons in a humanitarian crisis, but less easy to encapsulate in a sound-bite or single photograph. As a result, it has been argued that the concept of protection has not yet found its place within the humanitarian system.[87]

[84] The Nansen Initiative, *Cross-Border Displacement in the Context of Disasters and Climate Change: A Protection Agenda* (Draft for consultation) (8 April 2015) 6. Notably, this comment was removed from the final Protection Agenda adopted in October 2015.

[85] For a critique of the cluster approach for protection, see Ferris, *Politics of Protection*, above n 2, 119–23.

[86] Murray and Landry, *Placing Protection*, above n 1, 40–42.

[87] ibid, 44.

Part of the challenge in locating protection within the humanitarian system arises from the diverse origins of the responsibilities that protection activities entail. While some humanitarian actors have a specific legal mandate to engage in protection work, it must be recognised that the concept of protection is derived from both binding legal sources and non-binding operational and policy guidance that primarily rely on moral or ethical considerations. Indeed, international lawyers need to be consistently aware of the potential limitations of the law to provide protection. As noted by Authers and Charlesworth:

> In its repeated inability to prevent events described as crises from occurring, the law fails to uphold its promise of protection, proffering instead a self-reflexive (re)turn to its own norms and their reiteration in treaties and conventions. Crisis repeatedly appears as a catalyst for international human rights law, and the discipline's responses to this characterisation speak simultaneously to its potency and ineffectiveness in answer.[88]

Therefore, as a key institution of the international humanitarian framework established by UNGA Resolution 46/182 and an important driver of the normative development of humanitarian policy, the Inter-Agency Standing Committee's operational guidance on protection is particularly relevant.[89] In its comprehensive *Handbook for the Protection of Internally Displaced Persons*, the IASC sets out a tripartite understanding of protection as: a) an objective; b) a legal responsibility; and c) an activity.[90] Reflecting the expansive ICRC-IASC definition of protection, the IDP Handbook describes the objective of protection as the full and equal respect for the rights of all individuals, without discrimination, as provided for in national and international law. Protection therefore covers the full range of civil and political rights, such as the right to freedom of movement and the right to political participation, and economic, social and cultural rights, including the rights to education and health. The second element of the IASC tripartite understanding sets out that protection entails legal responsibility for a variety of different duty-bearers. For example, while the legal responsibility to provide protection falls primarily on the state and its agents, the IDP Handbook highlights that under the law of armed

[88] B Authers and H Charlesworth, 'The Crisis and the Quotidian in International Human Rights Law' (2013) 44 *Netherlands Yearbook of International Law* 19, 28.

[89] As noted by the IASC, given its inclusive membership, IASC guidelines, tools and documents carry a very broad consensus within the humanitarian community and guide the work of many UN and non-UN humanitarian agencies, http://interagencystandingcommittee.org/resources/iasc-products.

[90] IASC, *Handbook on the Protection of Internally Displaced Persons*, above n 5, 7 ('IDP Handbook').

conflict all parties, including non-state armed groups, have responsibilities to ensure the rights of protected persons.[91]

The third interconnected aspect of protection which the IDP Handbook examines are protection activities—in other words actions taken to ensure the enjoyment of rights. Such activities can be divided into three categories—those which are: a) responsive; b) remedial; or c) environment building. Responsive activities are those closest to the victims and the pattern of abuse to which they are subjected, and so aim to prevent imminent or stop on-going violations of rights. Remedial activities are primarily restorative, and assist and support people after violations to ensure redress, including through access to justice, reparations or rehabilitation. Protection as an environment-building activity is meanwhile intended to prevent or limit current and future violations and abuses, and so encompasses all actions to promote legal and institutional frameworks, plus political, social, cultural and institutional capacity and awareness raising about respect for human rights and the rule of law.[92] However, as the IASC stressed in its separate *Operational Guidelines on the Protection of Persons in Situations of Natural Disasters*, the exact type of protection activities will depend on the specific context of the humanitarian crisis. Therefore, the IASC has highlighted four protection tools (as opposed to activities) which are typically used for protection activities: monitoring; advocacy; capacity building; and the direct delivery of services.[93]

Based on this IASC model of protection, as set out in Figure 3.2 below, humanitarian actors should incorporate human rights principles into their overall objectives, and undertake activities based on these objectives to either prevent future human rights violations or to respond to previous or on-going violations. However, key to the IASC approach is the differentiation of responsibility. Not all humanitarian actors have a legal responsibility to provide protection, and the primary responsibility for protection falls on the affected state. As noted in the IDP Handbook: 'the role of international actors is to reinforce, not replace, national responsibility.'[94]

[91] ibid, 10.

[92] See also IASC, *Operational Guidelines*, above n 12, 5–6. In their seminal 1998 work examining internal displacement, Roberta Cohen and Francis Deng identified four similar methods whereby NGOs can engage in protection activities, namely: protection through presence; protection through community-building; protection through advocacy; and direct interventions to protect physical safety. R Cohen and F Deng, *Masses in Flight: The Global Crisis of Internal Displacement* (Brookings Institution Press, 1998) 128.

[93] IASC, *Operational Guidelines*, above n 12, 7.

[94] IASC, *IDP Handbook*, above n 5, 9.

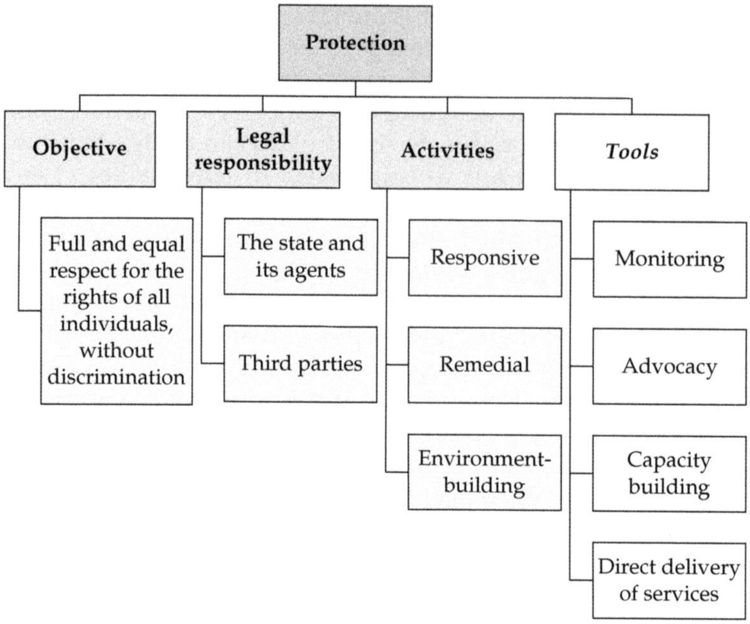

Figure 3.2: IASC model of protection

In addition to the IDP Handbook, and IASC policy guidelines covering topics such as sexual and gender-based violence and durable solutions for IDPs,[95] three other key operational manuals on the application of protection principles to humanitarian action are worth noting. The first attempt at introducing a comprehensive set of standards and indicators for humanitarian operations arose from the self-reflection amongst NGOs following the challenges faced during complex emergencies of the 1990s. The Sphere Project's *Humanitarian Charter and Minimum Standards in Humanitarian Response* (generally known as the *Sphere Handbook*) contains four interconnected sections: the Humanitarian Charter, Protection Principles, Core Standards and Minimum Standards.[96] The Core Standards refer to common process standards applicable across all thematic and technical sectors, including: participation by beneficiaries; co-ordination and collaboration; assessment and design of programmes; and key competences

[95] See: IASC, *Guidelines for Gender-based Violence Interventions in Humanitarian Settings* (September 2005); IASC, *Framework on Durable Solutions for Internally Displaced Persons*, The Brookings Institution-University of Bern Project on Internal Displacement (April 2010).

[96] *Sphere Handbook*, above n 3. Of note, the first two editions of the *Sphere Handbook* in 2000 and 2004 did not contain a specific section on protection principles, separate to the Humanitarian Charter, and were entitled 'Minimum Standards in Disaster Response' rather than the broader 'humanitarian response'.

for humanitarian workers. Detailed sector-specific Minimum Standards, with corresponding key indicators and suggested activities, cover: water supply, sanitation and hygiene promotion; food security and nutrition; shelter, settlement and non-food items; and health.

The Handbook aims to marry a traditional needs-based approach to humanitarian assistance (as set out in the Core Standards and Minimum Standards) with rights-based approaches premised on individual protection and entitlement (through the Humanitarian Charter and Protection Principles). So while recognising that specific humanitarian agencies may have more expansive protection mandates, four fundamental Protection Principles are highlighted as a means of operationalising the rights set out in the Handbook, namely:

1. To avoid causing harm.
2. To ensure access to impartial assistance.
3. To protect people from violence.
4. To assist with rights claims, access to remedies and recovery from abuse.[97]

The Humanitarian Charter forms the conceptual basis of the technical standards and protection principles set out in the Handbook. Drawing on international humanitarian, human rights and refugee law, the Charter asserts that civilians affected by armed conflicts or natural and human-made disasters have a right to life with dignity, and therefore a right to protection and assistance. The Charter continues by asserting that an individual's right to life entails the right to have steps taken to preserve life where it is threatened, and a corresponding duty on others to take such steps. Implicit in this is the duty not to withhold or frustrate the provision of life-saving assistance.[98] Nevertheless, the Charter is explicit in recognising that these rights are not formulated in the same terms under international law, and so argues that while they reflect international law, they ultimately derive their force from the moral principle of humanity.[99] This expansive understanding of the relevant legal obligations contained within the *Sphere Handbook* was one of the original concerns raised by organisations which questioned the legal validity of the Charter. For them, the Charter contained an arbitrary selection of articles of international law, mixed hard and soft law, and did not clearly state who was responsible for respecting the rights outlined.[100] Accordingly,

[97] ibid, 29–33.

[98] ibid, 20–22. For discussion of the wilful denial of material assistance or protection under international criminal law, see ch 7, Section III.

[99] ibid, 20–21.

[100] C Dufour et al, 'Rights, Standards and Quality in a Complex Humanitarian Space: Is Sphere the Right Tool?' (2004) 28(2) *Disasters* 124, 126.

the 2011 edition states: 'The *Sphere Handbook* is a voluntary code and a self-regulatory tool for quality and accountability.'[101] However, it has been argued that despite a rights-based approach providing a platform to appeal to political actors, the protection 'cornerstone' of the Handbook has been underutilised by humanitarian agencies in negotiations over access and relief provision.[102] Moreover, reflecting the increasing focus on the accountability of humanitarian actors themselves, a conceptual shift is still required by many organisations to utilise rights-based approaches as a means of empowering the victims of humanitarian crises, not just in appeals for humanitarian access with third parties.[103]

Reflecting its particular status in international law, and drawing on its legal mandate derived from the Geneva Conventions, the ICRC meanwhile has undertaken a comprehensive analysis of the principles behind and content of protection work in times of armed conflict. In its 2013 *Professional Standards for Protection Work*,[104] the ICRC elaborated a series of standards and guidelines for humanitarian actors engaged in protection work. As defined by the ICRC, the 'standards' were identified by practitioners as the minimum baseline of protection work for all operational humanitarian and human rights actors.[105] The corresponding 'guidelines' are described as useful or essential reference criteria. The key difference between the standards and guidelines is that an inherent flexibility is required in the application of the guidelines to reflect changing situations on the ground and the nature of different actors' work.[106] Of note, the first standard, or minimum requirement, is that protection actors 'must ensure that the principle of humanity is at the core of their protection work'.[107] The standards likewise note that work must be carried out with 'due respect for the dignity of individuals'.[108] So for the ICRC, the principle of humanity forms a fundamental aspect of the concept of protection, as respecting, safeguarding and promoting the dignity of persons signifies a recognition of our shared humanity. Subsequent standards stress the role of non-discrimination and impartiality, and the need to avoid harmful secondary effects, in particular through contributing to the capacity of other

[101] *Sphere Handbook*, above n 3, 8. For more on accountability mechanisms, see ch 4, Section III.

[102] J Darcy, 'Locating Responsibility: The Sphere Humanitarian Charter and Its Rationale' (2004) 28(2) *Disasters* 112, 118–19.

[103] As noted by the IASC, 'In all undertakings, primary consideration will be given to our accountability to affected populations, to identify, understand and support their own protection measures'. IASC, *The Centrality of Protection in Humanitarian Action*, above n 49.

[104] ICRC, *Professional Standards*, above n 15.

[105] ibid, 15.

[106] ibid.

[107] ibid, 22.

[108] ibid, 25.

actors and seeking to engage in dialogue with persons at risk and ensuring their participation.

Reflecting similarities with the typology of protection activities set out by the IASC, the ICRC has developed the so-called 'Protection Response Egg' as a means of visualising the main spheres of activities gravitating out from the point of violation.[109] As set out in Figure 3.3 below, the aim is to focus initially on the abuse itself, while subsequent protection activities should sequentially encompass responsive, remedial and environment-building actions.

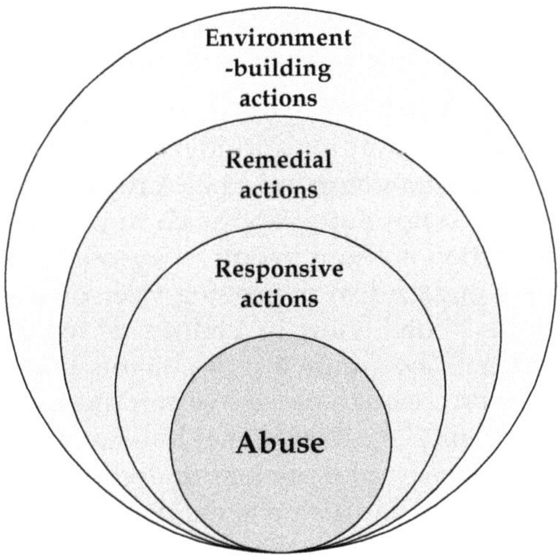

Figure 3.3: The ICRC Protection Response Egg

The fourth influential operational guidance manual comes from the Active Learning Network for Accountability and Performance in Humanitarian Action (ALNAP). Established in 1997 in the wake of the Rwandan genocide, ALNAP is intended to provide a learning forum for the humanitarian sector and uniquely comprises both UN and non-governmental humanitarian agencies, as well as the private sector and independent academic organisations and experts.[110] In addition to maintaining an extensive web-based electronic library of resources, ALNAP commissioned Hugo Slim and Andrew Bonwick to compile *Protection: An ALNAP Guide*

[109] The 'egg' framework was first elaborated in S Giossi Caverzasio, *Strengthening Protection in War: A Search for Professional Standards*, ICRC (2001). For analysis of the protection response egg in the conflict in Darfur, see S Pantuliano and S O'Callaghan, *The 'Protection Crisis': A Review of Field-based Strategies for Humanitarian Protection in Darfur*, Humanitarian Policy Group Discussion Paper, Overseas Development Institute, December 2006.

[110] For background to ALNAP, see www.alnap.org/who-we-are/our-role.

for Humanitarian Agencies to assist practitioners in understanding both the concepts that underpin protection and its operational elements.[111] Like the ICRC *Professional Standards for Protection Work*, the ALNAP Protection Guide commences with an analysis of the principle of humanity underpinning all humanitarian work. In eloquent language, which is worth reproducing in full, the Guide states:

> The emphasis in this principle on the whole human being is critical. It recognises that we are more than flesh and blood. When we are cut we bleed and when we cannot drink we thirst; but beyond our material needs, we also feel and care—about ourselves and others. This sense of self-worth, and the deep value of being together in family and community of some kind, are as important to protect and assist as are our physical needs. We live emotionally, socially and spiritually as well as physically, and so we suffer emotionally, socially and spiritually too.[112]

Drawing from this understanding of the motivation behind humanitarian action, the ALNAP Guide continues to identify the principles of safety, dignity and integrity as fundamental to all protection work. Moreover, the Guide takes a less state-centric approach to protection, and focuses on the fact that protection is about people. It stresses the need for beneficiaries to be actively engaged in improving their own situation, and so argues against the traditional view of 'charity' or top-down approaches to humanitarian action. The Guide also highlights that protection is not just a commodity or service but a process of empowerment.[113] It therefore advocates the applicability of international human rights law in times of war, disaster and emergency; in particular underlining that the non-derogable core of human rights law includes the right to life, the right to legal personality and due process of law, the prohibition of torture, slavery and degrading or inhuman treatment or punishment, and the right to freedom of religion, thought and conscience.[114]

Despite drawing on provisions of international law, none of these four handbooks and guides has the binding force of law. However, considering the lack of legal definitions of 'protection of persons' or 'humanitarian assistance', they provide important sources for understanding both the conceptual basis and protection strategies implemented by humanitarian actors. As the term 'protection' is widely used in regard to humanitarian action, it is therefore necessary to include such texts within the *acquis humanitaire*, as part of the evolving normative content influencing the policies and practices of states, inter-governmental and non-governmental

[111] Slim and Bonwick, *Protection: An ALNAP Guide*, above n 45.

[112] ibid 30.

[113] For discussion of human dignity as empowerment, see P Capps, *Human Dignity and the Foundations of International Law* (Hart Publishing, 2010) 108–09. Capps notes that: '[t]his conception of human dignity, then, is as a form of *empowerment*: human rights empower individuals so that they can exercise autonomy' 108 [emphasis in original].

[114] Slim and Bonwick, *Protection: An ALNAP Guide*, above n 45, 34.

humanitarian actors.[115] It follows that we should now examine the different strategies which humanitarian organisations use to apply such texts to their work.

ii. Implementing Protection Strategies

So far, we have seen how the concept of protection has strong roots in various branches of international law, forms a key component of the mandates of several inter-governmental organisations and the coordination mechanisms of the international humanitarian system, and has been the focus of influential non-binding operational standards and guidelines. It is clear that lawyers therefore do not have exclusive jurisdiction over either the concept or implementation of 'protection'. It follows that 'protection' is not just a legal concept. Bearing in mind the operational origin of the ICRC-IASC definition of protection, it is understandable that the spirit as well as the letter of the law is emphasised. However, the divergent legal and operational understandings of the term 'protection' highlight the need to understand how laws, policies and practices of the *acquis humanitaire* influence the actions of state and non-state actors. For example, the UN Human Rights Council takes an expansive view, arguing that protection is not limited to survival and security in the immediate emergency scenario post-disaster or post-conflict, but includes a requirement to guarantee all human rights to 'contribute to dignify the people affected'.[116] Such an all-encompassing approach corresponds with the perspective of many humanitarian agencies and practitioners. Yet there remains uncertainty and confusion between the legal obligations to provide protection set out in international law such as the 1949 Geneva Conventions and the 1951 Refugee Convention, and non-binding operational guidance. An expansive operational definition of protection of persons does not always correspond with existing positive international legal obligations. As noted in the Minimum Inter-Agency Standards for Protection Mainstreaming, developed by an NGO consortium led by World Vision:

> Not all humanitarian agencies are expected to implement protection programmes, or have the necessary staff and skills to do so. However, all humanitarian actors have an *ethical responsibility* to incorporate protection principles into their humanitarian response programmes.[117]

[115] For discussion of the UN Guiding Principles on Internal Displacement as a similarly influential non-binding text, see ch 9, Section II.B.

[116] HRC, *Final research-based report of the Human Rights Council Advisory Committee on best practices and main challenges in the promotion and protection of human rights in post-disaster and post-conflict situations*, 28th Session of the HRC (10 February 2015) A/HRC/28/76, para 6.

[117] World Vision, *Minimum Inter-Agency Standards for Protection Mainstreaming* (2012) 2 [emphasis added]. For discussion of the development of these standards, see L Searle and K Sutton, 'Standards in Incorporate Protection into Humanitarian Response: Do They Work?' (March 2010) 46 *Humanitarian Exchange* 13.

While it can be difficult to persuade a duty-bearer in the midst of a complex conflict, displacement or disaster setting that they have legal obligations to protect a particular group of people, it is even harder when such entreaties are only based on an ethical or moral understanding.[118] Elizabeth Ferris has stressed the interconnections between the three 'strands of protection' arising from IHL, refugee law and human rights law, and the continually expanding role each strand has taken towards the protection of specific groups.[119] However, like Marc DuBois, Ferris warns that an overly broad definition of protection, which encompasses activities such as building latrines or voter registration as well as safety and security, can raise unrealistic expectations on the part of affected communities. Such an approach may also encourage governments to avoid their obligations to provide physical safety to those in need.[120] Humanitarian staff are often acutely aware of the limitations of protection in humanitarian crises, and the risk that an increasing focus on protection by NGOs, without the necessary level of experienced field staff, can actually lead to greater risks for affected populations.[121] Moreover, the focus on protection activities by humanitarian agencies may ignore the root causes of violence, and the responsibility of state authorities to act. DuBois has pointedly asked: 'Have we lost sight of the fact that protection of civilians during periods of violent crisis (in the sense of providing physical safety) is not our job?'[122]

Although an expansive understanding of 'protection' provides considerable leeway for humanitarian actors to engage in activities beyond the provision of purely material assistance, it remains important to differentiate between humanitarian and human rights actions. Reflecting on the disproportionate impact of Hurricane Katrina on the predominantly poor African-American residents of New Orleans, Susannah Sirkin has argued that: 'a human rights analysis … differs from a humanitarian analysis in that it should lead us to look at the unacceptability of [vulnerabilities of minorities to natural disasters] in the first place. Such an analysis emphasizes and addresses how respect for the rights of all can reduce, minimize,

[118] Although humanitarian practitioners have lamented that: 'The focus on legal duty-bearers in the academic discourse on protection does not go far enough to acknowledge the part that non-formal actors, including affected communities themselves, play in protection.' See J Eby et al, 'Exploring the Role of Community Partnerships and Empowerment Approaches in Protection' (March 2010) 46 *Humanitarian Exchange* 10, 10.

[119] Ferris, *Politics of Protection*, above n 2, 61.

[120] E Ferris and C Stark, *Incorporating Protection into Humanitarian Action: Approaches and Limits*, paper presented at IFI-UNRWA International Conference, American University of Beirut, Lebanon, 8 October 2010 www.brookings.edu/papers/2010/1104_unrwa_ferris.aspx.

[121] R Thomson, 'Protection: A Good Idea Gone Too Far?' (8 December 2006) 8(1) *TalkBack Newsletter*, International Council of Voluntary Agencies 12.

[122] DuBois, 'Protection', above n 71, 2.

and in many cases eradicate such vulnerabilities.'[123] Since promoting and defending human rights can entail taking sides in a conflict or dispute, whether over access to resources or promoting the rights of vulnerable or marginalised groups, some humanitarian agencies prefer to focus on the neutral and impartial delivery of aid based on need alone.[124] Rather than try to change the root causes of inequality or discrimination through societal change, the argument goes that humanitarian actors should simply provide food, shelter and medical care following technical needs assessments. However, as noted by Robbie Thomson: 'It is now difficult to distinguish between human rights NGOs, whose principal tasks are the reporting of human rights violations and advocating for compliance to human rights law, and humanitarian NGOs whose principal task should be assistance to those in need, albeit delivered with an awareness of the wider context, including protection factors.'[125]

Despite the seeming dichotomy between rights-based and needs-based approaches to humanitarian action, combining both approaches within one humanitarian operation is conceptually valid and operationally achievable. The division of labour between humanitarian and human rights actors should not entail a value judgement as to the relative merits of each approach, and both have much to learn from each other.[126] Indeed, this is where coordination mechanisms, such as the Global and National Protection Clusters, can and should play an important role in bringing together disparate domestic and international actors working towards an overall goal of providing protection and assistance to persons in humanitarian crises. Coordination is particularly important to promote coherence in humanitarian action across all stages of preparation, response, recovery and rehabilitation. The final section of this chapter therefore argues that a rights-based approach to humanitarian action, based on the application

[123] S Sirkin, 'The Debacle of Hurricane Katrina: A Human Rights Response' (2006) 30 *The Fletcher Forum of World Affairs* 223, 225. See also HRC 'Concluding Observations on the United States' (2006) CCPR/C/USA/CO/3/Rev 1, para 26.

[124] Ferris, *Politics of Protection*, above n 2, 49. As argued by Jelena Pejic (ICRC): 'Only the principle of impartiality is laid down in the Geneva Conventions. Other fundamental principles such as neutrality and independence are principles of the Red Cross and Red Crescent Movement. Not all organizations working in conflict zones are neutral and not all should be so. It is therefore not advisable to lump all humanitarian organizations and human rights and development agencies together.' Quoted in 'Humanitarian Assistance in Armed Conflict', above n 67, 900.

[125] Thomson, 'Protection', above n 121, 13.

[126] As noted by the ICRC Director-General: 'Taking into account the complexity of the environment in which humanitarian action has to be carried out, the ICRC believes that the diversity of humanitarian agencies can be an asset if they are seen as complementary to each other.' A Gnaedinger, 'Humanitarian Principles—The Importance of their Preservation during Humanitarian Crises', speech delivered at the conference *Humanitarian Aid in the Spotlight: Upcoming Challenges for European Actors*, Lisbon, 12 October 2007, www.icrc.org/eng/resources/documents/statement/humanitarian-principles-statement-121007.htm.

of human rights principles to all humanitarian programming, is premised on a more limited understanding of the types of activities which should be classified as promoting the legal protection of persons in humanitarian crises. Such an approach aims to ensure that the fundamental principles of humanity and human dignity are respected, while simultaneously recognising the divergent operational approaches of different humanitarian organisations, and the necessary division of labour between humanitarian and human rights actors.

II. A RIGHTS-BASED APPROACH TO HUMANITARIAN ACTION

A. Promoting Coherence in Humanitarian Action

As discussed in chapter one, humanitarian action comprises activities at all stages of a humanitarian crisis, and encompasses both the protection of persons and the provision of material assistance. Therefore, pre-emergency preventative and risk reduction work is a fundamental aspect of contingency planning (whether to address natural disasters, forced displacements or outbreaks of armed conflict) to reduce the likelihood of an event occurring in the first place. Likewise, such activities can minimise the impact should a crisis occur (for example through stockpiling of material supplies or the establishment of early warning systems). Generally the most visible aspects of humanitarian action are emergency relief operations which occur during and in the immediate aftermath of a crisis. However, at least initially, most emergency responses are undertaken by local or domestic actors, and then based on the severity of the crisis (and other factors including political will and financial resources) the international community may decide to commit material assistance and protection support.[127] But even as the immediate emergency response activities are taking place, it is important to plan for the post-emergency recovery and reconstruction phase and establish links to broader development plans for the affected populations and localities.[128] The realisation of the need to promote coherence in humanitarian action has led to the development of conceptual and operational models to understand both the disaster cycle specifically and more generally the full cycle of protection required in all humanitarian crises.

[127] As noted by Beat Schweizer, ICRC Deputy Director-General: 'humanitarian organizations are constrained by the funds made available to them and are therefore subject to the political considerations of donor governments.' See B Schweizer, 'Moral Dilemmas for Humanitarianism in the Era of "Humanitarian" Military Interventions' (September 2004) 86(855) *International Review of the Red Cross* 547, 548–49.

[128] For discussion of various operational approaches, see: *VOICE Out Loud Newsletter No 15* (May 2012), including: J Costello, 'Joining the Dots: Ireland's Approach to Disaster Risk Reduction and Linking Relief, Recovery and Development'; P Örnéus and H Magnusson, 'Sweden's Flexible Approach Towards Linking Relief, Recovery and Development'.

i. The Disaster Cycle

As set out in Figure 3.4 below, there are four distinct phases to a disaster: pre-disaster risk reduction, prevention and preparedness; immediate humanitarian response; post-disaster recovery and rehabilitation; and the linking of humanitarian and development activities. These phases can be viewed as an interconnected 'disaster cycle'.[129] Reflecting the broader approach of humanitarian action, as opposed to simply material assistance, disaster risk reduction, prevention and preparedness activities (generally known as 'DRR') now play an increasingly fundamental role in the overall humanitarian response to natural and human-made hazards. For example, DRR was first included in the third edition of the *Sphere Handbook* as a cross-cutting theme of humanitarian action in 2011,[130] and the non-binding Sendai Framework for Action 2015–2030 highlights the international focus on DRR.[131] At the national level, the US Federal Emergency Management Agency (FEMA) defines 'preparedness' as 'a continuous cycle of planning, organizing, training, equipping, exercising, evaluating and taking corrective action in an effort to ensure effective coordination during incident response'.[132]

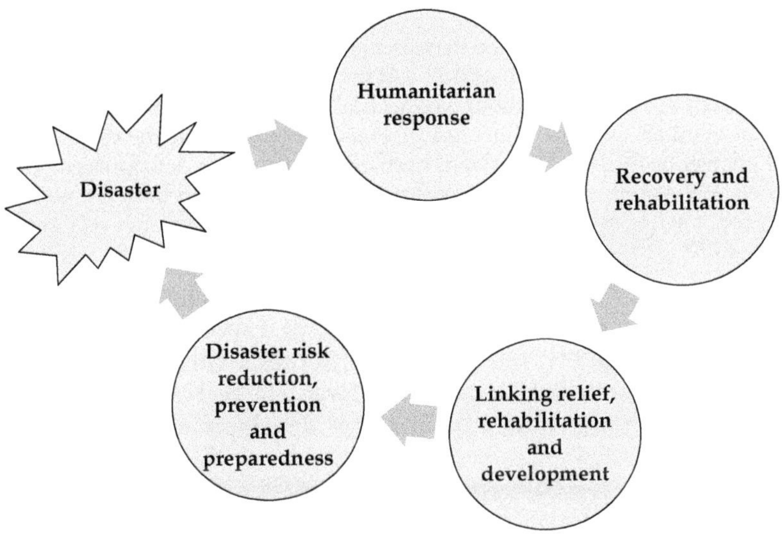

Figure 3.4: The disaster cycle

129 Adapted from: D Farber, 'Legal Scholarship, The Disaster Cycle, and the Fukushima Accident' (2012) 23(1) *Duke Environmental Law and Policy Forum* 1.

130 The Sphere Project, *Humanitarian Charter and Minimum Standards in Humanitarian Response* 3rd edn, April 2011, 14.

131 For further discussion of DRR, see ch 8, Section II.

132 US Department of Homeland Security/FEMA, *The Preparedness Cycle* www.fema.gov/plan-prepare.

Since work undertaken before a disaster strikes can reduce the vulnerabilities and increase the capacity and resilience of communities, and therefore the impact of the disaster, it follows that recovery and development planning must also incorporate DRR measures. The concept of 'linking relief, rehabilitation and development' (LRRD) arose in the 1990s as a means of bridging the funding and activities of emergency-focused humanitarian agencies and longer-term developmental agencies. While there have been practical difficulties in implementing the concept, particularly within states with weak infrastructure or during complex armed conflicts, the increasing focus on capacity and resilience has led to a revival of the concept.[133] As noted by Oxfam: 'building resilience will mean breaking down the barriers between humanitarian and development approaches more fundamentally than ever before. Responses to humanitarian and economic crises need to be brought together with responses to foster long-term development.'[134] Hugo Slim has argued against the false dichotomy between humanitarian and development work, noting that the perceived division breaks down when one adopts a rights-based approach to both humanitarian and developmental activities.[135] In promoting human rights as a common framework for elaborating values which underpin humanitarian action and development work, Slim cogently remarks:

> Perpetuating a rigid distinction between humanitarian values and development values opens the door to absurd questions of comparison between the two. Is humanitarian work only about saving life? Is development work 'long term' and humanitarian work 'short term'? Is one apolitical and the other political? The answer is, of course, that both humanitarianism and development are concerned with saving life, both are short and long term, and both are political in the proper sense of being concerned with the use and abuse of power in human relations.[136]

However, there is a need to ensure coherence between the evolving legal and policy frameworks for DRR, humanitarian response and development activities.[137] As noted by the UN Special Representative of the Secretary-General for Disaster Risk Reduction, Margareta Wahlström: 'Traditional barriers between the humanitarian and development fields—be they

[133] I Mosel and S Levine, *Remaking the Case for Linking Relief, Rehabilitation and Development*, Humanitarian Policy Group, Overseas Development Institute, March 2014, 3.

[134] D Hillier and G Castillo, *No Accident: Resilience and the Inequality of Risk*, Oxfam International, Briefing Paper No 172, May 2013, 5.

[135] H Slim, 'Dissolving the Difference between Humanitarianism and Development: The Mixing of a Rights-based Solution' (August 2000) 10(3–4) *Development in Practice* 491, 491.

[136] ibid, 492.

[137] D Cubie, 'Promoting Dignity for All: Human Rights Approaches in the Post-2015 Climate Change, Disaster Risk Reduction and Sustainable Development Frameworks' (2014) 8 *Human Rights and International Legal Discourse* 1.

institutional, funding-related or conceptual—should not be allowed to stifle the action, innovation and change needed to alleviate suffering and strengthen resilience.'[138]

ii. The Full Cycle of Protection

Just as Daniel Farber has elaborated the concept of a 'disaster cycle' to track the phases of preparation and response to natural and human-made disasters,[139] Walter Kälin has emphasised the need for a 'cycle of protection' for internally displaced persons:

> The challenge lies in forming a cycle of protection that constantly adapts to the challenges posed by natural hazards and optimizes protection to those affected in order to mitigate the impact of disasters, prevent displacement and other negative consequences ... The State is responsible for protecting the rights of its population in the context of all phases of a natural disaster. State responsibility covers not only the immediate response phase after a disaster has struck, but begins with preparedness before disaster strikes and extends to recovery, reconstruction and reinforced preparedness measures on the basis of lessons learned.[140]

As can be seen from Kälin's description, this view of protection is firmly rooted in international human rights law and stresses the fundamental role of the affected state—an approach Marlies Hesselman has called the 'full cycle of protection'.[141] Indeed, one can argue that the duality of material assistance and protection of persons in humanitarian crises mirrors the debate between needs-based and rights-based approaches—with the provision of material assistance premised on needs and protection based on rights. However, such an approach is too simplistic, and ignores the complex relationship between needs and rights in humanitarian activities and the divergent responsibilities of different actors. From a legal perspective, it appears clear that a twin-track of rights-based and needs-based approaches may be undertaken by humanitarian actors. Indeed, at times it can be difficult to separate the two approaches. So it is important to note that despite the existence of *lex specialis*, such as during an

[138] M Wahlström, *Chairperson's Summary*, Nansen Conference on Climate Change and Displacement in the 21st Century, Oslo, 6–7 June 2011, para 17.

[139] D Farber, 'The Disaster Cycle', above n 129.

[140] W Kälin, 'Report of the Representative of the Secretary-General on the Human Rights of Internally Displaced Persons: Addendum on Protection of Internally Displaced Persons in Situations of Natural Disasters' (5 March 2009) A/HRC/10/13/Add.1, para 21.

[141] M Hesselman, 'Establishing a Full "Cycle of Protection" for Disaster Victims: Preparedness, Response and Recovery according to Regional and International Human Rights Supervisory Bodies' (2013) 18 *Tilburg Law Review* 106. See also D Cubie and M Hesselman, 'Accountability for the Human Rights Implications of Natural Disasters: A Proposal for Systemic International Oversight' (2015) 33(1) *Netherlands Quarterly of Human Rights* 9.

armed conflict,[142] and operational requirements for the efficient running of humanitarian programmes, general human rights obligations of states and other duty-bearers continue to exist alongside specialised bodies of law.[143] Kälin's description of the cycle of protection therefore provides a coherent explanation for the application of protection activities across all stages of any humanitarian crisis.

Elizabeth Ferris meanwhile has highlighted the continuing lack of understanding of the substantive content of protection activities, despite the widespread acceptance of the ICRC-IASC definition and influential non-binding guidance documents. Ferris therefore developed a typology of protection activities, identifying three types of protection relevant in humanitarian crises:

1. ***Physical security or protection*** – protecting the life and integrity of a person; ensuring personal safety and security;
2. ***Humanitarian protection*** – providing adequate access to basic requirements of life (food, water, medical care, shelter etc.) on a non-discriminatory basis; and
3. ***Human rights protection*** – protecting individuals' full enjoyment of all rights.[144]

Ferris argues convincingly that humanitarian actors cannot and should not engage in physical security or protection activities, as they are ill-equipped to prevent violence from occurring.[145] One must never forget that the primary responsibility for all three types of protection (physical, humanitarian and human rights) lies squarely with the affected state. Ferris notes: 'Protection is about preventing people from getting hurt. But humanitarian assistance was intended to respond to people who already have been hurt, and functions best when that is what it does. In human rights terms, protection is about responding to violations of human rights, while relief is about alleviating the consequences of those violations.'[146] So can humanitarian agencies balance the need to respond to human suffering wherever it may occur based on greatest need, with a legal, ethical and moral responsibility to respect the rights of those affected by humanitarian crises? The following section argues that it is indeed possible to merge

[142] One could argue that *lex specialis* regarding international disaster laws are in the process of formation, not least driven by the current work of the ILC on the protection of persons in the event of disasters. However, the framework and parameters are still under development.
[143] For discussion of the substantive content of human rights law applicable in humanitarian crises, see ch 5, Section II.
[144] Ferris, *Politics of Protection*, above n 2, 278.
[145] It is beyond the scope of this book to examine the broader UN mandate to protect civilians under peacekeeping mandates. However, for detailed analysis see S Wills, *Protecting Civilians: The Obligations of Peacekeepers* (Oxford University Press, 2009).
[146] Ferris, *Politics of Protection*, above n 2, 273.

rights-based and needs-based approaches within humanitarian operations, through the application of human rights principles to humanitarian programming.

B. Merging Rights-based and Needs-based Approaches

The Inter-Agency Standing Committee has noted that in addition to respecting civil and political rights, humanitarian and development actors also play an important role in fulfilling economic, social and cultural rights through the provision of material assistance such as food, water and sanitation, shelter, healthcare and education.[147] Crucially, the IASC specifically highlights that:

> [D]istributing humanitarian goods and providing humanitarian services, while greatly contributing to the enjoyment of human rights by affected persons, are not as such protection activities. They become so insofar as they specifically aim at preventing future, stopping on-going and redressing past violations of such rights.[148]

Drawing on work conducted by Barnett and Weiss, Craig Allan and Thérèse O'Donnell have argued that 'while rights-based and needs-based approaches both focus on basic survival needs (including access to food, water and medicines), rights-discourse really reflects notions of political rights and rights to democracy. Thus, a difference emerges between those who favour survival and those who favour freedom.'[149] While agreeing that a focus on political and social transformation may accompany a rights-based approach, I would argue that both approaches can encompass survival and freedom objectives. As noted by David Forsythe: 'Some threats to human dignity call for diplomatic or legal representation, and some threats to human dignity call for the provision of socio-economic goods and services.'[150] Indeed, rights-based and needs-based approaches can be incorporated into the overall humanitarian response to a particular crisis, with different organisations playing distinct roles in the provision of material assistance or in monitoring and advocacy for the rights of the affected population. The two approaches can also be combined internally within each humanitarian actor's response. The development of

[147] IASC, *Operational Guidelines*, above n 12, 6.

[148] ibid.

[149] Allan and O'Donnell, 'An Offer You Cannot Refuse?, above n 64, 61. Barnett and Weiss have argued that: '[R]elief agencies will nearly always privilege survival over freedom, while the human rights community is willing, at times, to use relief as an instrument to foster rights.' Barnett and Weiss, *Humanitarianism Contested*, above n 68, 79.

[150] Forsythe, 'Humanitarian Protection', above n 11, 682.

beneficiary communications programmes within humanitarian responses, as illustrated in the following example, is a case in point.

i. Indonesia: Beneficiary Communications in Banda Aceh

Following the 2004 Indian Ocean Tsunami, the BBC World Service Trust highlighted the need for improved information provision for the local population from humanitarian actors in Aceh Province in Indonesia.[151] The Irish Red Cross Society (IRCS) therefore established an innovative programme across Aceh to promote two-way communication between humanitarian actors and the local population. Through the establishment of first a newsletter and then a newspaper, followed by a radio station and finally public-service TV broadcasting, an accountability forum was provided for the local population, who were faced with a multitude of national and international humanitarian agencies, to ask questions and relay concerns regarding protection and assistance activities. UN staff, government officials and NGO workers were regularly interviewed about the emergency and reconstruction programmes, for example a panel of local school girls quizzed the provincial Minister for Education on access to school on live TV.

Key to the success of the programme was the establishment of a Community Advocacy Unit (CAU), which provided one-to-one support to individuals so that issues of quality or appropriateness of protection and assistance activities could be raised directly with the service providers. A free SMS text service was provided so that individuals could contact the IRCS directly with questions. So if someone was concerned about the quality of their house reconstruction, they would be facilitated by IRCS staff to meet with the service provider (often another international NGO) in a non-confrontational manner to resolve any questions or issues. The CAU therefore ensured the practical application of rights-based principles of empowerment, participation, non-discrimination and accountability for all actors (whether local government officials or an international agency).[152]

The extensive programme set up in Banda Aceh was only possible due to the availability of resources. Yet it was not operational in the immediate phase of the emergency in early 2005 due to its innovative nature and the need to establish basic communication infrastructure. Nevertheless, the experiences of many organisations during the tsunami prompted

[151] *Left in the Dark: The Unmet Need for Information in Humanitarian Responses*, BBC World Service Trust, Policy Briefing No 2, October 2008.

[152] See *After the Wave: A Pictorial History of the Irish Red Cross Society Tsunami Relief & Recovery Programme 2005–2011* (Irish Red Cross Society, 2011) 22–27.

more focus on how to ensure better two-way communication between affected populations and humanitarian agencies. As a result, following the 2010 Haitian earthquake, beneficiary communications programmes were established in the initial phases of the humanitarian response, and are now a standard component of Red Cross operations.[153]

Moreover, reflecting the increasingly central role of beneficiary communication for all humanitarian actors, the global consultations for the 2016 World Humanitarian Summit emphasised that to empower people to cope and recover with dignity, 'people affected by crises should be enabled to exercise greater voice and choice in humanitarian action, including through better two-way communication and feedback mechanisms.'[154]

ii. Incorporating Human Rights Principles into Programming

Based on the preceding understanding of humanitarian action and protection of persons in humanitarian crises, it follows that human rights principles should be incorporated into the operational programmes of all humanitarian actors. This is not to say that each organisation should undertake human rights programmes—as noted by the OHCHR in the context of international development programmes:

> [H]uman rights cannot be expected to provide detailed recommendations for good development processes or clear answers to resource-allocation and policy choices. However, they can provide a conceptual framework for evaluating and improving practice and ensuring that decision-making is more reasonable, objective and transparent, and will benefit those living in poverty.[155]

Moreover, if rights-based and needs-based approaches are complementary, then human rights principles should inform even traditional 'pure' humanitarian responses premised on needs-based approaches during the immediate emergency phase. More explicitly political and transformative approaches may undertake a broader range of activities, but it must be recognised that humanitarian and human rights organisations play different roles. So organisations need to be conscious that it is possible to move away from humanitarian protection into the realm of human rights protection. To reiterate, this is not to argue that human rights protection

[153] IFRC, *What We Do—Beneficiary Communications*, www.ifrc.org/en/what-we-do/beneficiary-communications.

[154] World Humanitarian Summit secretariat, *Restoring Humanity: Synthesis of the Consultation Process for the World Humanitarian Summit* (New York, UN, 2015) ix.

[155] UNOHCHR, *Claiming the Millennium Development Goals: A Human Rights Approach* (2008) HR/PUB/08/3, 7.

should not be promoted during humanitarian operations, but simply that organisations need to be conscious of the differences between humanitarian protection activities and human rights protection activities.

One can furthermore distinguish human rights principles from human rights protection. As noted previously, a rights-based approach to humanitarian action would incorporate four key human rights principles into all humanitarian programming, in particular: a) empowerment of rights-holders; b) participation in decision-making processes; c) non-discrimination and prioritisation of vulnerable groups; and d) accountability of duty-bearers to rights-holders. Such an approach would prioritise procedural rights such as the right of access to information, the right to participate in decision-making, and the right of effective access to justice and administrative proceedings.[156] Such procedural rights are fundamental to promote participation and empowerment of local and affected communities on a non-discriminatory basis. As highlighted in the ICRC's Professional Standards for Protection Work:

> Measures to respect, safeguard and promote the dignity of persons at risk are not limited to engaging with them in a respectful manner. They also include facilitating their access to accurate and reliable information, ensuring their inclusion and meaningful participation in decision-making processes which affect them, and supporting their independent capacities, notably those of making free and informed choices, and of asserting their rights.[157]

It therefore follows that even agencies undertaking predominantly needs-based approaches can and should incorporate human rights principles, in particular procedural rights for local communities and the affected population, into all their humanitarian programming; while those taking a more explicitly rights-based approach to humanitarian protection should be free to incorporate more transformative objectives, while remaining conscious of the differences between humanitarian protection and human rights protection.

This chapter has focused on the operational nature of the prime objective of the *acquis humanitaire*, namely the protection of persons. However, before we can commence a more detailed examination of the normative content of the *acquis humanitaire* across various branches of international law in Part II of this monograph, we shall first review some of the challenges to the implementation and enforcement of humanitarian norms, in particular the need to ensure humanitarian access and the related concept of state sovereignty and non-intervention. The next chapter also examines Harold Koh's concept of transnational legal process as a means of

[156] See *Rio Declaration on Environment and Development* (12 August 1992) A/CONF.151/26 (Vol I), Principle 10.

[157] ICRC, *Professional Standards*, above n 15, 25.

understanding the creation and internalisation of humanitarian norms, and the role played by political, legal, administrative, professional and social accountability mechanisms. For, as noted by the IASC, the goals of protection and accountability are fundamentally linked and should be approached as 'essential, complementary and mutually reinforcing components of an effective humanitarian response'.[158]

[158] IASC, *Protection and Accountability to Affected Populations in the Humanitarian Programme Cycle* (2016) Emergency Directors Group (EDG), Preliminary Guidance Note, 5–6.

4

Strengthening the Web of International Legal Protection

I. CHALLENGES OF IMPLEMENTATION AND ENFORCEMENT

FOLLOWING DISCUSSION OF the conceptual basis of the *acquis humanitaire* in the form of the principles of humanity and human dignity in chapter two, and analysis of the protection of persons as the prime objective of humanitarian action in chapter three, this chapter examines the third constituent part of the *acquis humanitaire*, namely processes and mechanisms to promote compliance with international, regional and domestic norms. For despite the existence of multiple sources of binding international law and non-binding norms relating to the protection of persons, fundamental challenges remain for their actual implementation in humanitarian crises. As with many areas of the law, all too often the problem is not a lack of legal instruments per se, but their consistent application and lack of political will to implement agreed laws, norms and standards. As cogently noted by Jane McAdam in the context of the debate surrounding the need for a new legal instrument to address climate change-induced displacement:

> Even if a treaty were achieved, States would have to demonstrate sufficient political will to ratify, implement and enforce it. For example, the law on refugees is very well established and there are 148 parties to the Refugee Convention/Protocol. Yet there are still some 15 million refugees in the world without a durable solution. The problem, I would argue, is not an absence of law, but an absence of the will to implement the law.[1]

Louise Oswald-Beck has expressed similar concerns regarding the lack of enforcement, rather than lack of legal rules, in the context of armed conflicts.[2] Recognising which rights and obligations already exist in

[1] J McAdam, 'Legal Solutions: If a Treaty is Not the Answer, Then What Is?', paper presented at ClimMig Conference on Human Rights, Environmental Change, Migration and Displacement, Vienna, 20–21 September 2012, 1–2.

[2] Quoted in 'Humanitarian Assistance in Armed Conflict Conference of the Luxemburg Group, 24–25 May 2004, Graduate Institute of International Studies, Geneva' (2004) 86(856) *International Review of the Red Cross* 879, 900.

international law is a prerequisite for identifying potential gaps and lacunae for the protection of persons in humanitarian crises. As a consequence, the normative content of the *acquis humanitaire* can be viewed as a constantly evolving web of international legal protection for individuals caught up in conflict, displacement or disasters. However, the provisions that comprise this web of protection, by necessity, arise from both binding and non-binding sources, and from a range of recognised branches of international law. One must therefore take an expansive view of the sources that influence the operational practices of states and humanitarian actors. While lawyers principally consider the *lex lata* of binding obligations and rights, international law is by its nature dynamic and evolving. The normative force of international law influences the actions of state and non-state actors, and so codifying and developing *lex ferenda* for the international legal protection of persons in humanitarian crises is equally important.[3]

The objective of strengthening the normative content of the *acquis humanitaire* is linked to the processes and mechanisms for promoting the internalisation of norms and ultimately their compliance and implementation. Section II of this chapter therefore applies Harold Koh's theory of norm internalisation via transnational legal process to humanitarian action. Section III then examines key mechanisms of accountability for states and non-state actors. The chapter concludes by providing a summary of the arguments presented in Part I of this monograph setting out the conceptual framework of the *acquis humanitaire*, before we move onto an examination of selected aspects of the normative content of the *acquis humanitaire* in Part II. However, it is first necessary to examine challenges to the implementation of humanitarian action, not least the need to ensure humanitarian access for impartial humanitarian actors and the role of state sovereignty and non-intervention in domestic affairs.

A. Ensuring Humanitarian Access

The concept of humanitarian access is fundamental to the protection of persons, as well as for the operational activities of humanitarian actors.[4] Elizabeth Ferris has described this as 'one of the most difficult and

[3] As recognised by the ILC Special Rapporteur in the context of the protection of persons in the event of disasters. See E Valencia-Ospina, *Preliminary Report on the Protection of Persons in the Event of Disasters* (8 May 2008) A/CN.4/598, para 59.

[4] See, eg, Government of Switzerland, *Humanitarian Access in Situations of Armed Conflict: Handbook on the International Normative Framework*, Version 2, December 2014, 10.

highly politicized issues in humanitarian action today'.[5] Similarly, UN Secretary-General, Ban Ki-moon, emphasised that participants at the 2016 World Humanitarian Summit 'underscored that the denial of humanitarian access prevents an effective response to humanitarian needs and deprives people of human dignity. Unfettered humanitarian access is imperative, and humanitarian principles must be upheld and promoted with the utmost urgency'.[6] The concept therefore involves a dual focus: i) humanitarian actors' ability to reach populations affected by crisis; and ii) an affected population's ability to access humanitarian assistance and services.[7] Simply put, humanitarian access concerns the full and unimpeded ability of organisations (whether domestic or international) to meet, interact and provide protection and assistance to populations in need. A range of practical and political factors can restrict or deny humanitarian organisations from direct contact with populations during armed conflicts, displacement or disasters. UNOCHA has noted five distinct types of constraints on humanitarian access: a) bureaucratic restrictions on personnel and humanitarian supplies (whether intentional or unintentional); b) impediments related to climate, terrain or lack of infrastructure; c) the deliberate diversion of aid, and interference in the delivery of relief or implementation of activities; d) active fighting and military operations; and e) attacks on humanitarian personnel, goods and facilities.[8]

In many cases, a combination of factors impedes access for humanitarian agencies, which are compounded by logistical challenges. Major disasters and armed conflicts can destroy roads and bridges (for example, Oxfam International cleared more than 100 km of roads and built 31 bridges to access devastated communities following the 2004 Indian Ocean Tsunami),[9] or flood waters may impede travel into affected areas (for example, the ICRC used donkeys and human porters during the 2010 Pakistan floods to access the worst-affected areas which were also in the midst of active military operations).[10] The question of ensuring

[5] E Ferris, 'Humanitarian Perspectives on "Protection of Persons in the Event of Disasters"', paper presented at Roundtable on Canada and International Law, Department of Foreign Affairs and International Trade, 21 April 2009 www.brookings.edu/speeches/2009/0421_natural_disasters_ferris.aspx.

[6] 'Chair's Summary by the United Nations Secretary-General' in *Standing Up for Humanity: Committing to Action*, final version, World Humanitarian Summit, Istanbul, 23–24 May 2016 (2016) 4.

[7] UNOCHA, *OCHA on Message: Humanitarian Access*, April 2010, 1.

[8] ibid. See also UNSC, *Report of the Secretary-General on the Protection of Civilians in Armed Conflict* (13 May 2016) S/2016/447, 8–11.

[9] Oxfam, *The Indian Ocean Tsunami, 10 Years On: Lessons from the response and ongoing humanitarian funding challenges*, 18 December 2014, Oxfam Research Reports, 15.

[10] ICRC, *Pakistan: ICRC and Pakistan Red Crescent Ramp Up Aid Effort as Floods Spread to South*, 19 August 2010, Operational Update www.icrc.org/eng/resources/documents/news-release/2010/pakistan-news-190810.htm.

humanitarian access therefore needs to address both restrictions of an unintentional or environmentally induced nature and deliberate acts which impede or deny access. Such human actions may be bureaucratic, and so need to be addressed via consultation and awareness raising of the practical challenges in distributing material assistance and undertaking programmes of protection. This is the primary motivation behind the IFRC *Guidelines for the Domestic Facilitation and Regulation of International Disaster Relief and Initial Recovery Assistance*[11] and *Model Act for the Facilitation and Regulation of International Disaster Relief and Initial Recovery Assistance*,[12] which are intended to assist governments to prepare for regulatory issues surrounding international humanitarian activities.

Conversely, the denial of access may be a deliberate policy on the part of civil or military authorities so that external actors are unable to witness abuse and suffering, or as a means of coercing an affected population, for example to move from one area to another.[13] As discussed in chapter seven, these actions may ultimately amount to war crimes, crimes against humanity or genocide bearing individual criminal responsibility.[14] Such binding provisions of international law interact with non-binding norms to exert pressure on governments, non-state armed groups and local communities to allow humanitarian organisations to undertake activities for affected populations. However, even diplomatic or judicial pressure cannot always ensure humanitarian access.[15] The initial refusal of the military junta in Myanmar to permit Western and UN humanitarian agencies to access hundreds of thousands of people affected by Cyclone Nargis in 2008 highlighted the role state officials play in ensuring that external assistance reaches those affected. As in other cases of aid refusal, the actions of Myanmar's authorities led to calls for the provision of humanitarian assistance against their wishes, through the use of military force if necessary.[16] This brings us on to the controversial issue of state sovereignty and non-intervention in domestic affairs, and the need to distinguish between impartial humanitarian action and military humanitarian interventions.

[11] IFRC, *Introduction to the Guidelines for the Domestic Facilitation and Regulation of International Disaster Relief and Initial Recovery Assistance* (Geneva 2008) 3.

[12] IFRC, *Model Act for the Facilitation and Regulation of International Disaster Relief and Initial Recovery Assistance (with commentary)* (March 2013).

[13] See, eg, M Usmani, 'Restrictions on Humanitarian Aid in Darfur: The Role of the International Criminal Court' (2007–2008) 36 *Georgia Journal of International and Comparative Law* 257.

[14] See ch 7, Sections II and III.

[15] See, eg, UNSC, *Report of the Secretary-General*, above n 8.

[16] C Allan and T O'Donnell, 'An Offer You Cannot Refuse? Natural Disasters, the Politics of Aid Refusal and Potential Legal Implications' (2013) 5(1) *Amsterdam Law Forum* 36.

B. Sovereignty and Non-Intervention in Domestic Affairs

i. Distinguishing Humanitarian Action from Humanitarian Intervention

The conceptual and operational development of humanitarianism within international law has been fundamentally influenced by the changing importance placed on state sovereignty over the past 70 years. Modern views of state sovereignty, like many areas of international law, were redefined at the end of the Second World War. The horrors of war, atomic bombs and the Holocaust shocked an already stunned world into fundamental advances in international legal protections. The Universal Declaration of Human Rights, and International Covenants on Civil and Political Rights and on Economic, Social and Cultural Rights formed the basis for an international Bill of Rights, while the Conventions Against Genocide,[17] Torture,[18] and Racial Discrimination[19] led to the universal applicability of specific rights, irrespective of a government's formal acceptance through an international treaty. The superior status of *jus cogens* norms were given concrete expression in the 1969 Vienna Convention on the Law of Treaties,[20] while the developing understanding of international obligations owed *erga omnes* (that is to the community of states as a whole) reaffirmed that a state's actions in regard to both individuals and the international community could legitimately be constrained.[21]

These chinks in the armour of the traditional view of state sovereignty, firmly grounded in the principle of non-intervention set out in the 1970 UNGA Friendly Relations Declaration,[22] were further prised open following the end of the Cold War. For example, the 1998 UN Guiding Principles on Internal Displacement[23] were premised on the concept of 'sovereignty as responsibility' as developed by Francis Deng, the first Representative

[17] Convention on the Prevention and Punishment of the Crime of Genocide (adopted 9 December 1948, entered into force 12 January 1951) 78 UNTS 277.

[18] Convention against Torture and Other Cruel, Inhuman or Degrading Treatment or Punishment (adopted 10 December 1984, entered into force 26 June 1987) 1465 UNTS 85.

[19] International Convention on the Elimination of All Forms of Racial Discrimination (adopted 7 March 1966, entered into force 4 January 1969) 660 UNTS 195.

[20] Vienna Convention on the Law of Treaties (adopted 23 May 1969, entered into force 27 January 1980) 1155 UNTS 331.

[21] See generally J Crawford and S Olleson, 'The Nature and Forms of International Responsibility' in M Evans (ed), *International Law* 3rd edn (Oxford University Press, 2010) 441.

[22] UNGA Res 2625 (XXV), *Declaration on Principles of International Law concerning Friendly Relations and Co-operation among States in accordance with the Charter of the United Nations* (24 October 1970) A/RES/25/2625, which states: 'No State or group of States has the right to intervene, directly or indirectly, for any reason whatever, in the internal or external affairs of any other State.'

[23] UN Commission on Human Rights, *The Guiding Principles on Internal Displacement*, E/CN.4/1998/53/Add.2 (1998).

to the UN Secretary-General on Internally Displaced Persons.[24] The non-binding Guiding Principles set out that national authorities have the primary duty and responsibility to provide protection and humanitarian assistance to internally displaced persons within their jurisdiction.[25] Furthermore, if a government is unable to provide the necessary assistance, they should not arbitrarily refuse offers of international aid.[26] Roberta Cohen, one of the drafters of the Guiding Principles, has argued that the Guiding Principles reflect an effort to balance state sovereignty with humanitarian imperatives.[27] Cohen further notes that the concept of sovereignty as responsibility entails a corresponding obligation on the part of the international community 'to provide humanitarian assistance and protection to IDPs when the governments concerned are unable to fulfill their responsibilities'.[28]

However, what happens when a government is unable or unwilling to provide the necessary protection and assistance to persons caught up in humanitarian crises in its territory? The concept of external intervention for humanitarian purposes has a long pedigree.[29] For example, John Stuart Mill discussed the international regulation of interventions in 1859, although it should be noted that he distinguished interventions between 'civilised nations' and those between 'civilised' nations and 'barbarians'.[30] Nevertheless, he contended:

> There seems to be no little need that the whole doctrine of non-interference with foreign nations should be reconsidered ... There are few questions which more require to be taken in hand by ethical and political philosophers, with a view to establish some rule or criterion whereby the justifiableness of intervening in the affairs of other countries, and (what is sometimes fully as questionable) the

[24] F Deng et al, *Sovereignty as Responsibility: Conflict Management in Africa* (Brookings Institution Press, 1996).

[25] Principle 3(1), *Guiding Principles*, above n 23.

[26] See K Luopajärvi, 'Is there an Obligation on States to Accept International Humanitarian Assistance to Internally Displaced Persons under International Law?' (2003) 15(4) *International Journal of Refugee Law* 678.

[27] R Cohen, 'The Guiding Principles on Internal Displacement: An Innovation in International Standard Setting' (2004) 10 *Global Governance* 459, 466–67.

[28] ibid, 466.

[29] For discussion of Emer de Vattel's support for humanitarian interventions in the eighteenth century, see A Hurrell, 'Vattel: Pluralism and Its Limits' in I Clark and I Neumann (eds), *Classical Theories of International Relations* (St Martin's Press, 1996), in particular 242–45. See also J-P Fonteyne, 'The Customary International Law Doctrine of Humanitarian Intervention: Its Current Validity under the UN Charter' (1973–1974) 4 *California Western International Law Journal* 203, in particular 214–26.

[30] For critical analysis of the historical motivations of Western powers in undertaking interventions against 'uncivilised' or 'half-civilised' nations, see D Rodogno, 'Nineteenth-Century Humanitarian Intervention: A Short Overview' (November 2011) 15 *Quaderni di Relazioni Internazionali*.

justifiableness of refraining from intervention, may be brought to a definite and rational test.[31]

The ending of the Cold War in the early 1990s coincided with a series of complex humanitarian emergencies that provided one such opportunity for the international community to reconsider the rational for, and limitations of, military interventions for humanitarian purposes. The treatment of civilian Kurds in northern Iraq by Saddam Hussein's military at the end of the 1990–91 Gulf War prompted the UN Security Council to declare the repression of the Iraqi population as a threat to international peace and security.[32] While UNSC Resolution 688 did not explicitly authorise the use of force to protect the civilian population, the UK, US and other countries argued that international law provided a basis for the establishment of 'safe havens' and 'no-fly' zones in both northern and southern Iraq due to the severe humanitarian need faced by the Kurdish and Shi'ite populations who were opposed to Hussein.[33] The subsequent military interventions in Somalia, Liberia, Haiti, Bosnia, Kosovo and Timor Leste reflected post-Cold War aspirations that a new world order was possible whereby the international community could intervene to protect civilians from gross and systematic human rights abuses.[34] Unfortunately, the messy reality of these military interventions eroded much of the initial enthusiasm for an expansive doctrine of humanitarian intervention.[35] Consequently, subsequent interventions in Afghanistan and Iraq following the attacks on the World Trade Center and the Pentagon on 9/11 were premised on the 'war on terror' and collective self-defence, rather than humanitarian justifications per se.[36]

The long-running debate about the legality and morality of humanitarian interventions is instructive for two key reasons. First, humanitarian intervention has traditionally been viewed from the perspective of interventions to stop a government or other forces within a country from

[31] 'A Few Words on Non-Intervention (1859)' in J Robson (ed), *The Collected Works of John Stuart Mill, Volume XXI—Essays on Equality, Law, and Education* (University of Toronto Press/Routledge and Kegan Paul, 1984) http://oll.libertyfund.org/title/255/21666.

[32] UNSC Resolution 688 (5 April 1991) para 1.

[33] For succinct analysis, see C Greenwood, 'Is There a Right of Humanitarian Intervention?', *The World Today*, February 1993, 34.

[34] For arguments supporting a broad application of humanitarian interventions, see N Dorr, 'Humanitarian Intervention—Challenges for the International Community on the Eve of a New Century' (1999) *Trócaire Development Review* 17. For counter arguments, see F Weissman, '"Not In Our Name": Why Médecins Sans Frontières Does Not Support the "Responsibility to Protect"' (August 2010) 29(2) *Criminal Justice Ethics* 194.

[35] See A Nollkaemper, '"Failures to Protect" in International Law' (2013) SHARES Research Paper 26, ACIL 2013–15.

[36] See C Greenwood, 'International Law and the Pre-emptive Use of Force: Afghanistan, Al-Qaida, and Iraq' (2003) 4 *San Diego International Law Journal* 7.

subjecting the population to large-scale human rights abuses. This was predominantly understood to occur in times of armed conflict, either of an international or non-international nature.[37] There was little, if any, discussion of forcible humanitarian interventions in non-conflict settings until the perceived lack of response by the Myanmar government to the needs of the victims of Cyclone Nargis. Second, while there may be an understandable focus on military enforcement actions, interventions by one state into the affairs of another state do not necessarily require the use of force.[38] It is therefore important to distinguish 'humanitarian interventions' from 'humanitarian action'.[39]

At a theoretical level, the debate revolves around the respective weight to be ascribed to limitations on state sovereignty contrasted with individual rights as set out in international law. In advance of and during emergency relief operations, the arguments centre on the right of humanitarian access.[40] If state sovereignty takes precedence over human rights, then a state can lawfully deny humanitarian agencies access to people potentially in need of protection and assistance.[41] As noted by the ILC in the context of disasters: 'The principles of sovereignty and non-intervention contain two important corollaries: that disaster relief carried out by assisting actors is subject to the consent of the receiving State and that the receiving State has the primary responsibility for the protection of persons on its territory or subject to its jurisdiction or control during a disaster.'[42] However, if a state's actions are constrained by a narrower understanding of sovereignty and non-intervention, the international community can argue that there is a right of access to protect individual or group rights irrespective of the wishes of the affected state. The International Court of Justice provided a classic examination of the interplay between intervention and state sovereignty in the Nicaragua case.

[37] See, eg, J Dungel, 'A Right to Humanitarian Assistance in Internal Armed Conflicts Respecting Sovereignty, Neutrality and Legitimacy: Practical Proposals to Practical Problems' (May 2004) *Journal of Humanitarian Assistance*; Y Dinstein, 'The Right to Humanitarian Assistance' (Autumn 2000) *Naval War College Review* 77.

[38] R Cohen, 'The Burma Cyclone and the Responsibility to Protect', Brookings Institute, paper presented at the Congressional Briefing on Security for a New Century, 21 July 2008.

[39] Unfortunately, the two concepts can be conflated in theory; see, eg, L Fielding, 'Taking the Next Step in the Development of New Human Rights: The Emerging Right of Humanitarian Assistance to Restore Democracy' (1994–1995) 5 *Duke Journal of Comparative and International Law* 329.

[40] See, eg, R Hardcastle and A Chua, 'Humanitarian Assistance: Towards a Right of Access to Victims of Natural Disasters' (December 1998) 325 *International Review of the Red Cross* 589.

[41] See C Allan and T O'Donnell, 'A Call to Alms?: Natural Disasters, R2P, Duties of Cooperation and Uncharted Consequences' (2012) *Journal of Conflict and Security Law* 1.

[42] Memorandum by the Secretariat, *Protection of Persons in the Event of Disasters*, International Law Commission, 60th Session (11 December 2007) A/CN.4/590, Summary, p 2, and generally paras 20–24.

ii. Nicaragua: Humanitarian Assistance and the International Court of Justice

In 1986, the ICJ was called upon to examine the specific status of humanitarian assistance in the context of the US intervention into the domestic affairs of Nicaragua.[43] In its judgment, the Court separated military support for the contras provided by the US from 1981 to 1984 from subsequent non-military assistance provided once the US House of Congress restricted support to only humanitarian objectives.[44] The Court stated: 'There can be no doubt that the provision of strictly humanitarian aid to persons or forces in another country, whatever their political affiliations or objectives, cannot be regarded as unlawful intervention, or as in any other way contrary to international law.'[45] The Court went on to declare:

> An essential feature of truly humanitarian aid is that it is given 'without discrimination' of any kind. In the view of the Court, if the provision of 'humanitarian assistance' is to escape condemnation as an intervention in the internal affairs of Nicaragua, not only must it be limited to the purposes hallowed in the practice of the Red Cross, namely 'to prevent and alleviate human suffering', and 'to protect life and health and to ensure respect for the human being'; it must also, and above all, be given without discrimination to all in need in Nicaragua, not merely to the contras and their dependents.[46]

While representing the first international judicial pronouncement on humanitarian assistance, the Court undertook a limited examination of the issue. Despite examining state sovereignty and non-intervention from the perspective of the threat or use of force by one state against another, the ICJ did not clarify the implications of unilateral provision of humanitarian assistance.[47] Following the Court's reasoning, for humanitarian assistance to be provided without discrimination to all those in need, that is not just to the contras and their dependants, consent from the Nicaraguan authorities would have been required. Yet in the

[43] Military and Paramilitary Activities in and against Nicaragua (*Nicaragua v United States of America*), Merits, Judgment, ICJ Reports 1986, 14. See generally H Charlesworth, 'Customary International Law and the Nicaragua Case' (1984–1987) 11 *Australian Yearbook of International Law* 1; F Morrison, 'Legal Issues in the Nicaragua Opinion' (1987) 81 *American Journal of International Law* 160.

[44] 'Humanitarian assistance' was defined in the relevant US legislation as: 'the provision of food, clothing, medicine, and other humanitarian assistance, and it does not include the provision of weapons, weapons systems, ammunition, or other equipment, vehicles, or material which can be used to inflict serious bodily harm or death.' Quoted in Military and Paramilitary Activities in and against Nicaragua, above n 43, para 97.

[45] ibid, para 242.

[46] ibid, para 243.

[47] G Verdirame, 'Compliance with Human Rights in UN Operations' (2002) 2 *Human Rights Law Review* 265, 272. For discussion of cross-border humanitarian operations during armed conflicts, see ch 6, Section III.A.i.

context of the US support to the contras in Nicaragua, it was a deliberate policy of the US government not to support the Sandinista government. Conversely, the Nicaraguan government was unlikely to accept assistance for the contra rebels coming from another country which it believed was interfering in its domestic affairs. Such a stand-off highlights the challenges in providing humanitarian assistance to all those in need, and also the importance of impartial humanitarian actors who can operate in a non-discriminatory manner.

iii. The Responsibility to Protect Doctrine

The humanitarian crises and military interventions in the 1990s refocused the international debate on the limits of state sovereignty.[48] Following the NATO Kosovo bombing campaign in early 1999, UN Secretary-General Kofi Annan took up the theme of redefining sovereignty through his vision of 'two sovereignties'.[49] Under this concept, state sovereignty coexists with the concept of individual sovereignty drawn from the fundamental freedoms enshrined in the UN Charter and international human rights law. Annan stressed that the conflicts and genocide of the 1990s, and political changes resulting from the end of the Cold War, obliged the international community to rethink how the UN responded to humanitarian crises; and why states acted in some areas of conflict, but not in others even if the level of suffering was equally severe.

The UN responded to this call from the Secretary-General, and Canada supported the establishment of an International Commission on Intervention and State Sovereignty. Their final report in 2001 set forth the concept of the 'Responsibility to Protect' or 'R2P'.[50] While initially governments were reluctant to accept this interference in their national sovereignty, the Outcome Resolution of the Heads of State and Government at the 2005 World Summit included a modified version of the Responsibility to Protect doctrine.[51] The Resolution was accepted unanimously by all UN Member States, albeit in a non-binding instrument, thereby confirming the revised political view of the limits of state sovereignty.[52] In 2009, the UN

48 N Rodley and B Çali, 'Kosovo Revisited: Humanitarian Intervention on the Fault Lines of International Law' (2007) 7(2) *Human Rights Law Review* 275.

49 K Annan, 'Two Concepts of Sovereignty', *The Economist*, 18 September 1999.

50 *The Responsibility to Protect*, Report of the International Commission on Intervention and State Sovereignty, International Development Research Centre (December 2001).

51 UNGA, *2005 World Summit Outcome* (15 September 2005) A/60/L.1, paras 138–40.

52 For discussion of the evolving legal status of UN General Assembly Resolutions, see: B Sloan, 'The Binding Force of a "Recommendation" of the General Assembly of the United Nations' (1948) 25 *British Yearbook of International Law* 3 (1948); B Sloan, 'General Assembly Resolutions Revisited (Forty Years Later)' (1987) 58(1) *British Yearbook of International Law* 39.

Secretary-General clarified the three pillar structure to the R2P doctrine: a) states have the primary responsibility to protect their populations from genocide, war crimes, ethnic cleansing and crimes against humanity; b) the international community must support states in building capacity to protect their populations from such international crimes, as well as assisting states before crises and conflicts occur; and c) the international community ultimately has a responsibility to take timely and decisive action, including military actions, to prevent and halt such crimes when a state is manifestly failing to protect its population.[53]

However, while there have been calls to apply the R2P doctrine in a range of settings, including in Darfur, the Democratic Republic of Congo and Syria, governments and the UN have been slow to expressly invoke R2P, even in cases where international action ensues. In reality, there is limited international consensus on what R2P means in practice. Using the conflict in Darfur as an example, Luke Glanville has argued that despite the widespread political agreement that sovereignty entails responsibility, there remains a strong body of opinion and state practice against the international enforcement of sovereign responsibility during humanitarian crises in the absence of consent by the state in question.[54] Furthermore, the belief by some states that the invocation of R2P in 2011 to justify international military action in Libya was in fact a cover for regime change has resulted in an even more limited application of the doctrine—as evidenced by the lack of consensus on the actions to take in the long-running conflict in Syria.[55] The UN Secretary-General and the ILC have also clearly limited the extent of the doctrine, noting that it does not apply in situations such as climate change or natural disasters and remains restricted to the international crimes of genocide, war crimes, ethnic cleansing and crimes against humanity.[56] A potential opening for future changes was provided

[53] UNGA, *Implementing the Responsibility to Protect: Report of the Secretary-General*, Ban Ki-moon (12 January 2009) A/63/677.

[54] L Glanville, 'Darfur and the Responsibilities of Sovereignty' (2011) 15(3) *International Journal of Human Rights* 462. See also A Bellamy, *Global Politics and the Responsibility to Protect: From Words to Deeds* (Routledge, 2011) 52–54.

[55] S Butler, '"To Unite Our Strength to Maintain International Peace and Security": The International Response to the Syrian Civil War and the Global Discourse on State Sovereignty' *Irish Yearbook of International Law* (2017 forthcoming); G Cronogue, 'Responsibility to Protect: Syria, The Law, Politics, and Future of Humanitarian Intervention Post-Libya' (2012) 3(1) *Journal of International Humanitarian Legal Studies* 124.

[56] See Official Records of the General Assembly, Sixty-fourth Session, Report of the International Law Commission, *Supplement No 10* (A/64/10), para 164. For discussion of R2P and natural disasters, see: TR Saechao, 'Natural Disasters and the Responsibility to Protect: from Chaos to Clarity' (2006–2007) 32 *Brookings Journal of International Law* 663; J Wong, 'Reconstructing the Responsibility to Protect in the Wake of Cyclones and Separatism' (2009–2010) 84(2) *Tulane Law Review* 219; T Jackson, 'Bullets for Beans: Humanitarian Intervention and

by Ban Ki-moon when he noted that: 'The responsibility to protect applies, *until Member States decide otherwise*, only to the four specified crimes and violations.'[57]

As a result of this apparent buyers' remorse by some states towards the R2P doctrine, Ved Nanda has argued that for the third pillar covering military intervention to be operationalised, the UN General Assembly and Security Council need to elaborate common standards and principles for 'evaluating the risks, determining the urgency of the situation and concluding whether a state is actually "manifestly failing" to meet its responsibility to protect'.[58] Yet the political challenges of securing consensus are likely to remain. Therefore, while military interventions provide one form of accountability for a recalcitrant state unwilling to protect persons on its territory, this will always remain highly contentious, and may even exacerbate the suffering of the affected population.[59] Considering the limited applicability of military force to ensure humanitarian access, it is therefore necessary to analyse other norm creation processes to identify potential mechanisms for promoting compliance and implementation of international humanitarian laws, policies and practices.

II. NORM CREATION AND INTERNALISATION

As discussed in chapter two, the sources of the *acquis humanitaire* include traditional 'hard law' such as international conventions and judicial determinations of competent international courts and tribunals, but also includes non-binding norms arising from authoritative resolutions, guidelines and minimum standards which aim to improve the delivery of material assistance and the protection of persons in humanitarian crises.[60] While legal positivists may focus their analysis on binding international legal instruments, the role such non-binding norms play in the preparation and response to humanitarian crises necessitates an expanded view

the Responsibility to Protect in Natural Disasters' (2010) 59 *Naval Law Review* 1; J Harrington, 'R2P and Natural Disasters' in WA Knight and F Egerton (eds), *The Routledge Handbook of the Responsibility to Protect* (Routledge 2012); Allan and O'Donnell, 'A Call to Alms?', above n 41.

[57] *Implementing the Responsibility to Protect: Report of the Secretary-General*, Ban Ki-moon, A/63/677, January 2009, para 10(b) [emphasis added].

[58] VP Nanda, 'The Future under International Law of the Responsibility to Protect after Libya and Syria' (2013) 21(1) *Michigan State International Law Review* 1, 41–42. From a state perspective, see the proposal advanced by Brazil regarding 'responsibility while protecting': UNSC, *Letter dated 9 November 2011 from the Permanent Representative of Brazil to the United Nations addressed to the Secretary-General* (11 November 2011) A/66/551–S/2011/701, Annex.

[59] Cohen, 'Burma Cyclone', above n 38, 2.

[60] See ch 2, Section II.A.

of the sources of international law making.[61] In this section, I will argue that Harold Koh's theory of transnational legal process, which sets out to explain the creation and internalisation of norms, provides a cogent framework for understanding the dynamic and evolving range of sources, and therefore rights and obligations, contained within the *acquis humanitaire*. Moreover, in the context of a rights-based approach to humanitarian action, legal and non-legal mechanisms of accountability provide an important means of promoting compliance and enforcement of both binding and non-binding humanitarian norms.

However, before examining Koh's theory, it is important to note that other mechanisms of norm creation and international law making have been proposed. From an international relations perspective, the concept of constructivism focuses on 'the role of ideas, norms, knowledge, culture, and argument in politics, stressing in particular the role of collectively held or "intersubjective" ideas and understandings on social life'.[62] In other words, constructivists aim to understand how social facts change and influence politics. Indeed, Koh has drawn on a constructivist approach in some of his work on norm creation in international law.[63] Martha Finnemore, one of the leading theorists on constructivism, undertook a detailed analysis of military humanitarian interventions noting that '[t]he social nature of international politics creates normative understandings among actors that, in turn, coordinate values, expectations, and behavior'.[64] Finnemore concludes that mechanisms such as public opinion, the media and international institutions influence how norms are created and modified.[65] Hannah Entwisle meanwhile has applied Finnemore and Sikkink's constructivist concept of a 'norm-life cycle'[66] to the development

[61] See, eg, J Charney, 'Universal International Law' (1993) 87 *American Journal of International Law* 530; S Ratner, 'Does International Law Matter in Preventing Ethnic Conflict?' (2000) 32 NYU *Journal of International Law and Politics* 591; A Nollkaemper, 'The Distinction Between Non-Legal and Legal Norms in International Affairs: an Analysis with Reference to International Policy for the Protection of the North Sea from Hazardous Substances' (1998) 13 *International Journal of Marine and Coastal Law* 353.

[62] M Finnemore and K Sikkink, 'Taking Stock: The Constructivist Research Program in International Relations and Comparative Politics' (2001) 4 *Annual Review of Political Science* 391, 392.

[63] See, eg, H Koh, 'Review Essay: Why do Nations Obey International Law?' (June 1997) 106(8) *Yale Law Journal* 2599. For analysis of the relationship between international law and international relations, see H Koh, 'Transnational Legal Process' (1996) 75 *Nebraska Law Review* 181, 191–94.

[64] M Finnemore, 'Constructing Norms of Humanitarian Intervention' in PJ Katzenstein (ed), *The Culture of National Security: Norms and Identity in World Politics* (Columbia University Press, 1996) 157.

[65] ibid, 178.

[66] M Finnemore and K Sikkink, 'International Norm Dynamics and Political Change' (Autumn 1998) 52(4) *International Organization* 887.

of the UN Guiding Principles on Internal Displacement.[67] Entwisle argues that rather than focusing on the binding or non-binding nature of a specific norm, international lawyers should seek compliance via interactive processes between state and non-state actors.[68]

Meanwhile, back within the discipline of international law, as noted in chapter two, Pauwelyn et al have advanced the concept of informal law making, or IN-LAW, as a means of understanding process, output or actor informality in the development of international agreements.[69] From a humanitarian perspective, this concept was applied to the normative development of the Hyogo Framework for Action on disaster risk reduction by Luca Corredig.[70] Corredig argues that the UN International Strategy for Disaster Reduction provides a classic example of informal international law making as all three elements of an IN-LAW approach were present. In particular, Corredig highlights the informal nature of the process, actors and output, whereby the Hyogo Framework for Action was drafted and adopted by a loosely organised network of agents, incorporating a range of state and non-state actors and resulted in a non-binding text which comprised a collection of guidelines rather than a formal treaty.[71]

Both the international relations theory of constructivism and the legal theory of informal law making provide useful analytical lenses to examine the development and normative content of the *acquis humanitaire*. However, I would argue that neither fully incorporates the depth of analysis that Koh's theory of transnational legal process provides. For constructivism, the focus is primarily on the social and political relationships, rather than the legal processes per se. While it is important to understand the political context of humanitarian norms, the *acquis humanitaire* contains highly developed international legal regimes, such as the law of armed conflict, and so requires a legal focus. Likewise, although the *acquis humanitaire* contains non-binding or informal sources and processes for norm creation and implementation, the exclusive focus on such informal law making within an IN-LAW approach ignores the formal sources of the *acquis humanitaire* found in, inter alia, international human rights law,

[67] H Entwisle, 'Tracing Cascades: The Normative Development of the UN Guiding Principles on Internal Displacement' (2004–2005) 19 *Georgetown Immigration Law Journal* 369.

[68] ibid, 389–90.

[69] J Pauwelyn, 'Informal International Lawmaking: Framing the Concept and Research Questions' in J Pauwelyn, R Wessel and J Wouters (eds), *Informal International Lawmaking* (Oxford University Press, 2012).

[70] L Corredig, 'Effectiveness and Accountability of Disaster Risk Reduction Practices: An Analysis through the Lens of IN-LAW' in A Berman et al (eds), *Informal International Lawmaking: Case Studies* (Torkel Opsahl Academic Epublisher, 2012).

[71] ibid, 474.

refugee law and international criminal law. Therefore, the following sections will examine the theory of transnational legal process and apply this to humanitarian action as a means of understanding the substantive content and progressive development of binding and non-binding, formal and informal, humanitarian norms within the *acquis humanitaire*.

A. Koh's Theory of Transnational Legal Process

Philip Jessup popularised the phrase 'transnational law' in 1955 when he argued: 'I shall use the term "transnational law" to include all law which regulates actions or events that transcend national frontiers. Both public and private international law are included, as are other rules which do not wholly fit into such standard categories.'[72] In so doing, Jessup provided the title for a concept that had already been challenging the traditional view of international law as regulating the relations between sovereign states. Reflecting his experience as an academic, US diplomat and judge on the ICJ, Jessup promoted an understanding of international law which included the interactions of non-state actors, as well as a more interdisciplinary approach to scrutinising the creation of rules, norms and customs.[73] Despite Jessup's stature, the concept and phrase 'transnational law' was slow to take off. However, over the past 20 years Harold Koh has been a key promoter of the concept and has developed his own theory of 'transnational legal process' which includes Jessup's expansive view of international legal sources and influences.[74]

To understand Koh's theory of transnational legal process, one must first understand the legal process approach adopted in the middle of the twentieth century by US legal scholars to distinguish between objective law and subjective policy. As noted by Anne-Marie Slaughter,[75] this was

[72] Quoted in C Oliver, 'Philip C Jessup's Continuing Contribution to International Law' (November 1962) 62(7) *Columbia Law Review* 1132, 1134–35.

[73] Jessup's humanitarian credentials are evidenced from his involvement in drafting the UN Charter in 1945, and his role as Under-Secretary-General of the UN Relief and Rehabilitation Agency during the Second World War. See O Schachter, 'Philip Jessup's Life and Ideas' (October 1986) 80(4) *American Journal of International Law* 878, 882; P Zumbansen, 'Transnational Law' in J Smits (ed), *Encyclopaedia of Comparative Law* (Edward Elgar, 2006) 738–40.

[74] Koh initially developed his views on transnational legal process in Koh, 'Transnational Legal Process', above n 63, and has expanded his thesis in numerous texts including: Koh, 'Why do Nations Obey?', above n 63; H Koh, 'Bringing International Law Home' (1998–1999) 35 *Houston Law Review* 623; H Koh, 'How is International Human Rights Law Enforced?' (1998–1999) *Indiana Law Journal* 1397; H Koh, 'Transnational Legal Process after September 11th' (2004) 22 *Berkeley Journal of International Law* 339.

[75] A-M Slaughter-Burley, 'International Law and International Relations Theory: A Dual Agenda' (1993) 87 *American Journal of International Law* 205, 213–14.

a pragmatic response to the realist challenge to the relevance of (international) law in the face of power politics. Therefore, the international legal process approach is best seen as an expansion of legal positivism that prioritises understanding of how international law works in practice. It concentrates on how international legal rules are created, interpreted and applied, for example for governments' foreign policy purposes, rather than providing a descriptive analysis of the normative content of international law. Mary Ellen O'Connell has advanced a 'new' international legal process approach which goes beyond a mere description of existing legal rules and processes to include value-based judgements on the normative content of international law, arguing for 'dynamic decision-making in light of contemporary norms'.[76] In a similar vein, Rosalyn Higgins, a key figure in the adjudication of international law, has argued that '[i]nternational law is a process, a system of authoritative decision-making. It is not just the neutral application of rules.'[77] Nevertheless, the core question that (new) international legal process is primarily concerned with remains: 'How—and how far—do law, lawyers, and legal institutions operate to affect the course of international affairs?'[78]

Harold Koh's theory of transnational legal process meanwhile explains how the development and evolution of norms takes place through the multiple flow of ideas and principles between national, regional and international legal systems, and highlights the wide range of actors that influence the interpretation of contemporary norms. In other words, transnational legal process goes beyond the traditional legal process approach by examining not only the development of norms via the law, lawyers and legal institutions, but recognises the potential influence of a whole gamut of other actors within communities and across countries. Blending Jessup's concept of transnational law with the American legal process tradition, Koh defined his theory of 'transnational legal process' as:

> [T]he theory and practice of how public and private actors—nation-states, international organizations, multinational enterprises, non-governmental organizations, and private individuals—interact in a variety of public and private, domestic and international fora to make, interpret, enforce, and ultimately, internalize rules of transnational law.[79]

[76] M O'Connell, 'New International Legal Process' (April 1999) 93(2) *American Journal of International Law* 334, 346. See also A-M Slaughter, A Tulumello and S Wood, 'International Law and International Relations Theory: A New Generation of Interdisciplinary Scholarship' (1998) 92 *American Journal of International Law* 367, 379–81.

[77] R Higgins, *Problems and Process: International Law and How We Use it* (Oxford University Press, 1995) 267.

[78] Slaughter-Burley, 'International Law and International Relations', above n 75, 213.

[79] H Koh, 'Transnational Legal Process', above n 63, 183–84.

Key to Koh's conception are four specific aspects, namely that transnational legal processes are non-traditional, non-statist, dynamic and normative. Koh explains that transnational legal processes transcend the traditional dichotomies between domestic and international law, and between public and private law.[80] Furthermore, the relevant actors are not just, or even primarily, nation-states, but also include non-state actors. Meanwhile, as a dynamic and normative process, transnational law transforms, mutates, and percolates up and down, from public to private and from domestic to international. Koh describes the on-going process of norm percolation in the following manner:

> From this process of interaction, new rules of law emerge, which are interpreted, internalized, and enforced, thus beginning the process all over again. Thus, the concept embraces not just the descriptive workings of a process, but the normativity of that process. It focuses not simply upon how international interaction among transnational actors shapes law, but also on how law shapes and guides future interactions: in short, how law influences why nations obey.[81]

In other words, transnational legal process describes how international norms are created and complied with based on multiple interactions at the national, regional and international levels by a variety of actors. These interactions prompt legal interpretations which may ultimately lead to the internalisation of a new norm into either domestic, regional or international law thereby promoting obedience to the norm. Therefore, the concept of 'internalisation' plays a crucial part in understanding how norms can enter into domestic law and policy, and their associated compliance and enforcement mechanisms. While Koh focuses primarily on compliance and enforcement by states, his understanding of how norms may be internalised has parallels to Mark Bovens' five forms of accountability (political, legal, administrative, professional and social) discussed in Section III.A below, which are equally applicable to non-state actors.

Koh identifies three distinct forms of internalisation, namely: 'social internalisation', which occurs when a norm acquires so much public legitimacy that it gains widespread general adherence; 'political internalisation', which occurs when political elites accept an international norm and advocate its adoption as a matter of government policy; and 'legal internalisation', which occurs when an international norm is incorporated into the domestic legal system through the executive, legislature, or judiciary, or through a combination of all three. Koh argues that the sequencing

[80] See also M Reimann, 'From the Law of Nations to Transnational Law: Why We Need a New Basic Course for the International Curriculum' (2003–2004) 22 *Penn State International Law Review* 397, 406–08.

[81] Koh, 'Transnational Legal Process', above n 63, 184.

of internalisation will vary from case to case, with social internalisation occurring before political or legal internalisation in some instances, while legal internalisation may prompt social and political internalisation in others.[82]

i. Social, Political and Legal Internalisation of the Red Cross Symbol

An example of the three forms of internalisation identified by Koh can be seen in the development of the legally protected status of the distinctive emblems of the International Red Cross Movement. The concept of national relief societies to assist those injured in war originated from a short book self-published by a private businessman, Henri Dunant in 1862.[83] This idea was promptly taken up by a select group of prominent Swiss community leaders, leading to the establishment of the International Committee of the Red Cross and first diplomatic conference of states in 1863.[84] The founders quickly recognised the importance of having one distinctive emblem for their humanitarian activities. They proposed the inversion of the Swiss flag, that is a red cross on a white background. Military commanders and politicians from across Europe meanwhile recognised the mutual benefit for their own armed forces of having an independent, humanitarian symbol to protect those soldiers who were no longer able to fight (that is, were *hors de combat*), and this was promptly codified into international law in the first Geneva Convention in 1864.

Since then, the distinctive emblems of the Red Cross Movement have been given legal protection in the domestic law of numerous countries, and treaty-based and customary international law.[85] Enforcement of the norm is now provided via the Rome Statute of the International Criminal Court, which classifies their improper use, resulting in death or

[82] Koh, 'How is International Human Rights Law Enforced?', above n 74, 1413–14. For a case study of the internalisation of humanitarian norms in the UK, see D Cubie, 'Clarifying the "*Acquis Humanitaire*": A Transnational Legal Perspective on the Internalization of Humanitarian Norms' in D Caron, M Kelly and A Telesetsky (eds), *The International Law of Disaster Relief* (Cambridge University Press, 2014) 424–26.

[83] H Dunant, *A Memory of Solferino*, 1862 (American Red Cross, 1939, 1959).

[84] For a detailed overview of the Red Cross, see D Forsythe and B Rieffer-Flanagan, *The International Committee of the Red Cross: A Neutral Humanitarian Actor* 2nd edn (Routledge Global Institutions Series, 2016). See also: ICRC, *The History of the Emblems* (14 January 2007) www.icrc.org/eng/resources/documents/misc/emblem-history.htm.

[85] eg Art 53 GCI provides that unauthorised use of the distinctive emblems of the red cross and red crescent shall be 'prohibited at all times', while Art 38 API prohibits their 'improper use'. Meanwhile, Rule 30 of the ICRC Customary IHL Database states: 'Attacks directed against medical and religious personnel and objects displaying the distinctive emblems of the Geneva Conventions in conformity with international law are prohibited.'

serious personal injury, as a war crime.[86] The concept of an independent humanitarian organisation originated with one person, was socially promoted by like-minded individuals before being formalised into a private organisation which was politically accepted by states and that organisation's symbol was subsequently transposed into international law. Once the distinctive emblem of the red cross was formalised in international law, it was then adopted into domestic legal regimes. This widespread acceptance of a particular symbol through the practice of states and other actors led to legal accountability for its misuse bearing individual criminal responsibility under international law. Moreover, reflecting the dynamic nature of the norm, the original red cross symbol was subsequently joined by the red crescent and red crystal symbols, which state and non-state actors are equally required to respect.

In other words, the innovative norm of a distinctive emblem for humanitarian work first emerged as a rule of law via interactions between private individuals, states and the military. Over the course of the past 150 years, this rule has been interpreted and modified, while undergoing a process of social, political and legal internalisation in the vast majority of countries and institutions around the world, ultimately resulting in respect for the distinctive emblems of the Red Cross Movement bearing the force of international criminal law.

B. Applying a Transnational Legal Process Approach to Humanitarian Action

A transnational legal process approach recognises the multiple flows of influence, whereby domestic law, policies and practices can directly impact on international understandings of relevant norms and vice versa.[87] Consequently, a wide range of traditional international law topics are engaged in developing consensus on specific humanitarian norms, alongside the evolving body of non-binding norms of humanitarian action. These international laws and norms feed directly into regional and sub-regional structures, such as the EU's civil protection mechanisms[88] or the ASEAN

[86] For discussion, see ch 7, Section II.B.

[87] Koh, 'Transnational Legal Process', above n 63, 184.

[88] Since 2010, the European Communities Humanitarian Office (ECHO) has encompassed both external humanitarian aid and internal civil protection. See: Council Decision, 8 November 2007 establishing a Community Civil Protection Mechanism (recast) (2007/779/EC, Euratom) OJ L314/9; and *The European Consensus on Humanitarian Aid*, Joint Statement by the Council and Representatives of the Governments of Member States meeting within the Council, the European Parliament and the European Commission, OJ C25, 30 January 2008, p 1.

disaster management system,[89] as well as domestic law, policies and practices. This process reflects Koh's description of 'layered co-operation' within legal diplomacy, whereby in any given area of international co-operation, the choice between international agreements and non-legal alternatives is not binary, and states may choose non-legal mechanisms to facilitate international co-operation.[90]

In the context of sovereignty as responsibility, Francis Deng and his colleagues similarly referred to 'layers of assistance' whereby states exercise sovereignty at home, then turn to neighbours for assistance, and subsequently request assistance at a regional level before looking for a global response via the UN.[91] This layered approach to diplomacy and sovereignty reflects the reality of international humanitarian responses. If one takes Cyclone Nargis in 2008, it took a month until Western relief workers were allowed to access the stricken areas of Myanmar, while their governments argued over the legality of a military humanitarian intervention.[92] However, Indian, Chinese and other Asian neighbours were allowed earlier access to assist the Myanmar relief effort, and there were numerous local initiatives despite government restrictions. Clearly, by delaying much-needed international assistance the Myanmar government failed in its responsibilities as a sovereign state towards protecting persons on its territory. Nevertheless, the role played by regional bodies should not be underestimated. The ASEAN Agreement on Disaster Management and Emergency Response has regulated the regional responses to natural disasters since 2005, in a region well known for its strong views on the importance of state sovereignty and non-intervention, and it was through assistance from ASEAN states that international support first arrived in Myanmar.[93]

Koh's theory of transnational legal process is premised on the 'percolation' of norms between international, regional and domestic levels. Using an IT analogy, Koh argues that norms may be 'uploaded' into the international arena from the domestic law, policy or practice of a particular state or private actor, undergo confirmation or modification, before being 'downloaded' into various regional or domestic legal systems or internal rules of private actors.[94] For example, at the global level one can

[89] See *Disasters in Asia: the Case for Legal Preparedness*, IFRC (Geneva, 2010).

[90] H Koh, 'Twenty-First Century International Lawmaking', speech at Georgetown University Law Center, Washington, DC (17 October 2012) 10. See also ch 2, Sections II.A.i and ii.

[91] Deng et al, *Sovereignty as Responsibility*, above n 24, xviii.

[92] S Ford, 'Is the Failure to Respond Appropriately to a Natural Disaster a Crime Against Humanity? The Responsibility to Protect and Individual Criminal Responsibility in the Aftermath of Cyclone Nargis' (2009–2010) 38 *Denver Journal of International Law and Policy* 227, 230–33.

[93] For further discussion, see ch 7, Section III.B.i.

[94] Koh, 'Twenty-First Century International Lawmaking', above n 90, 14.

identify a range of top-down approaches regarding humanitarian norms initiated by the UN or other global bodies, including non-governmental actors. The political commitments made in the outcome texts from the 2016 World Humanitarian Summit are a case in point.[95] Likewise, even if the ILC draft articles on the protection of persons in the event of disasters are not adopted as a binding international convention, the final text resulting from the interactions and interpretations prompted by the ILC deliberations and corresponding input by states and humanitarian actors will have a major impact on our understanding of the norms and principles, as well as technical and operational modalities, of international humanitarian action. Yet the development of consensus within the UN or ILC is not only influenced by existing norms but simultaneously exerts its own influence on the operations and practice of state and non-state humanitarian agencies. For example, it is unclear what, if any, impact the removal of a 'right to humanitarian assistance' from the latest version of the (intergovernmental) IASC Operational Guidelines[96] will have on state practice when, conversely, the (non-governmental) *Sphere Handbook*[97] now bases its entire approach on the existence of such a right.

Concurrently, the practice of individual states or humanitarian actors may exert a strong influence on developing humanitarian norms. For example, the definition of humanitarian aid set out in the Swedish government's Humanitarian Aid Policy[98] (quoted in chapter one) provides a clear and articulate approach for other states to follow.[99] Yet there remains a lack of coherence between the responses to humanitarian crises around the world. As David Caron has noted, the haphazard response by states 'mirrors the fortuity of the catastrophes humanity encounters'.[100] From a transnational legal process perspective, multiple interactions between states and non-state humanitarian actors lead to interpretations of the appropriate *lex lata* and proposed *lex ferenda* applicable in humanitarian crises. Such interpretations help strengthen our understanding of the

[95] See 'Chair's Summary', above n 6.

[96] IASC, *Operational Guidelines on the Protection of Persons in Situations of Natural Disasters*, Brookings-Bern Project on Internal Displacement (January 2011).

[97] The Sphere Project, *Humanitarian Charter and Minimum Standards in Humanitarian Response* 3rd edn, April 2011.

[98] Swedish Ministry of Foreign Affairs, *The Government's Humanitarian Aid Policy*, Government Communication 2004/05:52 (16 December 2004) 6. See also ch 1, Section II.B.

[99] For discussion of the global influence of Scandinavian (including Swedish) approaches to the environment, global security and aid, see C Ingebritsen, 'Norm Entrepreneurs: Scandinavia's Role in World Politics' (March 2002) 37(1) *Cooperation and Conflict: Journal of the Nordic International Studies Association* 11, 18–20.

[100] D Caron, 'Addressing Catastrophes: Conflicting Images of Solidarity and Separateness' in *The International Aspects of Natural and Industrial Catastrophes*, Hague Academy of International Law (Martinus Nijhoff Publishers, 2001) 3–4.

normative content of the *acquis humanitaire*, thereby clarifying the applicable rights and responsibilities in humanitarian crises. The identification of binding and non-binding norms helps ensure compliance with those norms by promoting legal certainty. However, the social, political or legal internalisation of such norms does not guarantee the international legal protection of persons—a further layer of accountability mechanisms is required to encourage states and humanitarian actors to apply the concepts of humanity and human dignity, and their operational requirement to alleviate suffering, more clearly within their internal policy structures.

III. ACCOUNTABILITY MECHANISMS

A. Forms of Accountability

In chapter three we saw how rights-based and needs-based approaches may work in tandem, provided that fundamental human rights principles of empowerment, participation, non-discrimination and accountability are incorporated into all humanitarian programming. Following the preceding discussion of the overarching processes whereby norms may be created and internalised, this section focuses specifically on how to promote compliance and implementation of such norms. While the concept of accountability takes many forms, it is generally accepted to play a central role in providing critical oversight of public officials, non-state actors and humanitarian agencies. Peter Uvin has argued that: 'The move from needs to rights, and from charity to duties, also implies an increased focus on accountability. Indeed, at the heart of any rights-based approach to development are concerns with mechanisms of accountability, for this is precisely what distinguishes charity from claims.'[101] Likewise, the Office of the High Commissioner for Human Rights (OHCHR) has noted that human rights-based approaches place a focus on measurable and enforceable obligations through mechanisms of accountability since this strengthens political commitment and justifications for resource allocations, and improves incentives for the fair delivery of social services.[102] In the humanitarian context, the IASC has described accountability as the 'responsible use of power, combined with effective and quality

[101] P Uvin, 'From the Right to Development to the Rights-based Approach: How "Human Rights" Entered Development' (Aug 2007) 17 (4–5) *Development in Practice* 597, 602–03.

[102] *Towards Freedom from Fear and Want: Human Rights in the Post-2015 Agenda* (Thematic Think Piece, Office of the High Commissioner for Human Rights, May 2012, produced for the UN System Task Team on the Post-2015 UN Development Agenda) 6–7.

programming that recognizes the community's dignity, capacity, and ability for self-determination'.[103]

Mark Bovens has highlighted two key strands of academic and practitioner thinking surrounding the concept of 'accountability'.[104] The first approach views accountability as a normative concept which elaborates standards for the evaluation of the behaviour of public actors. Initiatives such as the 2014 *Core Humanitarian Standard on Quality and Accountability*,[105] which originated in an attempt by the British Red Cross in 1994 to establish an NGO peer review process, fall into this category (albeit with a broader understanding of the term 'public actor' than Bovens' focus on governmental officials and civil servants).[106] The Core Humanitarian Standard is intended to be used by humanitarian organisations to align their internal procedures to international standards, and as a means of facilitating greater accountability to communities and people affected by crisis.[107] However, as a voluntary code, there is no enforcement or compliance procedure built into the text.

This brings us to Bovens' second approach to accountability—accountability as a mechanism, that is an institutional relation or arrangement in which an agent can be held to account by another agent or institution.[108] Bovens has defined this narrower, sociological, understanding of accountability as 'a relationship between an actor and a forum, in which the actor has an obligation to explain and to justify his or her conduct, the forum can pose questions and pass judgement, and the actor may face consequences'.[109] Curtin and Nollkaemper concur, noting that while there is no single paradigm of accountability, the original or 'core' sense of accountability is that associated with 'the process of being called "to account" to some authority for one's actions'.[110] While both approaches to accountability may be

[103] IASC, *Protection and Accountability to Affected Populations in the Humanitarian Programme Cycle* (2016) Emergency Directors Group (EDG), Preliminary Guidance Note, 9.

[104] M Bovens, 'Two Concepts of Accountability: Accountability as a Virtue and as a Mechanism' (2010) 33(5) *West European Politics* 946.

[105] CHS Alliance, Groupe URD and the Sphere Project, *Core Humanitarian Standard on Quality and Accountability* (2014).

[106] See: D Peppiatt, 'The Ombudsman Project: Pilot Project to Investigate the Concept of an Ombudsman for Humanitarian Assistance' (Nov 1997) 9 *Humanitarian Exchange Magazine*; 'Update: Ombudsman for Humanitarian Accountability' (Dec 1999) 6 *Forced Migration Review* 43.

[107] *Core Humanitarian Standard*, above n 105, 2.

[108] Bovens, 'Two Concepts', above n 104, 948. From an IN-LAW perspective, Pauwelyn et al further differentiate between accountability mechanisms in the narrow sense (such as courts) and accountability promoting measures (such as transparency, decision-making rules, and participation of stakeholders). See: Berman et al, 'Introduction', above n 70, 5–6.

[109] M Bovens, 'Analysing and Assessing Accountability: A Conceptual Framework' (2007) 13(4) *European Law Journal* 447, 450.

[110] D Curtin and A Nollkaemper, 'Conceptualizing Accountability in International and European Law' (2005) 36 *Netherlands Yearbook of International Law* 3, 4.

relevant in humanitarian crises, the following discussion focuses specifically on accountability mechanisms for humanitarian actors. Reflecting the broad tent approach to sources for the *acquis humanitaire*, this monograph will not set out a prescriptive, or single, accountability mechanism as one approach cannot encompass all the various actors or types of humanitarian crisis. The accountability mechanisms required to hold state agencies to account, for example for breaches of legal obligations or human rights violations, may vary drastically from those required to ensure that non-governmental actors follow professional or industry codes and guidelines.[111]

B. Accountability Fora

A focus on accountability mechanisms raises the question of to whom an account must be made. One can split accountability mechanisms into two distinct forms: those addressing vertical accountability (that is, the rights and obligations of states in relation to persons within a state's territory and control), and horizontal accountability (that is, the rights and obligations of states in relation to one another and the international community). The ILC Special Rapporteur on the protection of persons in the event of disasters has classified this as a 'dual-axis approach'.[112] Reflecting the centrality of the protection of persons in the *acquis humanitaire*, the following discussion focuses particularly on vertical accountability between a state (or by analogy humanitarian agency) and individuals within its territory and control. Relevant vertical accountability mechanisms include judicial processes to enforce rights, such as before the European Court of Human Rights,[113] and non-judicial processes such as improved access and sharing of information, as evidenced by the increased focus on beneficiary communications in humanitarian operations.[114] However, this is not to diminish the importance of horizontal inter-state processes in promoting the protection of persons, for example through the general law of responsibility of states and international organisations[115] or international human rights monitoring mechanisms.[116] Indeed, the UN General Assembly has recognised that

111 For examples of practical and operational accountability mechanisms for humanitarian actors, see IASC, *Protection and Accountability*, above n 103, 12–18.

112 E Valencia-Ospina, *Sixth Report on the Protection of Persons in the Event of Disasters* (3 May 2013) A/CN.4/662, p 12.

113 See discussion in ch 5, Section II.C.i.

114 See discussion in ch 3, Section II.B.i.

115 For discussion of the evolving nature of state responsibilities, see A Nollkaemper, 'Constitutionalization and the Unity of the Law of International Responsibility' (2009) 16 *Indiana Journal of Global Legal Studies* 535. See also Section III.C.i below.

116 See, eg, D Cubie and M Hesselman, 'Accountability for the Human Rights Implications of Natural Disasters: A Proposal for Systemic International Oversight' (2015) 33(1) *Netherlands Quarterly of Human Rights* 9.

accountability is 'an integral part of effective humanitarian assistance' and emphasised the need to enhance the accountability of state and non-state humanitarian actors at all stages of humanitarian action.[117]

Julie Brunnée's examination of legal responsibility under international law highlighted that international legal accountability involves 'the *legal* justification of an *international* actor's performance *vis-à-vis* others, the assessment or judgment of that performance against *international legal* standards, and the possible imposition of consequences if the actor fails to live up to applicable *legal* standards'.[118] Such international legal accountability may take place at the state level, for example through contested cases before the International Court of Justice, or at the individual level, such as prosecutions before the International Criminal Court.[119] However, as with Koh's theory of norm internalisation, accountability mechanisms need not be purely legal in nature. Bovens has argued that, based on the nature of the forum, at least five forms of accountability exist, namely: political; legal; administrative; professional; and social.[120] While legal accountability before domestic or international courts may provide an obvious example of 'holding to account', in the humanitarian context a broad range of accountability mechanisms are applicable. At the international level, the proliferation of soft law sources (and non-state actors) may mean that other forms of accountability play a more important role than legal accountability based on hard law provisions or enforcement mechanisms.[121] For example, a truth and reconciliation commission following an internal armed conflict[122] may provide political and social accountability for state-sanctioned or individual breaches of international law; while a public enquiry following the collapse of buildings due to poor construction methods in an earthquake may provide administrative and professional accountability for public officials and private companies.[123]

[117] UNGA, *Res 67/87* (26 March 2013) A/RES/67/87, para 10.

[118] J Brunnée, 'International Legal Accountability through the Lens of the Law of State Responsibility' (2005) 36 *Netherlands Yearbook of International Law* 21, 24 [emphasis in original].

[119] M Koenig-Archibugi, 'Accountability in Transnational Relations: How Distinctive Is It?' (2010) 33(5) *West European Politics* 1142, 1149. See also L Moffett, 'Accountability for Forced Displacement in Democratic Republic of Congo and Uganda before the International Criminal Court' (2015) 1(2) *African Journal of International Criminal Justice* 129.

[120] Bovens, 'Analysing and Assessing Accountability', above n 109, 455–57. Helen Potts has likewise identified five mechanisms of accountability: judicial; quasi-judicial; administrative; political; and social. See H Potts, *Accountability and the Right to the Highest Attainable Standards of Health* (Human Rights Centre, University of Essex, 2008) 17.

[121] Koenig-Archibugi, 'Accountability in Transnational Relations', above n 119, 1150.

[122] Such as the Sierra Leone Truth and Reconciliation Commission established via the 1999 Lomé Peace Accord, following the 11-year civil war in Sierra Leone.

[123] Such as the Canterbury Earthquakes Royal Commission of Inquiry which was established to report on the causes of building failure, as well as legal and best-practice requirements for buildings in Central Business Districts, following the 22 February 2011 earthquake in Christchurch, New Zealand.

C. Impact of Accountability Mechanisms

Reflecting the full cycle of protection, accountability mechanisms can perform both prospective and retrospective functions.[124] As Bovens notes: 'Accountability is not only about ex post scrutiny, it is also about prevention and anticipation. Norms are (re)produced, internalised and, where necessary, adjusted through accountability.'[125] From an operational perspective, Helen Potts has argued that accountability processes require the incorporation of continuous monitoring into all aspects of policy development and implementation, while simultaneously promoting the involvement of non-governmental actors and civil society.[126] Similarly, Paul Hunt, the former UN Special Rapporteur on the Right to Health, has noted that accountability is a process that 'helps to identify what works, so it can be repeated, and what does not, so it can be revised. It is a way of checking that reasonable balances are fairly struck'.[127] This process-orientated view of accountability mirrors one of the three effects of accountability identified by Bovens—namely the learning perspective whereby administrators and policy-makers are confronted with information on the outcomes of their policies thereby forcing them to reflect on the successes and failure of their policies.[128] While such processes may take place in various formats at the international, regional and national level, Potts has argued that ultimately it is accountability at the national level which is most relevant to the day-to-day work of policy makers.[129]

Focusing on how accountability mechanisms can influence domestic policies also resonates with process-orientated understandings of human rights implementation and compliance. For example, Oona Hathaway has argued that there is little empirical evidence that poorly monitored and enforced human rights provisions positively influence a state's human rights practices, as there are few incentives for signatory governments to match their rhetoric with action. Hathaway therefore proposes a stronger system of international independent expert monitoring of the domestic human rights practices of states that sign up to human rights treaties.[130] One

[124] Potts, *Accountability*, above n 120, 13.

[125] Bovens, 'Analysing and Assessing Accountability', above n 109, 453.

[126] Potts, *Accountability*, above n 120, 5. See also IASC, *Protection and Accountability*, above n 103.

[127] HRC, 'Report of the Special Rapporteur on the right of everyone to the enjoyment of the highest attainable standard of physical and mental health' (31 January 2008) A/HRC/7/11, para 99.

[128] Bovens, 'Analysing and Assessing Accountability', above n 109, 463–64.

[129] Potts, *Accountability*, above n 120, 17.

[130] See O Hathaway, 'Making Human Rights Treaties Work: Global Legal Information and Human Rights in the 21st Century' (2003) 31 *International Journal of Legal Information* 312, 316; O Hathaway, 'Do Human Rights Treaties Make a Difference?' (2001–2002) 111 *Yale Law Journal* 1935, 2023.

can further argue that national authorities should not be the only subjects of monitoring and accountability processes. In the humanitarian context, while the affected state has the primary responsibility for protection and assistance for persons on their territory, other humanitarian actors (be they UN, inter-governmental or non-governmental) may also wield considerable influence, and so require external oversight. Mathias Koenig-Archibugi has argued that '[t]he idea that accountability is also due to those most directly and intensely affected by decisions is gaining ground as a potentially hegemonic global norm'.[131] However, ensuring that accountability mechanisms for states and other actors actually provide a forum for justification, judgement and consequences[132] remains challenging in humanitarian crises, as seen from the UN's response to the alleged introduction of cholera by UN peacekeepers following the 2010 Haiti earthquake.[133]

i. Haiti: Privileges and Immunities of the UN

The devastating earthquake which struck Haiti on 12 January 2010, measuring 7.0 on the Moment Magnitude Scale,[134] caused massive loss of life and destruction of property and infrastructure. While the total number of fatalities will probably never be known, the International Federation of Red Cross and Red Crescent Societies (IFRC) reported there were over 222,000 deaths and 300,000 injuries, while over 1.5 million people were made homeless.[135] The earthquake compounded pre-existing structural problems, severe poverty and low levels of development—even before the earthquake Haiti was one of the poorest countries in the world, with limited access to education, health and sanitation services.[136] As the capital Port-au-Prince was so extensively damaged, large numbers of state workers were killed or injured. Civil servants, teachers, medical staff and politicians were all severely affected, which compounded the difficulties in organising and implementing the extensive relief operation required. Even the National Disaster Risk Management System sustained heavy losses of staff and material resources. The official report on the response to the earthquake highlights the challenges faced by the national authorities:

> The buildings of the Ministry of the Interior, which housed the Emergency Operations Centre and the Direction de la Protection Civile, were destroyed,

[131] Koenig-Archibugi, 'Accountability in Transnational Relations', above n 119, 1159.

[132] Bovens, 'Analysing and Assessing Accountability', above n 109, 453.

[133] For discussion of the right to housing after the Haiti earthquake, see ch 5, Section II.B.i.

[134] The Moment Magnitude Scale (MMS or M_W) has generally replaced the older Richter scale for measuring earthquakes as a better reflection of the amount of energy released.

[135] IFRC, *Haiti: Earthquake*, Operations Update No 27, 16 June 2011.

[136] In 2010, Haiti was ranked 145 out of 169 countries by the UNDP; by 2015 Haiti was ranked 163 out of 188 countries. UNDP, *Human Development Report 2015*, 210.

the Port-au-Prince fire station was seriously damaged, and many Government vehicles were rendered unusable. Port-au-Prince had no municipal petrol reserves, and few Government officials had functioning mobile phones prior to the earthquake, which complicated communications and transportation in the immediate aftermath.[137]

While the Haitian Ministry of Health was commended for its response in the face of the major difficulties created by the destruction of infrastructure and loss of personnel, the lack of sanitation and healthcare facilities within the IDP camps established around Port-au-Prince was identified as a key factor in the rapid spread of cholera after it was allegedly introduced into the camps by UN peacekeepers.[138] Prior to the earthquake, cholera was unknown in Haiti, yet since 2010 over 770,000 people have been infected and more than 9,200 people are officially recorded as having died.[139] The introduction of cholera into the camps provides a stark reminder that humanitarian actors can wittingly or unwittingly cause severe harm, as well as good, in their humanitarian responses.[140]

Compounding the tragedy of the cholera epidemic was the fact that the UN Secretary-General invoked the 1946 Convention on Privileges and Immunities of the United Nations[141] to avoid potential compensation claims against the UN, thereby highlighting the challenges victims face in seeking accountability and redress.[142] As a result, a class action lawsuit was brought by victims and their families before the US District Court of New York (where the UN Headquarters is based).[143] In rejecting the case, the Court ruled that the UN had immunity from compensation claims via the 1946 Convention.[144] The case is currently under

[137] IASC, *Response to the Humanitarian Crisis in Haiti Following the 12 January 2010 Earthquake: Achievements, Challenges and Lessons To Be Learned* (July 2010) 7–8.

[138] See: *From Relief to Recovery: Supporting good governance in post-earthquake Haiti*, Oxfam Briefing Paper 142, 6 January 2011, 10; M Schuller, 'Haiti's Disaster after the Disaster: The IDP Camps and Cholera' (December 2010) *Journal of Humanitarian Assistance*.

[139] Ministère de la Santé Publique et de la Population, *Rapport de Cas* (9 February 2016) http://mspp.gouv.ht/site/downloads/Rapport%20Web%2009.02.2016_Avec_Courbes_departementales.pdf.

[140] Schuller, 'Haiti's Disaster', above n 138.

[141] UN Convention on the Privileges and Immunities of the United Nations (adopted 13 February 1946, entered into force 17 September 1946) 1 UNTS 15 and 90 UNTS 327 (corrigendum to vol 1).

[142] 'UN Rejects Haiti Cholera Compensation Claims', *BBC News Online* (21 February 2013) www.bbc.co.uk/news/world-latin-america-21542842. For challenges in organising domestic legal empowerment in post-disaster settings, see M Jagannath, N Phillips and J Shah, 'A Rights-Based Approach to Lawyering: Legal Empowerment as an Alternative to Legal Aid in Post-Disaster Haiti' (2011–2012) 10 *Northwestern Journal of International Human Rights* 7.

[143] M Doyle, 'UN Sued Over Haiti Cholera Epidemic', *BBC News Online* (9 October 2013) www.bbc.com/news/world-latin-america-24457195.

[144] R Gladstone, 'Haiti: Judge Throws Out Cholera Suit Against UN', *The New York Times* (10 January 2015).

consideration by the US Court of Appeals for the Second Circuit. While a final decision has not yet been reached, it was reported that during the appeal hearing the judges asked what other possible recourse could be available, as the victims were caught in a situation where nobody had been held accountable.[145] Moreover, while the UN apparently conceded its role in the cholera outbreak following an internal report by Philip Alston, in August 2016 the deputy spokesman for the Secretary-General, Farhan Haq, reiterated that the UN's legal position on diplomatic immunity and possible compensation had not changed.[146] At the same time, it was reported in the *New York Times* that Alston had concluded that the UN's continuing denial and refusal to make reparations to the victims 'upholds a double standard according to which the UN insists that member states respect human rights, while rejecting any such responsibility for itself'.[147]

While one can understand the need for the UN to protect itself from the myriad of potential cases that could arise from the actions of peacekeepers and UN humanitarian agencies, if the UN is able to claim immunity from lawsuits where does this leave the victims?[148] Should non-governmental implementing partners of the UN also be entitled to immunity when they were working as part of the UN Cluster system? While humanitarians generally wish to be seen as a positive force for good, this is not always the case. Therefore, what national and international accountability mechanisms should be in place to ensure that people caught up in humanitarian crises are not re-victimised, either directly or indirectly, by the very people attempting to assist them?

Guglielmo Verdirame has argued that: 'Assuming … that the rules on state responsibility apply mutatis mutandis to the responsibility of international organisations, aiding and assisting a state in the commission of an internationally wrongful act should engage the responsibility of an international organisation, provided that it did so with knowledge of the circumstances.'[149] Verdirame therefore concludes that the enforcement and compliance monitoring machinery of human rights law should be

[145] R Gladstone, 'Court Hears Suit Against UN on Haiti Cholera Outbreak', *The New York Times* (1 March 2016).

[146] 'UN Admits Role in Haiti's Deadly Cholera Outbreak', *BBC News Online* (19 August 2016) www.bbc.com/news/world-latin-america-37126747.

[147] JM Katzaug, 'UN Admits Role in Cholera Epidemic in Haiti', *The New York Times* (17 August 2016).

[148] For detailed discussion of the obligations of UN peacekeepers, see S Wills, *Protecting Civilians: The Obligations of Peacekeepers* (Oxford University Press, 2009), in particular 261–82.

[149] Verdirame, 'Compliance with Human Rights', above n 47, 274. See also G Verdirame, 'Testing the Effectiveness of International Norms: The Provision of Humanitarian Assistance by the UN and Sexual Apartheid in Afghanistan' (2001) 23 *Human Rights Quarterly* 733.

equally focused on the actions of international organisations, including the UN, as on states through an expanded understanding of the concept of accountability.[150]

IV. CONCLUSION: SUMMARY SO FAR

At this stage it is worthwhile to summarise the arguments advanced in Part I of this monograph outlining the three constituent parts of the *acquis humanitaire*, namely the prime objective, conceptual basis and accountability mechanisms. First of all, forces of destruction created by both human and natural hazards can create humanitarian crises, resulting in large-scale human suffering. This suffering, arising from armed conflict, forced displacement or disasters, may be exacerbated by pre-existing vulnerabilities or reduced by pre-existing capacities and resilience. Counter-balancing this destruction, the forces of production allow humans to plan, manage and deliver support and assistance to prevent or alleviate suffering. These actions are undertaken based on the forces of salvation, as signified by the principles of humanity and human dignity.

The forces of production and salvation combine through the concept of humanitarian action, which incorporates the twin aspects of material assistance for the basic necessities of life and protection activities that aim to protect the inherent dignity and rights of all persons. Humanitarian action therefore includes a broad range of activities at all stages of emergency preparation, response, recovery and rehabilitation to create a full cycle of protection. However, there are practical and conceptual limitations to the legal protection of persons in humanitarian crises, so it is important to separate activities covering physical, humanitarian and human rights protection. Moreover, there are factual differences and specific challenges that arise based on the type of humanitarian crisis, be it a conflict, displacement or disaster. The forces of production and salvation also include a multitude of governmental, inter-governmental and non-governmental actors, as well as the affected population themselves. Therefore, divergent approaches and activities may be undertaken by these different actors (along a spectrum of rights-based and needs-based approaches), and distinct legal obligations may exist for each.

Importantly, across all types of humanitarian crisis, the primary obligation to respect, protect and fulfil the human rights of all persons on its territory remains with the affected state and its various organs and agents. This includes the primary responsibility for organising or facilitating

150 Verdirame, 'Compliance with Human Rights', above n 47, 286. For a comparable argument in the context of disasters, see Cubie and Hesselman, 'Accountability for Human Rights Implications', above n 116.

material assistance and protection. If the state is unable or unwilling to provide the necessary levels of assistance and protection, it has a duty to request external support. Moreover, while it is not necessary or expected for each humanitarian actor to engage in all aspects of humanitarian action, it is not only possible but appropriate for humanitarian organisations to merge rights-based and needs-based approaches to their work. The key human rights principles of empowerment, participation, non-discrimination and accountability should therefore be incorporated into all humanitarian programming and operations.

Despite challenges to the implementation of humanitarian norms, such as limitations on access or reliance on state sovereignty and non-intervention in domestic affairs, the web of international legal protection set out in the *acquis humanitaire* is strengthened through the identification of norm creation processes and subsequent internalisation of humanitarian norms into domestic legal systems or the internal rules of private actors. Harold Koh's theory of transnational legal process provides a coherent framework for understanding how the multiple interactions between state and non-state actors can lead to interpretations of new international norms, which in turn may be socially, politically and/or legally internalised by relevant actors. Such internalisation can help to ensure the actual application of humanitarian norms in the potentially chaotic environment of a humanitarian crisis. Moreover, to promote compliance and enforcement of such norms, accountability mechanisms across a variety of fora (namely political, legal, administrative, professional or social) are required, albeit that the legal status of a particular actor (such as a state agency, intergovernmental organisation or private individual) will entail differential rights and obligations.

Therefore, while the concept of the *acquis humanitaire* is not intended as a prescriptive model, it provides a logical framework for the grouping together of laws, policies and practices relating to humanitarian action. The aim is to establish the overlaps and gaps in the international legal protection of persons in humanitarian crises and to assist operational actors in identifying the binding legal obligations and non-binding norms applicable to their humanitarian activities. Part II of this monograph therefore sets out key elements of the substantive content of the *acquis humanitaire* across a variety of existing branches of international law. This analysis will highlight the extent of existing laws, policies and practices relating specifically to the provision of material assistance and the protection of persons in humanitarian crises—a putative law of humanitarian assistance. However, reflecting the dynamic nature of international law, and the overarching humanitarian imperative to alleviate suffering wherever it may be found, this web of international legal protection should be constantly strengthened through detailed analysis of *lex lata* and proposed *lex ferenda* for humanitarian crises at the international, regional and local levels.

Part II

Normative Content of the *Acquis Humanitaire*

5

International Human Rights Law

I. INTRODUCTION

> [Humanitarians have] come to realize that humanitarian assistance involves far more than saving lives through the provision of material aid. It includes saving lives in other ways: by helping people to realise rights not yet achieved, by empowering people to regain rights that have been taken away—and by protecting people to the best of one's ability from suffering directly caused by armed conflict, repression and exploitation.
>
> Youssou N'Dour, 2002[1]

BY DEFINITION, A complex emergency entails extensive violence and loss of life, massive displacements of people, and widespread damage to societies and economies.[2] It follows that a wide range of human rights violations may occur during all stages of a humanitarian crisis—including threats to the rights to life and physical safety, the basic necessities of life such as water, food and shelter, or participation in decision making such as during reconstruction planning or the conclusion of peace settlements. Therefore, since the second part of this book introduces key examples of the normative content of the *acquis humanitaire* from a variety of branches of international law, it is important to first provide an overview of international human rights provisions directly applicable to humanitarian action.

Indeed, despite on-going debate regarding the exact status of human rights law during armed conflicts,[3] the UN Security Council noted back in 1967 that 'essential and inalienable human rights should be respected even during the vicissitudes of war'.[4] The International Court of Justice

[1] IASC, *Growing the Sheltering Tree: Protecting Rights through Humanitarian Action* (2002) xiii.
[2] UNOCHA Financial Tracking Service, *Glossary of Humanitarian Terms* https://fts.unocha.org/pageloader.aspx?page=AboutFTS-definitions.
[3] See, eg, M Dennis, 'Application of Human Rights Treaties Extraterritorially in Times of Armed Conflict and Military Occupation' (2005) 99 *American Journal of International Law* 119.
[4] UNSC Resolution 237 (14 June 1967) S/RES/237 (1967). For a more recent examination, see N Lubell, 'Challenges in Applying Human Rights Law to Armed Conflict' (December 2005) 87(860) *International Review of the Red Cross* 737.

refined this statement in its Advisory Opinion on the *Legal Consequences of the Construction of a Wall in the Occupied Palestinian Territory*, arguing that: 'some rights may be exclusively matters of international humanitarian law; others may be exclusively matters of human rights law; yet others may be matters of both these branches of international law.'[5] In recent years, the application of human rights law during natural or human-made disasters has also come to the fore, not least following the 2004 Indian Ocean Tsunami and Hurricane Katrina in 2005.[6] Therefore, the human rights impact of humanitarian crises is increasingly a source of academic study and practitioner concern,[7] and it is well recognised that states' binding human rights obligations apply at all times.[8] Moreover, as succinctly noted by UNOCHA:

> In situations of disaster or civil unrest, national authorities have primary responsibility for the well-being of those affected. In situations of armed conflict, the responsibility for the civilian population's well-being lies with all the parties to the conflict. If they are unable or unwilling to meet the basic needs of the affected population within their control, they are obliged to allow and facilitate the impartial provision of assistance.[9]

This chapter cannot examine every type of human rights violation that may occur in a humanitarian crisis.[10] Instead, it will analyse fundamental aspects of a state's core obligations relating to access to protection and assistance, the right to an adequate standard of living, and the right to

[5] *Legal Consequences of the Construction of a Wall in the Occupied Palestinian Territory (Advisory Opinion)*, ICJ Reports 2004, 131 ('Advisory Opinion on the Wall'), para 106.

[6] H Lewis, 'Human Rights and Natural Disaster: The Indian Ocean Tsunami' (Fall 2006) 33(4) *Human Rights* 12; H Lewis, 'Race, Class, and Katrina: Human Rights and (Un)Natural Disaster' (August 2009) *Northeastern Public Law and Theory Faculty Working Paper Series No 38*; S Sirkin, 'The Debacle of Hurricane Katrina: A Human Rights Response' (2006) 30 *The Fletcher Forum of World Affairs* 223.

[7] See, eg: T Meron, 'The Humanization of Humanitarian Law' (2000) 94 *American Journal of International Law* 239; G Verdirame, 'Compliance with Human Rights in UN Operations' (2002) 2(2) *Human Rights Law Review* 265; B Concannon and B Lindstrom, 'Cheaper, Better, Longer Lasting: a Rights-Based Approach to Disaster Response in Haiti' (2011) 25 *Emory International Law Review* 1145; IASC, *Operational Guidelines on the Protection of Persons in Situations of Natural Disasters* (Brookings-Bern Project on Internal Displacement, January 2011).

[8] See, eg, A D'Amato, 'The Concept of Human Rights in International Law' (1982) 82 *Columbia Law Review* 1110; H Koh, 'How is International Human Rights Law Enforced?' (1998–1999) *Indiana Law Journal* 1397.

[9] UNOCHA, *UNOCHA on Message: Humanitarian Access*, April 2010 https://docs.unocha.org/sites/dms/Documents/OOM_HumAccess_English.pdf.

[10] See generally H-J Heintze, 'On the Relationship between Human Rights Law Protection and International Humanitarian Law' (December 2004) 86(856) *International Review of the Red Cross* 789; IASC, *Frequently Asked Questions on International Humanitarian, Human Rights and Refugee Law in the Context of Armed Conflict* (2004) Task Force on Humanitarian Action and Human Rights; E Harper, *International Law and Standards Applicable in Natural Disaster Situations* (International Development Law Organization 2009).

physical security and integrity. However, considering the broad range of human rights applicable in humanitarian crises, the chapter will conclude by highlighting the role of international human rights law within the evolving normative content of the *acquis humanitaire*. It should also be noted that reflecting the interconnected nature of the different branches of international law contributing to the *acquis humanitaire*, various references will be made to relevant provisions of the law of armed conflict, refugee law and international criminal law. Before entering into this discussion of the substantive content of human rights law in humanitarian crises, it is useful to briefly review a state's overarching obligation to respect, protect and fulfil human rights, and when a state may legitimately place limitations on or derogate from human rights provisions.

A. State Obligations to Respect, Protect and Fulfil Human Rights

Considering the fundamental importance of the basic necessities for survival during humanitarian crises, it is appropriate that the tripartite typology of a state's obligations to respect, protect and fulfil all human rights was initially proposed by UN Rapporteur Asbjørn Eide in the context of the right to food.[11] In his 1987 report, Eide set out that states must respect the freedom of individuals to take action relating to the resources necessary for their livelihoods; and then protect that freedom of action and use of resources as against third parties. As a last resort, the state has an obligation to fulfil individuals' expectations for the enjoyment of the right to food.[12] This understanding of a state's obligations has since been widely accepted, and as a conceptual breakthrough has been credited with encouraging the justiciability of economic, social and cultural rights (ESCR).[13] In General Comment 14 on the right to the highest attainable standard of health, the UN Committee on Economic, Social and Cultural Rights (CESCR) reaffirmed the applicability of these three levels of obligation to all human rights (not just ESCR) and provided detailed analysis of the specific legal obligations for states regarding the right to health.[14]

[11] *Report on the Right to Adequate Food as a Human Right submitted by Mr Asbjørn Eide, Special Rapporteur*, Commission on Human Rights, Sub-Commission on Prevention of Discrimination and Protection of Minorities (7 July 1987) E/CN.4/Sub.2/1987/23.

[12] ibid, paras 112–14.

[13] O De Schutter, *International Human Rights Law* (Cambridge University Press, 2010) 248. See also M Dennis and D Stewart, 'Justiciability of Economic, Social and Cultural Rights: Should There be an International Complaints Mechanism to Adjudicate the Rights to Food, Water, Housing and Health?' (2004) 98 *American Journal of International Law* 462.

[14] CESCR, *General Comment No 14: The Right to the Highest Attainable Standard of Health* (11 August 2000) E/C.12/2000/4, paras 33–37.

In the context of humanitarian action, it follows that states first have an obligation to respect the rights of those affected, for example respecting religious requirements for the burial of the dead, or for types of food assistance provided.[15] Next, the state must take positive action to protect those affected from violations of their rights by third parties or arising from the emergency situation. For example, the state must genuinely attempt to protect people from the actions of non-state armed groups, proactively assist people to move to safer areas,[16] or ensure a minimum level of physical protection for residents of refugee or internally displaced persons (IDP) camps.[17] The state also has an obligation to ensure that violations do not occur as a direct result of humanitarian activities. As noted by the IASC, unequal access to assistance, discrimination in aid provision, enforced relocation, sexual and gender-based violence, loss of documentation, recruitment of children into fighting forces, unsafe or involuntary return or resettlement, and issues of property restitution may all occur during humanitarian operations.[18] Finally, states have a positive obligation to provide or facilitate support to ensure that persons affected by humanitarian crises can access their rights. In other words, the state must fulfil affected persons' rights either directly or with the assistance of others, be they third states or other humanitarian actors.[19] As noted by Walter Kälin in his examination of the protection of IDPs:

> The State has the primary responsibility not only to respect, but also to protect and fulfil the human rights of all the people living in its territory or jurisdiction, including the displaced. Therefore, international human rights law obliges States, to the extent possible, to prevent or at least mitigate the negative effects of natural hazards and, in particular, protect persons displaced by natural disasters from abuses and violations of human rights in the emergency, recovery and reconstruction phases.[20]

[15] *Strengthening of the Coordination of Humanitarian Emergency Assistance of the United Nations*, UNGA Res 46/182 (19 December 1991) A/RES/46/182, Annex, Guiding Principle I.4 states: 'Each State has the responsibility first and foremost to take care of the victims of natural disasters and other emergencies occurring on its territory.'

[16] For discussion of relocation options in the face of inter-communal violence, see J Zapater, 'Humanitarian Evacuations in the Central African Republic' (September 2014) 62 *Humanitarian Exchange*.

[17] For discussion of the right to housing following the Haiti earthquake, see Section II.B.i below.

[18] IASC, *Protecting Persons Affected by Natural Disasters: IASC Operational Guidelines on Human Rights and Natural Disasters* (June 2006) 8.

[19] CESCR, *General Comment No 14*, above n 14, para 40.

[20] W Kälin, *Report of the Representative of the Secretary-General on the Human Rights of Internally Displaced Persons: Addendum on Protection of Internally Displaced Persons in Situations of Natural Disasters* (5 March 2009) A/HRC/10/13/Add.1, para 9.

The obligation to fulfil rights is particularly pertinent in the context of humanitarian crises which entail widespread suffering and deprivation. Individuals affected will most likely face challenges in securing the basic necessities of life (such as food, drinking water or shelter), and risk a range of threats to their physical security and integrity (such as rape, assault or trafficking), or violations of other civil, political, economic, social or cultural rights (such as religious freedom, political participation or access to education). The obligation to fulfil can furthermore be sub-divided into obligations to facilitate, to provide and to promote rights. In other words, states are required to take positive measures to facilitate and enable individuals and communities to enjoy their rights. States are also required to directly provide specific rights when people are unable, for reasons beyond their control, to realise that right themselves by the means at their disposal.[21] Finally, the obligation to promote requires states to undertake actions to create, maintain and restore people's rights.[22] This implies the need for effective systems so that rights are fulfilled, and monitoring and accountability mechanisms so that such systems are responsive.[23]

i. The Right to Food in Emergencies[24]

If one takes the example of the right to food in emergencies, the first point to note is that despite the progressive realisation nature of this right, states have binding obligations via ICESCR to implement the right to adequate food 'to the maximum of [their] available resources … by all appropriate means'.[25] This means that states have a legal obligation to respect the right of individuals to source their own food through their own activities. A corollary of this is the state's obligation not to prevent access to food aid being provided by third parties. Meanwhile, a state's obligation to protect the right to adequate food requires them to undertake proactive measures to ensure that third parties (such as other individuals, armed groups or private enterprises) do not deprive rights-holders of their access to adequate food, for example through

[21] *Maastricht Guidelines on Violations of Economic, Social and Cultural Rights* (1997) (adopted by a group of academic experts meeting in Maastricht, 22–26 January 1997) para 6.

[22] CESCR, *General Comment No 14*, above n 14, para 34.

[23] For more on accountability mechanisms, see ch 4, Section II. See also D Cubie and M Hesselman, 'Accountability for the Human Rights Implications of Natural Disasters: A Proposal for Systemic International Oversight' (2015) 33(1) *Netherlands Quarterly of Human Rights* 9.

[24] For a detailed examination, see L Cotula and M Vidar, *The Right to Adequate Food in Emergencies* (2002) FAO Legislative Study 77, 22–52.

[25] Art 2(1) ICESCR.

misappropriation of food aid. Liability can also arise from a lack of due diligence on the part of the state in ensuring the protection of the right to food from violations by such third parties.

In regard to a state's obligation to fulfil the right to adequate food, in an emergency setting this can be broken down into the three components of facilitate, provide and promote. For example, the state must directly provide food to those who are unable to realise their right to adequate food through their own activities. If the state is unable to provide food directly to the affected population, it should facilitate the entry, transit and transport of food aid from third parties or countries to the affected areas.[26] Likewise, the state should promote private trade in food, for example by ensuring that the regulatory environment is supportive of this or even by introducing price controls to ensure that all persons are able to purchase basic foodstuffs. Indeed, if a state is unable to ensure the right to adequate food in an emergency setting it has a duty to request assistance from other states.[27]

International human rights law recognises both obligations of conduct and of result—which is intended to ensure that states consistently devote the necessary and available resources to comply with their international human rights obligations.[28] While a state may not be directly responsible for a humanitarian crisis which occurs on its territory, such as a natural disaster or forced displacement arising from the actions of a non-state armed group, its preparations for and responses to such risks will engage its direct responsibility. Yet in humanitarian crises persons affected are all too often seen as passive 'victims' rather than active rights holders.[29] This can result from the top-down approaches of humanitarian assistance as 'charity' as opposed to rights-based approaches to humanitarian

[26] For analysis of the international legal framework for food assistance, see A La Chimia, 'Food Security and the Right to Food: Finding Balance in the 2012 Food Assistance Convention' (2016) 65(1) *International and Comparative Law Quarterly* 99.

[27] See: E Valencia-Ospina, *Second Report on the Protection of Persons in the Event of Disasters* (7 May 2009) A/CN.4/615, paras 50–70; C Allan and T O'Donnell, 'An Offer You Cannot Refuse? Natural Disasters, the Politics of Aid Refusal and Potential Legal Implications' (2013) 5(1) *Amsterdam Law Forum* 36; C Allan and T O'Donnell, 'A Call to Alms?: Natural Disasters, R2P, Duties of Cooperation and Uncharted Consequences' (2012) *Journal of Conflict and Security Law* 1; K Luopajärvi, 'Is there an Obligation on States to Accept International Humanitarian Assistance to Internally Displaced Persons under International Law?' (2003) 15(4) *International Journal of Refugee Law* 678.

[28] *Towards Freedom from Fear and Want: Human Rights in the Post-2015 Agenda*, Thematic Think Piece, Office of the High Commissioner for Human Rights (May 2012) 9.

[29] For a damning indictment of the 'biased and arrogant rhetoric and history of the human rights enterprise,' see M Matua, 'Savages, Victims, and Saviours: The Metaphor of Human Rights' (2001) 42(1) *Harvard International Law Journal* 201, 202. See also U Baxi, 'Too Many, or Too Few, Human Rights?' (2001) 1 *Human Rights Law Review* 1.

action based on empowerment, participation, non-discrimination and accountability.[30] Yet changes are occurring within the humanitarian sector itself. For example, one of the core commitments made at the World Humanitarian Summit in May 2016 was to 'empower women and girls as change agents and leaders, including by increasing support for local women's groups to participate meaningfully in humanitarian action'.[31]

Despite the increasing focus on the agency and participation of individuals affected by humanitarian crises, the international humanitarian system remains stubbornly state-centric. The Guiding Principles of UNGA Resolution 46/182 clearly established that humanitarian assistance should be 'provided with the consent of the affected country and in principle on the basis of an appeal by the affected country', and that the affected country has the 'primary role in the initiation, organisation, coordination, and implementation of humanitarian assistance within its territory'.[32] Paul Harvey has argued that an affected state therefore has four broad responsibilities, namely: a) establishing that a crisis has occurred and inviting international aid; b) directly providing assistance and protection; c) monitoring and coordinating external assistance; and d) setting the regulatory and legal frameworks governing assistance.[33] Nevertheless, immediate assistance generally comes directly from the local community, while the majority of international responders to conflicts and disasters are NGOs. So there exists potential for disputes between the authorities of the affected state and those local and international humanitarian responders. For example, in the aftermath of Cyclone Nargis in Myanmar in 2008, which killed at least 138,000 people, private humanitarian responses were not only discouraged by the ruling junta but local people were penalised for undertaking such activities.[34]

While international human rights law clearly sets out a state's obligations to respect, protect and fulfil all human rights, this is predicated on the state undertaking these duties in good faith.[35] What happens when

[30] As discussed in ch 3, Section II.

[31] *Core Commitment 1*, 'Women and Girls: Catalysing Action to Achieve Gender Equality', High-Level Leaders' Roundtable, World Humanitarian Summit (May 2016).

[32] UNGA Res 46/182, above n 15, Annex, Guiding Principle I.4.

[33] P Harvey, *Towards Good Humanitarian Government: The Role of the Affected State in Disaster Response*, Humanitarian Policy Group Report 29, Overseas Development Institute, September 2009, 6. See also E Valencia-Ospina, *Third Report on the Protection of Persons in the Event of Disasters* (31 March 2010) A/CN.4/629, paras 63–101 (responsibility of the affected state); IFRC, *Introduction to the Guidelines for the Domestic Facilitation and Regulation of International Disaster Relief and Initial Recovery Assistance* (2008).

[34] 'Comic arrested for Burma aid runs', *BBC News Online*, 5 June 2008 http://news.bbc.co.uk/2/hi/asia-pacific/7437251.stm.

[35] eg Art 22 UDHR highlights not only an individual's entitlement to 'the economic, social and cultural rights indispensable for his dignity and the free development of his personality' but also the duty of national effort and international cooperation required for the realisation of these rights. *Universal Declaration of Human Rights* (adopted 10 December 1948) UNGA Res 217 A(III).

a state is unable or unwilling to respect, protect or fulfil the rights of people facing a humanitarian crisis? Despite the expanded understanding of duty-bearers in recent years, there is still doubt regarding whether non-state humanitarian agencies have identifiable legal human rights obligations.[36] Conversely, under the law of armed conflict, it is well recognised that non-state armed groups in control of territory have comparable obligations to state armed forces.[37] Notwithstanding the lack of clarity on the human rights obligations of humanitarian actors, many humanitarian agencies have adopted rights-based approaches to their work. Reflecting the overarching principles of humanity and human dignity, states and humanitarian organisations can and should apply human rights principles to all their humanitarian programming.

B. Limitations and Derogations to Human Rights

Built into international human rights law are the notions of legitimate limitations to economic, social and cultural rights (ECSR), and allowable derogations from certain civil and political rights during emergencies, as evidenced by the International Covenants on Civil and Political Rights (ICCPR) and Economic, Social and Cultural Rights (ICESCR). Although the ICESCR establishes that states have an obligation 'to take steps … to the maximum of its available resources, with a view to achieving progressively the full realisation of the rights recognised in the present Covenant by all appropriate means,' this is offset by Article 4:

> The States Parties … recognise that, in the enjoyment of those rights provided by the State in conformity with the present Covenant, the State may subject such rights only to such limitations as are determined by law only in so far as this may be compatible with the nature of these rights and solely for the purpose of promoting the general welfare in a democratic society.[38]

This limitation clause was introduced to ensure a balance between individual rights and community interests (the general welfare of society), and in recognition of the fact that ECSR are not necessarily absolute so may require policy choices.[39] Meanwhile, Dominick McGoldrick has

[36] See, eg, G Kent, 'The Human Rights Obligations of Intergovernmental Organizations' (2005) 3 *UN Chronicle*; N Schimmel, 'The International Human Rights Law Responsibilities of NGOs', *Oxford Human Rights Hub Blog* (20 March 2015) http://humanrights.dev3.oneltd.eu/the-international-human-rights-law-responsibilities-of-ngos.

[37] M Sassòli, 'Taking Armed Groups Seriously: Ways to Improve their Compliance with International Humanitarian Law' (2010) 1(1) *Journal of International Humanitarian Legal Studies* 5.

[38] Art 4 ICESCR.

[39] A Müller, 'Limitations to and Derogations from Economic, Social and Cultural Rights' (2009) 9(4) *HumanRights Law Review* 557.

defined a derogation as the complete or partial elimination of a right as an international obligation;[40] although certain fundamental guarantees, such as the prohibition against torture, are non-derogable. The non-binding *Paris Minimum Standards of Human Rights Norms in a State of Emergency* state: 'The basic rights and freedoms guaranteed by international law shall remain non-derogable even during emergency. As the minimum ... the rights recognised as non-derogable in international law may not be affected by a state of emergency.'[41] As derogation clauses set out which human rights provisions may be derogated from and the procedure for so doing, by definition all other human rights are non-derogable and non-compliance with procedural requirements (such as official proclamation of an emergency and non-discriminatory application) render the derogation void. Therefore, Article 4(1) ICCPR sets out that:

> In time of public emergency which threatens the life of the nation and the existence of which is officially proclaimed, the States Parties ... may take measures derogating from their obligations under the present Covenant to the extent strictly required by the exigencies of the situation, provided that such measures are not inconsistent with their other obligations under international law and do not involve discrimination solely on the ground of race, colour, sex, language, religion or social origin.[42]

Similar limitation and derogation clauses are included in regional human rights instruments.[43] However, states are not free to impose limitations or derogations without good cause, and their substantive content and temporal applicability may be restricted. In the ICJ's *Advisory Opinion on the Wall*, the Court considered an attempt by Israel to derogate certain rights under the ICESCR, and noted that 'the protection offered by human rights conventions does not cease in case of armed conflict, save through the effect of provisions for derogation of the kind found in Article 4 of the [ICCPR]'.[44] As there is no derogation clause in the ICESCR, this means that states are unable to derogate from economic, social and cultural rights. Indeed, many of the key rights relevant in humanitarian crises, such as the rights to food, healthcare and shelter, are ESCR. Despite Authers and Charlesworth's observation that 'economic, social and cultural rights are

[40] D McGoldrick, 'The Interface Between Public Emergency Powers and International Law' (2004) 2 *International Journal on Constitutional Law* 380, 383.

[41] Section B(2)(e). See 'The Paris Minimum Standards of Human Rights Norms in a State of Emergency' (1985) 79(4) *American Journal of International Law* 1072.

[42] Art 4(1) International Covenant on Civil and Political Rights (adopted 16 December 1966, entered into force 23 March 1976) 999 UNTS 171 ('ICCPR').

[43] Art 15 European Convention for the Protection of Human Rights and Fundamental Freedoms (adopted 4 November 1950, entered into force 3 September 1953) ETS 5; Art 32(2) American Convention on Human Rights (adopted 22 November 1969, entered into force 18 July 1978) 1144 UNTS 123; Art 14 African Charter on Human and Peoples' Rights (adopted 27 June 1981, entered into force 21 October 1986) 1520 UNTS 217.

[44] ICJ, *Advisory Opinion on the Wall*, above n 5, para 106.

associated with political choices rather than legal ones',[45] states retain binding legal obligations to undertake their progressive realisation, even in the face of a humanitarian crisis.

Moreover, CESCR has recognised that, despite the limitations clause, all rights contained within the ICESCR deserve minimum protection in the form of 'core obligations'. This means that any state party in which a significant number of individuals are deprived of 'minimum essential levels' of ESCR, such as 'essential foodstuffs, essential primary health-care, basic shelter and housing, or the most basic forms of education is, *prima facie*, failing to discharge its obligations under the Covenant'.[46] The CESCR has explicitly affirmed that states have 'a core obligation to take the necessary action to mitigate and alleviate hunger … even in times of natural or other disasters',[47] and if a state cannot fulfil its minimum core obligations there is an obligation to accept or request aid from other states.[48] Likewise, the non-binding Limburg Principles on the Implementation of the ICESCR, drafted by academics and practitioners in June 1986, stress that 'States parties are obligated, regardless of the level of economic development, to ensure respect for minimum subsistence rights for all'.[49] Consequently, Amrei Müller has argued it would be extremely difficult to limit the minimum core of subsistence rights (such as the right to food or basic emergency health care) without impacting the very nature of the rights in question.[50]

However, the derogations clause in the ICCPR confirms that certain rights may be limited 'in time of public emergency'. There could therefore be a temptation to restrict key civil and political rights during a humanitarian crisis, for example to reduce the fair trial guarantees of captured non-state combatants. Sarah Joseph has noted that terrorist insurgencies are the most common justification used by states to introduce a state of emergency.[51] By a coincidence of timing, the Human Rights Committee (HRC) updated its General Comment on derogations only months before the terrorist attacks of 11 September 2001, attacks which led to the so-called 'war on terror' and a range of countries introducing derogations

[45] B Authers and H Charlesworth, 'The Crisis and the Quotidian in International Human Rights Law' (2013) 44 *Netherlands Yearbook of International Law* 19, 36.

[46] See CESCR, *General Comment No 3: The Nature of States Parties' Obligations* (14 December 1990) E/1991/23, para 10; CESCR, *General Comment No 12: The Right to Adequate Food* (12 May 1999) E/C.12/1999/5, paras 6, 13, 15, 17, 38–39; CESCR, *General Comment No 14*, above n 14, paras 16, 40, 45.

[47] CESCR, *General Comment No 12*, above n 46, para 6.

[48] ibid, paras 15, 17. See also Allan and O'Donnell, 'Offer You Cannot Refuse?' above n 27.

[49] Art 25 Limburg Principles on the Implementation of the International Covenant on Economic, Social and Cultural Rights, June 1986.

[50] Müller, 'Limitations and Derogations', above n 39, 582–83.

[51] S Joseph, 'Human Rights Committee: General Comment 29' (2002) 2(2) *Human Rights Law Review* 81, 83.

(some officially proclaimed, others not) from key civil and political rights for persons suspected of terrorism.[52] The HRC stressed the interconnections between human rights and humanitarian law, noting that during all armed conflicts (whether international or non-international), the law of armed conflict remains applicable, as an additional method of accountability to prevent abuse of a state's emergency powers.[53]

Nevertheless, a state may have justifiable reasons for restricting a particular right, such as freedom of movement in the midst of a suspected viral pandemic spread through the air or physical contact such as Ebola or SARS, as large groups of people meeting together could exacerbate the spread of the disease. As with all limitations and derogations, any restrictions on free movement need to be proportionate to the risk posed. The HRC has stressed that in such situations, state parties should 'carefully consider the justification and why such a measure is necessary and legitimate in the circumstances'.[54] For example, Article 11(3) ICCPR already provides that states may impose restrictions on freedom of movement which are 'necessary to protect national security, public order (*ordre public*), public health or morals or the rights and freedoms of others'.[55] Therefore, situations where recourse to a formal derogation via Article 4 regarding freedom of movement are limited. Moreover, while derogations from certain civil and political rights may be permissible when the life of a nation is threatened, the threshold of threat is recognised as being sufficiently high that many humanitarian crises would not constitute such a threat.[56] The HRC has noted that: 'If States purport to invoke the right to derogate from the [ICCPR] during … a natural catastrophe … or a major industrial accident, they must be able to justify not only that such a situation constitutes a threat to the life of the nation, but also that all their measures derogating from the Covenant are strictly required by the exigencies of the situation.'[57] The HRC further notes that not every disturbance or catastrophe qualifies as a public emergency which threatens the life of the nation.[58] For example, most natural disasters such as flooding, hurricanes and landslides do not affect large sections of a country, but can have devastating impacts at the local level.[59]

[52] HRC, *General Comment No 29: States of Emergency (Article 4)* (31 August 2001) CCPR/C/21/Rev.1/Add.11.

[53] ibid, para 3.

[54] ibid.

[55] Art 11(3) ICCPR, above n 42.

[56] See, eg, W Kälin, 'The Human Rights Dimension of Natural or Human-Made Disasters' (2012) 55 *German Yearbook of International Law* 119, 128–31.

[57] HRC, *General Comment No 29*, above n 52, para 5.

[58] ibid, para 3.

[59] For specific discussion, see E Sommario, 'Derogation from Human Rights Treaties in Situations of Natural or Man-Made Disasters' in A de Guttry, M Gestri and G Venturini (eds), *International Disaster Response Law* (TMC Asser Press, 2012).

Müller has identified four key considerations for states before the introduction of any derogation, namely: the existence of an exceptional threat; the non-derogability of certain rights; non-discriminatory application; and proportionality between the expected threat and proposed restrictions.[60] Moreover, the interplay between human rights law and international criminal law has been highlighted by the HRC, with General Comment 12 noting that: 'If action conducted under the authority of a State constitutes a basis for individual criminal responsibility for a crime against humanity by the persons involved in that action, Article 4 of the Covenant cannot be used as justification that a state of emergency exempted the State in question from its responsibility in relation to the same conduct.'[61] Therefore, while a state may provide justifications for limiting or derogating certain rights during a humanitarian crisis, the UN human rights monitoring bodies have stressed their supervisory role through the requirements for the emergency to be officially proclaimed to ensure international accountability of whether the measures taken were strictly required by the exigencies of the situation, and to permit other states to monitor their compliance with international human rights law.[62] Notwithstanding the possibility of limitations or derogations to human rights, we will now examine some of the core substantive human rights provisions which are applicable before, during and after a humanitarian crisis.

II. SUBSTANTIVE HUMAN RIGHTS PROVISIONS IN HUMANITARIAN CRISES

The humanitarian impact of Hurricane Katrina in New Orleans in 2005 was a stark reminder that even countries with extensive infrastructure and resources can face serious challenges in the face of a major humanitarian crisis. Susannah Sirkin launched a scathing attack on the official response when she argued:

> [N]eglect of the basic human rights to education, food, a healthy and secure environment, access to health care, housing, and decent employment is the manmade cause of the obscene impact of the hurricane's disaster for the underserved residents of New Orleans and other areas of Louisiana and Mississippi. Neglect of these rights has ultimately resulted in failure to protect the right to life of many hurricane victims.[63]

[60] Müller, 'Limitations and Derogations', above n 39, 561–64. On non-discrimination, see also Kälin, above n 56, 131.

[61] HRC, *General Comment No 29*, above n 52, para 12.

[62] See, eg, HRC, *General Comment No 29*, above n 52, para 17.

[63] Sirkin, 'The Debacle of Hurricane Katrina', above n 6, 225.

Indeed, the current text of the ILC draft articles on the protection of persons in the event of disasters explicitly reiterates that: 'Persons affected by disasters are entitled to the respect for and protection of their human rights in accordance with international law.'[64] But what does international human rights law say regarding the application of human rights norms in times of humanitarian crisis? The non-binding 1993 IIHL Guiding Principles on the Right to Humanitarian Assistance proposed that a specific right to humanitarian assistance could be invoked when essential humanitarian needs were not being met, arguing that the abandonment of victims without assistance would constitute a threat to human life and a grave offence to human dignity.[65] Conversely, Yoram Dinstein has asserted that: 'It is impossible to assert, *at the present point*, that a general right to humanitarian assistance has actually crystallized in positive international law.'[66] Whether international law has progressively developed in the years since Professor Dinstein made this comment will be discussed further in chapter ten. Yet it is undeniable that human rights law plays an important role before, during and after humanitarian crises. Reflecting the different stages of humanitarian action, the IASC has identified four categories of rights which are particularly relevant in the context of natural disasters:

1. Rights related to protection of life; security and physical integrity; and the protection of family ties in the context of evacuations.
2. Rights related to the provision of food; health; shelter; and education.
3. Rights related to housing, land and property; and livelihoods.
4. Rights related to documentation, free movement in the context of durable solutions for internally displaced persons; re-establishment of family ties, expression and opinion; and elections.[67]

Hugo Slim and Andrew Bonwick have likewise identified the non-derogable core of human rights law applicable in times of war, disaster and emergency as 'the right to life, the right to legal personality and due process of law, the prohibition of torture, slavery and degrading or inhuman treatment or punishment, and the right to freedom of religion, thought

[64] Draft Art 5. For the final text of the preamble, draft articles and commentaries adopted by the ILC, see Official Records of the General Assembly, Seventy-first Session, *Supplement No 10* (A/71/10), Chapter IV: Protection of Persons in the Event of Disasters (2016).

[65] *Guiding Principles on the Right to Humanitarian Assistance*, International Institute of Humanitarian Law (IIHL), April 1993, Principle 3, arising from the XVIIth Round Table on Current Problems of Humanitarian Law: 'The Evolution of the Right to Assistance', San Remo, Italy, 2–4 September 1992.

[66] Y Dinstein, 'The Right to Humanitarian Assistance' (Autumn 2000) *Naval War College Review* 77, 77 [emphasis added].

[67] IASC, *Operational Guidelines on the Protection of Persons in Situations of Natural Disasters*, Brookings-Bern Project on Internal Displacement (January 2011) 9.

and conscience'.[68] Drawing on such formulations, the following sections will examine three core obligations of a state, namely: the right of access to protection and assistance; the right to an adequate standard of living; and the right to physical security and integrity. The chapter will conclude with a broader discussion of the role of human rights law within the *acquis humanitaire*.

A. Right of Access to Protection and Assistance

As discussed in chapter four, ensuring humanitarian access is fundamental for the protection of persons in humanitarian crises. If domestic or international agencies are unable to physically provide material assistance and protection activities to those affected, then any rights to assistance, such as those set out in the Geneva Conventions for civilians in international and non-international armed conflicts,[69] are meaningless. Yet, as the debate surrounding the existence of a general right to humanitarian assistance signifies, there are limited provisions in binding international law expressly mandating the right of access to protection and assistance. Moreover, one has to distinguish between an individual's right to receive humanitarian protection and assistance, and an impartial humanitarian organisation's right to offer their services.[70] However, certain international human rights law instruments contain binding obligations regarding the provision of assistance and protection. For example, UNGA Resolution 44/25, which introduced the 1989 Convention on the Rights of the Child (CRC), called for urgent and effective national and international action due to the critical situation of children resulting from, inter alia, natural disasters and armed conflicts.[71] In particular, the CRC sets out specific requirements in regard to refugee children, namely:

Article 22 (CRC)

1. States Parties shall take appropriate measures to ensure that a child who is seeking refugee status or who is considered a refugee in accordance with applicable international or domestic law and procedures shall, whether unaccompanied or accompanied by his or her parents or by any other person, receive appropriate protection and humanitarian assistance in the enjoyment of applicable rights set forth in the present Convention and in

[68] H Slim and A Bonwick, *Protection: An ALNAP Guide for Humanitarian Agencies* (August 2005) Overseas Development Institute, 34.

[69] For discussion of these rights, see ch 6, Sections II and III.

[70] For further discussion of this distinction, see ch 10, Sections II and III.

[71] UNGA Res 44/25, 12 December 1989.

> other international human rights or humanitarian instruments to which the said States are Parties.[72]

The CRC therefore clearly articulates the right of all refugee and asylum-seeking children to both assistance and protection, and the corresponding responsibility of all state parties. Considering that the CRC has obtained near-universal ratification, this provision represents an authoritative right to humanitarian assistance for refugee children. At the regional level, a similarly worded provision in Article 23(4) of the African Charter on the Rights and Welfare of the Child[73] expressly states that provisions on refugee children apply equally to children displaced internally due to, inter alia, natural disasters, internal armed conflicts or civil strife. Furthermore, Article 25(2)(b) places obligations on state parties to take 'all necessary measures' to trace and reunite families of separated children, including separation caused by displacement arising from armed conflicts and natural disasters.

The right to access education (at all stages from pre-primary to secondary level) is of crucial importance for children as disruption for whatever reason can be particularly traumatic for young children. Therefore, the re-establishment of educational systems provides an element of continuity and stability.[74] Additional protection for children is provided by the Optional Protocol to the CRC on the Involvement of Children in Armed Conflict which requires state parties to provide appropriate assistance for the physical and psychological recovery and social reintegration of former child soldiers.[75] These binding state obligations have received scrutiny from the UN human rights monitoring bodies in the context of individual country reports, with the Committee on the Rights of the Child highlighting that effective protection of children should include: the implementation of disaster preparedness in school curricula;[76] the development and implementation of action plans or strategies on assistance and protection;[77] and the setting up of 'strategic budgetary lines' protecting vulnerable and disadvantaged children 'even in situations of economic crisis, natural disasters or other emergencies'.[78]

[72] Art 22(1) Convention on the Rights of the Child (adopted 20 November 1989, entered into force 2 September 1990) 1577 UNTS 3 ('CRC').

[73] OAU, African Charter on the Rights and Welfare of the Child (adopted 11 July 1990, entered into force 29 November 1999) CAB/LEG/24.9/49 (1990).

[74] S Nicolai, S Hine and J Wales, *Education in Emergencies and Protracted Crises: Toward a Strengthened Response* (July 2015) Overseas Development Institute.

[75] Art 6 Optional Protocol to the Convention on the Rights of the Child on the Involvement of Children in Armed Conflict (adopted 25 May 2000, entered into force 12 February 2002) UNGA Res A/RES/54/263.

[76] See, eg, CRC 'Concluding Observations Djibouti' (2009) CRC/C/DJI/CO/2, para 63.

[77] CRC 'Concluding Observations The Philippines' (2009) CRC/C/PHL/CO/3-4, para 60(d).

[78] See, eg, CRC 'Concluding Observations Madagascar' (2012) CRC/C/MDG/CO/3-4, para 18; CRC 'Concluding Observations Canada' (2012) CRC/C.CAN/CO/3-4, para 17; CRC 'Concluding Observations Myanmar' (2012) CRC/C/MMR/CO/3-4, para 18(c).

Meanwhile for adults and children alike, the Universal Declaration of Human Rights[79] provides for the right to 'seek and to enjoy in other countries asylum from persecution'. By so doing, the UDHR recognises the right to access the international refugee protection regime which in turn contains specific rights to material assistance and protection for refugees.[80] In addition to children and refugees, international human rights law has recognised other specific groups as in need of particular attention during humanitarian crises. The most recent international human rights convention, the Convention on the Rights of Persons with Disabilities, which entered into force in 2008, uniquely provides an operative article explicitly recognising the potential vulnerability of persons with disabilities:

Article 11 (CRPD)

> States Parties shall take, in accordance with their obligations under international law, including international humanitarian law and international human rights law, all necessary measures to ensure the protection and safety of persons with disabilities in situations of risk, including situations of armed conflict, humanitarian emergencies and the occurrence of natural disasters.[81]

Reflecting the evolving nature of international human rights law, this provision may form a template for dedicated articles on humanitarian protection and assistance in future global, regional or national human rights instruments. Indeed, the Committee on the Rights of Persons with Disabilities has required state parties to report measures taken to ensure the protection and safety of disabled persons, including measures taken to include persons with disabilities in national emergency protocols, and those taken:

> to ensure that humanitarian aid relief is distributed in an accessible way to people with disabilities caught in humanitarian emergency, in particular measures taken to ensure that sanitation and latrine facilities in emergency shelters and refugee camps are available and accessible for persons with disabilities.[82]

Such recommendations have been bolstered by the endorsement of the Charter on the Inclusion of Persons with Disabilities in Humanitarian Action by the World Humanitarian Summit in May 2016. The signatories

[79] Art 14(1) UDHR, above n 35.

[80] Convention relating to the Status of Refugees (adopted 28 July 1951, entered into force 22 April 1954) 189 UNTS 137. For further discussion, see ch 9, Section II.A.

[81] Art 11 Convention on the Rights of Persons with Disabilities (adopted 13 December 2006, entered into force 3 May 2008) 2515 UNTS 3. See also 'Statement of the Committee on the Rights of Person with Disabilities on the Situation in Haiti' in *Report of the Committee on the Rights of Persons with Disabilities to the General Assembly* (2011) A/66/55, Annex XI.

[82] CRPD, *Guidelines on Treaty-Specific Document to be Submitted by States Parties under Article 35, paragraph 1, of the Convention on the Rights of Persons with Disabilities* (18 November 2009) CRPD/C/2/3, 9.

to the Charter, which include states, inter-governmental and non-governmental actors, reaffirm their determination to 'make humanitarian action inclusive of persons with disabilities and to take all steps to meet their essential needs and promote the protection, safety and respect for the dignity of persons with disabilities in situations of risk, including situations of armed conflict, humanitarian emergencies and the occurrence of natural disasters'.[83] Moreover, the Charter signatories commit to 'strive to ensure that persons with disabilities have access to humanitarian response, both in terms of protection and assistance, without discrimination, and allowing them to fully enjoy their rights'.[84]

Another recognised group which may be particularly vulnerable in the context of humanitarian crises are women and girls—a shocking 60 per cent of preventable maternal deaths take place in settings of conflict, displacement or disaster.[85] It is therefore noticeable that the 1979 Convention on the Elimination of Discrimination Against Women[86] makes no express reference to discrimination in humanitarian crises. Reflecting changing levels of awareness, the UN Commission on the Status of Women concluded a specific Resolution on Gender Equality and the Empowerment of Women in Natural Disasters in 2012.[87] In addition to recognising the vital role that women play in the prevention and response to natural disasters, the Resolution explicitly urges governments to: 'Ensure the full enjoyment by women and girls of all human rights in every phase of disaster risk reduction (prevention, mitigation and preparedness), response and recovery.'[88] Likewise, the Committee on the Elimination of all Forms of Discrimination Against Women has pronounced several times on issues relating to women's access to assistance and protection in disaster

[83] Art 1.1 Charter on the Inclusion of Persons with Disabilities in Humanitarian Action, May 2016. Reflecting the non-binding status of the text, the Charter states: 'This document expresses our common political intention and intended course of action, however, it does not establish legally binding obligations to the States and other actors and does not affect the signatories' existing obligations under applicable international and domestic law.'

[84] ibid, Art 1.2. For analysis of violence against women with disabilities, including in times of conflict and disaster, see S Ortoleva and H Lewis, 'Forgotten Sisters—A Report on Violence Against Women with Disabilities: An Overview of its Nature, Scope, Causes and Consequences' (2012) *Northeastern Public Law and Theory Faculty Research Papers Series No 104.*

[85] UN Women, *Promoting the Rights, Needs and Agency of Women and Girls in Humanitarian Action* (May 2016) 2.

[86] Convention on the Elimination of Discrimination Against Women (adopted 18 December 1979, entered into force 3 September 1981) 1249 UNTS 13 ('CEDAW').

[87] The Resolution was proposed by Japan, and was jointly sponsored by 49 other states. See: *Japan: Draft Resolution, Gender Equality and the Empowerment of Women in Natural Disasters* (6 March 2012) E/CN.6/2012/L.4.

[88] UN Commission on the Status of Women, Res 56/2, 'Gender Equality and the Empowerment of Women in Natural Disasters' (March 2012). UN Commission on the Status of Women, *Report on the fifty-sixth session* (14 March 2011, 27 February–9 March and 15 March 2012), Economic and Social Council, Official Records, Supplement No 7 (2012) E/CN.6/2012/16, 9.

situations.[89] Meanwhile, the severe challenges faced by women and girls in armed conflicts and displacement settings are reflected in the on-going focus on women, peace and security commenced via UNSC Resolution 1325.[90] Therefore, the World Humanitarian Summit endorsed five core commitments on gender equality, set out in Table 5.1 below.[91]

Table 5.1: World Humanitarian Summit Commitments to Catalyse Action to Achieve Gender Equality

Commitment 1	Empower women and girls as change agents and leaders, including by increasing support for local women's groups to participate meaningfully in humanitarian action.
Commitment 2	Ensure universal access to sexual and reproductive health and reproductive rights as agreed in accordance with the Programme of Action of the International Conference on Population and Development and the Beijing Platform for Action and the Outcome documents of their review conferences for all women and adolescent girls in crisis settings.
Commitment 3	Implement a coordinated global approach to prevent and respond to gender-based violence in crisis contexts, including through the Call to Action on Protection from Gender-based Violence in Emergencies.
Commitment 4	Ensure that humanitarian programming is gender responsive.
Commitment 5	Fully comply with humanitarian policies, frameworks and legally binding documents related to gender equality, women's empowerment, and women's rights.

As with all human rights law, recognition that particular groups of people may need specific protection or assistance aids in the identification of the legal obligations due to such rights holders. Moreover, our evolving understanding that humanitarian action may take place before, during and after a humanitarian crisis (reflecting Walter Kälin's concept of a cycle of protection) requires us to broaden our understanding of when such obligations are triggered. Humanitarian action entails much more than just food and clothing delivered in the immediate aftermath of a crisis.

[89] For discussion of the substantive human rights implications of disasters for women, see E Ferris, 'How Can International Human Rights Law Protect us from Disasters?' (2014) *Proceedings of the 108th Annual Meeting of the American Society of International Law* 10–16.

[90] UNSC Resolution 1325 (31 October 2000) S/RES/1325 (2000), as supplemented by UNSC Resolution 1820 (2008), UNSC Resolutions 1888 and 1889 (2009), UNSC Resolution 1960 (2010) and UNSC Resolutions 2106 and 2122 (2013).

[91] *Core Commitments*, World Humanitarian Summit, above n 31.

However, material assistance comprises a core component of humanitarian action, and so the following section will examine the substantive content of the right to an adequate standard of living.

B. Right to an Adequate Standard of Living

In a humanitarian operation, the concept of adequacy, as developed by the CESCR in the context of adequate housing and adequate food, means that all goods and services are: a) available; b) accessible; c) acceptable; and d) adaptable.[92] As explained by the IASC,[93] availability means that goods and services are provided to the affected population in sufficient quantity and quality; while accessibility requires that goods and services are provided to all according to their needs and without discrimination; are within safe reach and can be physically accessed by everyone, including persons with specific needs; and are known to the beneficiaries. Acceptability requires that goods and services are respectful of the culture of individuals, minorities, peoples and communities, and sensitive to gender and age requirements; while adaptability requires that goods and services are provided flexibly to adapt to changing needs in different phases of emergency relief and recovery.[94]

This concept of 'adequacy' plays a fundamental role in one of the key human rights for persons in humanitarian crises. While one can debate what should be considered 'adequate' in the midst of massive destruction and suffering, international law and non-binding norms have attempted to provide some guidance. As noted above, both the CESCR and IASC have examined the concept of adequacy, and the technical standards of the *Sphere Handbook* are intended to provide a baseline in humanitarian operations. Under international law, Article 25(1) UDHR sets out that everyone has the right to a standard of living adequate for their health and well-being, including food, clothing, housing, medical care and necessary social services. Moreover the UDHR recognises the right to security in the event of 'unemployment, sickness, disability, widowhood, old age or other lack of livelihood in circumstances beyond his control'.[95] While no specific definition is provided for 'lack of livelihood in circumstances beyond his control' it is clear that an individual's ability to provide for themselves in the midst of a humanitarian crisis is likely to be severely curtailed. At a bare minimum, the right to an adequate standard of living must therefore

[92] See CESCR, *General Comment No 4: The Right to Adequate Housing* (13 December 1991) E/1992/23, and *General Comment No 12*, above n 46.

[93] IASC, *Operational Guidelines*, above n 9, 30–31.

[94] See also W Kälin and J Künzli, *The Law of International Human Rights Protection* (Oxford University Press, 2009) 303–04.

[95] Art 25(1) UDHR, above n 35.

include the basic necessities for survival.[96] More specifically, Article 11(1) ICESCR sets out that:

Article 11 (ICESCR)

> 1.The States Parties to the present Covenant recognise the right of everyone to an adequate standard of living for himself and his family, including adequate food, clothing and housing, and to the continuous improvement of living conditions. The States Parties will take appropriate steps to ensure the realisation of this right, recognising to this effect the essential importance of international cooperation based on free consent.[97]

Moreover, the ICESCR also expressly provides for the rights to 'the highest attainable standard of physical and mental health'[98] and the right of 'everyone to education'.[99] The close connection between an individual's right to life and violations of the rights to food, clothing, housing, sanitation, healthcare and water in disasters has been recognised for nearly 40 years.[100] Expanding upon the specific rights set out in the Covenant, the CESCR has highlighted a state's obligation to take steps to ensure that refugees, asylum seekers, displaced persons, victims of disaster and persons living in disaster-prone areas are provided with safe and sufficient water.[101] Additionally, the CESCR has stressed that priority should be given to 'the provision of international medical aid, distribution and management of resources, such as safe and potable water, food and medical supplies, and financial aid … to the most vulnerable or marginalized groups of the population' which by implication would include persons caught up in humanitarian crises.[102] The CESCR has furthermore indicated that the right to health includes the creation of 'a system of urgent medical care in cases of accidents, epidemics and similar health hazards, and the provision of disaster relief and humanitarian assistance in emergency situations'.[103] Ensuring access to such basic necessities for survival is one of the key priorities of all humanitarian operations. However, the challenges of respecting, protecting and fulfilling these rights were brought into stark focus by the 2010 Haitian earthquake.[104]

[96] See A Eide, 'Adequate Standard of Living' in D Moeckli, S Shah and S Sivakumaran, *International Human Rights Law* 2nd edn (Oxford University Press, 2014) 195–216; Kälin and Künzli, *International Human Rights Protection*, above n 94, 303–19.

[97] Art 11(1) ICESCR, as elaborated in *General Comment No 12*, above n 46 and *General Comment No 15: The Right to Water* (20 January 2003) E/C.12/2002/11.

[98] Art 12(1) ICESCR, as elaborated in *General Comment No 14*, above n 14.

[99] Art 13(1) ICESCR, as elaborated in CESCR, *General Comment No 13: The Right to Education* (8 December 1999) E/C.12/1999/10.

[100] P MacAlister-Smith, 'Human Rights and Disaster Relief' (1980) 5 *Holdsworth Law Review* 173.

[101] CESCR, *General Comment No 15*, above n 97, para 16.

[102] CESCR, *General Comment No 14*, above n 14, paras 40, 65.

[103] ibid, para 16.

[104] See, eg, AM Abebe, 'Human Rights in the Context of Disasters: The Special Session of the UN Human Rights Council on Haiti' (2011) 10 *Journal of Human Rights* 99.

i. Haiti: The Right to Housing

The earthquake which hit Haiti on 12 January 2010 caused massive loss of life and destruction of infrastructure. In addition to over 222,000 recorded deaths and 300,000 peopled injured, over 1.5 million people were made homeless.[105] The poor quality of many of the shanty towns around the capital, Port-au-Prince, contributed to the high death and injury toll, and also highlighted the precarious title to land of many residents. Inadequate construction standards and land tenure in advance of the earthquake contributed to the humanitarian impact, which in turn was exacerbated by the organisational and logistical challenges of responding to the earthquake. As a result, by the end of May 2010, 1,342 internally displaced persons (IDP) sites had been identified in the area affected by the earthquake.[106] The subsequent reconstruction efforts were similarly constrained, despite the extensive international financial and operational response.[107] Consequently, six years later, 14,679 IDP households, or 59,720 individuals, remained in 39 sites. Over 50 per cent of these sites were still composed of tents and makeshift shelters,[108] despite the right to housing being recognised as a component of the right to an adequate standard of living contained within Article 11(1) ICESCR. The Human Rights Council expressly called upon the international community to 'ensure adequate and coordinated support to the government and the people of Haiti in their efforts to overcome the challenges arising from the earthquake, keeping in mind the importance of integrating a human-rights approach.'[109]

The UN Guiding Principles on Internal Displacement likewise reiterate that core subsistence rights for IDPs, which must be provided without discrimination and regardless of the circumstances, include safe access to basic shelter and housing.[110] In the aftermath of any major

[105] IFRC, *Haiti: Earthquake*, Operations Update No 27, 16 June 2011.

[106] IASC, *Response to the Humanitarian Crisis in Haiti following the 12 January 2010 Earthquake: 6-Month Report* (July 2010) 5, 12.

[107] For analysis of common challenges to reconstruction, see S Leckie, *Regulatory Obstacles to Rapid and Equitable Emergency and Interim Shelter Solutions after Natural Disasters* (July 2011) Displacement Solutions.

[108] IOM, *Displacement Tracking Matrix (DTM) Haiti: Round 24 Report as of 31st December 2015*, 1.

[109] HRC Res A/HRC/S-13/2 (2 February 2010) para 1. The UN Special Rapporteur on the Right to Housing has been particularly active in highlighting the right to housing in disaster contexts. See, eg, R Rolnik, *Report of the Special Rapporteur on Adequate Housing as a Component of the Right to an Adequate Standard of Living* (5 August 2011) A/66/270, which has as its main focus the right to adequate housing in disaster relief efforts.

[110] UN Commission on Human Rights, *The Guiding Principles on Internal Displacement*, E/CN.4/1998/53/Add.2 (1998), Principle 18(2). See also W Kälin, *Guiding Principles on Internal Displacement: Annotations*, ASIL and Brookings-Bern Project on Internal Displacement, Studies in Transnational Legal Policy, No 38 (2008) 82–86.

natural disaster it is necessary to immediately provide shelter for those who have lost their homes. As highlighted by the IASC, the establishment of communal shelters (such as schools or community centres) or temporary camps (generally using tents and tarpaulins) should be a last resort when the possibility of host family arrangements, self-sustainability or rapid rehabilitation does not exist.[111] However, in recognition of the fact that rebuilding sustainable and appropriate housing for all those affected may take several years, an intermediate phase of more secure transitional shelters or semi-permanent housing is often required.[112] Nevertheless, the CESCR has stressed that:

> Adequate housing must be accessible to those entitled to it. Disadvantaged groups must be accorded full and sustainable access to adequate housing resources. Thus, such disadvantaged groups as … victims of natural disasters, people living in disaster-prone areas and other groups should be ensured some degree of priority consideration in the housing sphere.[113]

By definition, 'temporary' IDP sites are not adequate long-term housing for victims of a natural disaster. Indeed, the CESCR has stressed that the right to adequate housing means more than merely having a roof over one's head, but should be seen as 'the right to live somewhere in security, peace and dignity'.[114] Ensuring permanent sustainable housing is just as important as emergency temporary shelters. So while recognising the logistical and resource constraints faced in the context of large-scale property destruction and homelessness after a major natural disaster, ensuring that the right to adequate housing is fulfilled is fundamental to the rehabilitation of communities and individual lives.[115] Moreover, disaster risk reduction measures to identify and remedy pre-existing vulnerabilities, such as in the field of urban planning and construction, are required prior to a disaster occurring.[116]

While the right to an adequate standard of living provides a key baseline for the protection of persons, it is recognised that logistical,

[111] IASC, *Operational Guidelines*, above n 18, 32. See also R Barber, 'Protecting the Right to Housing in the Aftermath of Natural Disaster: Standards in International Human Rights Law' (2008) 20(3) *International Journal of Refugee Law* 432.

[112] Shelter Centre, *Transitional Shelter Guidelines*, inter-agency consensus publication (May 2012).

[113] CESCR, *General Comment No 4*, above n 92, para 8(e).

[114] ibid, para 7.

[115] C Gould, 'The Right to Housing Recovery After Natural Disasters' (2009) 22 *Harvard Human Rights Journal* 169, 180–81. See also Concannon and Lindstrom, 'Cheaper, Better, Longer Lasting', above n 7.

[116] C Wamsler, 'Mainstreaming Risk Reduction in Urban Planning and Housing: A Challenge for International Aid Organisations' (2006) 30(2) *Disasters* 151. See also discussion of a state's obligations to prevent or mitigate disasters in Section II.C.i below.

financial and operational constraints may limit the extent of material assistance and protection activities which can be undertaken in a humanitarian crisis. Nevertheless, states have binding legal obligations to ensure that the core subsistence rights of the basic necessities for survival are provided, either directly or via the support of other actors. Yet the provision of food and shelter is not sufficient. As memorably noted in the context of the siege of Sarajevo during the Bosnian war, material assistance without physical protection simply results in the 'well-fed dead'.[117] So we will now turn to the third core right: the right to physical security and integrity.

C. Right to Physical Security and Integrity

As far back as 697AD, more than 50 Scottish and Irish kings agreed, at the instigation of the Abbot of Iona, to a prohibition on attacking non-combatants during war through the introduction of the *Cáin Adomnáin* or Law of the Innocents. In a particularly far-sighted move, to promote compliance and accountability, the agreement also contained a series of fines for unlawful acts including wounding or slaying innocent children, clerics and women.[118] Despite the precedent that the Law of the Innocents may have set locally, unfortunately throughout history it is well recognised that civilians are often not only the unintended victims of war, but are targeted as part of a deliberate policy.[119] In addition to direct attacks against civilians, humanitarian crises present other serious challenges for the safety and security of those caught up in them.

The right to physical security and integrity therefore incorporates proactive measures to protect the right to life. Such measures can include early warning and alert systems, so that persons in danger have time to move to a safer location—this would apply equally to providing warnings of impending military action in a particular area as to warnings of foreseeable natural disasters. In addition to warnings, an effective and non-discriminatory evacuation plan should be in place, as evidenced by the UN Human Rights Committee's (HRCtee) concern at the US preparations for and response to Hurricane Katrina. In particular, the Committee noted that poor people, primarily African-Americans, were disproportionally disadvantaged by the rescue and evacuation plans for New Orleans which were based on private car ownership. The HRCtee called on the US to review its practices and policies in relation to disaster prevention and

[117] 'The Well-Fed Dead in Bosnia', Opinion, *The New York Times* (15 July 1992).

[118] Education Scotland, *Scotland's History: Law of the Innocents* www.educationscotland.gov.uk/scotlandshistory/britonsgaelsvikings/lawoftheinnocents/index.asp.

[119] H Slim and D Mancini-Griffoli, *Interpreting Violence: Anti-Civilian Thinking and Practice and How to Argue Against it More Effectively*, Centre for Humanitarian Dialogue (2007).

preparedness, emergency assistance and relief, and to bring them into line with requirements of the right to life and the prohibition of direct or indirect discrimination.[120] At a regional level, the European Court of Human Rights has ruled in a series of cases that failure to take feasible measures to prevent or mitigate the consequences of foreseeable disasters amounts to a violation of the right to life and therefore incurs the state responsibility under the ECHR.

i. Disaster Risk Reduction: The Right to Life and the European Court of Human Rights

The *Öneryildiz v Turkey*[121] case concerned a methane explosion in a municipal rubbish dump. Despite warnings from officials who investigated the dump in 1991 regarding the proximity of houses, an explosion occurred on 23 April 1993 causing refuse to erupt from the mountain of waste and engulf some 10 slum dwellings situated below. Thirty-nine people were killed. Reviewing the warning which had been received, and the limited actions taken by the municipal authorities, the Court reiterated that the right to life set out in Article 2 ECHR does not solely concern deaths resulting from the use of force by state agents but also lays down a positive obligation on states to take appropriate steps to safeguard the lives of those within their jurisdiction.[122]

This case was soon followed by *Budayeva and others v Russia*,[123] which concerned a mudslide that swept through the town of Tyrnauz in July 2000, resulting in the destruction of property and a number of deaths. Just as in the *Öneryildiz* case, warnings from officials regarding the risk of an impending disaster were ignored, including from the Mountain Institute and the District Administration. In finding a breach of Article 2, the Court ruled that not only were the applicant's substantive rights violated due to the resulting deaths, but their procedural rights under Article 2 were violated as there was a lack of an adequate judicial investigation into the disaster once it had occurred.

The Court subsequently developed its jurisprudence in two further cases. In *Kolyadenko and others v Russia*[124] the Court held that a sudden

[120] HRC' Concluding Observations on the United States' (2006) CCPR/C/USA/CO/3/Rev.1, para 26. See also Sirkin, 'Debacle of Hurricane Katrina', above n 6.

[121] *Öneryildiz v Turkey*, ECtHR, Application 48939/99, judgment of 30 November 2004.

[122] ibid, paras 18 and 72.

[123] *Budayeva and others v Russia*, ECtHR, Applications 15339/02, 21166/02, 20058/02, 11673/02 and 15343/02, judgment of 20 March 2008.

[124] *Kolyadenko and others v Russia*, ECtHR, Applications 17423/05, 20534/05, 20678/05, 23263/05, 24283/05, 35673/05, judgment of 28 February 2012.

large-scale release of water from the Pionerskoye reservoir near the city of Vladivostok which resulted in flooding of properties and risk to life (although no deaths) was a violation of Article 2 due to the lack of evacuation warnings or subsequent rescue operations. Moreover, the deliberate release of water also violated the applicants' right to respect for private and family life and the home under Article 8, and their right to protection of property in Article 1, Protocol 1.

Of note, the most recent relevant case to come before the Court was held to be inadmissible. In the case of *Hadzhiyska v Bulgaria*,[125] which concerned property damage due to flooding resulting directly from a storm (as opposed to the deliberate release of water from a reservoir), the Court stressed that:

> natural disasters, which are as such beyond human control, do not call for the same extent of State involvement as dangerous activities of a man-made nature. Accordingly, the State's positive obligations to protect property against the former do not necessarily extend as far as those in the sphere of the latter.[126]

While noting the fundamental importance of the right to life, the Court emphasised that the positive obligations under Article 2 include a duty on the state to do 'everything within the authorities' power in the sphere of disaster relief for the protection of that right'.[127] Conversely, the obligation to protect the right to property was not absolute. Moreover, the Court observed that in deciding what measures to take in order to protect private possessions from weather hazards, the authorities enjoy a wider margin of appreciation than in deciding on measures needed to protect lives.

These cases highlight the European Court's awareness and interest in the human rights implications of natural and human-made disasters. In clear and unambiguous terms, the Court has clarified that states have binding legal obligations under the ECHR to proactively undertake disaster risk reduction and response activities. These obligations are balanced by a state's margin of appreciation, particularly in natural disasters, regarding the appropriate measures to take. It should be noted, though, that none of the events in these four cases would have fallen within the definition of a 'disaster' set out in the current text of the ILC draft articles on the protection of persons in the event of disasters.[128] While there were serious local impacts, namely destruction

[125] *Hadzhiyska v Bulgaria*, ECtHR, Application 20701/09 (15 May 2012).
[126] ibid, para 15.
[127] ibid.
[128] For analysis of the ILC draft articles, see ch 8.

of property, injuries and deaths, these could not be described as 'seriously disrupting the functioning of society'. This disparity is understandable. The ILC draft articles set out the framework for international humanitarian assistance, while the Court was examining the domestic obligations of an affected state. Nevertheless, the clear limitations set out by the Court in the *Hadzhiyska* case may foreshadow a more restrictive approach that the Court could adopt in future cases.

As recognised by the UN Human Rights Council, threats to an individual's physical security and integrity in humanitarian crises do not just relate to the right to life, but encompass the right to be free from assault, rape, arbitrary detention and kidnapping.[129] Of particular concern in many refugee and IDP camp settings is the high incidence of sexual and gender-based violence, with one woman in five likely to experience sexual violence in humanitarian settings.[130] This was particularly true in Haiti following the earthquake.[131] The vast majority of IDP sites had little security or lighting available, and were desperately overcrowded. As is well recognised by humanitarian organisations, such conditions create vulnerability to sexual violence for women and children.[132] Consequently, local grassroots women's groups took direct action by submitting an application to the Inter-American Commission on Human Rights requesting precautionary measures by the Haitian Government to prevent sexual violence in the IDP sites. Ruling in their favour, the Commission called on the Haitian Government to implement a series of measures to reduce the risk of sexual violence in the aftermath of the earthquake, and stressed the state's responsibility to prevent third-party violence against women and children.[133]

Unfortunately, the range of threats to an individual's physical security and integrity in a humanitarian crisis extend well beyond those outlined here. However, this brief overview highlights that international human rights law plays a fundamental role in the protection of persons

[129] HRC, *Final research-based report of the Human Rights Council Advisory Committee on best practices and main challenges in the promotion and protection of human rights in post-disaster and post-conflict situations*, 28th Session of the HRC (10 February 2015) A/HRC/28/76, para 98.

[130] UN Women, *Humanitarian Action*, above n 85, 2. For discussion of sexual and gender-based violence in the Bhutanese refugee camps in Nepal, see ch 9, Section II.A.i.

[131] L Davis, 'Still Trembling: State Obligation Under International Law to End Post-Earthquake Rape in Haiti' (2010–2011) 65 *University of Miami Law Review* 867.

[132] See, eg, the chapter on 'Camp Coordination and Camp Management' in IASC, *Guidelines for Integrating Gender-Based Violence Interventions in Humanitarian Action: Reducing Risk, Promoting Resilience and Aiding Recovery* (2015).

[133] IACHR, *Women and girls victims of sexual violence living in 22 internally displaced persons camps*, Precautionary Measures No MC-340-10 Haiti (22 December 2010).

in humanitarian crisis, and is a core component of the *acquis humanitaire*. Therefore, the final section of this chapter will highlight additional human rights of relevance in humanitarian crises, and will draw some general conclusions regarding the role that international human rights law plays in advancing our understanding of the normative content of the *acquis humanitaire*.

III. CONCLUSION: HUMAN RIGHTS AND THE *ACQUIS HUMANITAIRE*

The three core aspects of a state's obligations discussed above are intended to provide examples of the normative content of international human rights law relevant to the protection of persons in humanitarian crises contained within the *acquis humanitaire*. An individual's right to life is threatened if they are not able to access life-saving assistance or protection, and this implies that either the state or third parties must be in a position to provide the necessary support. Likewise, the right to physically access services must be understood in conjunction with the substantive content of human rights law covering the basic necessities of survival. Moreover, even if an individual is able to access sufficient goods and services, a state must ensure their physical safety and security. The well-fed dead of Bosnia still haunt international humanitarian operations.[134] However, in addition to these core rights, a range of additional civil and political rights may be impacted by a humanitarian crisis. Such rights include, but are not limited to: the rights to religious freedom and freedom of speech; personal documentation; political participation and elections; access to courts; free movement; re-establishment of family ties; and freedom of expression and opinion.[135] While recognising the universality and indivisibility of all human rights, the IASC has noted that these types of rights 'may become more important the longer the recovery phase lasts'.[136] Meanwhile, although the basic necessities for survival are of immediate concern for those caught up in humanitarian crises, and of primary importance for the domestic and international humanitarian agencies working with those affected, other ESCR are equally important once the emergency phase of the operation is completed—for example, the rights relating to restitution or compensation for housing, land and property, as well as

[134] For a comprehensive account of the Yugoslav wars in the 1990s, see A Little and L Silber, *The Death of Yugoslavia* 2nd edn (Penguin Books, 1996).

[135] See IASC, *Operational Guidelines*, above n 18, 45–54; HRC, *Final Research-based Report*, above n 129, para 98.

[136] IASC, above n 135, 9–10.

rights to livelihoods, skills training, and higher and further education.[137] Likewise, as highlighted by the European Court of Human Rights, states are required to undertake advance warning and risk-reduction measures to minimise potential human rights violations which may occur in future humanitarian crises.

Yet Elizabeth Ferris has cautioned against the conflation of humanitarian and human rights protection. As discussed in chapter three, there are important differences between broader human rights activities and a narrower set of activities which can be classified as humanitarian. One can identify concrete provisions of international human rights law relating specifically to humanitarian assistance and protection, such as those in Article 22 CRC for refugee children and Article 11 CRPD for persons with disabilities. Academic, practitioner and judicial interpretations of other core human rights provisions also clarify state obligations towards persons in their territory in humanitarian crises. The rights to food, shelter and healthcare are clearly of direct relevance in a humanitarian crisis, as are rights to family unity, documentation, livelihoods and restitution for lost or damaged property. However, from the perspective of the normative content of the *acquis humanitaire*, two observations must be made. First, the existence or otherwise of a stand-alone general right to humanitarian assistance applicable in all types of humanitarian crisis is contested. As will be seen over the course of the following chapters, and summarised in chapter ten, there are hard law provisions at the international and regional levels relating specifically to humanitarian activities. However, whether or not these have crystallised into a general right to humanitarian assistance is not so obvious. Arguably, a more consistent application and implementation of existing international human rights law in humanitarian crises would be a more effective way to promote the protection of persons.[138] Second, it is important to stress that human rights law is not necessarily the panacea for strengthening the protection of persons in humanitarian crises. While the substantive content of international human rights law contains some specific provisions on humanitarian crises, the interplay between different branches of international law remains relevant. For example, in certain circumstances the *lex specialis* of armed conflict will be applicable, and may even provide a greater level of protection than existing human rights law. It follows that the *acquis humanitaire* is not only a human rights framework.

Nevertheless, human rights law plays a fundamental role in the protection of persons, and as argued in chapter three all humanitarian

[137] ibid, 33–44; HRC, *Final Research-based Report*, above n 129, para 98.

[138] For an analogous argument in the context of the right to development, see A Vandenbogaerde, 'The Right to Development in International Human Rights Law: A Call for its Dissolution' (2013) 31(2) *Netherlands Quarterly of Human Rights* 187.

operations should incorporate human rights principles into their operational programming. Reflecting the diversity of humanitarian actors, and approaches to humanitarian action that this entails, the legal obligations of actors will differ. A state agency, such as a Ministry for Health, may have a legal obligation to ensure that specific human rights are respected, protected and fulfilled, even in the midst of a complex emergency. Likewise, certain inter-governmental agencies have specific protection mandates for identified groups, such as refugees, children or protected groups under the law of armed conflict; while all UN and partner agencies have a general obligation to integrate human rights into their work. Conversely, NGOs lack clear-cut legal obligations as duty-bearers toward specific rights holders. Nevertheless, they should apply a rights-based approach to humanitarian action incorporating the human rights principles of empowerment, participation, non-discrimination and accountability. Such a rights-based approach prioritises the internalisation of procedural rights into the decision-making processes of all humanitarian actors, without limiting organisations from undertaking more transformative human rights advocacy and activities should they so wish. However, human rights are not the only source of obligations for the *acquis humanitaire*. Indeed, the next branch of international law we will examine, the law of armed conflict, pre-dates modern international human rights law by 85 years.

6

Law of Armed Conflict

I. INTRODUCTION

ALTHOUGH WIDELY USED to denote the body of law, policy and practice applicable during international or non-international armed conflicts, the phrase 'international humanitarian law' (IHL) obscures the complexity of the interconnected branches of law relating to the commencement and conduct of armed hostilities and the use of lethal force between and within states. Moreover, the use of the word 'humanitarian' concurrently overlooks other branches of law relating to non-conflict humanitarian crises, while implying a precedence of humanitarian considerations over military aims and objectives.[1] In reality, a symbiotic relationship between the twin objectives of military necessity and humanitarian considerations rests at the heart of the regulation of all armed conflicts.[2] As a result, the original terminology of the 'laws of war' or the contemporary phrase 'law of armed conflict' more accurately describe the entirety of the international legal provisions relating to the commencement and use of lethal force by states and non-state actors in conflict settings (that is, outwith internal civil disturbances or other legitimate uses of force by state authorities).[3] The specific provisions focusing on material assistance and the protection of civilians and those *hors de combat* in conflicts can be viewed as a sub-set of the law of armed conflict (primarily, but not exclusively, found within the so-called Geneva Law), and form a key source of law, policy and practice within the *acquis humanitaire*.[4]

[1] See Y Dinstein, *The Conduct of Hostilities under the Law of International Armed Conflict* 2nd edn (Cambridge University Press, 2010) 4–6. Since the terms 'international humanitarian law' and 'IHL' are widely used, they retain their normal meaning here unless otherwise specified.

[2] M Schmitt, 'Military Necessity and Humanity in International Humanitarian Law: Preserving the Delicate Balance' (2010) 50 *Virginia Journal of International Law* 795, 796.

[3] For discussion of violence not reaching the threshold of an internal armed conflict, see E Crawford, 'The Road to Nowhere? The Future for the Declaration on Fundamental Standards of Humanity' (2012) 3 *Journal of International Humanitarian Legal Studies* 43.

[4] Considering the voluminous writing on the law of armed conflict, it is not possible to elaborate all the specific provisions of relevance to the *acquis humanitaire* in this monograph. However, the Swiss government has provided an excellent analysis of the international

The law of armed conflict is generally split into the *jus ad bellum* (that is, the legality of the commencement of hostilities) and the *jus in bello* (that is, the conduct of hostilities). The *jus in bello* is further sub-divided into the 'Hague Law' and 'Geneva Law' covering the means and methods of warfare and the protection of civilians and non-combatants. The International Court of Justice (ICJ) has noted that the terminology of 'Hague' and 'Geneva' law masks the fluid relationship between these two aspects of the *jus in bello*, arguing that: '[t]hese two branches of the law applicable in armed conflict have become so closely interrelated that they are considered to have gradually formed one single complex system.'[5] Considering the various terminologies in use, a convenient taxonomy of the law of armed conflict is set out in Figure 6.1 below.

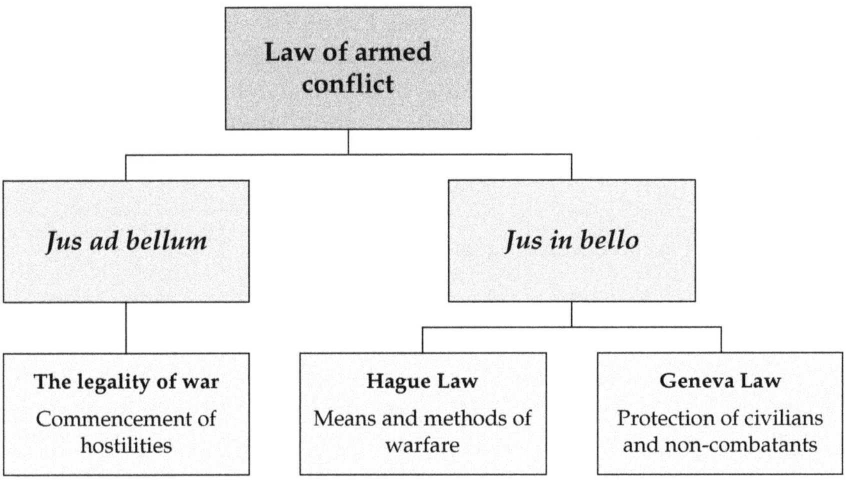

Figure 6.1: Taxonomy of the law of armed conflict

Despite the interconnected nature of these branches of the law of armed conflict, each has a set of core functions, legal instruments and objectives. States and armed groups have an understandable self-interest in ensuring that their soldiers are protected from the worst excesses of human nature and technological innovations during combat operations, and are

normative framework and practical challenges for humanitarian actors in the context of armed conflicts. See Government of Switzerland, *Humanitarian Access in Situations of Armed Conflict: Handbook on the International Normative Framework*, Version 2, December 2014; Government of Switzerland, *Humanitarian Access in Situations of Armed Conflict: Practitioners' Manual*, Version 2, December 2014.

[5] ICJ, *Legality of the Threat or Use of Nuclear Weapons*, Advisory Opinion, 1996, ICJ Reports (8 July 1996) para 75.

treated humanely should they be injured or captured. Likewise, non-combatants require fundamental guarantees that their inherent dignity will be respected and protected should they find themselves either directly targeted or caught in the cross-fire of an armed conflict. Therefore, the fundamental aim of the four Geneva Conventions concluded at the end of the Second World War was to identify and reinforce minimum levels of material assistance and protection for civilians and former combatants who were wounded, sick, shipwrecked or prisoners of war (that is, who were *hors de combat*). Of particular importance is the fact that these binding obligations apply to both state and non-state parties to a conflict. Moreover, the ICRC has a legal mandate to support and advocate on behalf of protected persons via the 1949 Geneva Conventions and subsequent Additional Protocols,[6] augmented by their operational mandate to provide material assistance and protection activities.[7] We will now examine the substantive content of the *acquis humanitaire* in armed conflicts in more detail, first by examining the *lex specialis* nature of the law of armed conflict and its customary law status, before analysing key provisions for humanitarian protection and assistance in international and non-international armed conflicts.

A. The Law of Armed Conflict as *Lex Specialis*

The primary motivation of the 1864 Geneva Convention for the Amelioration of the Condition of the Wounded in Armies in the Field,[8] and the Hague Conventions and Declarations of 1899 and 1907[9] regulating the laws of war, was the protection and reduction of suffering arising

[6] Common Art 10 GCIV states: 'The provisions of the present Convention constitute no obstacle to the humanitarian activities which the International Committee of the Red Cross or any other impartial humanitarian organisation may, subject to the consent of the Parties to the conflict concerned, undertake for the protection of civilian persons and for their relief.' The three other Geneva Conventions contain identical wording via Common Art 9, subject to the final clause reflecting the primary focus of each Convention, ie wounded and sick on land, at sea and POWs.

[7] Y Sandoz, 'The International Committee of the Red Cross as Guardian of International Humanitarian Law' ICRC, Geneva, 31 December 1998 www.icrc.org/eng/resources/documents/misc/about-the-icrc-311298.htm.

[8] Convention for the Amelioration of the Condition of the Wounded in Armies in the Field, Geneva, 22 August 1864.

[9] The first international peace conference was held in The Hague in May 1899, and resulted in three international treaties covering the peaceful settlement of disputes, the laws and customs of war, and maritime warfare, plus three Declarations on exploding bullets, poisonous gases and the first regulation of aerial bombardments. Thirteen international treaties were concluded at the second Hague Convention in October 1907 covering various aspects of the laws of war, plus a Declaration prohibiting the discharge of projectiles and explosives from balloons.

for soldiers (in modern parlance 'combatants'), rather than civilians.[10] As noted by Siobhán Wills, the weight placed on state sovereignty during the nineteenth and twentieth centuries meant that a breach of the laws of war was not treated as a violation of the individual soldier's rights per se but a breach of the obligations due to the enemy state.[11] Nevertheless, even these early international conventions did not neglect the role of civilians—as set out in Article 5 of the 1864 Geneva Convention: 'Inhabitants of the country who bring help to the wounded shall be respected and shall remain free.' This codified Henri Dunant's vision of national relief societies providing aid to the wounded on the battlefield proposed in his ground-breaking work, *A Memory of Solferino*, which had led to the establishment of the Red Cross Movement.[12] Likewise, the so-called Martens clause included in the Preamble to the Hague Conventions of 1899 and 1907 clearly established the overarching application of the 'laws of humanity and the dictates of the public conscience' as a limitation on the methods and means of warfare.[13]

While the law of armed conflict was progressively codified between 1864 and 1939, the horrific global experiences of the Second World War reinforced the need to protect not just combatants but all those caught up in the calamities of war. The four Geneva Conventions of 1949 therefore expanded the international legal protections for wounded and sick combatants on land[14] and at sea,[15] and for prisoners of war,[16] and introduced

[10] David Rieff has argued that the 1864 Geneva Convention derived from the increased lethality of weapons which meant that western (colonial) powers had a real interest in reducing the impact of wars on their own troops, rather than an explicit concern for the suffering of individuals caused by war. D Rieff, *A Bed for the Night: Humanitarianism in Crisis* (Vintage, 2002) 68–70.

[11] S Wills, 'The Legal Characterization of the Armed Conflicts in Afghanistan and Iraq: Implications for Protection' (2011) 58(2) *Netherlands International Law Review* 173, 180.

[12] H Dunant, *A Memory of Solferino*, 1862 (American Red Cross 1939, 1959) 126.

[13] See, eg, Preamble, Convention with Respect to the Laws of War on Land (Hague II), 29 July 1899. For discussion of the Martens clause, see A Cassese, 'The Martens Clause: Half a Loaf or Simply Pie in the Sky?' (2000) 11 *European Journal of International Law* 187; T Meron, 'The Martens Clause, Principles of Humanity, and Dictates of Public Conscience' (2000) 94 *American Journal of International Law* 78. Meron notes that it is 'undeniable that the principle of humanity has had a major influence on the development of international humanitarian law and that some humanitarian restraints can be regarded as its offspring', 88–89.

[14] Geneva Convention I for the Amelioration of the Condition of the Wounded and Sick in Armed Forces in the Field (adopted 12 August 1949, entered into force 21 October 1950) 75 UNTS 31 ('GCI'). Note that the ICRC issued an updated online Commentary to GCI in March 2016 https://ihl-databases.icrc.org/ihl/full/GCI-commentary.

[15] Geneva Convention II for the Amelioration of the Condition of Wounded, Sick and Shipwrecked Members of Armed Forces at Sea (adopted 12 August 1949, entered into force 21 October 1950) 75 UNTS 85 ('GCII').

[16] Geneva Convention III Relative to the Treatment of Prisoners of War (adopted 12 August 1949, entered into force 21 October 1950) 75 UNTS 135 ('GCIII').

detailed legal provisions for civilians.[17] Article 27 of Geneva Convention IV Relative to the Protection of Civilian Persons in Times of War provides an overarching obligation on parties to the conflict that civilians 'shall at all times be humanely treated, and shall be protected especially against all acts of violence or threats thereof'.[18] The international community's intention to provide all victims of war with fundamental guarantees of humane treatment is reinforced by Common Article 3 covering non-international armed conflicts, which provides that 'persons taking no active part in the hostilities … shall in all circumstances be treated humanely'.[19] Despite this increasing breadth and depth of binding obligations on states and non-state armed groups in the conduct of armed conflicts, the limitations of positive international law were subsequently acknowledged through Article 1(2) of Additional Protocol I in 1977, which contains a modern version of the Martens clause:

> In cases not covered by this Protocol or by other international agreements, civilians and combatants remain under the protection and authority of the principles of international law derived from established custom, from the principles of humanity and from the dictates of public conscience.[20]

However, while the 1949 Geneva Conventions and 1977 Additional Protocols provide the fundamental basis for the protection of civilians and non-combatants, the law of armed conflict does not stand alone.[21] As noted by the ICJ in its Advisory Opinion on the *Legality of Nuclear Weapons*, international humanitarian law represents *lex specialis* in times of armed conflict,[22] so while additional protections may arise from international human rights law, questions of a specific nature (such as defining the arbitrary

[17] Geneva Convention IV Relative to the Protection of Civilian Persons in Times of War (adopted 12 August 1949, entered into force 21 October 1950) 75 UNTS 287 ('GCIV').

[18] Art 27 GCIV.

[19] Art 3(1) common to all four Geneva Conventions 1949.

[20] Art 1(2) Protocol Additional to the Geneva Conventions of 12 August 1949, and relating to the Protection of Victims of International Armed Conflicts (adopted 8 June 1977, entered into force 7 December 1978) 1125 UNTS 3 ('API').

[21] For discussion of interconnections between the law of armed conflict and other branches of international law, see: S Jaquemet, 'The Cross-Fertilization of International Humanitarian Law and International Refugee Law' (September 2001) 83(843) *International Review of the Red Cross* 651; R Brett and E Lester, 'Refugee Law and International Humanitarian Law: Parallels, Lessons and Looking Ahead' (September 2001) 83(843) *International Review of the Red Cross* 713; H-J Heintze, 'On the Relationship between Human Rights Law Protection and International Humanitarian Law' (December 2004) 86(856) *International Review of the Red Cross* 789.

[22] Although it should be noted that following a detailed analysis of the written and oral pleadings in the Nuclear Weapons Advisory Opinion, and of pre-1996 academic commentary, Marko Milanovic has highlighted the paucity of references to the law of armed conflict as *lex specialis* before the ICJ's Advisory Opinion. See M Milanovic, 'The Lost Origins of *Lex Specialis*: Rethinking the Relationship between Human Rights and International Humanitarian Law' in JD Ohlin (ed), *Theoretical Boundaries of Armed Conflict and Human Rights* (Cambridge University Press, 2016).

deprivation of life) need first to be examined through the law of armed conflict.[23] This is of particular importance when non-state armed groups are involved. While international human rights law is often viewed as stubbornly state-centric, the law of armed conflict has long recognised that non-state armed forces face similar obligations as state armed forces to encourage reciprocity and the realistic application of the law by all parties to a conflict.[24] The International Commission of Inquiry on Darfur noted the complementary nature of international human rights law and IHL, arguing that:

> [T]hey both aim to protect human life and dignity, prohibit discrimination on various grounds, and ... to ensure basic rights including those related to health, food and housing. They both include provisions for the protection of women and vulnerable groups, such as children and displaced persons. The difference lies in that whilst human rights law protects the individual at all times, international humanitarian law is the *lex specialis* which applies only in situations of armed conflict.[25]

Likewise, mixed humanitarian responses are necessary when natural disasters occur in areas of armed conflict. Complex emergencies which include aspects of armed conflict and disaster are not uncommon, as seen in eastern Sri Lanka and in Indonesia's Aceh Province following the 2004 Indian Ocean Tsunami, or in Pakistan during the massive flooding of 2010.[26] In these situations, binding obligations from the law of armed conflict remain limited to mitigating the consequences of war, not of the natural disaster per se.[27] Indeed, the ILC draft articles on the protection of persons in the event of disasters highlight the *lex specialis* nature of the

[23] *Legality of Nuclear Weapons*, above n 5, para 25. See also ICJ, *Legal Consequences of the Construction of a Wall in the Occupied Palestinian Territory*, Advisory Opinion, 2004, ICJ Reports (9 July 2004), para 106.

[24] See, eg: T Rodenhäuser, 'Human Rights Obligations of Non-State Armed Groups in Other Situations of Violence: The Syria Example' (2012) 3(2) *Journal of International Humanitarian Legal Studies* 263; J Mahon, 'The Evolution of Non-State Military Actors from the Cold War Era to the Contemporary Age' (2014) *Irish Defence Forces Review* 89; M Sassòli, 'Taking Armed Groups Seriously: Ways to Improve their Compliance with International Humanitarian Law' (2010) 1 *Journal of International Humanitarian Legal Studies* 5.

[25] *Report of the International Commission of Inquiry on Darfur to the United Nations Secretary-General pursuant to Security Council Resolution 1564 of 18 September 2004* (Geneva, 25 January 2005), para 143.

[26] See, eg: E Ferris, 'Natural Disasters and Human Rights: Comparing Responses to Haiti and Pakistan' Presentation at Center for Human Rights and International Justice, Boston College, 3 November 2010 www.brookings.edu/research/speeches/2010/11/03-natural-disasters-human-rights-ferris; G Venturini, 'Disasters and Armed Conflict' in A de Guttry, M Gestri and G Venturini, *International Disaster Response Law* (TMC Asser Press 2012) 251.

[27] For discussion of the nexus requirement, see D Gavshon, 'The Applicability of IHL in Mixed Situations of Disaster and Conflict' (2009) 14(1) *Journal of Conflict and Security Law* 243, 248–52. For discussion of the impact of natural disasters on specific armed conflicts, see P Le Billon and A Waizenegger, 'Peace in the Wake of Disaster? Secessionist Conflicts and the 2004 Indian Ocean Tsunami' (2007) 32(3) *Transactions of the Institute of British Geographers* 411.

law of armed conflict, clearly stating: 'The present draft articles do not apply to the extent that the response to a disaster is governed by the rules of international humanitarian law.'[28] The Commentaries clarify that while the law of armed conflict takes precedence in situations where they are applicable, the complete exclusion of the draft articles' applicability in situations of co-existing armed conflicts and disasters would be detrimental to the protection of the victims of the disaster; especially when the onset of the disaster predates the armed conflict.[29] Therefore, the draft articles are intended to apply to the disaster preparation and response components of humanitarian action in situations of armed conflict to the extent that existing rules of international law, particularly the rules of IHL, do not apply. As Daniela Gavshon has noted, an entire body of law is not *lex specialis* vis-à-vis another body of law, but rather when there is a conflict between two specific rules on a particular issue, the more specialised one will take precedence.[30] For example, if a disaster occurs in an African Union country where an internal armed conflict is on-going, the more detailed provisions on humanitarian assistance in the AU Convention on Internal Displacement may take precedence over Article 18 APII.[31]

Despite extensive normative and operational guidance provided by non-binding norms, the law of armed conflict remains primarily driven by dedicated international agreements, covering issues such as the prohibition of specific types of weapons[32] and operational modalities such as the use of protected emblems by humanitarian actors.[33] The applicable law in any given conflict must therefore first be determined by the nature of the conflict, second by the status of the combatants, and finally by the binding international obligations which the relevant parties to the conflict have ratified. While the four Geneva Conventions have almost universal ratification by states around the world, 174 states have currently ratified Additional Protocol I, and 168 states have ratified Additional Protocol II.[34]

[28] Draft Art 18(2) (Relationship to other rules of international law). For the final text of the preamble, draft articles and commentaries adopted by the ILC, see Official Records of the General Assembly, Seventy-first Session, *Supplement No 10* (A/71/10), Chapter IV: Protection of Persons in the Event of Disasters (2016).

[29] ibid, 73.

[30] Gavshon, 'Applicability of IHL', above n 27, 261.

[31] Art 3(1)(c) African Union Convention for the Protection and Assistance of Internally Displaced Persons in Africa (adopted 22 October 2009, entered into force 6 December 2012).

[32] eg Convention on Cluster Munitions (adopted 30 May 2008, entered into force 1 August 2010) 2688 UNTS 39.

[33] Protocol Additional to the Geneva Conventions of 12 August 1949, and relating to the Adoption of an Additional Distinctive Emblem (adopted 8 December 2005, entered into force 14 January 2007) 2404 UNTS 261 ('APIII').

[34] Protocol II Additional to the Geneva Conventions of 12 August 1949 and relating to the Protection of Victims of Non-International Armed Conflicts (adopted 8 June 1977, entered into force 7 December 1978) 1125 UNTS 609 ('APII'). Reflecting its more recent adoption, APIII on distinctive emblems currently only has 70 state parties. See: https://treaties.un.org.

The potential challenges of identifying the applicable law were most notable during the conflicts in Iraq and Afghanistan, where the lead military power, the United States, had not ratified either Additional Protocol I or II.[35] Indeed, it was the uncertainty regarding the applicable legal framework governing specific conflicts which prompted the ICRC to identify which provisions of the law of armed conflict had passed into customary international law.

B. Customary International Law

As noted in chapter two, customary international law based on state practice and *opinio juris* is of particular importance in determining the applicable rules during armed conflicts.[36] The massive human suffering arising from large-scale internal conflicts in places such as Colombia,[37] Sri Lanka[38] and Uganda,[39] combined with the more limited express treaty provisions covering non-international armed conflicts, vividly highlights the potential lack of protection for civilians and combatants alike in conflict zones. The ICRC Customary International Humanitarian Law database, originally published in 2005, was therefore intended to plug some of the gaps in the law of armed conflict brought about by the varying levels of ratification of international conventions, and differential provisions for international and non-international armed conflicts, by identifying universally applicable rules.[40] Of note, the authors concluded that extensive state practice in line with the basic humanitarian principles set out in API reflects their broad international acceptance, irrespective of the level of ratifications.[41] Specifically in regard to non-international armed conflicts, the study concludes that customary international law rules are now more extensive than the existing treaty-based regime.[42] Such conclusions have

[35] See, eg, Wills, 'Legal Characterization', above n 11.

[36] See ch 2, Section II.B.

[37] See, eg, Human Rights Watch, *Beyond Negotiation: International Humanitarian Law and its Application to the Conduct of the FARC-EP* (August 2001) Vol 13, No 3(B).

[38] See, eg, Human Rights Watch, *War on the Displaced: Sri Lankan Army and LTTE Abuses against Civilians in the Vanni* (February 2009).

[39] See, eg, Human Rights Watch, *Uprooted and Forgotten: Impunity and Human Rights Abuses in Northern Uganda* (September 2005) Vol 17, No 12(A).

[40] JM Henckaerts and L Doswald-Beck, *Customary International Humanitarian Law: Rules and Practice* (Cambridge University Press, 2005). For background, see J-M Henckaerts, 'Customary International Humanitarian Law: Taking Stock of the ICRC Study' (2010) 78 *Nordic Journal of International Law* 435. See also T Meron, 'The Continuing Role of Custom in the Formation of International Humanitarian Law' (1996) 90 *American Journal of International Law* 238.

[41] Chatham House, *The Law of Armed Conflict: Problems and Prospects*, Transcripts and summaries of presentations and discussions, 18–19 April 2005, 5.

[42] ibid, 9.

a profound impact on the obligations of parties in all forms of armed conflict, as well as for those in need of humanitarian protection and assistance. Therefore, the ICRC CIL database is divided into two sections—the first setting out a series of 161 rules which the ICRC posits have passed into customary international law, and the second which supports the ICRC's contentions by elaborating the relevant state practice.

Of particular interest from the perspective of the *acquis humanitaire* are the rules the ICRC has identified which specifically relate to the protection of and assistance for civilians and those *hors de combat*. As an overarching foundation, which also reflects human rights principles, the ICRC has stressed that civilians and those *hors de combat* are entitled to humane treatment at all times,[43] and that discrimination on the basis of characteristics such as race, religion or sex is prohibited.[44] The ICRC then focused on specifically protected persons and objects, and identified customary international law rules obliging parties to all conflicts to respect and protect both humanitarian relief personnel and objects used for humanitarian relief operations.[45] Reflecting the extensive state practice and universal nature of the obligations to protect and assist, the ICRC identified a central customary international law rule applicable in both international and non-international armed conflicts:

> The parties to the conflict must allow and facilitate rapid and unimpeded passage of humanitarian relief for civilians in need, which is impartial in character and conducted without any adverse distinction, subject to their right of control.[46]

However, the devil is in the detail, not least a party's 'right of control'—in other words their right to control humanitarian access.[47] Rule 56 therefore provides that parties to all conflicts must ensure the freedom of movement of authorised humanitarian relief personnel for the essential exercise of their functions. Crucially, the ICRC has determined that only in case of imperative military necessity may the movement of humanitarian personnel be temporarily restricted. The ICRC likewise examined specific methods of warfare and determined that not only is the deliberate starvation of the civilian population as a method of warfare prohibited,[48]

[43] Henckaerts and Doswald-Beck, *Customary IHL*, above n 40, Rule 87.
[44] ibid, Rule 88.
[45] ibid, Rules 31 and 32. For discussion, see S Breau, 'Protected Persons and Objects' in E Wilmshurst and S Breau, *Perspectives on the ICRC Study on Customary International Humanitarian Law* (Cambridge University Press, 2007) 179–82. Breau concurs with the ICRC that the rules on humanitarian relief personnel set out in Rules 31 and 32 are customary international law, subject to the proviso regarding the consent of the party concerned.
[46] Henckaerts and Doswald-Beck, *Customary IHL*, above n 40, Rule 55.
[47] For discussion of humanitarian access, see ch 4, Section I.A.
[48] Henckaerts and Doswald-Beck, *Customary IHL*, above n 40, Rule 53.

but that attacking, destroying, removing or rendering useless objects indispensable to the survival of the civilian population is likewise contrary to customary international law.[49] The obligation not to attack or damage civilian objects therefore supplements the positive obligation to provide assistance to civilians when required.[50] As Simone Hutter has noted, the law of armed conflict imposes prohibitions on action, while international human rights law imposes positive obligations on states to respect, protect and fulfil.[51] As set out below, the ICRC CIL database elaborates a series of customary international law rules covering the treatment of civilians and humanitarian actors in international and non-international armed conflicts.

i. Particularly Relevant Rules from the ICRC CIL Database

Rule 31: Humanitarian relief personnel must be respected and protected.

Rule 32: Objects used for humanitarian relief operations must be respected and protected.

Rule 53: The use of starvation of the civilian population as a method of warfare is prohibited.

Rule 54: Attacking, destroying, removing or rendering useless objects indispensable to the survival of the civilian population is prohibited.

Rule 55: The parties to the conflict must allow and facilitate rapid and unimpeded passage of humanitarian relief for civilians in need, which is impartial in character and conducted without any adverse distinction, subject to their right of control.

Rule 56: The parties to the conflict must ensure the freedom of movement of authorised humanitarian relief personnel essential to the exercise of their functions. Only in case of imperative military necessity may their movements be temporarily restricted.

Rule 87: Civilians and persons *hors de combat* must be treated humanely.

Rule 88: Adverse distinction in the application of international humanitarian law based on race, colour, sex, language, religion or belief, political or other opinion, national or social origin, wealth, birth or other status, or on any other similar criteria is prohibited.

[49] ibid, Rule 54.

[50] For discussion of individual criminal responsibility for deliberate attacks on humanitarian personnel and equipment, see ch 7, Section II.

[51] S Hutter, *Starvation as a Weapon: Domestic Policies of Deliberate Starvation as a Means to an End under International Law* (Brill-Nijhoff, 2015) 249.

Rule 131: In case of displacement, all possible measures must be taken in order that the civilians concerned are received under satisfactory conditions of shelter, hygiene, health, safety and nutrition and that members of the same family are not separated.
Rule 135: Children affected by armed conflict are entitled to special respect and protection.
Rule 138: The elderly, disabled and infirm affected by armed conflict are entitled to special respect and protection.

The ICRC study and database (which is updated regularly) have been widely welcomed and few would argue with many of the legal obligations it advances. Notably, the ICRC found a broad correlation between the provisions for protection and assistance to civilians in both international and non-international armed conflicts.[52] Indeed, prior to its publication in 2005, Jelena Pejic, a senior ICRC legal advisor, stressed that the database was likely to show that the rules governing the provision of relief were 'practically the same in international and non-international armed conflicts'.[53] It has further been argued that a general convergence of the laws for international and non-international armed conflicts, via the greater application of customary international law rules, is currently taking place. Emily Crawford has highlighted the increasing harmonisation of the rules relating to the permissible means and methods of combat, in particular the key principles of distinction, proportionality, military necessity, and the prohibition of indiscriminate attacks or employing means of armed conflict which cause unnecessary suffering.[54] Theodore Meron has gone further, arguing that: 'as a matter of law, some important Hague rules already apply to non-international armed conflicts and that, as a matter of policy, most, perhaps all Hague rules should be applicable *mutatis mutandis*.'[55]

However, there remains a divergence regarding the treaty-based rights of civilians to humanitarian action. While there is extensive state practice in the provision of domestic and international humanitarian activities

[52] The ICRC originally proposed identical wording for the provision of protection and assistance to civilians in international and non-international armed conflicts, but this was not accepted by states at the 1977 diplomatic conference, resulting in the divergent language of Art 70 API and Art 18 APII. D Plattner, 'Assistance to the Civilian Population: The Development and Present State of International Humanitarian Law' (1992) 288 *International Review of the Red Cross* 249, 260.

[53] Quoted in 'Humanitarian Assistance in Armed Conflict Conference of the Luxemburg Group, 24–25 May 2004, Graduate Institute of International Studies, Geneva' (2004) 86(856) *International Review of the Red Cross* 879, 900.

[54] E Crawford, 'Blurring the Lines between International and Non-International Armed Conflicts—The Evolution of Customary International Law Applicable in Internal Armed Conflicts' (2008) 15 *Australian International Law Journal* 29.

[55] Meron, 'Continuing Role of Custom', above n 40, 242–43.

for internal armed conflicts (as evidenced by the fact that in 2014 nearly US$3.5 billion was provided to assist persons affected by the Syrian conflict in Syria, Jordan and Lebanon, representing 12.5 per cent of total global humanitarian funding)[56] there has been conflicting *opinio juris* on this point. For example, Joakim Dungel has specifically challenged the ICRC's interpretation of the customary law status of Article 18 APII regarding the right of humanitarian agencies to provide services in internal armed conflicts, rather than simply a customary law right to offer their services.[57]

Moreover, despite its evident authority, the ICRC's analysis of customary international law is not necessarily definitive of actual state practice or *opinio juris*.[58] As highlighted by Daniel Bethlehem in his critique of the ICRC study, states which object to particular treaty-based rules are just as likely to object to those rules if they are reformulated in the language of customary international law.[59] It therefore remains to be seen which of the customary international law rules relating to humanitarian relief operations are accepted as *lex lata* by international judicial bodies such as the ICJ or ICC.[60] Nonetheless, the ICRC database provides a key source for identifying the rights and obligations of states, combatants and those affected by armed conflicts. However, considering the treaty-based nature of the law of armed conflict, the following two sections will examine some of the key provisions set out in the 1949 Geneva Conventions and 1977 Additional Protocols regarding humanitarian action. It should be noted that international law, policy and practice regarding assistance and protection for former combatants (that is combatants who are *hors de combat* as a result of injury, sickness, shipwreck or prisoner of war status) and civilian internees can also be included within the *acquis humanitaire*. For example, Article 72 GCIII on prisoners of war includes the right of individual relief shipments (traditionally known as 'Red Cross parcels'), and Article 73 provides for collective relief measures for POWs. However, for the context of this monograph, I will focus specifically on the provisions in the law of armed conflict covering the civilian population.

[56] Development Initiatives, *Global Humanitarian Assistance Report 2016*, 54.

[57] J Dungel, 'A Right to Humanitarian Assistance in Internal Armed Conflicts Respecting Sovereignty, Neutrality and Legitimacy: Practical Proposals to Practical Problems' (May 2004) *Journal of Humanitarian Assistance*.

[58] François Bugnion noted that the study 'reflects the authors' view of the present state of customary international humanitarian law, and not what they would like or what the ICRC would like this law to be; in other words, the authors refrained from wishful thinking and the ICRC respected the academic freedom of the authors and experts.' See Chatham House, *Law of Armed Conflict*, above n 41, 3.

[59] D Bethlehem, 'The Methodological Framework of the Study' in Wilmshurst and Breau, *Perspectives on ICRC Study*, above n 45, 7.

[60] For a classic study, see T Meron, 'The Geneva Conventions as Customary Law' (1987) 81 *American Journal of International Law* 348.

II. INTERNATIONAL ARMED CONFLICTS

A. Geneva Convention IV Relative to the Protection of Civilians (1949)

Geneva Convention IV Relative to the Protection of Civilian Persons in Times of War and Additional Protocols I and II provide the only universal treaty provisions in any branch of international law explicitly recognising a right to receive humanitarian assistance for civilians, albeit the enumerated rights are limited in scope.[61] Under Part II GCIV, civilian populations are entitled to a minimum level of protection against some of the consequences of war, and crucially these provisions cover all persons in a conflict zone, without adverse distinction, inter alia, based on race, nationality, religion or political opinion.[62] Key protections exist for hospitals and 'neutral zones',[63] while particularly vulnerable groups including the sick, wounded, children and the elderly should receive explicit protection and be afforded privileged treatment.[64] The majority of protections within GCIV relate to the conduct of hostilities by parties to the conflict, for example the requirement not to attack civilian hospitals or medical personnel unless they are committing acts harmful to the enemy.[65] However, express provisions, in particular Articles 23 and 24, detail the type of assistance that civilians are entitled to, and the methods by which this assistance should be provided.

> ***Article 23—Consignments of medical supplies, food and clothing***
>
> Each High Contracting Party shall allow the free passage of all consignments of medical and hospital stores and objects necessary for religious worship intended only for civilians of another High Contracting Party, even if the latter is its adversary. It shall likewise permit the free passage of all consignments of essential foodstuffs, clothing and tonics intended for children under fifteen, expectant mothers and maternity cases.

[61] See: P MacAlister-Smith, *International Humanitarian Assistance: Disaster Relief Actions in International Law and Organization* (Martinus Nijhoff, 1985) 28–34; K Mackintosh, *The Principles of Humanitarian Action in International Humanitarian Law*, Humanitarian Policy Group Report 5, Overseas Development Institute, March 2000 (Study 4 in *The Politics of Principle: The Principles of Humanitarian Action in Practice*); Y Dinstein, 'The Right to Humanitarian Assistance' (Autumn 2000) *Naval War College Review* 77; R Stoffels, 'Legal Regulation of Humanitarian Assistance in Armed Conflict: Achievements and Gaps' (September 2004) 86(855) *International Review of the Red Cross* 515.

[62] Part II (General Protection of Populations Against Certain Consequences of War), Arts 13–26 GCIV. For ICRC commentary, see J Pictet (ed), *Commentary: Fourth Geneva Convention relative to the Protection of Civilian Persons in Time of War* (1958) 118–98.

[63] Arts 14 and 15 GCIV.

[64] Arts 16 and 24 GCIV.

[65] Arts 18–20 GCIV.

> The obligation of a High Contracting Party to allow the free passage of the consignments indicated in the preceding paragraph is subject to the condition that this Party is satisfied that there are no serious reasons for fearing:
>
> (a) that the consignments may be diverted from their destination,
> (b) that the control may not be effective, or
> (c) that a definite advantage may accrue to the military efforts or economy of the enemy through the substitution of the abovementioned consignments for goods which would otherwise be provided or produced by the enemy or through the release of such material, services or facilities as would otherwise be required for the production of such goods.
>
> The Power which allows the passage of the consignments indicated in the first paragraph of this Article may make such permission conditional on the distribution to the persons benefited thereby being made under the local supervision of the Protecting Powers.
>
> Such consignments shall be forwarded as rapidly as possible, and the Power which permits their free passage shall have the right to prescribe the technical arrangements under which such passage is allowed.

In terms of ensuring the protection of civilians through the provision of relief supplies, Article 23 confirms that the entire population in a conflict zone is entitled to receive medical supplies and objects necessary for religious worship. Reflecting the language of the time of its adoption, the provision of essential foodstuffs, clothing and tonics is limited to particularly vulnerable groups such as children under 15, expectant mothers and maternity cases.[66] A deliberate distinction was made in Article 23 between different types of goods, based on military considerations. In reviewing the *travaux préparatoires* to the Geneva Conventions, Jean Pictet highlighted that contracting states were keen to ensure a distinction between goods which might reinforce the war economy, and strictly 'humanitarian' goods such as medical supplies and objects necessary for religious worship. Pictet notes: 'The intention is to keep a strict check on the destination of provisions which might reinforce the economic potential of the enemy if used for other purposes.'[67]

Furthermore, Article 23 explicitly states that parties to the conflict are only required to ensure free passage of consignments if they are satisfied the supplies will not be diverted, used for military or economic advantage, and that humanitarian agencies retain effective control over the supplies. This means that combatants are able to refuse access to humanitarian actors

[66] Y Dinstein, 'Siege Warfare and the Starvation of Civilians' in A Delissen and G Tanja (eds), *Humanitarian Law of Armed Conflict: Challenges Ahead*, Essays in Honour of Frits Kalshoven (Martinus Nijhoff, 1991) 148.

[67] Pictet, *Commentary: GCIV*, above n 62, 180.

if they have evidence that the supplies will not be used for the intended purposes, or if the humanitarian agency itself is unable to ensure delivery to the intended beneficiaries. As noted in chapter four, debate has raged between academics, practitioners, the military, diplomats and politicians regarding the legality and utility of forcefully providing humanitarian assistance against the wishes of parties to a conflict.[68] Despite, or perhaps because of, the specific wording of Article 23, balancing the need to respect state sovereignty with humanitarian considerations remains a challenge for both international law and diplomacy.[69] However, Article 23 does not sit in isolation. GCIV also contains specific provisions for the protection of children, set out in Article 24.

> ***Article 24—Measures relating to child welfare***
>
> The Parties to the conflict shall take the necessary measures to ensure that children under fifteen, who are orphaned or are separated from their families as a result of the war, are not left to their own resources, and that their maintenance, the exercise of their religion and their education are facilitated in all circumstances. Their education shall, as far as possible, be entrusted to persons of a similar cultural tradition.
>
> The Parties to the conflict shall facilitate the reception of such children in a neutral country for the duration of the conflict with the consent of the Protecting Power, if any, and under due safeguards for the observance of the principles stated in the first paragraph.
>
> They shall, furthermore, endeavour to arrange for all children under twelve to be identified by the wearing of identity discs, or by some other means.

The provisions for children in GCIV were particularly far-sighted. By highlighting the need to ensure the ability for children to exercise their religion and right to education in all circumstances, GCIV moved beyond the strict provision of material assistance to the broader protection activities required in a conflict zone. The importance placed on identification of children in Article 24, particularly those orphaned or separated from their families, remains a key concern for humanitarian agencies in current conflicts. In March 2016, UNICEF reported that during the course of five years of conflict, 15,525 unaccompanied or separated children had crossed Syria's borders into neighbouring countries. Additionally, a staggering 306,000 Syrian children had been born as refugees over the same period.[70]

Reflecting the potential vulnerability of children in armed conflicts, Article 38(4) of the Convention on the Rights of the Child reaffirms that 'in

[68] See ch 4, Section I.B.

[69] Dungel, 'Right to Humanitarian Assistance', above n 57.

[70] UNICEF, *No Place for Children: The Impact of Five Years of War on Syrian's Children and their Childhoods* (March 2016) 5.

accordance with their obligations under international humanitarian law to protect the civilian population in armed conflicts, State Parties shall take all feasible measures to ensure protection and care of children who are affected by an armed conflict'.[71] Likewise, at a regional level Article 22(3) of the African Union Charter on the Rights and Welfare of the Child provides that state parties shall 'take all feasible measures to ensure the protection and care of children who are affected by armed conflicts'.[72] Of note, this provision applies equally to children in 'situations of internal armed conflicts, tension and strife'.[73]

B. Additional Protocol I (1977)

Protection for civilians during international armed conflicts was enhanced with the conclusion of Additional Protocol I in 1977—in particular by expanding the concept of relief activities beyond areas considered as occupied territories and by including a range of measures to ensure respect and protection for civilian civil defence organisations and their personnel.[74] David Marcus has argued that until the adoption of the Additional Protocols, Article 23 GCIV simply provided a moral obligation and not a blanket prohibition against the starvation of civilians, either as a deliberate military tactic or as an unintended consequence of the conflict arising from a lack of the basic necessities of life.[75]

> ***Article 54—Protection of objects indispensable to the survival of the civilian population***
>
> 1. Starvation of civilians as a method of warfare is prohibited.
> 2. It is prohibited to attack, destroy, remove or render useless objects indispensable to the survival of the civilian population, such as foodstuffs, agricultural areas for the production of foodstuffs, crops, livestock, drinking water installations and supplies and irrigation works, for the specific purpose of denying them for their sustenance value to the civilian population or to the adverse Party, whatever the motive, whether in order to starve out civilians, to cause them to move away, or for any other motive.

[71] Art 38(4) Convention on the Rights of the Child (adopted 20 November 1989, entered into force 2 September 1990) 1577 UNTS 3.

[72] Art 22(3) OAU, African Charter on the Rights and Welfare of the Child (adopted 11 July 1990, entered into force 29 November 1999) CAB/LEG/24.9/49.

[73] ibid.

[74] Part IV (Civilian Population), Section I, Chapter VI: Civil Defence (Arts 61–67).

[75] D Marcus, 'Famine Crimes in International Law' (April 2003) 97(2) *American Journal of International Law* 245, 266–68.

3. The prohibitions in paragraph 2 shall not apply to such of the objects covered by it as are used by an adverse Party:
   (a) As sustenance solely for the members of its armed forces; or
   (b) If not as sustenance, then in direct support of military action, provided, however, that in no event shall actions against these objects be taken which may be expected to leave the civilian population with such inadequate food or water as to cause its starvation or force its movement.

Article 54 API now explicitly prohibits the deliberate starvation of the civilian population during international armed conflicts, and an arbitrary refusal of access to impartial humanitarian agencies may therefore fall foul of this provision. Moreover, Article 8(2)(b)(xxv) of the Rome Statute of the International Criminal Court (ICC) prohibits actions aimed at 'intentionally using starvation of civilians as a method of warfare by depriving them of objects indispensable to their survival, *including wilfully impeding relief supplies* as provided for under the Geneva Conventions' during international armed conflicts.[76] Any deliberate withholding of food or other indispensable objects therefore is a war crime bearing individual criminal responsibility. The ICRC Commentaries to Article 54 note that starvation of civilians could also amount to genocide if undertaken with intent to destroy, in whole or in part, a national, ethnic, racial or religious group as per the Genocide Convention.[77] From the perspective of the law of armed conflict, as opposed to international criminal law, API extends the range of materials Parties must provide to include clothing, bedding, shelter and other supplies necessary for the survival of civilians, plus objects necessary for religious worship, as well as establishing key protections for relief personnel engaged in the distribution of assistance to civilians.[78]

Article 70—Relief actions

1. If the civilian population of any territory under the control of a Party to the conflict, other than occupied territory, is not adequately provided with the supplies mentioned in Article 69, relief actions which are humanitarian and impartial in character and conducted without any adverse distinction shall be undertaken, subject to the agreement of the Parties concerned in such relief actions. Offers of such relief shall not be regarded as interference in the armed conflict or as unfriendly acts. In the distribution of relief

[76] Art 8(2)(b)(xxv) Rome Statute of the International Criminal Court (adopted 17 July 1998, entered into force 1 July 2002) 2187 UNTS [emphasis added].

[77] Y Sandoz, C Swinarski and B Zimmermann (eds), *Commentary on the Additional Protocols of 8 June 1977 to the Geneva Conventions of 12 August 1949* (Martinus Nijhoff, 1987) 654. For discussion of international criminal responsibility for the use of starvation as a means of warfare, see ch 7, Section II.C.

[78] Part IV (Civilian Population), Section II: Relief in Favour of the Civilian Population (Arts 68–71), API.

consignments, priority shall be given to those persons, such as children, expectant mothers, maternity cases and nursing mothers, who, under the Fourth Convention or under this Protocol, are to be accorded privileged treatment or special protection.

2. The Parties to the conflict and each High Contracting Party shall allow and facilitate rapid and unimpeded passage of all relief consignments, equipment and personnel provided in accordance with this Section, even if such assistance is destined for the civilian population of the adverse Party.
3. The Parties to the conflict and each High Contracting Party which allow the passage of relief consignments, equipment and personnel in accordance with paragraph 2:
   (a) Shall have the right to prescribe the technical arrangements, including search, under which such passage is permitted;
   (b) May make such permission conditional on the distribution of this assistance being made under the local supervision of a Protecting Power;
   (c) Shall, in no way whatsoever, divert relief consignments from the purpose for which they are intended nor delay their forwarding, except in cases of urgent necessity in the interest of the civilian population concerned.
4. The Parties to the conflict shall protect relief consignments and facilitate their rapid distribution.
5. The Parties to the conflict and each High Contracting Party concerned shall encourage and facilitate effective international co-ordination of the relief actions referred to in paragraph 1.

As the primary operative article on relief operations, the non-discretionary language of Article 70(1) is of particular importance: 'relief actions … *shall* be undertaken'.[79] However, despite the mandatory language, Article 70(1) also introduces specific limitations on the delivery of relief: first and foremost that humanitarian assistance must be 'subject to the agreement of the Parties concerned'. The ICRC Commentary states that any refusals must be exceptional, and notes that the clause requiring the agreement of the Parties concerned was added during the Diplomatic Conference to protect the national sovereignty of the state receiving the relief. Nevertheless this reservation does not imply that the Parties concerned have 'absolute and unlimited freedom to refuse their agreement to relief actions. A Party refusing its agreement must do so for valid reasons, not for arbitrary or capricious ones.'[80] Moreover, Denise Plattner from the ICRC Legal Division has argued that humanitarian relief provided by a third state without the consent of the affected state, following their persistent and arbitrary refusal of access, should not be classified as interference

[79] Art 70 API [emphasis added].
[80] Sandoz et al, *Commentary*, above n 77, 819–20.

in the domestic affairs of the affected state and could even amount to a legitimate counter-measure under general international law.[81]

Reflecting the overarching military considerations influencing the Geneva Conventions, Contracting Parties retain the right of control via Article 70(3).[82] This includes the right to prescribe technical arrangements, including search procedures, under which the passage of humanitarian supplies are permitted as a means of ensuring that such supplies do not fall into the hands of the enemy. Parties to a conflict can also make humanitarian access conditional on the distribution taking place under the local supervision of a Protecting Power.[83] However, reflecting the balancing of military necessity with humanitarian considerations, Article 70(3)(c) provides that the parties to the conflict shall not divert or delay relief consignments from the purpose for which they are intended, although diversion is allowed in cases of urgent necessity if, and only if, this is in the interest of the civilian population concerned. The final provisions of Article 70(3) require parties to the conflict to protect relief supplies and to encourage and facilitate international co-operation for humanitarian relief.

i. Maritime Blockades: The Gaza Freedom Flotilla

The Israeli Navy's interception of six boats carrying humanitarian supplies, the 'Gaza Freedom Flotilla', in May 2010 highlights the potential tensions between non-governmental groups wishing to provide humanitarian assistance and the rights of states to prescribe the arrangements for its distribution. The Gaza Freedom Flotilla was attempting to break the Israeli naval blockade of Gaza by sailing directly into the territorial waters off Gaza without the consent of the Israeli authorities.[84] The Israeli military boarded the vessels and met with resistance aboard the lead ship, the MV Mavi Marmara, which resulted in the deaths of nine Turkish civilian activists and injuries to dozens of others including Israeli soldiers. The incident led to strained relations between Turkey

[81] D Plattner, 'ICRC Neutrality and Neutrality in Humanitarian Assistance' (March–April 1996) 311 *International Review of the Red Cross* 161, 176.

[82] Art 70(3) API.

[83] As the Protecting Powers system envisaged in the 1949 Geneva Conventions has never formally been adopted, parties to a conflict may argue that distribution of assistance should take place subject to their own supervision, although impartial humanitarian organisations such as the ICRC have a strong claim to act via Common Article 10/10/10/11, which states: 'The High Contracting Parties may at all times agree to entrust to an organisation which offers all guarantees of impartiality and efficacy the duties incumbent on the Protecting Powers by virtue of the present Convention.'

[84] For analysis of the events surrounding the Gaza Freedom Flotilla, see UN Human Rights Council, *Report of the international fact-finding mission to investigate violations of international law, including international humanitarian and human rights law, resulting from the Israeli attacks on the flotilla of ships carrying humanitarian assistance* (27 September 2010) A/HRC/15/21.

and Israel, including the withdrawal of diplomatic representatives, which were only resolved in March 2013 following the intervention of US President Barack Obama.[85]

A series of reports into the incident were conducted by the Turkish and Israeli governments and by the UN. The UN Human Rights Council expert report into the events found that 'at no stage was a request made by the Israeli Navy for the cargo to be inspected'.[86] While the HRC report did not expressly examine the provisions of Article 23 GCIV or Article 70 API, the experts did conclude that potential grave breaches of the Geneva Conventions occurred as a result of the loss of life and disproportionate use of force by the Israeli military.[87]

While there are serious questions regarding the manner in which the Israeli military conducted the operation, and also evidence that a small group of the passengers were willing to use force, the strict wording of Article 70(3) API does provide states with the right to inspect cargoes and proscribe technical arrangements for their distribution.[88] As a result, one of the recommendations made by the UN Secretary-General's Panel of Inquiry, headed by the former New Zealand Prime Minister Geoffrey Palmer, was that while 'States maintaining a naval blockade must abide by their obligations with respect to the provision of humanitarian assistance', conversely 'humanitarian vessels should allow inspection and stop or change course when requested'.[89]

The Gaza Freedom Flotilla also highlights the need to ensure the neutral and impartial nature of humanitarian action. Denise Plattner has noted that the neutrality of humanitarian operations exists as a legal concept via the wording of Articles 70(1) API and 18(2) APII, which stress the humanitarian and impartial character of relief operations.[90] As noted in the HRC report: 'A distinction must be made between activities taken to alleviate crises and action to address the causes creating the crisis. The latter action is characterized as political action and therefore inappropriate for groups that wish to be classified as humanitarian.'[91] Such a comment reflects the need to clearly distinguish between human rights and humanitarian protection discussed in chapter three.[92]

85 'Q&A: Israeli Deadly Raid on Aid Flotilla', *BBC News Online* (22 March 2013) www.bbc.com/news/10203726.

86 UNHRC, *Report of fact-finding mission*, above n 84, para 109.

87 ibid, para 182.

88 Israel has not signed or ratified either API or II. For general discussion of maritime blockades, see Dinstein, 'Right to Humanitarian Assistance', above n 61, 81–83.

89 G Palmer et al, *Report of the Secretary-General's Panel of Inquiry on the 31 May 2010 Flotilla Incident* (September 2011) 6.

90 Plattner, 'Neutrality in Humanitarian Assistance', above n 81, 173.

91 UNHRC, *Report of fact-finding mission*, above n 84, para 277.

92 See ch 3, Section I.A.iii.

Article 71—Personnel participating in relief actions

1. Where necessary, relief personnel may form part of the assistance provided in any relief action, in particular for the transportation and distribution of relief consignments; the participation of such personnel shall be subject to the approval of the Party in whose territory they will carry out their duties.
2. Such personnel shall be respected and protected.
3. Each Party in receipt of relief consignments shall, to the fullest extent practicable, assist the relief personnel referred to in paragraph 1 in carrying out their relief mission. Only in case of imperative military necessity may the activities of the relief personnel be limited or their movements temporarily restricted.
4. Under no circumstances may relief personnel exceed the terms of their mission under this Protocol. In particular they shall take account of the security requirements of the Party in whose territory they are carrying out their duties. The mission of any of the personnel who do not respect these conditions may be terminated.

Notwithstanding the provisions regulating the delivery of humanitarian assistance to civilians, Article 71 API places mutual obligations on Contracting Parties in receipt of relief consignments to assist relief personnel to the greatest extent practicable and to respect and protect such personnel in the discharge of their functions. Relief personnel meanwhile are required not to exceed the terms of their mission, in particular by taking into account the security requirements of the state in whose territory they are carrying out their duties.[93] Additional protection for certain categories of humanitarian workers was created via the 1994 Convention on the Safety of United Nations and Associated Personnel and its 2005 Optional Protocol; however, their limited ratification by states restricts the protection afforded.[94] Nevertheless, the recognition in the ICC Rome Statute that a deliberate attack against humanitarian personnel amounts to a war crime has provided an alternative legal accountability mechanism for humanitarian workers.[95]

C. Specific Provisions for Occupying Powers

Geneva Convention IV and Additional Protocol I also place obligations on Contracting Parties which control territory as an Occupying Power by

[93] Art 71 API.

[94] UN Convention on the Safety of United Nations and Associated Personnel (adopted 9 December 1994, entered into force 15 January 1999) 2051 UNTS 363, currently 93 state parties; UN, Optional Protocol to the Convention on the Safety of United Nations and Associated Personnel (adopted 8 December 2005, entered into force 19 August 2010) A/60/518, currently 30 state parties.

[95] For further discussion of the protection of humanitarian personnel, see ch 7, Section II.A.

setting out the basic necessities for sustaining life that must be provided for the local civilian population.[96] In particular, Article 49 GCIV confers rights to accommodation, hygiene, health, safety and nutrition during transfers or evacuations of civilians by an Occupying Power, while Article 50 covers the situation of children, particularly unidentified, orphaned or separated children. The provision of material assistance for civilians is set out in Articles 55 and 56, which confer rights to food and medical supplies; Article 58 ensures access to ministers of religion and religious books and articles. Finally, Articles 59–63 provide for the establishment of relief schemes, consignments and relief deliveries for civilian populations, and access for humanitarian agencies.

Article 55 (GCIV)—Food and medical supplies for the population

> To the fullest extent of the means available to it, the Occupying Power has the duty of ensuring the food and medical supplies of the population; it should, in particular, bring in the necessary foodstuffs, medical stores and other articles if the resources of the occupied territory are inadequate.
>
> The Occupying Power may not requisition foodstuffs, articles or medical supplies available in the occupied territory, except for use by the occupation forces and administration personnel, and then only if the requirements of the civilian population have been taken into account. Subject to the provisions of other international Conventions, the Occupying Power shall make arrangements to ensure that fair value is paid for any requisitioned goods.
>
> The Protecting Power shall, at any time, be at liberty to verify the state of the food and medical supplies in occupied territories, except where temporary restrictions are made necessary by imperative military requirements.

While formal declarations of occupation may be rare, these provisions were particularly relevant during the Iraq and Afghanistan conflicts (2004–2014), where the US-led multinational forces were acknowledged as occupying powers. As highlighted by Siobhán Wills, the Afghan and Iraqi conflicts started as situations of occupation as a result of an international armed conflict when the multinational forces invaded both countries, and therefore GCIV and API were applicable to the extent that the Parties to the conflict had ratified both texts.[97] However, the establishment of national governments who invited the allied forces to remain to support the on-going fight against 'militants' such as the Taliban and Al-Qaeda meant one could arguably only classify these conflicts as 'occupation' for a short period of time. Once the conflict was classified as a non-international

[96] For detailed discussion of the law of occupation, see Y Dinstein, *The International Law of Belligerent Occupation* (Cambridge University Press, 2009); and the special edition of the *International Review of the Red Cross* on occupation, Vol 94, No 885, Spring 2012.

[97] Wills, 'Legal Characterization', above n 11, 192–206.

conflict, only the provisions of Common Article 3 and APII (for those states which had ratified APII, which did not include the US) were applicable. Therefore, despite the on-going nature of the conflict and presence of international forces, the civilian populations and those *hors de combat* in Afghanistan and Iraq had very limited treaty-based rights to material assistance and protection. The importance of recognising customary international law provisions therefore took on a particular relevance, as well as states' overarching human rights obligations.[98]

> ***Article 59 (GCIV)—Collective relief***
>
> If the whole or part of the population of an occupied territory is inadequately supplied, the Occupying Power shall agree to relief schemes on behalf of the said population, and shall facilitate them by all the means at its disposal.
>
> Such schemes, which may be undertaken either by States or by impartial humanitarian organisations such as the International Committee of the Red Cross, shall consist, in particular, of the provision of consignments of foodstuffs, medical supplies and clothing.
>
> All Contracting Parties shall permit the free passage of these consignments and shall guarantee their protection.
>
> A Power granting free passage to consignments on their way to territory occupied by an adverse Party to the conflict shall, however, have the right to search the consignments, to regulate their passage according to prescribed times and routes, and to be reasonably satisfied through the Protecting Power that these consignments are to be used for the relief of the needy population and are not to be used for the benefit of the Occupying Power.

Besides the provisions on food, health, safety and spiritual assistance, GCIV recognises that an Occupying Power must undertake such activities to the 'fullest extent of the means available to it' (Articles 55 and 56) or 'by all the means at its disposal' (Article 59). If it is unable to provide sufficient support for the civilian population, Article 59 specifically requires an Occupying Power to facilitate relief schemes and consignments by other states or by impartial non-military humanitarian organisations, such as the ICRC.[99] Articles 59–63 continue by establishing explicit rules for the operation of such relief schemes, including a ban on the diversion of relief supplies from their intended recipients, a requirement to allow free passage to relief goods, to exempt relief consignments from all charges, taxes

[98] See, eg, A Müller, 'States' Obligations to Mitigate the Direct and Indirect Health Consequences of Non-international Armed Conflicts: Complementarity of IHL and the Right to Health' (2013) 95(889) *International Review of the Red Cross* 129.

[99] For discussion of ICRC's role in providing humanitarian assistance in armed conflicts, see D Forsythe, 'The International Committee of the Red Cross and Humanitarian Assistance—A Policy Analysis' (October 1996) 36(314) *International Review of the Red Cross* 512.

and customs duties unless necessary for the economy of the occupied territory, and a requirement to permit individual relief consignments subject to security checks on packages received. Article 63, in particular, recognises the status of non-military humanitarian organisations, such as national Red Cross and Red Crescent Societies, and provides that humanitarian organisations should be entitled to undertake humanitarian activities, subject only to temporary and exceptional measures imposed for urgent reasons of security. As can be seen, the specific obligations of state parties to provide the basic necessities of life are considerably more detailed in situations of occupation (that is the military occupation of a territory by a third state), than for non-occupied territories. This division between occupied and non-occupied territories was reinforced by Article 69 API in 1977, which extended the types of material assistance which should be provided in occupied territories, and reiterated that the relevant provisions in GCIV and API 'shall be implemented without delay'.

Article 69 (API)—Basic needs in occupied territories

1. In addition to the duties specified in Article 55 of the Fourth Convention concerning food and medical supplies, the Occupying Power shall, to the fullest extent of the means available to it and without any adverse distinction, also ensure the provision of clothing, bedding, means of shelter, other supplies essential to the survival of the civilian population of the occupied territory and objects necessary for religious worship.
2. Relief actions for the benefit of the civilian population of occupied territories ... shall be implemented without delay.

Moreover, fundamental guarantees of humane treatment apply to all civilians and non-combatants during situations of occupation. Authoritative guidance was provided by the ICJ in the contentious case between the Democratic Republic of Congo (DRC) and Uganda in 2005.[100] The DRC argued that despite the express invitation to Ugandan troops to occupy parts of eastern DRC in late 1997, following the overthrow of Mobutu Sese Seko in May 1998 the Ugandan troops engaged in massive human rights violations and grave breaches of IHL.[101] Of particular relevance were the ICJ's findings in regard to breaches of the principles of humane treatment of civilians and non-combatants by an occupying power. The ICJ ruled that there was credible evidence that Ugandan troops had committed, inter alia, acts of killing, torture, destruction of villages, training of child soldiers, and failed to take measures to ensure respect for human rights and

[100] ICJ, *Armed Activities on the Territory of the Congo (Democratic Republic of the Congo v Uganda)*, Judgment of 19 December 2005.

[101] See L Moffett, 'Accountability for Forced Displacement in Democratic Republic of Congo and Uganda before the International Criminal Court' (2015) 1(2) *African Journal of International Criminal Justice* 129.

IHL in Ituri Province.[102] In particular, the ICJ ruled that Uganda breached the requirement of humane treatment and protection of civilians and non-combatants set out in Article 27 GCIV and Article 75 API,[103] although the Court specifically noted that the actions of 'various parties in the complex conflict in the DRC have contributed to the immense suffering faced by the Congolese population'.[104]

i. Iraq: State-building and the Law of Occupation

The US-led invasion of Iraq in March 2003 was premised on the authoritarian nature of Saddam Hussein's regime and his acquisition and potential use of weapons of mass destruction.[105] Irrespective of the debateable legality of the use of force against Iraq, the successful completion of the coalition's military objectives with the overthrow of Saddam Hussein on 10 April 2003 resulted in the US and UK taking on the responsibilities of occupying powers under the law of armed conflict, as they explicitly acknowledged in UNSC Resolution 1483.[106]

The law of occupation has a long legal history, dating back to the original 1899 and 1907 Hague Conventions, which placed specific obligations on states that militarily conquer the territory of another state. In particular, Article 43 of the Hague Conventions provides that: 'The authority of the legitimate power having in fact passed into the hands of the occupant, the latter shall take all the measures in his power to restore, and ensure, as far as possible, public order and safety, while respecting, unless absolutely prevented, the laws in force in the country.'[107] Based on this provision, alongside Article 64 GCIV, the traditional understanding of occupation is that the occupying power acts as a mere trustee and therefore does not assume the legislative competence of the former regime.[108] From this 'conservationist' perspective, the role of the

[102] *Armed Activities*, above n 100, 'Violations of International Human Rights Law and International Humanitarian Law: Findings of the Court', paras 205–21.

[103] ibid, para 219.

[104] ibid, para 221.

[105] The legality of the decision to invade Iraq has been subject to extensive public, media and academic debate. For two contrasting opinions, see J Yoo, 'International Law and the War in Iraq' (2003) 97(3) *American Journal of International Law* 563; S Murphy, 'Assessing the Legality of Invading Iraq' (2003–2004) 92 *Georgetown Law Journal* 173.

[106] UNSC, *Resolution 1483 (2003) on the situation between Iraq and Kuwait* (22 May 2003) S/RES/1483.

[107] See M Sassòli, 'Article 43 of the Hague Regulations and Peace Operations in the Twenty-first Century' (2004) International Humanitarian Law Research Initiative, Background Paper prepared for Informal High-Level Expert Meeting on Current Challenges to International Humanitarian Law, Cambridge, 25–27 June 2004.

[108] G Fox, 'Transformative Occupation and the Unilateralist Impulse' (Spring 2012) 94(885) *International Review of the Red Cross* 237, 238.

occupying force is simply to undertake 'humanitarian objectives that essentially preserve the status quo'.[109] Such an understanding can be contrasted with the concept of 'transformative occupation' whereby the occupying power's stated purpose is to 'change states that have failed, or have been under tyrannical rule'.[110]

In the first few weeks of the Iraqi occupation, the newly established Coalition Provisional Authority (CPA) led by Paul Bremer undertook a series of wide-ranging economic, political and legal reforms that substantially changed the structures and institutions of the Iraqi authorities.[111] Yet humanitarian agencies (amongst others) severely criticised the lack of support for basic services which paralysed their ability to provide emergency relief during this time. MSF stressed the responsibility of occupying powers to re-establish services disrupted during and in the immediate aftermath of the war, while noting that 'the provision of relief such as medical care, water, and food to civilians in areas an advancing military brings under its control is not humanitarian action but part of a belligerent's obligations under the Geneva Conventions'.[112] Indeed, US military officers have acknowledged that severe shortcomings in strategic planning and advance training resulted in their failure to undertake their responsibilities as an occupying force, which contributed to the alienation of the Iraqi population and commencement of an increasingly violent insurgency from late 2004 onwards.[113]

Although the Interim Government of Iraq took full governmental authority on 28 June 2004, Siobhán Wills has argued that the de facto situation on the ground meant that the Multi-National Forces-Iraq (MNF-I) were exercising actual authority in Iraq until at least January 2009.[114] Wills argues that the political reclassification of an international armed conflict and occupation into a non-international armed conflict,

[109] DJ Scheffer, 'Beyond Occupation Law' (2003) 97 *American Journal of International Law* 842, 851.

[110] A Roberts, 'Transformative Military Occupation: Applying the Laws of War and Human Rights' (2006) 100(3) *American Journal of International Law* 580, 580.

[111] R Buchan, 'International Community and the Occupation of Iraq' (2007) 12(1) *Journal of Conflict and Security Law* 37, 37–40.

[112] N de Torrente, 'Humanitarian Action Under Attack: Reflections on the Iraq War' (2004) 17 *Harvard Human Rights Journal* 1, 15, 20–21. The debate surrounding the politicisation of humanitarian action in the Iraq war was stoked by Colin Powell's infamous statement that NGOs were 'such a force multiplier for us, such an important part of our combat team': *Remarks to the National Foreign Policy Conference for Leaders of Nongovernmental Organizations* (26 October 2001). For an alternative perspective from CARE International, see P O'Brien, 'Politicized Humanitarianism: A Response to Nicolas de Torrente' (2004) 17 *Harvard Human Rights Journal* 31.

[113] MR Hover, 'The Occupation of Iraq: A Military Perspective on Lessons Learned' (Spring 2012) 94(885) *International Review of the Red Cross* 339, 346.

[114] Wills, 'Legal Characterization', above n 11, 201.

where international forces are invited to remain in the territory to assist a new government, can have serious consequences for legal certainty, and leads to the sudden loss of protection for civilians granted under the law of international armed conflicts, including the law of occupation. Wills concludes that in situations where the UN Security Council has authorised or endorsed the continuance of military operations in a particular state, it has the authority to assert that the law of international armed conflicts remains applicable to foreign forces for as long as they remain engaged in active combat operations.[115]

The experience in Iraq highlights the dangers of prematurely pronouncing 'mission accomplished' and the need to ensure that protections granted to civilians under the law of occupation are not prematurely removed. Moreover, the transformative focus of the CPA not only distracted from the re-establishment of essential basic services, but also went far beyond what is permissible under the law of occupation. As noted by David Scheffer, the occupation clauses in the law of armed conflict are 'far more relevant to a belligerent occupation than to an occupation designed to liberate a society from its repressive governance and transform it as a nation guided by international norms and the self-determination of its liberated populace'.[116] In other words, the law of occupation is not suited for long-term occupations where a primary objective is to promote the rule of law and human rights, or to restore democracy. As seen in Bosnia-Herzegovina, Kosovo, Timor Leste and Afghanistan, other international instruments, most notably UN Security Council authorisation in the form of a resolution, are more appropriate legal vehicles to use for these objectives.[117]

III. NON-INTERNATIONAL ARMED CONFLICTS

A. Additional Protocol II (1977)

Internal armed conflicts can present specific challenges for undertaking humanitarian activities. Reliance on state sovereignty by the governing authorities is likely to be enhanced when the state apparatus is fighting an 'internal' enemy; conversely, non-state armed groups may have limited knowledge or interest in abiding by international law. Accordingly, the minimum obligations of parties during non-international armed conflicts were originally set out in Common Article 3 of the 1949 Geneva

[115] ibid, 207.
[116] Scheffer, 'Beyond Occupation', above n 109, 849.
[117] ibid, 852.

Conventions, which requires humane treatment of all persons taking no active part in the hostilities, including those members of the armed forces who have laid down their arms or are *hors de combat*. Common Article 3 expressly prohibits all 'outrages upon personal dignity, in particular humiliating and degrading treatment' against civilians and non-combatants, and provides that the wounded and sick shall be collected and cared for. As with international armed conflicts, the right of initiative is expressly reaffirmed in Common Article 3(2), which states that: 'An impartial humanitarian body, such as the International Committee of the Red Cross, may offer its services to the Parties to the conflict.' Despite the limited nature of Common Article 3, by reading these provisions together, it is clear that even in internal armed conflicts all parties to the conflict have an obligation to ensure that protection and material assistance are provided to those not directly participating in the hostilities, and that both domestic and international humanitarian organisations have a right to offer their services in an impartial manner.[118] However, with the increasing incidence of internal or non-international armed conflicts during the 1960s and 1970s, it was recognised that the 'Convention in miniature'[119] set out in Common Article 3 was insufficient.

The Red Cross Movement first proposed a dedicated convention covering the protection of persons during civil wars back in 1912,[120] but it took until 1977 before a text which was agreeable to the majority of states was adopted. Despite state concerns about sovereignty and undue recognition being granted to small groups of 'rebels' or 'terrorists' via such an international agreement,[121] the fundamental principle of humanity prevailed and remains at the core of Additional Protocol II. Yet the stark reality of balancing state sovereignty and humanitarian considerations meant that APII reflected a more limited set of legal responsibilities towards civilians.[122] Unlike API for international armed conflicts, APII does not contain the

[118] Dungel, 'Right to Humanitarian Assistance', above n 57.

[119] As described by one of the original Delegates to the 1949 Diplomatic Conference. For discussion of the genesis of Common Article 3, see Pictet, *Commentary: GCIV*, above n 62, 26–44.

[120] ibid, 27.

[121] The divergence in ratifications between API and APII suggests on-going concerns from some states. For example, the US has signed but not ratified APII; the UK only ratified APII in 1998, after the conclusion of the Good Friday Agreement relating to the 'Troubles' in Northern Ireland, reflecting the UK Government's position that the violence in Northern Ireland during the 1960s–1990s was an internal matter, rather than subject to the provisions of APII. For analysis by the ICRC's Head of Mission for UK and Ireland, see G Loane, 'A New Challenge or a New Role? The ICRC in Northern Ireland' (Winter 2012) 94(888) *International Review of the Red Cross* 1481.

[122] Wills, 'Legal Characterization', above n 11, in particular 187–92 on aspects of humanitarian access and protection in non-international armed conflicts.

same level of detail regarding relief activities, and only contains one article specifically on the role and content of relief actions in non-international armed conflicts, although, as noted previously, there is a strong argument regarding the convergence of the customary rules applicable in international and non-international armed conflicts.[123] Moreover, key provisions of APII expand upon Common Article 3 and reiterate that persons who do not take a direct part, or who have ceased to take part, in hostilities are entitled to respect and humane treatment.[124]

> ***Article 18—Relief societies and relief actions***
>
> 1. Relief societies located in the territory of the High Contracting Party, such as Red Cross (Red Crescent, Red Lion and Sun)[125] organisations, may offer their services for the performance of their traditional functions in relation to the victims of the armed conflict. The civilian population may, even on its own initiative, offer to collect and care for the wounded, sick and shipwrecked.
> 2. If the civilian population is suffering undue hardship owing to a lack of the supplies essential for its survival, such as foodstuffs and medical supplies, relief actions for the civilian population which are of an exclusively humanitarian and impartial nature and which are conducted without any adverse distinction shall be undertaken subject to the consent of the High Contracting Party concerned.

In addition to the general right of initiative set out in Common Article 3,[126] Article 18 APII expressly provides that relief societies may offer their services to the victims of the armed conflict. In similar mandatory language to Article 70(1) API, Article 18(2) provides that if civilians are suffering undue hardship due to a lack of essential supplies, humanitarian and impartial relief actions shall be conducted—subject to the consent of the party concerned.[127] This means that a government could potentially refuse consent for the provision of humanitarian assistance to the victims of an internal armed conflict. In a situation where territory is controlled by an armed group within a country, the national government or another party to the conflict could deny access to this area for humanitarian agencies, even if it was recognised there was a humanitarian need. As noted by Dinstein: 'as long as consent is essential … authorities can usually find plausible excuses for delaying humanitarian assistance, and even for frustrating it

[123] See, eg, 'Humanitarian Assistance in Armed Conflict', above n 53; Crawford, 'Blurring the Lines', above n 54; Meron, 'Continuing Role of Custom', above n 40.

[124] Part II: Humane Treatment (Arts 4–6) and Part IV: Civilian Population (Arts 13–18).

[125] The Red Lion and Sun was the official emblem of the Iranian national society from its establishment in 1922 until 1980, when it adopted the Red Crescent symbol.

[126] eg the ICRC's activities in Northern Ireland are based on the Common Art 3 right of initiative, rather than APII. See Loane, 'New Challenge or New Role', above n 121.

[127] See also Common Art 9/9/9/10 Geneva Conventions.

altogether.'[128] However, the ICRC Commentary to Article 18(2) highlights that in exceptional cases, where due to the nature of the conflict it is not possible to determine who are the relevant authorities, consent should be presumed due to the fact that 'assistance for the victims is of paramount importance and should not suffer any delay'.[129]

The ICRC Commentary further stresses that refusals of consent must be based on 'good grounds', and notes that such a refusal may constitute a violation of Article 14 APII,[130] namely the prohibition of the use of starvation as a method of combat.[131] David Marcus has argued that the express prohibition of starvation in both international and non-international armed conflicts means that failure to provide relief to civilians would always amount to a breach of either API or APII.[132] However, the ICC Rome Statute only classifies starvation as a method of warfare as a war crime in situations of international armed conflicts—as Yoram Dinstein has noted, this was 'by no means accidental'.[133] War crimes in non-international armed conflicts under Article 8(2)(c) Rome Statute are limited to serious violations of Common Article 3, namely: i) violence to life and person; ii) committing outrages upon personal dignity; iii) taking of hostages; and iv) the passing of extra-judicial sentences and the carrying out of executions.[134] One would therefore have to argue that the deliberate denial of humanitarian assistance in an internal armed conflict fell within either of the first two of these scenarios for it to be classified as a war crime under the Rome Statute.[135]

It is equally noticeable that Article 18 APII does not contain equivalent express obligations on state parties in regard to the protection of humanitarian personnel and objects, or the requirement to facilitate humanitarian relief for civilians as set out in API. However, Jean-Marie Henckaerts has argued that these requirements are implicit in the mandatory language of Article 18(2), and have additionally crystallised into rules of customary international law.[136] In particular, the ICRC's Customary International Law Rule 55 states that parties to a conflict must allow and facilitate

[128] Dinstein, 'Right to Humanitarian Assistance', above n 61, 85–86.
[129] ICRC, *Commentary*, above n 77, 1479.
[130] Art 14 (Protection of Objects Indispensable to the Survival of the Civilian Population) APII.
[131] ICRC, *Commentary*, above n 77, 1478–81.
[132] Marcus, 'Famine Crimes', above n 75, 266–68.
[133] Dinstein, 'Right to Humanitarian Assistance', above n 61, 85. See also Plattner, 'Assistance to the Civilian Population', above n 52, 260–61.
[134] Art 8(2)(c)(xxv) Rome Statute, above n 76.
[135] For further discussion, see ch 7, Section II.C.
[136] Chatham House, *Law of Armed Conflict*, above n 41, 6.

the rapid and unimpeded passage of humanitarian relief for civilians in need,[137] while Rule 56 states that Parties to a conflict must ensure the freedom of movement of authorised humanitarian personnel.[138] Only in case of imperative military necessity may their movements be temporarily restricted. Yet practice shows that humanitarian agencies are often frustrated or denied access to civilians. Katja Luopajärvi has argued that although Article 18 does not impose an obligation on parties to accept humanitarian aid, some form of relief action must be undertaken for civilian populations to alleviate suffering.[139] This raises the question of whether third states or humanitarian agencies should undertake cross-border humanitarian operations against the express wishes of the affected state or of non-state armed groups in control of territory.

i. Syria: Cross-border Humanitarian Operations

The complex nature of the long-running conflict in Syria and surrounding areas has posed particular challenges for humanitarian access. In the context of an armed conflict, humanitarian action can take place either 'in-country cross-line' (that is, by agencies operating within the affected state with the consent of the various armed groups to provide assistance across the frontlines) or 'cross-border' from a neighbouring state (that is, agencies based in a neighbouring state provide assistance on the territory of the affected state by consistently crossing the border). Examples of large-scale cross-border operations in the past include the 'air bridge' into Biafra during the Nigerian civil war of 1967–1970, and the UN-organised Operation Lifeline Sudan from Kenya into southern Sudan during the 1990s.[140]

From an ethical and moral perspective, based on the humanitarian imperative to prevent and alleviate suffering, the provision of humanitarian action without the consent of the relevant authorities is justifiable. However, from a legal and operational perspective, there are greater challenges, not least in ensuring the safety and security of humanitarian staff. Since the Syrian conflict began in early 2011, nearly 5 million Syrian refugees and other displaced persons have fled to Turkey,

[137] The ICRC *Customary IHL Project*, Rule 55 (Access for Humanitarian Relief for Civilians in Need).

[138] ibid, Rule 56 (Freedom of Movement of Humanitarian Relief Personnel).

[139] K Luopajärvi, 'Is there an Obligation on States to Accept International Humanitarian Assistance to Internally Displaced Persons under International Law?' (2003) 15(4) *International Journal of Refugee Law* 678.

[140] H Slim and E Gillard, 'Ethical and Legal Perspectives on Cross-border Humanitarian Operations' (November 2013) 59 *Humanitarian Exchange* 6.

Egypt, Lebanon, Iraq and Jordan.[141] Millions more remained trapped, both within besieged towns and cities,[142] or in hard-to-reach areas controlled by the government or one of the numerous armed opposition or jihadi groups. The combined effects of armed conflict, extremely limited domestic assistance, and lack of external access to people within Syria has resulted in wide-spread hunger and the 'worst humanitarian crisis of our time'.[143]

In February 2014, UNSC Resolution 2139 unanimously demanded that all parties, in particular the Syrian authorities, 'promptly allow rapid, safe and unhindered humanitarian access for UN humanitarian agencies and their implementing partners, including across conflict lines and across borders, in order to ensure that humanitarian assistance reaches people in need through the most direct routes'.[144] The UN Emergency Relief Coordinator, Valerie Amos, commended the UNSC Resolution, and stressed that the 'continued withholding of consent to cross-border or cross-line relief operations, particularly of commodities privileged throughout the Geneva Conventions—like food, water, medical treatment and supplies, or shelter—is arbitrary and unjustified'.[145] Likewise, 35 leading international lawyers signed an open letter in *The Guardian* calling on the UN to directly undertake cross-border humanitarian operations into Syria, and condemning the 'overly cautious interpretation of international humanitarian law, which has held UN agencies back from delivering humanitarian aid across borders for fear that some member states will find them unlawful'.[146]

[141] Regional Refugee and Resilience Plan, *Mid-Year Report: 2016* (June 2016) 9. The Regional Refugee and Resilience Plan (3RP) brings together the plans developed under the leadership of national authorities of Egypt, Iraq, Jordan, Lebanon, and Turkey to ensure protection, humanitarian assistance and strengthen resilience. The 3RP brings together over 200 governments, UN agencies, inter-governmental and non-governmental organisations for a coordinated region-wide response to the Syrian crisis. See www.3rpsyriacrisis.org.

[142] For discussion of besieged cities, see ch 7, Section II.C.i. See also E Ferris and K Kirişci, 'From Turkey to Syria: The Murky World of Cross-border Assistance' Opinion, 20 July 2015, Brookings Institute www.brookings.edu/research/opinions/2015/07/20-syria-turkey-crossborder-assistance-ferris-kirisci.

[143] *Remarks by António Guterres, UN High Commissioner for Refugees*, 142nd ministerial meeting of the Council of the League of Arab States, Cairo, 7 September 2014. In terms of population displacement and the denial of humanitarian access, the situation in Syria mirrors southern Sudan in the early 2000s, which Francis Deng cited in late 2001 as 'the worst humanitarian disaster in the world today'. F Deng, 'Sudan—Civil War and Genocide' (Winter 2001) 8(1) *Middle East Quarterly* 13, 13.

[144] UNSC, *Resolution 2139 (2014)* (22 February 2014) S/RES/2139.

[145] UNOCHA, *Emergency Relief Coordinator and Under-Secretary-General for Humanitarian Affairs, Valerie Amos Statement to the Press on Syria* (28 March 2014).

[146] 'There is No Legal Barrier to UN Cross-border Operations in Syria', *The Guardian*, 28 April 2014.

As a result of this pressure, and the obvious humanitarian need within Syria, in July 2014 the UN authorised the delivery of cross-border humanitarian assistance without the consent of the Syrian government through four designated crossing points in Turkey.[147] This authorisation has been renewed annually as a result of the on-going nature of the conflict and humanitarian need.[148] As noted by Elizabeth Ferris and Kemal Kirişci, while the staff of Syrian NGOs undertake the vast majority of the work inside Syria, and therefore face the highest level of threats to their physical safety and security, this provides some hope that domestic humanitarian organisations will be well placed to undertake recovery and rehabilitation activities once the conflict ends.[149]

Yet this also highlights the fact that, by definition, cross-border humanitarian operations without the consent of the authorities are undertaken in challenging and dangerous environments. As Hugo Slim and Emanuela-Chiara Gillard have argued, despite their potential legality, from an operational perspective humanitarian agencies need to carefully weigh up the impact of cross-border activities on both in-country activities (whether undertaken by themselves or other humanitarian agencies) and the feasibility and risk to humanitarian principles that may occur. Slim and Gillard conclude that humanitarian agencies are duty bound to consider the best use of their resources, and in some situations may determine that focusing their relief activities on wider regional programmes, such as refugee support or lobbying for peace, may ultimately have a larger and more immediate impact.[150]

IV. CONCLUSION: BALANCING HUMANITARIAN CONSIDERATIONS AND MILITARY NECESSITY

Following this overview of key positive law obligations set out in the Geneva Conventions, Additional Protocols and customary international law, it is worthwhile to reflect on the interconnections between the law of armed conflict and international human rights law. As discussed in chapter five, a state's international obligations to respect, protect and fulfil specific provisions of international human rights law, such as the right to life, an adequate standard of living, and physical security and integrity, continue to apply during both international and non-international armed conflicts. Despite the well-recognised impact that war and violence have

[147] UNSC, *Resolution 2165 (2014)* (14 July 2014) S/RES/2165.

[148] Most recently, UNSC, *Resolution 2258 (2015)* (22 December 2015) S/RES/2258 renewed the authorisation until January 2017.

[149] Ferris and Kirişci, 'From Turkey to Syria', above n 142.

[150] Slim and Gillard, 'Ethical and Legal Perspectives', above n 140, 8–9.

on civilians and other non-combatants, Yoram Dinstein has argued against a general individual right to humanitarian assistance in armed conflicts, noting:

> Surely, civilians do not have an absolute right to demand relief from the outside, applicable *erga omnes* (that is, vis-à-vis the entire international community) … [I]t would be absurd to contend that every state in the world is duty bound to come up, on demand, with relief aid to civilians embroiled in any armed conflict, wherever it is raging.[151]

Indeed, although Geneva Convention IV expressly contains a right for individuals to request humanitarian assistance during international armed conflicts,[152] this is constrained as Contracting Parties' may respond 'within the bounds set by military or security considerations' and only need to facilitate access to protected persons 'as much as possible'. The ICRC clearly acknowledges that military considerations are part and parcel of decisions surrounding the provision of humanitarian assistance to civilians in conflict zones,[153] despite Article 70(1) API highlighting that '[o]ffers of such relief shall not be regarded as interference in the armed conflict or as unfriendly acts'. Humanitarian access in war zones is often a highly contentious issue, and can present serious dangers for both humanitarian personnel and civilians they are trying to assist. However, reflecting the ICRC's dual role as the guardian of international humanitarian law[154] and as one of the largest humanitarian organisations in conflict settings, the ICRC has reiterated that belligerents in all forms of armed conflict (occupation, other situations of international armed conflict, and non-international armed conflicts) have an obligation to meet the basic needs of persons under their control. The ICRC has stressed that this all-encompassing obligation can be inferred from 'the object and purpose of IHL'.[155]

Positive international law in the form of GCIV and API and II, plus identified customary international law, has therefore enshrined the right of initiative for humanitarian agencies, particularly the Red Cross Movement. In other words, an impartial humanitarian organisation's right to *offer* humanitarian assistance to civilians and non-combatants is clearly identifiable in international law. Yet despite this, as noted by Stoffels:

151 Dinstein, 'Right to Humanitarian Assistance', above n 61, 78.

152 Art 31 GCIV: 'Protected persons shall have every facility for making application to the Protecting Powers, the International Committee of the Red Cross, the National [Red Cross/Red Crescent] Society of the country where they may be, as well as to any organisation that might assist them.'

153 Pictet, *Commentary: GCIV*, above n 62, 180.

154 Sandoz, 'ICRC as Guardian of IHL', above n 7. Sandoz notes that: 'a guardian is not a guarantor, and the ICRC must not and cannot feel responsible for every violation of international humanitarian law.'

155 ICRC, *International Humanitarian Law and the Challenges of Contemporary Armed Conflicts* (October 2015) Report prepared for the 32nd International Conference of the Red Cross and Red Crescent (32IC/15/11) 27.

'The first conclusion that can be drawn from an analysis of implementation mechanisms established under IHL is that individuals are largely dependent on the political will of States to use the means at their disposal to ensure implementation and enforcement [of a right to humanitarian assistance].'[156] Of equal concern to humanitarian actors engaged in humanitarian action in armed conflicts is the fact that:

> Whatever the law on the books might say about who can deliver assistance in what situation, and who is entitled to receive it, many warring parties in the post-Cold War world have never heard of the Geneva Conventions, are not familiar with the ICRC and the Red Cross/Red Crescent symbol, or regard civilian death and suffering as weapons for attaining their personal and political objectives.[157]

So although the law of armed conflict contains both an organisational right to offer and an individual's right to receive humanitarian assistance in certain circumstances, these rights are limited and vary considerably between international and non-international conflicts. Furthermore, humanitarian agencies or those entitled to such assistance are likely to face considerable difficulty in seeking the enforcement of their rights in the chaotic environment of a war zone.[158] However, the provisions on protection and material assistance set out in the law of armed conflict represent the modern source for many themes found in other branches of international law and non-binding norms contained within the *acquis humanitaire,* such as the RCRC Code of Conduct and the *Sphere Handbook.* Running throughout the law of armed conflict is a balancing of the binding responsibilities of states and non-state armed groups towards civilians and non-combatants under their control, with an acceptance that these rights can be legitimately constrained, either for military necessity or security reasons or due to insufficient resources. International law also recognises that material assistance alone is not sufficient, and so provides for activities such as spiritual assistance and the identification and registration of separated children.

Whilst subject to numerous, and horrific, breaches in conflicts around the world, the fundamental importance of humanity and human dignity in the midst of war remains the defining characteristic of the law of armed conflict. The need for corresponding legal accountability mechanisms for those who breach international standards of humane treatment resulted in the attribution of individual criminal responsibility via the statutes of a series of international criminal tribunals from Nuremberg to The Hague. Therefore, it is to this separate but inter-connected branch of international law that we turn next.

[156] Stoffels, 'Legal Regulation', above n 61, 528.
[157] Forsythe, 'ICRC and Humanitarian Assistance', above n 99, 513.
[158] See D Fisher, 'Domestic Regulation of International Humanitarian Relief in Disasters and Armed Conflict: A Comparative Analysis' (June 2007) 89(866) *International Review of the Red Cross* 345, 355–67.

7

International Criminal Law

I. INTRODUCTION

IN RECOGNITION OF the differing levels of legal protection for civilians in international and non-international armed conflicts, soon after the fall of the Berlin Wall a group of experts met in Turku, Finland to identify minimum non-derogable humanitarian standards applicable in all conflicts, including internal violence, disturbances, tensions, and public emergencies.[1] Of note, the group highlighted that the deliberate deprivation of access to necessary food, drinking water and medicine was prohibited under international law.[2] Likewise, the group stressed that medical and religious personnel should be respected and protected, and that humanitarian agencies should be granted all the facilities necessary to enable them to carry out their humanitarian activities.[3]

As reflected in the overall approach of the Turku Declaration, it is well recognised that deliberate attacks on humanitarian personnel or the wilful denial of humanitarian assistance or protection to those in dire need is not just unacceptable but constitutes potentially criminal behaviour. It follows that there is a symbiotic relationship between the law of armed conflict and international criminal law (Robert Cryer has defined war crimes as 'the criminal phase of humanitarian law'),[4] as well as potential overlaps between international human rights law and international criminal responsibility.[5] The *acquis humanitaire* therefore also includes provisions from international criminal law relating specifically to material assistance and humanitarian protection for civilians and non-combatants.

[1] Declaration of Minimum Humanitarian Standards, adopted by an expert meeting convened by the Institute for Human Rights, Åbo Akademi University, in Turku/Åbo Finland, 2 December 1990. See E Crawford, 'The Road to Nowhere? The Future for the Declaration on Fundamental Standards of Humanity' (2012) 3 *Journal of International Humanitarian Legal Studies* 43, 52–55.

[2] Declaration, above n 1, Art 3(2)(f).

[3] ibid, Arts 14 and 15.

[4] R Cryer, 'International Criminal Law' in M Evans (ed), *International Law* 4th edn (Oxford University Press, 2014) 761.

[5] See R Cryer, 'International Criminal Law' in D Moeckli, S Shah and S Sivakumaran (eds), *International Human Rights Law* 2nd edn (Oxford University Press, 2014) 496–512.

However, a distinction must be made between 'international crimes' directly established in international law which authorise the prosecution of individual offenders in international criminal tribunals, and 'transnational crimes' which place obligations on states to criminalise breaches of certain international laws through their domestic legal regimes. The first category of 'international crimes' arose from the horrendous crimes committed against combatants and civilians during the Second World War, and subsequent jurisprudence of the Nuremberg and Tokyo International Military Tribunals. Despite a hiatus of 50 years during the Cold War, the renewed focus on individual criminal responsibility for actions undertaken in armed conflicts during the 1990s arising from the breakup of the former Yugoslavia and Rwanda's genocidal rampage has ensured the rapid development of the field of international criminal law over the past 20 years. In particular, international criminal law has strengthened the legal accountability mechanisms for the perpetrators of crimes deemed of concern to humanity as a whole, and which potentially threaten international peace and security.[6] The second category of 'transnational crimes' can be classified as a state's obligation to either prosecute or extradite an individual suspected of a crime included within a multilateral treaty regime, such as slavery or piracy, as understood by the maxim *aut dedere aut judicare*.[7] For instance, the UN Convention Against Torture[8] contains express obligations for states to ensure that all acts of torture are offences under their criminal law, establish mechanisms of inquiry to determine jurisdiction over an alleged offender, and co-operate with other potential states with jurisdiction to establish within which state the individual will be prosecuted.[9]

As with other branches of international law contributing to the *acquis humanitaire*, the focus of this chapter is on those components of international criminal law which directly impact the protection of persons in humanitarian crises. Indeed, the fact that individual criminal liability exists for acts or omissions relating to the provision of material assistance or protection activities in humanitarian crises highlights the fundamental importance placed on humanitarian action within the international legal system. As with our analysis of the law of armed conflict, particular focus will be placed on the law surrounding humanitarian activities for

[6] For a detailed overview of international criminal law, see A Cassese et al (eds), *Cassese's International Criminal Law* 3rd edn (Oxford University Press, 2013).

[7] For discussion of universal jurisdiction regarding international and transnational crimes, see C Kreß, 'Universal Jurisdiction over International Crimes and the *Institut de Droit international*' (2006) 4 *Journal of International Criminal Justice* 561.

[8] Convention against Torture and Other Cruel, Inhuman or Degrading Treatment or Punishment (adopted 10 December 1984, entered into force 26 June 1987) 1465 UNTS 85.

[9] ibid, Arts 4–6.

civilians (as opposed to persons *hors de combat* such as prisoners of war or the sick and wounded). Furthermore, while the vast majority of the practice and jurisprudence of international criminal law focuses on actions during armed conflict (both international and non-international), this chapter also examines criminal liability during peacetime humanitarian crises, such as Cyclone Nargis which hit Myanmar in 2008. As discussed in the previous chapter, Geneva Convention IV[10] and Additional Protocols I and II[11] provide binding rights to humanitarian assistance for identified groups of protected persons, and the ICRC has identified a range of potential customary international law rules applicable in armed conflicts.[12] Yet there are currently no equivalent internationally binding treaty provisions for humanitarian assistance in situations of natural or human-made disaster.[13] Therefore, in addition to enumerated war crimes, a key question for this chapter is in what other circumstances can an individual be held criminally liable under international law for acts or omissions that deny or impede access to life-saving support in a humanitarian crisis?

A. Rome Statute of the International Criminal Court

The 1998 Rome Statute of the International Criminal Court (ICC),[14] which codified four international crimes (war crimes, crimes against humanity, genocide and aggression)[15] and their subsequent elaboration through official publications and criminal prosecutions, provides the foundational basis for identifying which actions or inactions within humanitarian crises might engage individual criminal liability. The Rome Statute establishes a regime of complementarity—whereby state parties are expected to prosecute persons suspected of breaching international criminal law through

[10] Geneva Convention IV Relative to the Protection of Civilian Persons in Times of War (adopted 12 August 1949, entered into force 21 October 1950) 75 UNTS 287 ('GCIV').

[11] Protocol Additional to the Geneva Conventions of 12 August 1949 and relating to the Protection of Victims of International Armed Conflicts (adopted 8 June 1977, entered into force 7 December 1978) 1125 UNTS 4 ('API'); Protocol II Additional to the Geneva Conventions of 12 August 1949 and relating to the Protection of Victims of Non-International Armed Conflicts (adopted 7 June 1977, entered into force 7 December 1978) 1125 UNTS 610 ('APII').

[12] See ch 6, Section I.B.

[13] For discussion of the key binding and non-binding normative texts relevant in natural and human-made disaster contexts, see ch 8.

[14] Rome Statute of the International Criminal Court (adopted 17 July 1998, entered into force 1 July 2002) 2187 UNTS 3 ('Rome Statute').

[15] ibid, Art 5. The crime of 'aggression' relates to the illegal use of force by a state (ie the *jus ad bellum* branch of the law of armed conflict), and so falls out with the scope of this investigation into the normative context of the *acquis humanitaire*. Note also that the crime of aggression was only codified in 2010 via the Kampala Review Conference of the State Parties to the ICC, and will only enter into force during 2017.

their domestic legal system first, and only if a state is unable or unwilling to initiate investigations or prosecutions should the case be internationalised to the ICC.[16] Although international prosecutions are symbolically important, questions of criminal liability regarding humanitarian activities should ideally be addressed at the domestic level, provided there is the political will and resources available to conduct such prosecutions in a fair manner. A cogent example comes from the Colombian Penal Code, which criminalises both an individual's failure to provide humanitarian assistance when they are under an obligation to do so, and the deliberate obstruction of medical or relief personnel.[17]

Considering the individual criminal liability which may arise, it follows that international criminal law is by definition more reliant on case law and judicial interpretation than other branches of international law within the *acquis humanitaire*.[18] Yet it is noticeable that to date there has been limited judicial examination or discussion of many of the breaches of international criminal law discussed below. While direct attacks on humanitarian personnel (such as attacks on hospitals in war zones) or the deliberate starvation of civilians (such as through militarily besieging cities) have come to the fore in recent years, particularly in media and academic commentary, the protection of persons in humanitarian crises would benefit from a greater level of judicial analysis.[19] It should also be noted that the wording of the statutes of the International Tribunals for the Former Yugoslavia (ICTY) and Rwanda (ICTR) adopted in the early 1990s vary in places from that agreed in the 1998 Rome Statute. Therefore, this chapter will focus to a large extent on the crimes set out in the Rome Statute as the ICC is the only global judicial body for international crimes, and its statute and jurisprudence are likely to form the basis of any future domestic or hybrid criminal tribunals. Joakim Dungel has even argued that the ICC should be given an advisory role with respect to any UN Security Council

[16] ibid, Arts 1 and 17. See also JK Kleffne, 'The Impact of Complementarity on National Implementation of Substantive International Criminal Law' (2003) 1 *Journal of International Criminal Justice* 86.

[17] Arts 152 and 153, *Colombia: Penal Code*, Law No 599, 24 July 2000.

[18] The establishment of the International Tribunals for the former Yugoslavia and Rwanda in the mid-1990s and subsequent hybrid domestic-international tribunals such as in Sierra Leone, Lebanon and Cambodia provide a range of jurisprudential analysis of international criminal law. While the jurisprudence from the ICC remains limited, the range of on-going cases under investigation or trial will provide a rich vein of judicial decisions over the coming years.

[19] Theodor Meron, as President of the ICTY, examined some of the implications of international criminal law for humanitarian operations in 2004. See 'Humanitarian Assistance in Armed Conflict, Conference of the Luxemburg Group, 24–25 May 2004' (2004) 86(856) *International Review of the Red Cross* 879, 895–97.

determination on the unlawfulness of a refusal of humanitarian assistance during internal armed conflicts.[20]

During the tense negotiations that led to the establishment of the ICC, both the Inter-Agency Standing Committee and UNHCR argued that the wilful denial of humanitarian assistance in international and non-international armed conflicts should be included within the Court's jurisdiction as a war crime.[21] Citing its practical experience of providing assistance in conflict settings, UNHCR argued that the tactic of deliberately starving vulnerable populations through the denial of humanitarian assistance with the aim of weakening, demoralising or pressurising a party to the conflict was 'particularly reprehensible'.[22] Experience has shown that the suffering of civilians may actually be a specific military objective.[23] The premeditated denial of humanitarian assistance and violence towards civilians was witnessed during the break-up of the former Yugoslavia, and more recently the conflict in Syria has seen the deliberate besiegement of towns and cities containing large numbers of civilians.[24] While the final text of the Rome Statute did not include a general crime of the denial of humanitarian assistance in all circumstances, there are a range of scenarios where such denial could amount to genocide, war crimes or crimes against humanity in both conflict or non-conflict settings.[25] For example, attacking objects or persons using the distinctive emblems of the Geneva Conventions or wilfully impeding relief supplies are both confirmed as specific war crimes in international armed conflicts. Supplementing the Rome Statute and judicial decisions, the ICC's explanatory 'Elements of Crimes stresses the intentional nature of these actions required for them to attract individual criminal responsibility.[26]

[20] J Dungel, 'A Right to Humanitarian Assistance in Internal Armed Conflicts Respecting Sovereignty, Neutrality and Legitimacy: Practical Proposals to Practical Problems' (May 2004) *Journal of Humanitarian Assistance*.

[21] IASC, 'Communication received from Inter-Agency Standing Committee to the United Nations Diplomatic Conference of Plenipotentiaries on the Establishment of an International Criminal Court, Note by the Secretary-General' (11 June 1998) A/CONF.183/INF/4.

[22] UNHCR, 'Statement by the Assistant High Commissioner for Refugees, Mr Søren Jessen-Petersen, at the United Nations Diplomatic Conference of Plenipotentiaries on the Establishment of an International Criminal Court' Rome, 16 June 1998.

[23] See H Slim and D Mancini-Griffoli, *Interpreting Violence: Anti-civilian thinking and practice and how to argue against it more effectively*, Centre for Humanitarian Dialogue (2007).

[24] See Section II.C.i below.

[25] C Rottensteiner, 'The Denial of Humanitarian Assistance as a Crime Under International Law' (Sept 1999) 835 *International Review of the Red Cross* 555–82. See also L Moffett, 'Accountability for Forced Displacement in Democratic Republic of Congo and Uganda before the International Criminal Court' (2015) 1(2) *African Journal of International Criminal Justice* 129.

[26] *Elements of Crimes*, Official Records of the Review Conference of the Rome Statute of the International Criminal Court, Kampala, 31 May to 11 June 2010 (ICC publication, RC/11) 30–31.

B. International Humanitarian Fact-finding Commission

Not all states have signed or ratified the Rome Statute, with notable non-participants including three permanent members of the UN Security Council (China, Russia and the US), as well as countries such as India, Israel and Pakistan. Nevertheless, the grave breaches regime of the Geneva Conventions and Additional Protocols[27] provides an alternative avenue of legal accountability as the majority of states have signed and ratified the four GCs and at least API. Overseeing the grave breaches regime, the International Humanitarian Fact-finding Commission (IHFFC) was established in 1991 under Article 90 API to independently investigate allegations of grave breaches and serious violations of the law of armed conflict. Reflecting its legal basis in API, the IHFFC can only investigate allegations formally requested by state parties which have recognised the competence of the Commission, and only against another state having made the same declaration.[28] To date, only 76 states have made such a declaration, which equates to around half the parties to API and a third of the parties to the Geneva Conventions.[29]

Nevertheless, all state parties to the Geneva Conventions and Additional Protocols have the right to legislate for universal jurisdiction over war crimes in their domestic courts, and moreover have a responsibility to investigate war crimes allegedly committed by their nationals or armed forces, or on their territory, and, if appropriate, prosecute the suspects. States must investigate other war crimes over which they have jurisdiction and, if appropriate, prosecute the suspects.[30] The ICRC has determined that these obligations amount to customary international law, and so are binding on all states irrespective of their lack of signature of the relevant conventions.[31] The former President of Chad, Hissène Habré, was prosecuted by an African Union-backed Extraordinary African Chambers in Senegal on the basis of such universal jurisdiction arising from Chad's domestic ratification of the Geneva Conventions. Habré was convicted in May 2016 of torture, war crimes and crimes against humanity and sentenced to life imprisonment.[32] Therefore, irrespective of a state's lack of

[27] Set out in Arts 50/51/130/147 Geneva Conventions and Arts 11 and 85 API.

[28] Rules 20 and 21, *Rules of the International Humanitarian Fact-Finding Commission* (as adopted on 8 July 1992 and amended on 11 March 2003, 13 February 2009, 11 February 2011 and 26 March 2014).

[29] For further information see www.ihffc.org.

[30] Arts 49/50/129/146 Geneva Conventions.

[31] JM Henckaerts and L Doswald-Beck, *Customary International Humanitarian Law: Rules and Practice* (Cambridge University Press, 2005), Rules 157 and 158.

[32] D Searcey, 'Hissène Habré, Ex-President of Chad, Is Convicted of War Crimes', *The New York Times*, 30 May 2016.

signature or ratification of the Rome Statute or declaration of competence for the IHFFC, specific international legal obligations exist to prosecute or extradite any war crimes suspect on their territory. Specific war crimes in the Geneva Conventions and Additional Protocols which could be interpreted to incorporate the wilful denial of humanitarian assistance include wilful killing or violence to life and person; torture or inhuman treatment; and wilfully causing great suffering, or serious injury to body or health.[33]

Respecting the inherent dignity of each individual, whatever their role or circumstances in a humanitarian crisis, motivated the elevation of certain criminal behaviours to the international sphere, and provides the basis for action by states and the international community in the face of war crimes, crimes against humanity and genocide. Yet such a stance is not without its critics. Fabrice Weissman of MSF has argued that 'few organizations have drawn the logical conclusion that only a clear, transparent policy of non-cooperation with the ICC is compatible with the goal of helping, with total impartiality, the victims of war'.[34] This does not mean that MSF avoids engagement in debates about criminal liability in times of war, but simply reflects their approach to the humanitarian principles of impartiality and neutrality. As discussed below, following the air attack on the MSF Kunduz Trauma Centre in Afghanistan in October 2015, MSF called on the US and Afghan Governments to appoint the IHFFC to oversee an independent investigation to establish the facts behind the event.[35] Therefore, the following sections examine our current understanding of the criminal liability for acts or omissions in regard to providing material assistance and protection activities to victims of humanitarian crises. We commence with examining the relevant obligations regarding humanitarian action in the law of armed conflict via war crimes, before analysing the broader categories of genocide and crimes against humanity which can occur in both times of war and peace.[36]

II. WAR CRIMES

Whilst it is true that the law of armed conflict provides a detailed framework for regulating access to persons in need of material assistance and

[33] Government of Switzerland, *Humanitarian Access in Situations of Armed Conflict: Handbook on the International Normative Framework*, Version 2, December 2014, 52.

[34] F Weissman, *Humanitarian Aid and the International Criminal Court: Grounds for Divorce* (2009) Foundation MSF/CRASH, 3.

[35] See Section II.A.i below.

[36] As noted by the ICTY: 'It is by now a settled rule of customary international law that crimes against humanity do not require a connection to international armed conflict.' ICTY, *The Prosecutor v Tadiç* (IT-94-1-A72) Appeal on Jurisdiction, 2 October 1995, para 141.

protection in situations of armed conflict,[37] the express treaty-based rules regarding the protection of civilians and humanitarian personnel are markedly different between international and non-international armed conflicts. Geneva Convention IV specifically sets out the requirement of parties to an international armed conflict to permit the free passage of relief consignments (in particular foodstuffs, medical supplies and clothing) organised by impartial humanitarian organisations such as the ICRC and to guarantee their protection.[38] No such express provisions are set out in Additional Protocol II for non-international armed conflicts. Nevertheless, the ICRC has stressed that irrespective of the nature of the conflict, the general framework for humanitarian action under the law of armed conflict consists of four interdependent 'layers', namely:

1. Each party to an armed conflict bears the primary obligation to meet the basic needs of the population under its control.
2. Impartial humanitarian organisations have the right to offer their services in order to carry out humanitarian activities, in particular when the needs of the population affected by an armed conflict are not fulfilled.
3. Impartial humanitarian activities undertaken in situations of armed conflict are generally subject to the consent of the parties to the conflict concerned.
4. Once impartial humanitarian relief schemes have been agreed to, the parties to the armed conflict, as well as all other states, are expected to allow and facilitate the rapid and unimpeded passage of the relief schemes, subject to their right of control.[39]

Moreover, the overarching requirement of humane treatment set out in Common Article 3 can be read to include a proactive requirement to ensure that all those not taking part in hostilities receive minimum levels of protection, irrespective of the legal status of the conflict itself. As the original 1952 ICRC Commentaries memorably put it:

> It would … be pointless and even dangerous to try to enumerate things with which a human being must be provided for his normal maintenance as distinct from that of an animal, or to lay down in detail the manner in which one must behave towards him in order to show that one is treating him 'humanely', that is to say as a fellow human being and not as a beast or a thing.[40]

Since the Nuremberg and Tokyo war crimes trials, it has been accepted that individuals, whether military or civilian, should be held legally accountable for deliberate or negligent breaches of these fundamental guarantees.

[37] ICRC, *International Humanitarian Law and the Challenges of Contemporary Armed Conflicts* (October 2015) Report prepared for the 32nd International Conference of the Red Cross and Red Crescent (32IC/15/11) 27.

[38] Art 59 GCIV.

[39] ICRC, *IHL Report*, above n 37, 27.

[40] J Pictet (ed), *Commentary on the Geneva Conventions of 12 August 1949: Volume I* (1952) 53.

By definition, war crimes must take place during armed hostilities between two or more parties, as opposed to during periods of internal disturbances or sporadic acts of violence, or during peacetime humanitarian crises such as natural disasters. As set out in the Rome Statute, 'war crimes' can be divided into two categories. For international armed conflicts, war crimes are committed as a result of grave breaches of the 1949 Geneva Conventions and other enumerated serious violations of the laws and customs applicable in international armed conflict.[41] Meanwhile, in non-international armed conflicts, war crimes are defined as serious violations of Common Article 3 and other enumerated serious violations of the laws and customs applicable in armed conflict not of an international character.[42]

The primary responsibility for the prosecution of war crimes rests with national authorities—either the state of nationality of the alleged perpetrator or the state where the alleged offences took place. At a secondary level, all states have an obligation to prosecute grave breaches of the Geneva Conventions through the provisions on universal jurisdiction.[43] Moreover, the international community retains an interest in ensuring that particularly grievous breaches of international criminal law are identified and prosecuted. Therefore, based on the principle of complementarily,[44] the Rome Statute provides that the ICC has jurisdiction in respect of war crimes, in particular when such acts are committed as part of a specific plan or policy, or are particularly widespread, as opposed to individual incidences of breaches of the laws of war.[45] While many of the envisaged violations relate to illegal military action against military objectives, war crimes also encompass a range of actions against civilian protected persons and objects. Therefore, the following sections will examine four potential modalities of international criminal liability in times of conflict, namely: a) attacks against humanitarian personnel and equipment; b) misuse of the distinctive emblems of the Geneva Conventions; c) starvation as a means of warfare; and d) grave breaches of Geneva Convention IV.

A. Attacks Against Humanitarian Personnel and Equipment

While a specific legal requirement to protect humanitarian supplies was established through Article 59 GCIV, the protection of civilian humanitarian

[41] Art 8(2)(a) and (b) Rome Statute.
[42] Art 8(2)(c) and (e) Rome Statute.
[43] Kreß, 'Universal Jurisdiction', above n 7.
[44] As per Art 17(1)(a) and (b) Rome Statute the ICC will deem a case to be inadmissible if the case is being or has been investigated or prosecuted by a state which has jurisdiction over it, unless that state is unwilling or unable genuinely to carry out the investigation or prosecution.
[45] Art 8(1) Rome Statute.

personnel was only codified by API in 1977, with Article 71(2) stating that '[relief] personnel shall be respected and protected'. Of note, consequent to the fundamental principle of distinction between combatants and civilians,[46] military actors engaged in the delivery of humanitarian assistance are not covered by this clause.[47] Reflecting the more limited provisions in the law of armed conflict for non-international armed conflicts, APII does not contain similar protections for civilian humanitarian personnel; nevertheless, the ICRC Customary IHL Study identified broad condemnation of attacks against humanitarian personnel in both international and non-international armed conflicts. The ICRC Study concludes that:

> In addition to the prohibition of attacks on [civilian humanitarian relief] personnel, practice indicates that harassment, intimidation and arbitrary detention of humanitarian relief personnel are prohibited … [State] practice also contains examples in which the following acts against humanitarian aid personnel have been condemned: mistreatment, physical and psychological violence, murder, beating, abduction, hostage-taking, harassment, kidnapping, illegal arrest and detention.[48]

The Rome Statute further strengthened international criminal liability for offences committed against humanitarian personnel. Despite the disparities between API and APII, attacks against humanitarian personnel during both international and non-international armed conflicts are deemed to be war crimes, with Article 8(2)(b)(iii) of the Rome Statute criminalising:

> [i]ntentionally directing attacks against personnel, installations, material, units or vehicles involved in a humanitarian assistance or peacekeeping mission in accordance with the Charter of the United Nations, as long as they are entitled to the protection given to civilians or civilian objects under the international law of armed conflict.[49]

The only case before the ICC to date examining this provision is the Abdallah Banda case concerning war crimes committed during an attack against the African Union Peacekeeping Mission at the Haskanita Military Group Site in Darfur.[50] Despite originally voluntarily presenting himself in March 2011 for the Pre-Trial Hearings, Banda did not subsequently re-appear in Court. While an arrest warrant was issued on 11 September 2014, he currently remains at large so judicial examination of the charges is stalled.[51]

[46] Art 48 API.

[47] M Schmitt, 'Targeting in Operational Law' in T Gilland and D Fleck (eds), *The Handbook of the International Law of Military Operations* 2nd edn (Oxford University Press, 2015) 290.

[48] Henckaerts and Doswald-Beck, *Customary IHL*, above n 31, Rule 31.

[49] The same wording is used in Art 8(2)(e)(iii) Rome Statute for non-international armed conflicts.

[50] *The Prosecutor v Abdallah Banda Abakaer Nourain*, ICC-02/05-03/09.

[51] *The Prosecutor v Abdallah Banda Abakaer Nourain: Case Information Sheet*, ICC-PIDS-CIS-SUD-04-006/15 (23 March 2015).

These provisions of the Rome Statute are supplemented by specific protections afforded for certain humanitarian personnel via the 1994 Convention on the Safety of United Nations and Associated Personnel and its 2005 Optional Protocol.[52] The 1994 Convention sets out clear duties on the part of sending and receiving states to ensure the protection of UN and associated personnel, equipment and premises from attack or any action preventing them from discharging their mandate.[53] Moreover, state parties are required to establish specific criminal sanctions for such actions, and to implement measures to ensure prosecution or extradition of those accused of attacking or preventing UN and associated personnel from conducting their work.[54] A key criticism of the 1994 Convention was its restrictive definition of 'UN operations' to those under direct UN authority and control for the purpose of maintaining or restoring international peace and security, or where the Security Council or General Assembly has declared there is an exceptional risk to the safety of personnel participating in the operation.[55] Likewise, the definition of 'personnel' is restricted to UN personnel (that is, persons deployed specifically by the UN as police, military or civilian components of a UN operation) and associated personnel (that is, persons deployed by a humanitarian organisation with a formal UN agreement to carry out activities in support of the fulfilment of the mandate of a UN operation). Responding to these criticisms (not least by the UN Secretary-General), the 2005 Optional Protocol expanded the range of UN missions covered to include all other UN operations conducted under UN authority and control for the purposes of: a) delivering humanitarian, political or development assistance in peacebuilding; or b) delivering emergency humanitarian assistance.[56] However, there are currently only 92 state parties to the main Convention and 29 state parties to the Optional Protocol, thereby limiting this additional avenue of protection for UN and associated personnel.

Despite these criminal provisions, attacks on humanitarian personnel remain a common threat in complex emergencies. The Aid Worker Security Database documents over 3,900 incidents of serious violence against aid workers since 1997, including the deaths of 1,486 humanitarian

[52] UN Convention on the Safety of United Nations and Associated Personnel (adopted 9 December 1994, entered into force 15 January 1999) 2051 UNTS 363; UN Optional Protocol to the Convention on the Safety of United Nations and Associated Personnel (adopted 8 December 2005, entered into force 19 August 2010) A/60/518.

[53] Arts 9 and 11 1994 Convention.

[54] Art 13 1994 Convention.

[55] Art 1(c) 1994 Convention. See H Llewellyn, 'The Optional Protocol to the 1994 Convention on the Safety of United Nations and Associated Personnel' (2006) 55 *International and Comparative Law Quarterly* 718.

[56] Art II(1) Optional Protocol.

personnel.[57] Furthermore, former UN Under-Secretary-General for Humanitarian Affairs Jan Egeland has noted that attacks on humanitarian personnel tripled between 2000 and 2010, and stressed that governments, parties to armed conflicts and other influential actors have not done enough to reduce the threats to humanitarian personnel.[58]

i. Afghanistan: Attacks against Medical Facilities

The bombing of MSF medical facilities in Kunduz, Afghanistan in October 2015 provided a stark reminder of the risks for all humanitarian personnel working in conflict zones, as well as the responsibilities of parties to a conflict to undertake all reasonable precautions in their target selection. The MSF Kunduz Trauma Centre was treating patients from both the Afghan Government forces and the Taliban during the fighting for the city of Kunduz in September 2015. On 3 October 2015, US Air Force planes undertook 'precise and repeated airstrikes' against the MSF medical facility, killing at least 42 people including 24 patients and 14 staff.[59] MSF strongly condemned the attack, noting they had repeatedly provided the hospital's GPS coordinates to the US and Afghan military forces. In the immediate aftermath, the President of MSF, Dr Joanne Liu stated: 'Under International Humanitarian Law hospitals in conflict zones are protected spaces. Until proven otherwise, the events of last Saturday amount to an inexcusable violation of this law. We are working on the presumption of a war crime.'[60] The next day US President Barack Obama issued a personal apology to MSF for the 'mistaken bombing'.[61]

Initial reports suggested that the attack had occurred due to faulty intelligence from the Afghan military regarding the presence of active

[57] Database available at https://aidworkersecurity.org/incidents. The risks for national humanitarian staff are far greater than for international staff, with 1,304 national staff members killed and 182 international staff killed between 1997 and August 2016. Note: these deaths are the direct result of deliberate attacks, as opposed to other fatalities, such as a result of road traffic incidents.

[58] J Egeland et al, *To Stay and Deliver: Good Practice for Humanitarians in Complex Security Environments*, UNOCHA Policy and Studies Series, 2011, viii, 1. The number of humanitarian personnel working in highly dangerous conflict settings has also increased dramatically in the past 20 years. See S Collinson and S Elhawary, 'Humanitarian Space: A Review of Trends and Issues', Overseas Development Institute, Humanitarian Policy Group Report No 32, April 2012, 9–10.

[59] Médecins Sans Frontières (MSF), *MSF Factsheet—Kunduz Hospital Attack*, updated 8 February 2016.

[60] 'Médecins Sans Frontières (MSF) denounces blatant breach of International Humanitarian Law', statement by Dr Joanne Liu, President, MSF International, 6 October 2015.

[61] M Shear and S Sengupta, 'Obama Issues Rare Apology Over Bombing of Doctors Without Borders Hospital in Afghanistan', *The New York Times*, 7 October 2015.

Taliban combatants in the facility.[62] The subsequent internal Pentagon investigation into the attack rejected this and apportioned responsibility to the US soldiers and commanders, but stopped short of criminal charges. General Joseph L Votel of the US Central Command stressed their actions were unintentional, but accepted that communication and equipment failures and human error, compounded by the stress of combat, contributed to the mistaken airstrike.[63] Sixteen US military personnel received administrative or disciplinary action, including suspension and removal from command, letters of reprimand, formal counselling and extensive retraining.[64] In criticising the Pentagon report, Human Rights Watch noted that war crimes may be committed as a result of 'reckless behaviour' not just intentional acts, and called for appropriate criminal prosecutions for those acknowledged in the report to have acted in a reckless manner.[65]

Unfortunately, the attack on the MSF medical facilities in Kunduz is just one of many high-profile attacks on humanitarian personnel and operations in the past few years.[66] The World Health Organisation (WHO) recorded 594 attacks on healthcare facilities and personnel during 2014 and 2015, resulting in 959 deaths and 1,561 injuries in 19 countries. WHO reported that 62 per cent of these were intentional attacks, with the highest number of attacks occurring in Syria, Iraq and Pakistan.[67] Reflecting the rapid increase in attacks on humanitarian medical operations, the UN Security Council unanimously adopted Resolution 2286 on 3 May 2016, which strongly condemned all 'acts of violence, attacks and threats against the wounded and sick, medical personnel and humanitarian personnel exclusively engaged in medical duties, their means of transport and equipment, as well as hospitals and other medical facilities'.[68] The Resolution stressed that the fight against impunity and accountability for war crimes and other serious violations of IHL has been strengthened by the international criminal justice system, and called on states to co-operate with international courts and tribunals.

[62] Y Torbati, 'Afghan Forces Called for Air Strike in Kunduz: US General', *Reuters*, 5 October 2015.

[63] J Garamone, 'Centcom Commander: Communications Breakdowns, Human Errors Led to Attack on Afghan Hospital', *Department of Defence News*, Defense Media Activity, 29 April 2016.

[64] ibid.

[65] J Shifton, 'Pentagon Hospital Attack Report Falls Short', Human Rights Watch, 4 May 2016.

[66] See, eg, F Terry, 'Violence Against Health Care: Insights from Afghanistan, Somalia, and the Democratic Republic of the Congo' (2013) 95(889) *International Review of the Red Cross* 23.

[67] WHO, *Attacks on Health Care: Report on Attacks on Health Care in Emergencies 2014–2015* (2016) 6.

[68] UNSC *Resolution 2286* (3 May 2016) S/Res/2286 (2016).

In welcoming the Resolution, UN Secretary-General Ban Ki-moon stated: 'When so-called surgical strikes are hitting surgical wards, something is deeply wrong.'[69] He urged the Security Council and states to 'do more than condemn such attacks. They must use every ounce of influence to press parties to respect their obligations'.[70] However, at the same event, the MSF President noted that while the Security Council was responsible for maintaining peace and security, four of its five permanent members had been associated with coalitions responsible for attacks on health structures over the last year. Likewise the ICRC President, Peter Maurer, stated: 'To demand [the laws of war] are respected through practical measures is the most decisive next step this Council can take to ensure humanity in war is a reality and not just an ideal.'[71]

B. Misuse of the Emblems of the Geneva Conventions

One of the key sources of protection for humanitarian personnel is their clear identification as impartial actors not engaged in the conflict. Since the establishment of the Red Cross Movement in the nineteenth century, the symbol of the red cross or red crescent (and latterly the red crystal) signified the non-combatant status of its bearers.[72] The expansion in humanitarian organisations active in war zones beyond national red cross/red crescent societies and the ICRC has posed serious challenges for these other humanitarian organisations to ensure recognition of their particular status on the battlefield. Considering the multiplicity of organisations working to provide material assistance and protection in armed conflicts, a key task for them has been ensuring their logo and 'brand' recognition by parties to the conflict. Following the attack on the MSF Kunduz Trauma Centre, the US Air Force alleged that the Centre did not have an internationally recognised symbol to identify it as a medical facility, 'such as a Red Cross or Red Crescent that was readily visible to the aircrew at night'.[73] MSF countered by noting the facility had a large MSF flag and logo on its roof.[74] Under international law, the Geneva Conventions and

[69] UNSC, *Security Council Adopts Resolution 2286 (2016), Strongly Condemning Attacks against Medical Facilities, Personnel in Conflict Situations*, Press Release, 3 May 2016 (SC/12347).
[70] ibid.
[71] ibid.
[72] For discussion of the social, political and legal internalisation of the distinctive emblems of the Red Cross Movement, see ch 4, Section II.A.i.
[73] US Central Command, *Summary of the Airstrike on the MSF Trauma Center in Kunduz, Afghanistan on October 3, 2015; Investigation and Follow-on Actions* (April 2016) 3.
[74] J Goldstein, 'Doctors Without Borders Says Clues Point to "Illegal" US Strike on Afghan Hospital', *The New York Times*, 5 November 2015.

Additional Protocols only recognise the distinct emblems of two specific groups: the Red Cross Movement, and civil defence organisations.[75] As set out in the three Additional Protocols:

> ***Article 8—Additional Protocol I***
>
> 'Distinctive emblem' means the distinctive emblem of the red cross, red crescent or red lion and sun on a white ground when used for the protection of medical units and transports, or medical and religious personnel, equipment or supplies.
>
> ***Article 12: The distinctive emblem—Additional Protocol II***
>
> Under the direction of the competent authority concerned, the distinctive emblem of the red cross, red crescent or red lion and sun on a white ground shall be displayed by medical and religious personnel and medical units, and on medical transports. It shall be respected in all circumstances. It shall not be used improperly.
>
> ***Article 2: Distinctive emblems—Additional Protocol III***
>
> 1. This Protocol recognises an additional distinctive emblem in addition to, and for the same purposes as, the distinctive emblems of the Geneva Conventions. The distinctive emblems shall enjoy equal status.
> 2. This additional distinctive emblem, composed of a red frame in the shape of a square on edge on a white ground, shall conform to the illustration in the Annex to this Protocol. This distinctive emblem is referred to in this Protocol as the 'third Protocol emblem'.
> 3. The conditions for use of and respect for the third Protocol emblem are identical to those for the distinctive emblems established by the Geneva Conventions and, where applicable, the 1977 Additional Protocols.
> 4. The medical services and religious personnel of armed forces of High Contracting Parties may, without prejudice to their current emblems, make temporary use of any distinctive emblem referred to in paragraph 1 of this Article where this may enhance protection.

Recognising the importance of clearly identifiable emblems and signals, a specific Annex was appended to API to provide template identity cards, specific provisions for emblems, audio and visual signals for medical and other personnel, and symbols for works and installations containing dangerous forces such as dams and nuclear facilities (three orange circles placed on the same axis).[76] Likewise, the distinctive emblem of civil defence organisations (an equilateral blue triangle on an orange background) is specifically recognised in API for international armed conflicts,[77] although

[75] For discussion of the Framework Convention on Civil Defence Assistance and civil defence organisations generally, see ch 8, Section III.B.ii.

[76] Annex I: Regulations Concerning Identification, API. A second annex covers identify cards for journalists on dangerous professional missions.

[77] Art 66 API.

no such express recognition is provided in APII. Moreover, although APIII clearly states that 'the distinctive emblems shall enjoy equal status', the Rome Statute only criminalises their improper use in international armed conflicts as a war crime.

Article 8(2)(b)—Rome Statute

vii. Making improper use of a flag of truce, of the flag or of the military insignia and uniform of the enemy or of the United Nations, as well as of the distinctive emblems of the Geneva Conventions, resulting in death or serious personal injury.[78]

Nevertheless, the ICRC Customary International Humanitarian Law project concluded that the improper use of both the distinctive emblems of the Geneva Conventions and of the UN is prohibited in both international and non-international armed conflicts.[79] Moreover, the project concluded that improper use of 'other internationally recognised emblems', such as the letters 'PW' or 'PG' used to mark prisoner-of-war camps or 'IC' used to mark civilian internment camps, were also prohibited in all forms of armed conflict.[80] As with many of the ICRC customary law rules, while extremely persuasive their customary legal status is still debatable vis-à-vis non-state parties to the Additional Protocols or in situations of non-international armed conflicts.

C. Starvation as a Means of Warfare

As discussed in chapter six, Article 54 API explicitly prohibits the deliberate starvation of the civilian population during international armed conflicts and an arbitrary refusal of access to impartial humanitarian agencies may fall foul of this provision.[81] The Rome Statute likewise links the prohibition of starvation with the provision of humanitarian assistance, by determining that intentionally using starvation of civilians as a method of warfare, including wilfully impeding relief supplies provided under the Geneva Conventions, is a war crime.[82] However, this is limited

[78] See also ICC, *Elements of Crimes*, above n 26, 21–22.

[79] Henckaerts and Doswald-Beck, *Customary IHL*, above n 31, Rules 59 and 60.

[80] ibid, Rule 61. The ICRC defines 'other internationally recognised emblems' as including: 'the protective emblem of cultural property, the international distinctive sign of civil defence and the international special sign for works and installations containing dangerous forces. It also includes the protective emblem for hospital zones and localities, the protective emblem for hospital and safety zones and localities, the letters "PW" or "PG" used to mark prisoner-of-war camps and the letters "IC" used to mark civilian internment camps.'

[81] See ch 6, Section II.B.

[82] Art 8(2)(b)(xxv) Rome Statute.

to international armed conflicts, and no such provision exists for non-international armed conflicts.[83] Nevertheless, Article 14 APII reiterates the prohibition of starvation as a method of warfare in non-international armed conflicts, noting that:

> It is therefore prohibited to attack, destroy, remove or render useless for that purpose, objects indispensable to the survival of the civilian population such as food-stuffs, agricultural areas for the production of food-stuffs, crops, livestock, drinking water installations and supplies and irrigation works.[84]

While there are limited references to relief supplies or humanitarian assistance in APII, the deliberate denial of assistance in internal armed conflicts has been extensively condemned by states, for example during the Syrian conflict.

i. Syria: Besieged Communities

The long-running conflict in Syria, which commenced in 2011, has become one of the worst humanitarian crises in the past 50 years. In April 2016, the UN Special Envoy for Syria Staffan de Mistura estimated that 400,000 people have been killed over the course of the conflict;[85] in July 2016 UNHCR estimated there were 4.8 million Syria refugees in neighbouring countries and 8.7 million IDPs within Syria.[86] In late 2015 two NGOs (PAX and the Syria Institute) launched an initiative called 'Siege Watch' to highlight the plight of persons trapped within besieged areas in Syria, and reported that as of May 2016 there were 1 million people trapped in 46 besieged communities.[87]

Yoram Dinstein defines siege warfare as 'encircling an enemy military concentration, a strategic fortress or any other location defended by the enemy, cutting it off from channels of support and supply'.[88] Dinstein highlights that the essence of siege warfare is to capture a location through the starvation of its inhabitants.[89] Such a military tactic has been used for centuries, with medieval fortified castles designed to

[83] See: Y Dinstein, 'The Right to Humanitarian Assistance' (Autumn 2000) *Naval War College Review* 77, 84; S Wills, 'The Legal Characterization of the Armed Conflicts in Afghanistan and Iraq: Implications for Protection' (2011) 58(2) *Netherlands International Law Review* 173, 198–99.

[84] Art 14 APII.

[85] 'Syria death toll: UN envoy estimates 400,000 killed', *Al Jazeera*, 23 April 2016.

[86] UNHCR, *Syria Emergency* www.unhcr.org/syria-emergency.html.

[87] Siege Watch, *Second Quarterly Report on Besieged Areas in Syria*, May 2016, 8.

[88] Y Dinstein, *The Conduct of Hostilities under the Law of International Armed Conflict* 2nd edn (Cambridge University Press, 2010) 220.

[89] ibid. See also Y Dinstein, 'Siege Warfare and the Starvation of Civilians' in A Delissen and G Tanja (eds), *Humanitarian Law of Armed Conflict: Challenges Ahead*, Essays in Honour of Frits Kalshoven (Martinus Nijhoff, 1991) 148.

withstand prolonged sieges by opposing forces. However, Dinstein is quick to point out that the prohibition of starvation as a method of warfare means that 'a siege laid to a defended town inhabited by civilians must be differentiated from one encircling a military fortress'.[90]

In the Syrian conflict, the vast majority of besieged areas are predominantly civilian towns and communities, including major urban areas such as Homs and Madaya. While armed groups are likely to be present alongside the trapped civilian population, this does not reduce the besieging forces' obligations to ensure that the civilian population is not used as a pawn against combatants. As provided for in GCIV back in 1949:

> The parties to the conflict shall endeavour to conclude local agreements for the removal from besieged or encircled areas, of wounded, sick, infirm, and aged persons, children and maternity cases, and for the passage of ministers of all religions, medical personnel and medical equipment on their way to such areas.[91]

The modern equivalent language would be to promote the evacuation of civilians from besieged areas and to ensure humanitarian access. Since 2014, the UN Security Council has adopted a series of increasingly strongly worded resolutions condemning the denial of humanitarian access by both pro-Syrian government forces and opposition groups, and highlighting that depriving civilians of objects indispensable to their survival, including wilfully impeding relief supplies and access, can constitute a violation of IHL.[92] Yet Marianne Gasser, head of the ICRC delegation in Syria, has stressed the need for not just words but practical actions to ensure humanitarian access—in particular for humanitarian workers to be allowed to return repeatedly to besieged areas to provide humanitarian assistance.[93] Likewise, while acknowledging a significant increase in aid deliveries to besieged areas in Syria during 2016, the Siege Watch report highlights that they have been 'inconsistent, insufficient, and unbalanced due to continuing access restrictions, limiting their effectiveness'.[94]

In May 2014, 58 states called on the UN Security Council to refer the situation in Syria to the ICC so the Prosecutor could 'investigate crimes committed by the Syrian authorities and pro-government militias, as well as by non-State armed groups, all committed in the course of the

[90] ibid, 221.

[91] Art 17 GCIV.

[92] See, eg, UNSC Resolutions 2139 (22 February 2014), 2165 (14 July 2014), 2191 (17 December 2014), 2258 (22 December 2015).

[93] M Gasser, *Syria Conflict: Siege and Suffering*, ICRC, 1 February 2016 www.icrc.org/en/document/syria-conflict-siege-warfare-and-suffering-madaya.

[94] Siege Watch, *Second Quarterly Report*, above n 88, 9.

ongoing conflict in the Syrian Arab Republic since March 2011'.[95] Yet this call was vetoed by Russia and China as Permanent Members of the Security Council. This does not mean there will be impunity for crimes committed within the Syrian conflict. For example, Carla Del Ponte, former chief prosecutor of the ICTY and member of the Independent International Commission of Inquiry on the Syrian Arab Republic, has called for the establishment of an ad hoc criminal tribunal similar to the ICTY.[96] However, to date, no such decision has been made. In the face of on-going armed conflict, it is likely that the exact accountability mechanisms and criminal prosecutions will only be determined once the conflict is over, but the deliberate starvation and denial of access to besieged areas are likely to be a key charge against both Government and opposition forces in Syria.

D. Grave Breaches of the Geneva Conventions

As noted above, in addition to the Rome Statute, all states are bound to respect the Geneva Conventions through customary international law, and to prosecute grave breaches of them. While this method of legal accountability for war crimes has been in existence since 1949, there has been limited judicial examination of individual responsibility for the direct denial of humanitarian assistance for the civilian population in times of war. However, as discussed below, the International Criminal Tribunal for the former Yugoslavia examined criminal liability for the denial of food, medicine and other essentials and the creation of inhumane living conditions in the context of civilian detainees.

i. Civilian Detainees: The Čelebići and Stakiç Cases (ICTY)

The *Čelebići* case (named after a prison camp in Čelebići village, central Bosnia) was the second to be completed by the International Criminal Tribunal for the former Yugoslavia (ICTY) in 1998.[97] The initial indictment of the four accused covered a range of grave breaches of the 1949 Geneva Conventions and violations of the laws or customs of war arising from the treatment of civilian Bosnian-Serb detainees in the Čelebići prison camp, run at various points by both Bosnian and Croatian armed

[95] Human Rights Watch, *Letter: 58 States Call on UN Members to Co-Sponsor the French Resolution Referring Syria to the ICC*, 19 May 2014.

[96] J Borger, 'Call for Special Tribunal to Investigate War Crimes and Mass Atrocities in Syria', *The Guardian*, 17 March 2015.

[97] ICTY, *The Prosecutor v Delalic et al* ('*Čelebići*') (IT-96-21-T) Judgment 16 November 1998. For a summary of the case, see *Judgment Summary: Statement of the Trial Chamber at the Judgement Hearing, The Prosecutor v Delalic et al* ('*Čelebići*'), 16 November 1998. See also Rottensteiner, 'Denial of Humanitarian Assistance', above n 25.

groups. Amongst the various charges against the accused (either directly or due to their role as superiors) was that they subjected:

> the detainees at the Čelebići camp between May and October 1992, to an atmosphere of terror created by the killing and abuse of other detainees and to inhumane living conditions through deprivation of adequate food, water, medical care as well as sleeping and toilet facilities, which conditions caused the detainees to suffer severe psychological and physical trauma.[98]

In finding three of the accused guilty of grave breaches of GCIV, the Tribunal held that the offence of wilfully causing great suffering or serious injury to body or health constitutes 'an act or omission that is intentional, being an act which, judged objectively, is deliberate and not accidental, which causes serious mental or physical suffering or injury. It covers those acts that do not meet the purposive requirements for the offence of torture, although clearly all acts constituting torture could also fall within the ambit of this offence'.[99] The Tribunal also stressed the requirement for humane treatment set out in all four Geneva Conventions. In particular, the Tribunal noted the provisions of GCIII on prisoners of war, and held that: 'the prohibition on inhumane treatment also extends to the living conditions of protected persons and would be violated if adequate food, water, clothing, medical care and shelter, were not provided in light of the protected persons' varying habits and health.'[100]

The *Čelebići* case was subsequently followed by the *Stakiç* case, concerning Bosnian-Serb run prison camps which held Bosnian-Muslim and Bosnian-Croat civilians in Prijedor District between April and September 1992.[101] In particular, the conditions for civilian detainees in three camps (Omarska, Keraterm and Trnopolje) were examined by the ICTY. In 1992, Dr Stakiç was President of the Municipal Authority in Prijedor District, and a leading politician in the area. The Trial Chamber held Dr Stakiç responsible as a co-perpetrator due to his political authority for more than 1,500 killings in the three camps and was able to identify 486 victims by name.[102] While finding the accused not guilty of genocide due to the lack of the necessary *dolus specialis*, the Trial Chamber found Dr Stakiç guilty of crimes against humanity and war crimes.

[98] *Delalic et al judgment*, above n 97, paras 10, 16, 25. Both the Trial Chamber and Appeals Chamber also held that the accused had unlawfully confined civilians contrary to Arts 42 and 42 GCIV. ICTY, *The Prosecutor v Delalic et al ('Čelebići')* (IT-96-21-T) Judgment, Appeals Chamber, 20 February 2001, paras 323–30.

[99] ibid, para 511.

[100] ibid, para 530.

[101] ICTY, *The Prosecutor v Milomir Stakiç* (IT-97-24-T) Judgment, 31 July 2003.

[102] ibid, para 654. For discussion of the 'joint criminal enterprise' element of the conviction, see ME Badar, '"Just Convict Everyone!" Joint Perpetration: From Tadić to Stakiç and Back Again' (2006) 6 *International Criminal Law Review* 293.

In particular, the Trial Chamber focused on the conditions for civilian detainees in camps under the authority of Dr Stakiç, and the definition of persecution as a crime against humanity.

The Tribunal held that although the phrase 'physical violence' was not included in the ICTY Statute, it was a broad term which 'focuses inter alia on the conditions in which detainees were forced to live, such as overcrowded conditions, deprivation of food, water and sufficient air, exposure to extreme heat or cold, random beating of detainees as a general measure to instil terror amongst them and similar forms of physical assaults not amounting to torture'.[103] The accused was therefore convicted of the crime against humanity of persecution based on the inhumane conditions for detainees in the camps, physical, verbal and sexual assaults on detainees, and constant humiliation and degradation. The Trial Chamber concluded that the perpetuation of the inhumane conditions constituting cruel and inhuman treatment of the non-Serb detainees 'was carried out by the direct perpetrators with the intent to cause serious physical suffering to the victims and to attack their human dignity' amounting to a crime against humanity.[104] This conviction was upheld by the Appeals Chamber.[105]

As evidenced by these judgements, inflicting inhumane conditions on civilian detainees amounts to a grave breach of the Geneva Conventions, either as a war crime or as a crime against humanity. While the ICC has not yet specifically examined this issue, it is likely that they would follow the jurisprudence of the ICTY in this regard.

III. WILFUL DENIAL OF HUMANITARIAN ASSISTANCE

The previous section examined the potential criminal liability of individuals and armed groups for overt attacks on humanitarian actors, operations or protected persons in the context of international or non-international armed conflicts. However, international criminal law also recognises that heinous crimes may take place during peacetime. In particular, the Rome Statute recognises that individuals can be prosecuted for genocide and crimes against humanity without there being a specific nexus to an armed conflict.[106] It follows that the deliberate or negligent prolongation

[103] *Stakiç judgment*, above n 101, para 752.

[104] ibid, para 790.

[105] ICTY, *The Prosecutor v Milomir Stakiç* (IT-97-24-T) Judgment, Appeals Chamber, 22 March 2006, p 141.

[106] As confirmed by the ICTY: 'The obsolescence of the nexus requirement is evidenced by international conventions regarding genocide and apartheid, both of which prohibit particular types of crimes against humanity regardless of any connection to armed conflict.'

or exacerbation of suffering of the victims of humanitarian crises may engage individual criminal liability. In other words, if genuine efforts are not made to provide material assistance and protection to the victims of a humanitarian crisis, whether arising from an armed conflict, displacement or disaster scenario, this may lead to criminal liability under international criminal law.[107] As discussed further below, the limited and delayed response of the Myanmar military junta to the widespread destruction caused by Cyclone Nargis in May 2008 provides a case in point. Despite knowledge that there were tens of thousands of people killed, and hundreds of thousands displaced as a result of the storm, the junta severely restricted access for most international humanitarian actors for several weeks following the cyclone. Whether, on the specific facts, their actions amounted to a crime against humanity is debatable. However, it starkly highlighted the reality that governments will not always put the needs of their population first, and may erect unnecessary restrictions for both domestic and international actors, irrespective of the potential deaths and suffering which may occur.[108]

A. Genocide

In an extreme case, it is possible that deliberate acts or omissions resulting in the wilful denial of material assistance or protection may amount to the crime of genocide. The Rome Statute mirrors the language of the Genocide Convention,[109] defining genocide as:

> ***Article 6 (Rome Statute)—Genocide***
>
> … any of the following acts committed with intent to destroy, in whole or in part, a national, ethnical, racial or religious group, as such:
>
> (a) Killing members of the group;
> (b) Causing serious bodily or mental harm to members of the group;
> (c) Deliberately inflicting on the group conditions of life calculated to bring about its physical destruction in whole or in part;

ICTY, *The Prosecutor v Tadiç* (IT-94-1-AR72) Decision on the Defence Motion for Interlocutory Appeal on Jurisdiction, 2 October 1995, para 140. This was subsequently reflected in the ICC *Elements of Crimes* which state that the prohibited acts for a crime against humanity need not constitute a military attack. ICC, *Elements of Crimes*, above n 26, 5.

[107] See F Russo, 'Disasters Through the Lens of International Criminal Law' in A de Guttry, M Gestri and G Venturini, *International Disaster Response Law* (TMC Asser Press, 2012) 441.

[108] See C Allan and T O'Donnell, 'An Offer You Cannot Refuse? Natural Disasters, the Politics of Aid Refusal and Potential Legal Implications' (2013) 5(1) *Amsterdam Law Forum* 36.

[109] Art II Convention on the Prevention and Punishment of the Crime of Genocide (adopted 9 December 1948, entered into force 12 January 1951) 78 UNTS 277.

(d) Imposing measures intended to prevent births within the group;
(e) Forcibly transferring children of the group to another group.

The first point to note is that the ICC *Elements of Crimes* highlight that the word 'killing' in Article 6(a) is interchangeable with the term 'caused death'.[110] In other words, genocide does not only occur through deliberate actions traditionally viewed as murder, but may also occur through policies which restrict or deny people's access to life-sustaining services. Article 6(a) is therefore closely connected to Article 6(c) and the deliberate infliction of conditions of life calculated to bring about the physical destruction of a group. As noted in the *Elements of Crimes*: 'The term "conditions of life" may include, but is not necessarily restricted to, deliberate deprivation of resources indispensable for survival, such as food or medical services, or systematic expulsion from homes.'[111]

In highlighting the need to move beyond a limited understanding of humanitarian assistance, Pulitzer Prize winning journalist Nicholas Kristof made an impassioned plea for justice after meeting Darfuri refugees in Chad in 2006: 'After more than three years of such brutality, it seems incredibly inadequate for the international community simply to hand out bandages when old women are roasted in their huts and young men have their eyes gouged out. What we need isn't more bandages, but the will to stand up to genocide.'[112] Although the evidential burdens would be high, the crime of genocide, as per Article 6 of the Rome Statute, includes acts committed with the intent to destroy a national, ethnic, racial or religious group through killing, causing serious bodily harm or deliberately inflicting on the group conditions of life calculated to bring about its physical destruction. The ICRC has highlighted that deliberate starvation by a state may amount to genocide.[113] Therefore, should a state be unwilling to provide life-saving material assistance to a specific group within its territory during an armed conflict or following a natural or human-made disaster, in extreme cases this could qualify as an act of genocide.[114]

In the *Akayesu* case before the International Criminal Tribunal for Rwanda (ICTR), the judges examined the equivalent wording from the

[110] ICC, *Elements of Crimes*, above n 26, 2.

[111] ibid, 3.

[112] N Kristof, 'Bandages and Bayonets', *The New York Times*, 12 November 2006.

[113] Y Sandoz, C Swinarski and B Zimmermann (eds), *Commentary on the Additional Protocols of 8 June 1977 to the Geneva Conventions of 12 August 1949* (Martinus Nijhoff, 1987) 654.

[114] David Marcus has noted that the international community has never called for international criminal trials for officials responsible for creating, inflicting, or prolonging famine even when such famines could be classified as genocide, and argues for codification of international law via a famine crimes convention. See D Marcus, 'Famine Crimes in International Law' (April 2003) 97(2) *American Journal of International Law* 245.

ICTR Statute concerning the crime of genocide.[115] While the case did not specifically address the deliberate denial of humanitarian assistance, the judges held that the expression 'deliberately inflicting on the group conditions of life calculated to bring about its physical destruction in whole or in part' encompasses methods of destruction by which the perpetrator does not immediately kill the members of the group, but which, ultimately, seek their physical destruction.[116] Moreover, the Tribunal noted that such methods include, inter alia, 'subjecting a group of people to a subsistence diet, systematic expulsion from homes and the reduction of essential medical services below minimum requirement'.[117]

Yet the evidential requirements to secure a conviction for the crime of genocide for the deliberate withholding or denial of material assistance or protection would be high. As the 'crime of crimes', genocide requires a *dolus specialis*, in other words the specific 'eliminationist intent'.[118] Robert Cryer has highlighted the high burden of proof for the specific intent required for genocide compared to the *mens rea* requirement for a crime against humanity based on persecution or ethnic cleansing.[119] In the *Bosnian Genocide* case, the International Court of Justice examined Article II(c) of the Genocide Convention concerning deliberately inflicting on a group conditions of life calculated to bring about its physical destruction in whole or in part.[120] In particular, Bosnia-Herzegovina alleged that the encirclement, shelling and starvation of the civilian population of Sarajevo during the Yugoslavia conflict were evidence of a genocidal intent on the part of Serbia-Montenegro.[121] However, while accepting that civilian members of the protected group were deliberately targeted by Serb forces in Sarajevo and other cities, including through the denial of humanitarian access, the Court held there was insufficient evidence to show that the alleged acts were committed with the specific intent to destroy the protected group in whole or in part.[122] The long-running attempts to prosecute the President of Sudan, Omar Al-Bashir, before the International Criminal Court provides another example of potential criminal liability for the wilful denial of humanitarian assistance.

[115] ICTR, *The Prosecutor v Jean-Paul Akayesu*, ICTR-96-4-T, Trial Chamber 1, 2 September 1998.

[116] ibid, para 505.

[117] ibid, para 506.

[118] R Cryer, 'The Definitions of International Crimes in the *Al-Bashir* Arrest Warrant Decision' (2009) 7 *Journal of International Criminal Justice* 283, 293.

[119] ibid.

[120] ICJ, Case Concerning Application of the Convention on the Prevention and Punishment of the Crime of Genocide (*Bosnia and Herzegovina v Serbia and Montenegro*), Judgment of 26 February 2007.

[121] ibid, paras 323–28.

[122] ibid, para 328.

i. Sudan: The ICC Arrest Warrant for Omar Al-Bashir

Extensive international attention and pressure has been placed on Sudan at various points over the past 30 years. In the late 1980s, Operation Lifeline Sudan was launched as a cross-border humanitarian operation by UN agencies and 35 humanitarian organisations to provide assistance to civilians caught up in the prolonged Sudanese civil war which ultimately led to the creation of South Sudan as an independent country in 2011.[123] While South Sudan gained independence, the region of Darfur in the southwest of Sudan has likewise seen bloody scenes of conflict, with many commentators arguing that a policy of genocide has been committed in the region.[124]

According to Human Rights Watch, since early 2003 Sudanese government forces and allied Janjaweed militias were engaged in crimes against humanity, war crimes and ethnic cleansing in Darfur as part of a counter-insurgency campaign against two rebel movements, the Sudan Liberation Army/Movement (SLA/M) and the Justice and Equality Movement (JEM).[125] Human Rights Watch, amongst others, documented how this campaign included targeted killing, summary execution and systematic rape of civilians, as well as the destruction of hundreds of villages, theft of millions of livestock and forced displacement of more than two million people.[126] Following concerted international pressure, in March 2005 the UN Security Council referred the situation in Darfur to the ICC Prosecutor.[127] Following investigations, on 9 March 2009 the Prosecutor issued an arrest warrant for the President of Sudan, Omar Hassan Ahmad Al-Bashir, for war crimes and crimes against humanity. The Prosecutor argued: '[Al-Bashir] is suspected of being criminally responsible, as an indirect (co-)perpetrator, for intentionally directing attacks against an important part of the civilian population of Darfur, Sudan, murdering, exterminating, raping, torturing and forcibly

[123] See: D Maxwell, M Santschi and R Gordon, *Looking Back to Look Ahead? Reviewing Key Lessons from Operation Lifeline Sudan and Past Humanitarian Operations in South Sudan* (October 2014) Working Paper 24, Secure Livelihoods Research Consortium (SLRC); A Wiebalck, 'International Humanitarian Law and the ICRC in the Republic of the Sudan' (2003) 36 *Comparative and International Law Journal of Southern Africa* 198; F Deng, 'Sudan—Civil War and Genocide' (Winter 2001) 8(1) *Middle East Quarterly* 13.

[124] See, eg, J Hagan and W Rymond-Richmond, *Darfur and the Crime of Genocide* (Cambridge University Press, 2009). For discussion of the implications for the Responsibility to Protect doctrine, see L Glanville, 'Darfur and the Responsibilities of Sovereignty' (2011) 15(3) *International Journal of Human Rights* 462.

[125] Human Rights Watch, *Lack of Conviction: The Special Criminal Court on the Events in Darfur*, Briefing Paper, June 2006, 3.

[126] ibid.

[127] UNSC *Resolution 1593* (31 March 2005) S/RES/1593.

transferring large numbers of civilians, and pillaging their property.'[128] The charges were subsequently amended in July 2010 to include three counts of genocide committed against the Fur, Masalit and Zaghawa ethnic groups, namely: genocide by killing; genocide by causing serious bodily or mental harm; and genocide by deliberately inflicting on each target group conditions of life calculated to bring about the group's physical destruction.[129]

Discussion of the implications of the first ICC arrest warrant for a serving Head of State, and the non-implementation of the arrest warrant by various countries, is beyond the scope of this book.[130] However, of particular relevance to the *acquis humanitaire* is the ICC's examination of the third count of genocide: genocide by deliberate infliction on members of the target groups conditions of life calculated to bring about the physical destruction of the group in whole or in part. Humanitarian workers had faced severe restrictions in their work in Darfur for many years, including flight bans, denials or excessive delays in the processing of travel permits, limitations on staff numbers, and unnecessarily bureaucratic or arbitrary procedures for importing and transporting relief materials.[131] More direct forms of intimidation and harassment included arrests and detention of humanitarian personnel, as well as direct attacks on humanitarian operations.[132] Indeed, immediately following the issuance of the ICC's arrest warrant in March 2009, President Al-Bashir expelled 13 international NGOs and revoked the licences of three domestic NGOs.[133] All humanitarian activities in the region were directly affected by these expulsions, including food distribution, food security, nutrition, water and sanitation, health, shelter and protection.

[128] ICC, *ICC Issues a Warrant of Arrest for Omar Al-Bashir, President of Sudan*, Press Release, 4 March 2009.

[129] ICC, *Pre-Trial Chamber I Issues a Second Warrant of Arrest against Omar Al-Bashir for Counts of Genocide*, Press Release, 10 July 2010. See also Cryer, '*Al-Bashir Arrest Warrant* Decision', above n 119.

[130] See, eg, A Ciampi, 'The Proceedings against President Al-Bashir and the Prospects of their Suspension under Article 16 ICC Statute' (2008) 6 *Journal of International Criminal Justice* 885.

[131] Human Rights Watch, *Darfur: Humanitarian Aid under Siege*, May 2006, 15. The UN Committee on Economic, Social and Cultural Rights had expressed concern regarding similar tactics in southern Sudan in 2000 regarding 'the reported resort to the weapon of deprivation of food and the creation of a man-made famine as an instrument of war, coupled with the diversion of humanitarian food aid supplies from groups of the population in need'. CESCR, *Concluding Observations regarding Sudan* (1 September 2000) E/C.12/1/Add.48, para 25.

[132] M Usmani, 'Restrictions on Humanitarian Aid in Darfur: The Role of the International Criminal Court' (2007–2008) 36 *Georgia Journal of International and Comparative Law* 257, 258.

[133] Overseas Development Institute, *Where to Now? Agency Expulsions in Sudan: Consequences and Next Steps*, Humanitarian Policy Group and ALNAP (March 2009).

At the time, it was stressed that '[w]ater, sanitation and healthcare are expected to be of particular concern'.[134]

A key basis for the third count of genocide according to the Prosecutor were the alleged policies of President Al-Bashir and the Sudanese Ministry for Humanitarian Affairs. The ICC Prosecutor, Luis Moreno-Ocampo, advanced as evidence of genocidal intent that Al-Bashir and his subordinates systematically refused to provide any meaningful aid, and hindered other efforts to bring humanitarian aid to nearly 2.5 million IDPs. The Prosecutor argued that the cumulative effect of physical attacks, forced displacement and the denial of humanitarian assistance was that 'mortality rates among civilians, including principally members of the target groups, remained at critical levels'.[135] However, in their first decision on the arrest warrant, the ICC judges noted that the hindrance of humanitarian assistance, as well as cutting off supplies of food and other essential goods, could be carried out for a variety of reasons other than an intention to destroy in whole or in part a targeted group.[136] Moreover, the majority of judges disagreed with the Prosecutor as to the extent of hindrance of humanitarian aid for IDPs in Darfur, noting that there were 'reasonable grounds to believe that the extent, systematicity and consequences of the [Government of Sudan] hindrance of medical and humanitarian assistance in IDP Camps in Darfur varied greatly over time'.[137] As a result, the Pre-Trial Chamber rejected the counts of genocide against Al-Bashir as the Prosecution had failed to provide reasonable grounds to believe that he acted with a specific intent to destroy in whole or in part the Fur, Masalit and Zaghawa groups.[138]

While the charges of genocide were re-introduced following the Prosecutor's appeal, despite the detailed discussion of the denial of humanitarian assistance during the first arrest warrant decision, the Pre-Trial Chamber's appeal judgment focused primarily on direct attacks and killing of civilians, rather than the denial of humanitarian assistance, to identify the required *dolus specialis*.[139] So while the second arrest warrant for Al-Bashir includes the three charges of genocide, the weight

[134] ibid, 4.

[135] The Office of the Prosecutor, *Situation in Darfur, The Sudan: Summary of the Case, Prosecutor's Application for Warrant of Arrest under Article 58 Against Omar Hassan Ahmad Al-Bashir*, 6–7.

[136] ICC, *Situation in Darfur, Sudan in the Case of the Prosecutor v Omar Hassan Ahmad Al-Bashir ('Omar Al-Bashir'), Decision on the Prosecution's Application for a Warrant of Arrest against Omar Hassan Ahmad Al-Bashir*, 4 March 2009, ICC-02/05-01/09, para 181.

[137] ibid, para 189.

[138] ibid, para 206.

[139] ICC, *Situation in Darfur, Sudan in the Case of the Prosecutor v Omar Hassan Ahmad Al-Bashir, Second Decision on the Prosecution's Application for a Warrant of Arrest*, 12 July 2010, ICC-02/05-01/09, paras 37–40.

that may be put on evidence of hindrance of humanitarian operations in Darfur and the IDP camps is unclear. Moreover, despite the on-going status of the case, whether Al-Bashir will ever come to trial before the ICC is debatable and will likely result from a political decision, rather than a legal one. Nevertheless, through the Al-Bashir case the ICC has attempted to shine a light on the criminal liability of individuals for policies which result in the denial of humanitarian assistance and consequent human suffering. One can foresee future cases where similar such evidence is brought forward, for example arising from the besieged communities in Syria. We therefore await more detailed judicial analysis of the criminal implications of the denial of humanitarian assistance. Arguably, the factual evidence presented in the Al-Bashir arrest warrant could also have been used to support a charge of crimes against humanity; therefore it is to this crime that we turn next.

B. Crimes Against Humanity

Irrespective of a genocidal intent to destroy a particular group or the existence of an armed conflict, the non-provision or misappropriation of material assistance or protection activities can additionally be classified as a crime against humanity. As per Article 7 Rome Statute, a crime against humanity includes acts committed as part of a widespread or systematic attack against any civilian population that results in, inter alia, murder, extermination, torture, persecution of an identifiable group, or other inhumane acts causing great suffering or serious injury to body or to mental or physical health. The *Elements of Crimes* explain that the crime against humanity of extermination set out in Article 7(1)(b) covers inflicting conditions that destroy life including the deprivation of access to food and medicine.[140] Depending on the specific circumstances, the denial of humanitarian assistance could also fall under Article 7(1)(f) torture, Article 7(1)(h) persecution or Article 7(1)(k) other inhumane acts.

Article 7 (Rome Statute)—Crimes against humanity

1. For the purpose of this Statute, 'crime against humanity' means any of the following acts when committed as part of a widespread or systematic attack directed against any civilian population, with knowledge of the attack:
    (b) Extermination …
    (f) Torture …
    (h) Persecution against any identifiable group or collectivity on political, racial, national, ethnic, cultural, religious, gender … or other grounds

[140] ICC, *Elements of Crimes*, above n 26, 6.

that are universally recognised as impermissible under international law …

(k) Other inhumane acts of a similar character intentionally causing great suffering, or serious injury to body or to mental or physical health.

Key to determining whether or not a crime against humanity has occurred is the phrase 'acts when committed as part of a widespread or systematic attack directed against any civilian population'. In the *Limaj* case, the ICTY held that in the context of a crime against humanity, the term 'attack' is not limited to the use of armed force but also encompasses 'any mistreatment of the civilian population'.[141] Although the attack must be 'widespread' (that is, of a large-scale nature and the number of victims) or 'systematic' (that is, organised acts of violence), the ICTY held that whilst the existence of a policy or plan may be evidentially relevant, it is not a legal requirement.[142] As with the crime of genocide, the evidentiary hurdles to prove that a denial of humanitarian assistance amounted to a widespread or systematic attack on a civilian population would be high. Nevertheless, they are not insurmountable. It is feasible that either a deliberate or negligent lack of response to a major humanitarian crisis, such as a large-scale population displacement or natural disaster, could be held to be mistreatment of the civilian population even in the absence of a specific policy or plan to exacerbate the suffering of the victims.[143] The delayed response by the Myanmar government to the suffering caused by Cyclone Nargis provides a strong example of such a situation.

i. Myanmar: Delayed Response to Cyclone Nargis

On 2–3 May 2008, Cyclone Nargis hit the Irrawaddy Delta in Myanmar having crossed the Indian Ocean from Sri Lanka in the preceding days. Although the cyclone was originally expected to make landfall in Bangladesh, knowledge of its impending arrival in Myanmar had led to some limited advance warnings being provided by the Government.[144] Cyclone Nargis was classified as a Category 4 storm, with sustained winds of over 210 km per hour recorded.[145] Inadequate preparation and poor construction of housing and infrastructure meant that the powerful winds, heavy rainfall and large-scale sea surge created a humanitarian

[141] ICTY, *The Prosecutor v Limaj et al* (IT-03-66-T) Judgment 30 November 2005, para 182.

[142] ibid, para 184.

[143] See, eg, L Moffett, 'Accountability for Forced Displacement', above n 25.

[144] S Ford, 'Is the Failure to Respond Appropriately to a Natural Disaster a Crime Against Humanity? The Responsibility to Protect and Individual Criminal Responsibility in the Aftermath of Cyclone Nargis' (2009–2010) 38 *Denver Journal of International Law and Policy* 227, 253–54.

[145] NASA Visible Earth, *Cyclone Nargis* http://visibleearth.nasa.gov/view.php?id=19863.

catastrophe. At least 138,000 people were killed, and 2.4 million people were affected in the Ayeyarwady and Yangon regions of Myanmar.[146]

When the cyclone struck, the ruling military junta was preparing a national referendum to amend the Constitution, and in the aftermath of the Iraq and Afghan invasions was suspicious of Western states' motivations. As a result, the government waited four days before appealing for international assistance, and then imposed a series of onerous conditions on humanitarian activities resulting in allegations of refusal of access and confiscation of humanitarian aid by the military.[147] It took nearly a month before many UN and Western agencies were allowed to operate in the worst affected areas, and efforts by local Myanmar citizens were severely restricted, with criminal charges brought against individuals who attempted to provide 'unofficial' assistance.[148]

Several Western governments, most notably France, the UK and the US, argued that the delayed response by the national authorities was leading to an increased and unnecessary level of suffering in the affected regions. Bernard Kouchner, founder of MSF and then French Minister for Humanitarian Affairs, argued that the obstruction of aid could amount to a crime against humanity.[149] However, such an argument leads one to the debate surrounding humanitarian interventions, the applicability of the Responsibility to Protect doctrine and the international communities' right or obligation to intervene to prevent mass atrocities.[150] Garth Evans, one of the co-authors of the original ICISS report following the Kosovo intervention, has argued that:

> natural disasters, as such, are not per se 'responsibility to protect' situations, but they can be if mass atrocity crimes are also involved. While the Burma/Myanmar reaction could have been the case here—and the issue certainly deserved close scrutiny—in the event itself it was not.[151]

Evans' view that Cyclone Nargis did not entail mass atrocity crimes has been challenged by several authors, who argue that the inaction of the Myanmar government amounted to a crime against humanity and

[146] IFRC, *Myanmar: Cyclone Nargis Emergency Appeal Final Report* (18 November 2011) 5.

[147] J Wong, 'Reconstructing the Responsibility to Protect in the Wake of Cyclones and Separatism' (2009–2010) 84(2) *Tulane Law Review* 219, 242–43.

[148] Ford, 'Failure to Respond', above n 144, 230–33; 'Comic arrested for Burma aid runs', *BBC News Online*, 5 June 2008 http://news.bbc.co.uk/2/hi/asia-pacific/7437251.stm.

[149] C Allan and T O'Donnell, 'A Call to Alms?: Natural Disasters, R2P, Duties of Cooperation and Uncharted Consequences' (2012) *Journal of Conflict and Security Law* 1, 12–13.

[150] For discussion of the Responsibility to Protect doctrine, see ch 4, Section I.B.iii. See also: T Jackson, 'Bullets for Beans: Humanitarian Intervention and the Responsibility to Protect in Natural Disasters' (2010) 59 *Naval Law Review* 1; J Junk, 'Testing Boundaries: Cyclone Nargis in Myanmar and the Scope of R2P' (2016) 30(1) *Global Society* 78.

[151] G Evans, 'The Responsibility to Protect in Environmental Emergencies' (2009) 103 *American Society of International Law Proceedings* 27, 30.

therefore created individual criminal responsibility.[152] However, as such a determination by the UN Security Council would explicitly lead to calls for the application of the Responsibility to Protect doctrine, and potential military intervention, it is clear that some states would be extremely reluctant to take such a step during the emergency phase of a disaster. In the immediate aftermath of a large-scale disaster it is challenging to identify the exact number of people in need (as seen in Hurricane Katrina three years previously),[153] and most states will respond at least minimally to a disaster within their territory. Even in the case of Cyclone Nargis, Indian, Chinese and other Asian neighbours were allowed access to assist the (admittedly limited) domestic Myanmar relief effort in advance of UN and Western actors through the regionally binding the ASEAN Agreement on Disaster Management and Emergency Response.[154]

In reality, obtaining international consensus for humanitarian action without the consent of the government concerned or contrary to their express views in such circumstances would be challenging. However, it is conceivable that a subsequent international or domestic criminal prosecution could be initiated against government or military officials if evidence came to light that a deliberate policy of denial of humanitarian assistance had been in place. Clearly, by delaying much-needed international assistance the Myanmar government failed in its responsibilities as a sovereign state towards persons on its territory. Yet the fact that the international community decided not to pursue international criminal charges against the Myanmar authorities reflects the political nature of such determinations, and the fact that criminal prosecutions are not necessarily the most effective accountability mechanism. Arguably, the subsequent political transformation within Myanmar since 2010 may be linked to the failed domestic response to Cyclone Nargis. While causation is hard to determine, the re-engagement with the authorities of Myanmar by ASEAN, the UN and Western states following Cyclone Nargis provides an example of 'disaster diplomacy' in action.[155]

[152] See, eg, Ford, 'Failure to Respond', above n 144; Wong, 'Cyclones and Separatism', above n 149; R Cohen, 'The Burma Cyclone and the Responsibility to Protect', Brookings Institute, speech at the *Congressional Briefing on Security for a New Century*, 21 July 2008 www.brookings.edu/research/speeches/2008/07/21-myanmar-cohen.

[153] See, eg, MI Medina, 'Confronting the Rights Deficit at Home: Is the Nation Prepared in the Aftermath of Katrina? Confronting the Myth of Efficiency' (2006–07) 43 *California Western Law Review* 9.

[154] M Jacques, 'His Master's Voice', *The Guardian*, 15 May 2008. See also: *Post-Nargis Joint Assessment*, report prepared by the Tripartite Core Group comprised of Representatives of the Government of Myanmar, ASEAN and the UN, July 2008.

[155] See T Kovach, 'The Politics of Disaster Response: Disaster Diplomacy and the Responsibility to Protect after Cyclone Nargis' (April 2013) *American University School of International Service Working Paper*.

IV. CONCLUSION: LEGAL ACCOUNTABILITY VIA INTERNATIONAL CRIMINAL LAW

This chapter has shown that international criminal law provides a series of avenues for individual criminal liability for acts and omissions regarding humanitarian action in times of war and peace. There is increasing recognition that humanitarian actors and civilians are protected as a result of explicit war crimes and grave breaches set out in the Geneva Conventions and Additional Protocols addressing deliberate attacks on humanitarian personnel, the use of starvation of a method of warfare, misuse of protected humanitarian emblems, and the treatment of civilian detainees. Moreover, even outside an armed conflict, the wilful denial of humanitarian assistance in a humanitarian crisis may amount to a crime against humanity or even genocide. Reflecting the evolving nature of international criminal law, we currently lack the depth of case law and judicial interpretation of individual liability for such acts or omissions. While the *Banda* and *Al-Bashir* cases before the ICC provide potential sources of future judicial analysis, it is not clear when or if these cases will ever come to court. Likewise, the Syrian conflict may provide a source of international criminal jurisprudence, not least on the humanitarian impact for civilians in besieged communities. But there is currently no obvious route for such prosecutions to take place.

Despite inaction over these high-profile cases, explicit recognition of the wilful denial of humanitarian assistance in armed conflicts and natural or human-made disasters as an international crime could help ensure that other governments and armed groups act in accordance with international law to ensure humanitarian access. Indeed, by highlighting that individual criminal responsibility may arise from actions taken by responsible parties, this may also prompt those individuals to ensure a fair and efficient distribution of humanitarian assistance.[156] In most cases, the possibility of imposing criminal sanctions will only occur once the emergency phase of a humanitarian operation is completed. Indeed, the evidential burdens for criminal cases before the ICC mitigate against hasty charges being brought. Nevertheless, the symbolic capacity of international prosecution and punishment to express international abhorrence for breaches of international criminal law relating to the protection of persons in humanitarian crisis should not be overlooked, as it can provide an important deterrent effect.[157]

[156] Although Fabrice Weissman has cautioned: 'As far as relying on the fear of international criminal charges to protect humanitarian relief efforts is concerned, we can only stress that it is a risky bet.' Weissman, *Humanitarian Aid and the ICC*, above n 34, 6.

[157] See, eg, R Sloane, 'The Expressive Capacity of International Punishment: The Limits of the National Law Analogy and the Potential of International Criminal Law' (2007) 43 *Stanford Journal of International Law* 39.

In the meantime, our understanding of the criminal responsibilities of those in control of humanitarian access could be advanced by an amendment to the ICC's *Elements of Crimes* to elaborate the circumstances when the wilful denial of humanitarian assistance falls within the proscribed actions of war crimes, crimes against humanity and genocide. Alternatively, a judicial pronouncement that the wilful denial of humanitarian assistance in humanitarian crises falls within the current definitions of international crimes may be the best way to advance our understanding of actions that entail international criminal responsibility. Considering the international outcry concerning the besieged communities in Syria and increasing attacks against humanitarian medical facilities it is likely that the international criminal responsibility of state and non-state actors for ensuring the protection of persons via humanitarian action will be raised in the ICC in the foreseeable future. This should be welcomed and while such international criminal responsibility will not stop governments, officials and armed groups from withholding, attacking, misappropriating or simply stealing aid intended for civilian populations, it can provide another tool in the fight to ensure those facing overwhelming humanitarian needs receive the protection they require in a timely and respectful manner.

8

International Disaster Laws

I. INTRODUCTION: THE CONCEPT OF INTERNATIONAL DISASTER LAWS

IN PRINCIPLE, THE interplay between the severity of any humanitarian crisis (whether natural or human-made) and the vulnerabilities, capacity and resilience of the affected communities should determine the extent of the domestic and international humanitarian responses required. Of course, this is not always the case. Lack of funding, political will or public interest all play a fundamental role in the actual responses by states and humanitarian actors. As a result, different humanitarian crises receive vastly different priorities, directly impacting on the level of assistance affected states and humanitarian agencies can provide to individuals. Although large-scale natural disasters, such as the 2004 Indian Ocean Tsunami or 2010 Haiti earthquake, receive extensive media coverage and political and financial support, on average the UN requests funding for 37 disasters per year.[1] Most of these disasters do not hit the global headlines. Yet the UN has highlighted that communities, households and businesses can be particularly affected by recurring small-scale or slow-onset disasters, and such events constitute a high percentage of the total human and financial loss.[2] Catastrophic sudden-onset disasters such as earthquakes, tropical storms and major landslides are generally easier to identify as there is a clear causal link between the suffering caused and the event. However, slow-onset disasters such as droughts can pose particular challenges for local communities and humanitarian agencies as they do not emerge from a single, distinct event but emerge gradually over time, often based on a confluence of different events.[3] Moreover, there is not necessarily a precise distinction between different types of disaster. As noted

[1] Figures from the UN Financial Tracking Service, *Natural Disasters, 2000–2015* http://fts.unocha.org. Total funding received varies considerably annually depending on the disasters that occur. For example, under $58 million was received as a result of UN appeals in 2003, but over $7.6 billion was received in 2005 following the December 2004 Indian Ocean Tsunami, August 2005 Hurricane Katrina, and October 2005 major earthquake in Kashmir.

[2] UN, Sendai Framework for Disaster Risk Reduction 2015–2030 (18 March 2015) A/CONF.224/CRP.1, Section I(4).

[3] UNOCHA, *OCHA and Slow-onset Emergencies* (April 2011) Occasional Policy Briefing Series No 6, 3.

by UNOCHA, flooding is generally categorised as a sudden-onset event, but it may take weeks of heavy rain before the water flows into rivers and floods downstream communities.[4]

The variety of natural and human-made hazards which can result in a 'disaster' poses challenges to humanitarian agencies in developing consistent and coherent operational responses. Moreover, as noted by the IFRC in 2007: 'many of the most troublesome legal problems that arise in disaster operations do so not in the initial days but in the several weeks or months that follow, as "normal" rules of business re-emerge, and the consequences of faulty mechanisms of coordination, quality and accountability become more apparent.'[5] Ten years later, a legal lacuna remains in many countries regarding the entry and management of humanitarian goods, equipment and personnel,[6] and at the international level there is not yet a universal binding legal framework for natural or human-made disasters.

However, despite its apparent recent emergence as a field of academic and practitioner study, the concept of international disaster laws has a long pedigree. Indeed, a range of initiatives have been undertaken in the past 100 years to develop a specific body of international law surrounding natural and human-made disasters. Therefore, this chapter commences by examining the concept of a 'disaster', before reviewing attempts at codification of international disaster laws during the twentieth century. The chapter then examines some of the key provisions of existing law regarding disaster risk reduction, prevention and preparedness (DRR), before concluding with an analysis of provisions covering humanitarian response and recovery found in binding and non-binding sources.

A. Defining a 'Disaster'

Before commencing any analysis of international law and norms at play in disaster settings, it is necessary to determine what is meant by a 'disaster'. Despite the widespread use of the phrase 'natural disaster', it is hard to identify catastrophic events which result purely from 'natural' causes.[7]

[4] ibid, 4.

[5] IFRC, *Law and Legal Issues in International Disaster Response: A Desk Study* (Geneva 2007) 24.

[6] See, eg, research commissioned by the IFRC to update the operational experiences in natural and human-made disasters since 2007: HERE-Geneva, *The Impact of Regulatory Problems and the Gains from Legal Preparedness in Recent Response Operations* (March 2015).

[7] As set out in ch 1, Section II.C, in recognition of this widespread usage and the divergent legal and policy approaches taken to the concepts of 'hazard', 'vulnerability' and 'disaster', for consistency this book uses the terminology of 'natural and human-made disasters'. See also HRC, *Final research-based report of the Human Rights Council Advisory Committee on best*

As noted by the Internal Displacement Monitoring Centre (IDMC), so-called natural disasters are often strongly influenced by human actions, including urban development, deforestation, dam-building, release of flood waters and anthropogenic climate change.[8] As a result, a range of rapid or slow-onset events precipitated by natural, technological or human-made hazards exist. Such hazards only become a 'disaster' when they negatively affect human life, livelihoods or property. The practical and operational challenges of responding to such natural hazards are well known.[9] Severe human suffering and infrastructure damage can occur in high-income countries, for example in New Zealand[10] or the USA;[11] and the humanitarian challenges are magnified many times over in medium- and low-income countries such as the Philippines[12] or Haiti.[13] Moreover, the interconnection between natural hazards and human-made disasters, such as major technological accidents, were starkly highlighted by the 2011 Japanese earthquake and tsunami, and resulting nuclear emergency at the Fukushima power plant.[14]

Therefore, one needs to examine the specific impact of a natural or human-made hazard before one can determine that a 'disaster' has occurred. A hurricane far out to sea which has little impact on humans should be viewed differently from a similar hurricane in a densely populated coastal area. Hence, as set out in chapter one, a broadly accepted definition of a 'disaster' is a natural hazard plus vulnerability.[15] Such an

practices and main challenges in the promotion and protection of human rights in post-disaster and post-conflict situations (10 February 2015) A/HRC/28/76, paras 20–21.

[8] IDMC, *Global Estimates 2012: People Displaced by Disasters*, May 2013, 10.

[9] V Bannon and D Fisher, 'Legal Lessons in Disaster Relief from the Tsunami, the Pakistan Earthquake and Hurricane Katrina' (March 2006) 10(6) *ASIL Insights*.

[10] A Kaiser et al, 'The Mw 6.2 Christchurch Earthquake of February 2011: Preliminary Report' (2012) 55(1) *New Zealand Journal of Geology and Geophysics* 67.

[11] MI Medina, 'Confronting the Rights Deficit at Home: Is the Nation Prepared in the Aftermath of Katrina? Confronting the Myth of Efficiency' (2006–07) 43 *California Western Law Review* 9.

[12] T Branigan and K Hodal, 'Typhoon Haiyan: Frustration at Slow Pace of Relief Effort', *The Guardian* (15 November 2013).

[13] IASC, *Response to the Humanitarian Crisis in Haiti following the 12 January 2010 Earthquake: Achievements, Challenges and Lessons to be Learned* (2010).

[14] D Farber, 'Legal Scholarship, The Disaster Cycle, and the Fukushima Accident' (2012) 23(1) *Duke Environmental Law and Policy Forum* 1.

[15] T Cannon, 'Reducing People's Vulnerability to Natural Hazards: Communities and Resilience', United Nations University, World Institute for Development Economic Research, Research Paper No 2008/34, April 2008, 2. As noted by the IDMC, *Global Estimates Report 2012*, above n 8: 'Disasters result from a combination of risk factors: the exposure of people and critical assets to single or multiple hazards together with existing conditions of vulnerability, including insufficient capacity or measures to reduce or cope with potential negative consequences', 10.

approach is intended to highlight that people are affected differently by the same event, and recognises the differential vulnerabilities and capabilities within and between populations to diverse natural hazards. The impact a natural, technological or human-made hazard has on a particular community not only depends on its severity, but also can be exacerbated by underlying vulnerabilities of individuals or groups within the community or ameliorated by their capacity and resilience. Beyond these individual or community-level determinants, a different spread of risk and hazards is faced depending where in the world one lives (for example, close to an earthquake fault line, in an area prone to hurricanes or tornadoes, or in a mountainous area that experiences avalanches and mudslides). Therefore, a general typology of natural and human-made or technological hazards, drawn from the categories used by the Centre for Research on the Epidemiology of Disasters (CRED) in their Emergency Events Database (EM-DAT), is set out in Table 8.1 below.[16]

Table 8.1: Typology of natural and human-made or technological hazards

Natural hazards	Human-made or technological hazards
— **Geophysical**: earthquakes, landslides, tsunamis and volcanic activity — **Hydrological**: avalanches and floods — **Climatological**: extreme temperatures, drought and wildfires — **Meteorological**: cyclones and storms or wave surges — **Biological**: disease epidemics and insect or animal plagues	Events caused by humans occurring in or close to human settlements, such as: — Famine and food shortages — Forced population displacement — Major industrial or transport accidents — Environmental degradation and pollution — Complex emergencies: a combination of several hazards

The text of the International Law Commission's draft articles on the protection of persons in the event of disasters proposes a legal definition of a 'disaster' as: 'a calamitous event or series of events resulting in widespread loss of life, great human suffering and distress, mass displacement, or large-scale material or environmental damage, thereby seriously

[16] The Centre for Research on the Epidemiology of Disasters (CRED) has maintained an Emergency Events Database (generally known as 'EM-DAT') since 1988 which contains statistical data on the occurrence and effects of over 18,000 disasters from 1,900 to the present www.emdat.be/explanatory-notes. See also: IFRC, *Types of disasters: Definition of hazard* www.ifrc.org/en/what-we-do/disaster-management/about-disasters/definition-of-hazard; IDMC, *Global Estimates Report 2012*, above n 8, 9.

disrupting the functioning of society.'[17] The ILC Commentaries note that a conscious decision was made to focus on disasters as specific events, due to the legal nature of the definition, rather than a more policy-orientated definition focusing on the consequences of an event.[18] Conversely, the UN Office for Disaster Risk Reduction (UNISDR) defines a 'disaster' as: 'a serious disruption of the functioning of a community or a society involving widespread human, material, economic or environmental losses and impacts, which exceeds the ability of the affected community or society to cope using its own resources.'[19] The UNISDR approach therefore stresses the coping strategies of the local community or state authorities, and the potential need for external assistance to respond to the disruption caused. While the ILC definition is likely to gain considerable authority as a legal formulation of the concept of a 'disaster', the IFRC has highlighted that operational humanitarian organisations have generally adopted a broad approach to the term 'disaster', reflecting the complexity of different disaster scenarios.[20]

B. Early Attempts to Develop International Disaster Laws

Despite Emer de Vattel's recognition in 1758 that 'every Nation should give its aid to further the advancement of other Nations and save them from disaster and ruin',[21] the concept of international disaster laws has generally been of secondary consideration to other legal humanitarian challenges covering the maintenance of peace and security, and international co-operation to respond to armed conflicts and forced displacement.[22] While the establishment of the International Relief Union (IRU) in 1927 provided an early opportunity for a coherent body of law to emerge, in reality the legal regulation of responses to natural and human-made

[17] Draft Art 3(a). For the final text of the preamble, draft articles and commentaries adopted by the ILC, see Official Records of the General Assembly, Seventy-first Session, *Supplement No 10* (A/71/10), Chapter IV: Protection of Persons in the Event of Disasters (2016).

[18] For the final text of the Commentaries to draft articles adopted in August 2016, see Official Records of the General Assembly, A/71/10 (n 17), pp 17–73. For discussion of the legal definitions and approaches in various international texts, see E Valencia-Ospina, *Preliminary Report on the Protection of Persons in the Event of Disasters*, 8 May 2008, A/CN.4/598, paras 44–49.

[19] UNISDR, *Terminology* www.unisdr.org/we/inform/terminology.

[20] IFRC, *Desk Study*, above n 5, 22.

[21] E de Vattel, *The Law of Nations or the Principles of Natural Law Applied to the Conduct and to the Affairs of Nations and of Sovereigns*, text of 1758, Books I–IV, vol iii, 114.

[22] D Fidler, 'Disaster Relief and Governance after the Indian Ocean Tsunami: What Role for International Law?' (2005) 6 *Melbourne Journal of International Law* 458, 459–61.

disasters (as opposed to improving disaster management per se)[23] remained limited for much of the twentieth century.[24] Indeed, notwithstanding an on-going focus on humanitarian issues within the UN system, including by the specialised agencies and General Assembly,[25] there were limited attempts to codify international law surrounding disasters between the 1920s and the 1980s. This partly reflected the overarching Cold War tensions, and the resultant insistence on non-interference in the internal affairs of states. Nevertheless, with the winding down of the IRU in 1967, and in recognition of the need for mechanisms within the UN for disaster relief, Resolution 2816 (XXVI) of 1972[26] established the Office of the UN Disaster Relief Co-ordinator (UNDRO) with a broad mandate to lead UN operational responses to natural and other disasters. The period from 1972 also saw important advances in disaster management, with the recognition by disaster-prone states, donors and humanitarian agencies of the need for dedicated focal points and units responsible for disaster preparedness, response and prevention activities.[27]

Building on Resolution 2816 (XXVI) and the 1977 ECOSOC recommendation on Measures to Expedite International Relief,[28] in 1982 the UN Institute for Training and Research (UNITAR) developed a series of Model Rules for Disaster Relief Operations.[29] The primary focus was on

[23] The IFRC defines 'disaster management' as: 'the organisation and management of resources and responsibilities for dealing with all humanitarian aspects of emergencies, in particular preparedness, response and recovery, in order to lessen the impact of disasters.' See IFRC, 'About Disaster Management', www.ifrc.org/en/what-we-do/disaster-management/about-disaster-management.

[24] See KN Bookmiller, 'Closing "The Yawning Gap"? International Disaster Response Law at Fifteen' in S Breau and K Samuel, *Research Handbook on Disasters and International Law* (Edgar Elgar, 2016) 48–51.

[25] The General Assembly has produced numerous resolutions on humanitarian issues, in particular Resolutions entitled: International Cooperation on Humanitarian Assistance in the Field of Natural Disasters, from Relief to Development, most recently UNGA Res 70/107, 10 December 2015; Strengthening of the Coordination of Humanitarian Emergency Assistance of the United Nations, most recently UNGA Res 70/106, 10 December 2015; Safety and Security of Humanitarian Personnel and Protection of United Nations Personnel, most recently UNGA Res 70/104, 10 December 2015.

[26] Assistance in Cases of Natural Disaster and other Disaster Situations, UNGA Res 2816 (XXVI), 10 January 1972.

[27] R Kent, 'Reflecting upon a Decade of Disasters: The Evolving Response of the International Community' (Autumn 1983) 59(4) *International Affairs* 693, 698–99.

[28] Measures to Expedite International Relief, ECOSOC Res 2102 (LXIII), 3 August 1977 called on governments, inter-governmental agencies and NGOs to adopt appropriate legislative, administrative or operational measures to remove obstacles and expedite international relief assistance to the victims of disasters.

[29] M el Baradei, *Model Rules for Disaster Relief Operations*, Policy and Efficacy Studies No 8 (UN Institute for Training and Research 1982).

technical and operational aspects of international disaster responses to 'overcome some of the legal restrictions and bureaucratic impediments which are often major obstacles to the success of a relief operation'.[30] UNITAR examined four options when developing the Model Rules: the first was a multilateral convention on disaster relief assistance; second was the conclusion of regional or sub-regional agreements on disaster relief; third was a stand-by agreement to be concluded on a bilateral basis in anticipation of a disaster; and the final option was model rules for bilateral agreements which states and humanitarian agencies could incorporate into situation-specific agreements. Taking into account the political and legal realities of the time, UNITAR concluded that voluntary model rules were the most practical and feasible.[31] In fact, three separate Model Rules were developed covering co-operation between an assisting state and a receiving state; between an assisting organisation and a receiving state; and between an assisting state or organisation or a receiving state and a transit state. The issues covered by the Model Rules reflect the technical practicalities of international relief operations, with specific rules outlining the requirements for customs duties,[32] transportation, communications and visa requirements.

Despite this focus on model rules, the next logical step for the UN Disaster Relief Co-ordinator was the drafting of a multilateral convention on disaster relief. Therefore, relying on the 1977 ECOSOC Resolution which called on UNDRO to 'promot[e] measures designed to remove obstacles and to expedite international relief assistance', the Disaster Relief Co-ordinator took the initiative to develop a draft Convention on Expediting the Delivery of Emergency Assistance.[33] Following a report by Professor Jiri Toman, UNDRO convened an informal group of experts to draft the convention. Writing immediately after the development of the 1984 draft Convention, Peter MacAlister-Smith reviewed the possibilities of codification:

> An advantage of the approach based on a multilateral convention is found in the potentially universal and uniform nature of the results intended to be achieved. On the other hand, it can be feared that in practice the problems resulting from reservations and non-universal acceptance of a multilateral relief convention

[30] ibid, 3.

[31] Y Beigbeder, *The Role and Status of International Humanitarian Volunteers and Organizations: The Right and Duty to Humanitarian Assistance* (Martinus Nijhoff, 1991) 375–77.

[32] In 1990, the World Customs Organisation concluded the Convention on Temporary Admission, which provides a specific Annex setting out procedures for the admission of humanitarian goods in an emergency setting; Convention relating to Temporary Admission (adopted 26 June 1990, entered into force 27 November 1993). The Convention itself has 67 contracting parties; however, states must individually sign the Annexes, and as of November 2014 the relevant annex (Annex B.9) had only been signed by 45 states.

[33] Beigbeder, *Role and Status*, above n 31, 377–79.

might even increase the difficulties faced by those involved in humanitarian actions.[34]

Such fears were premature, though. While there was initial support for the draft Convention from governmental delegations in the General Assembly,[35] it faced serious criticism from some of the largest humanitarian NGOs such as Caritas International, Oxfam and the Red Cross Movement. These NGOs jointly wrote to UNDRO expressing their concern about their exclusion from the consultation and drafting process. They also criticised the substantive content of the draft Convention, in particular the state-centric approach adopted and the fact that the text neither mentioned the victims of disasters nor NGOs active in humanitarian responses. Furthermore, they highlighted that an excessive invocation of state sovereignty could paralyse humanitarian action, particularly as the political climate of the day did not favour the conclusion of a multilateral convention and so could potentially reinforce barriers to co-operation.[36] Government representatives subsequently also raised concerns, with the German Democratic Republic (GDR) arguing that existing bilateral and multilateral arrangements were sufficient to improve the effectiveness of relief. Reflecting Cold War tensions of the time, the GDR also warned that 'certain states' should cease using emergency relief as a coercive measure.[37] While the draft Convention was referred to the UN General Assembly Sixth Committee for consideration, these state reservations, coupled with the lack of support from major humanitarian actors, sounded the death knell for this attempt at codification of international disaster laws.

Nevertheless, although the UNITAR Model Rules were not widely used in practice, and the draft Convention was ultimately not acceptable to either states or humanitarian actors, these initiatives during the 1970s and 1980s prompted the emergence of a body of normative texts aimed at improving the effectiveness and co-ordination of international humanitarian operations.[38] Since the mid-1980s, and in particular following the conflicts in the former Yugoslavia, Rwanda and Somalia in the early 1990s, a range of disaster-specific non-binding resolutions, guidelines and minimum standards have been developed by inter-governmental and non-governmental agencies, including the IFRC *Guidelines for the Domestic*

[34] P MacAlister-Smith, *International Humanitarian Assistance: Disaster Relief Actions in International Law and Organization* (Martinus Nijhoff, 1985) 159–60.

[35] ibid, 159.

[36] Beigbeder, *Role and Status*, above n 31, 378.

[37] IFRC, *Desk Study*, above n 5, 27–28.

[38] Kirsten Bookmiller has highlighted the tensions during this period between those who advocated a technical and operational approach, and those who favoured a more normative approach. See Bookmiller, 'Closing "The Yawning Gap"?', above n 24, 53–55.

Facilitation and Regulation of International Disaster Relief and Initial Recovery Assistance,[39] and the IASC *Operational Guidelines on the Protection of Persons in Situations of Natural Disasters*.[40]

C. Constructing a Coherent Body of International Disaster Laws

In recent years, the concept of a global system of international disaster laws has been substantially advanced. In particular, the IFRC *World Disasters Report 2000* highlighted the lack of coordinated international legal mechanisms for disaster responses. The Report stressed that there was 'no definitive, broadly accepted source of international law which spells out legal standards, procedures, rights and duties pertaining to disaster response and assistance. No systematic attempt has been made to pull together the disparate threads of existing law, to formalize customary law or to expand and develop the law in new ways'.[41] Drawing on its functional responsibility within the International Red Cross Movement to take the lead on natural and human-made disasters (as a counterpart to the ICRC's primary responsibility for the humanitarian impact of armed conflicts), in 2001 the IFRC commenced such a systematic attempt to research existing laws and to advocate for a more consistent approach to global disaster laws. In 2007, the Director of the IFRC's Disaster Law Programme, David Fisher, argued that many of the operational challenges which arise in disaster response exist because international disaster relief resembles a 'swashbuckler's paradise', with a scattered and under-used international legal regime and scant applicable law at the national level.[42] The following year, the ILC Special Rapporteur on the Protection of Persons in the Event of Disasters, Eduardo Valencia-Ospina, likewise lamented the 'amorphous state of the law relating to international disaster response', noting that it is often difficult to distinguish between *lex lata* and *lex ferenda*.[43] Such statements reflected the reality of persistent legal and regulatory challenges faced by humanitarian agencies in disaster contexts, as summarised in Table 8.2 below.

[39] The Guidelines are aimed at state authorities to assist them in developing their domestic legal preparedness for disasters, and provide a practical approach to legal issues in disaster relief. As such, they resemble the technical and operational approach of the UNITAR Model Rules.

[40] IASC, *Operational Guidelines on the Protection of Persons in Situations of Natural Disasters*, Brookings-Bern Project on Internal Displacement, January 2011.

[41] IFRC, *World Disasters Report 2000* (Geneva, 2000) 145.

[42] D Fisher, 'International Disaster Relief: A Growing Regulatory Dilemma' (2007) 101 *Proceedings of the Annual Meeting (ASIL)* 114.

[43] Valencia-Ospina, *Preliminary Report*, above n 18, para 59.

Table 8.2: Summary of common regulatory challenges in international disaster operations

Regulatory issues for international disaster response[44]	
Initiation and termination	— The form and timing of a state's official request for international assistance, and subsequent declaration of the end of an emergency
Personnel, goods and equipment	— Delays in the entry of international humanitarian personnel, goods and equipment (for example foodstuffs, telecommunications equipment or vehicles) due to the requirements of customs and immigration laws which are not adapted to a situation of urgency — Imposition of duties, tolls and taxes on relief items and activities — Problems granting legal recognition of foreign qualifications for specialised professional personnel (for example doctors or search and rescue personnel)
Transport and movement	— Delays in the entry and exit of international humanitarian personnel, goods and equipment through transit states — Imposition of duties, tolls and taxes on relief items in transit
Operations	— Difficulties in granting legal recognition for foreign humanitarian organisations, which mean they may not be able to open bank accounts, hire local staff, lease premises, or other legal actions necessary for efficient in-country assistance
Quality and accountability	— Importation of unnecessary or inappropriate relief items — Use of inadequately trained personnel — Culturally unacceptable behaviour — Proselytising
Coordination	— Failure to coordinate with domestic authorities and other relief providers — Failure to consult with beneficiaries

Yet in the past decade or so, not least as a result of work conducted by the IFRC and ILC, a wide range of bilateral, trilateral and regional instruments relating to DRR, civil defence and mutual assistance have

[44] Drawn from: IFRC, Model Act for the Facilitation and Regulation of International Disaster Relief and Initial Recovery Assistance (with commentary) (March 2013) 8–9. For country-specific examples of regulatory challenges during humanitarian operations see HERE-Geneva, *Impact of Regulatory Problems*, above n 6.

been concluded.[45] Additionally, a plethora of non-binding texts have been developed to regulate or clarify the organisation, planning and implementation of national, regional and international responses to disasters, from UN General Assembly Resolutions to minimum standards and guiding principles elaborated by non-governmental humanitarian actors.[46]

Such national and regional binding and non-binding instruments are supplemented by a growing body of binding international law of direct relevance to disaster preparation and response. For example, the Convention on Assistance in the Case of Nuclear Accident or Radiological Emergency, concluded in the aftermath of the Chernobyl nuclear disaster, promotes international information sharing and the provision of assistance for a state party facing a nuclear accident on its territory.[47] Concurrently, the Convention on Early Notification of a Nuclear Accident provides that states utilising nuclear power must notify the International Atomic Energy Agency and neighbouring states of any nuclear accident.[48] Similar international conventions have been concluded covering oil pollution and industrial accidents.[49] Moreover, a range of other international conventions have included specific provisions for disaster response. For example, the Convention on Facilitation of International Maritime Traffic provides that public authorities must facilitate the arrival and departure of vessels engaged in natural disaster relief work, and to the greatest extent possible facilitate the entry and clearance of persons and cargo arriving in such vessels.[50] Nevertheless, the thematic nature of these provisions highlights the challenges of developing a unified international legal framework. As Eduardo Valencia-Ospina noted in his Preliminary Report on the protection of persons in the event of disasters:

> The importance of a coherent framework in terms of rights and obligations becomes apparent when considering the wide range of specific issues to which

[45] IFRC, *Desk Study*, above n 5, 62–84; ILC, 'Secretariat Memorandum on the Protection of Persons in the Event of Disasters' 60th Session (11 December 2007) A/CN.4/590, 10–11, 29–36. Examples of regional frameworks include the 1991 OAS Inter-American Convention to Facilitate Disaster Assistance and the 2005 ASEAN Agreement on Disaster Management and Emergency Response.

[46] D Cubie, 'An Analysis of Soft Law Applicable to Humanitarian Assistance: Relative Normativity in Action?' (2012) 2 *Journal of International Humanitarian Legal Studies* 177.

[47] Convention on Assistance in the Case of Nuclear Accident or Radiological Emergency (adopted 26 September 1986, entered into force 26 February 1987) 1457 UNTS 133.

[48] Convention on Early Notification of Nuclear Accidents (adopted 26 September 1986, entered into force 27 October 1986) 1439 UNTS 276.

[49] International Convention on Oil Pollution Preparedness, Response and Cooperation (adopted 30 November 1990, entered into force 13 May 1995) 1891 UNTS 77; Convention on the Transboundary Effects of Industrial Accidents (adopted 17 March 1992, entered into force 19 April 2000) 2105 UNTS 457.

[50] Convention on Facilitation of International Maritime Traffic (adopted 9 April 1965, entered into force 5 March 1967) 591 UNTS 265, Arts 5(11) and 5(12).

providing disaster assistance gives rise through successive phases, not only of disaster response but also pre-disaster and post-disaster: prevention and mitigation on the one hand, and rehabilitation on the other.[51]

The following sections therefore aim to provide an overview of the key binding international law relating specifically to the provision of material assistance and the protection of persons in natural and human-made disasters.[52] However, reflecting the evolving nature of international disaster laws as a coherent body of laws, reference will also be made to some of the most important non-binding policy and guidance documents. The sections trace the disaster cycle itself,[53] by initially examining DRR measures, before moving on to review provisions relating specifically to humanitarian response and recovery. Before examining the existing law, it is useful to consider one of the most devastating natural disasters to occur in the past 100 years—the 2004 Indian Ocean Tsunami.

i. Legal Impact of the 2004 Indian Ocean Tsunami

On 26 December 2004, the most powerful earthquake in a generation struck off the coast of Indonesia's Aceh Province, triggering a massive tsunami wave. Measuring over 9.1 M_W, the earthquake released the equivalent energy of 23,000 Hiroshima bombs. The tsunami radiated out across the Indian Ocean causing devastation across 14 countries. More than 226,000 people were killed, particularly along beachfront areas in Indonesia, Thailand, Sri Lanka, the Maldives, India and Bangladesh. Indonesia bore the brunt of the tsunami, with over 166,000 people killed and over 600,000 people made homeless in Aceh Province in a matter of minutes.[54]

Local actors were key to the initial response, but the extent of the human impact and physical destruction was beyond the capacity of any

[51] Valencia-Ospina, *Preliminary Report*, above n 18, 20. See also: Council Regulation (EC) No 1257/96 of 20 June 1996 concerning humanitarian aid (OJ L.163/6), which similarly emphasises that humanitarian assistance must cover the full duration of a crisis and its aftermath, Preamble.

[52] Some key regional provisions will also be noted. However, the extent of bilateral and multilateral regional agreements on civil defence and co-operation in accidents and disasters precludes detailed examination in this book.

[53] For discussion of the disaster cycle, see ch 3, Section II.A.i.

[54] *After the Wave: A Pictorial History of the Irish Red Cross Indian Ocean Tsunami Relief and Recovery Programme 2005–2011* (Irish Red Cross Society, 2011) 8. Having worked on the Irish Red Cross Tsunami operations between 2008 and 2010, I saw first-hand the dedication of the national Red Cross staff and volunteers in Aceh Province and eastern Sri Lanka, as well as the commitment of the International Red Cross Movement.

one agency or country.[55] The subsequent international response to the tsunami was impressive, but also highlighted many of the strengths and weaknesses of the international humanitarian system.[56] In particular, the challenge of simultaneously providing protection and assistance to affected communities in so many countries reinforced the need for comprehensive national, regional and international legal mechanisms and instruments to improve responses to natural disasters.[57] The subsequent international co-operation to establish tsunami early warning mechanisms can be seen as one of the immediate structural changes brought about by the tsunami, as well as recognition of the need for disaster risk reduction and preventative measures.[58] From an operational perspective, the tsunami also prompted the Humanitarian Response Review (HRR), which commenced in February 2005. This review of the international humanitarian system as a whole led to the introduction of the UN Cluster system to improve coordination and co-operation on the ground during disaster operations.[59]

Soon after the tsunami, David Fidler argued that its likely impact on international law would be limited, as both assisting and affected states would be keen to stress their sovereignty, and therefore would be 'hesitant to negotiate and accept far-reaching treaties that impose legally binding responsibilities with respect to disaster preparedness, protection and response'.[60] This early assessment has partly been borne out—as reflected in the non-binding Sendai Framework for disaster risk reduction (2015–2030), and the potential challenges of converting the ILC draft articles on the protection of persons in the event of disasters into a binding international instrument.

However, there was a swift response at the regional level, with the adoption of the comprehensive ASEAN Agreement on Disaster Management and Emergency Response in July 2005. Its entry into force in December 2009 marked a key development in the legal response to the tsunami (which directly affected four ASEAN countries), and highlights the role of multilateral regional treaty-based systems in conjunction with

[55] For analysis of the overall response, see J Telford and J Cosgrave, 'The International Humanitarian System and the 2004 Indian Ocean Earthquake and Tsunamis' (2007) 31(1) *Disasters* 1.

[56] Bannon and Fisher, 'Legal Lessons', above n 9.

[57] Fidler, 'Disaster Relief', above n 22.

[58] ibid, 470.

[59] For discussion of the Cluster system, see ch 3, Section I.B.ii.

[60] Fidler, 'Disaster Relief', above n 57, 473.

general international law.[61] Likewise, experience has shown that major natural disasters such as the Indian Ocean Tsunami prompt national authorities to develop and implement new domestic laws.[62] Finally, the Indian Ocean Tsunami provided a particularly visual and shocking reminder of the risks many countries face from natural disasters, thereby providing a strong impetus to heed the call for action set out in the Red Cross *World Disasters Report 2000* to develop international disaster laws. The inclusion of the protection of persons in the event of disasters onto the long-term programme of work of the ILC in 2006 can therefore be traced directly back to the tsunami. So while a comprehensive global binding legal text has not yet been concluded, the catalytic effect of the tsunami on national, regional and international laws is undeniable.

II. DISASTER RISK REDUCTION, PREVENTION AND PREPAREDNESS

A. From Yokohama to Hyogo

In parallel to the reflection and analysis prompted by the international community's failures in Rwanda, Somalia and the former Yugoslavia to prevent or mitigate some of the worst armed conflicts since the end of the Second World War, the 1990s was also designated the International Decade of Natural Disaster Reduction. Just as it was recognised that civilian casualties and suffering as a result of war had increased exponentially since the beginning of the twentieth century, there was an increasing awareness of the massive pain and suffering caused by 'natural' disasters.[63] Major geological or hydro-meteorological events, such as the eruption of Krakatoa in 1883 and the San Francisco earthquake in 1906, had always garnered both international awareness and support for those affected.[64] However, the major technological advances in the second half of the

[61] The member states of the Association of Southeast Asian Nations (ASEAN) are: Brunei Darussalam, Cambodia, Indonesia, Lao PDR, Malaysia, Myanmar, Philippines, Singapore, Thailand and Viet Nam. For information on the ASEAN Agreement on Disaster Management and Emergency Response (AADMER), see: *AADMER Work Programme 2016–2020* (April 2016) ASEAN Secretariat.

[62] Bannon and Fisher, 'Legal Lessons', above n 9.

[63] It should be noted that the International Relief Union in the 1920s was also mandated to 'encourage the study of preventative measures against disasters' and this knowledge base was one of the IRU's more enduring legacies. For discussion, see ch 1, Section III.B.

[64] J Hutchinson, 'Disasters and the International Order I: Earthquakes, Humanitarians, and the Ciraolo Project' (March 2000) 22(1) *International History Review* 1, 10–14.

twentieth century allowed a much wider range of people and organisations to not only highlight the humanitarian impacts of such disasters but to prepare for and respond to them directly.[65]

According to the Government of Japan, 21 per cent of the world's earthquakes of magnitude 6 or greater have occurred in Japan, despite Japan's landmass comprising only 0.25 per cent of the world total.[66] It is therefore no surprise that Japan has taken a global leadership role in disaster management and risk reduction measures. As part of the International Decade of Natural Disaster Reduction, the first World Conference on Natural Disaster Reduction, held in May 1994, adopted the Yokohama Strategy and Plan of Action comprising a series of guidelines for disaster prevention, preparedness and mitigation.[67] The need to focus on DRR, not just provision of emergency aid after an event had occurred, was starkly highlighted soon afterwards with the Great Hanshin-Awaji Earthquake of January 1995. The earthquake caused massive destruction in the Japanese Prefecture of Hyogo and surrounding areas, including 6,434 deaths and the economic cost of ten trillion yen was equal to around 2.5 per cent of Japanese GDP.[68] Of particular importance, Japanese and global authorities noted that despite the proximity of the three cities of Kobe, Osaka and Kyoto, 71 per cent of all fatalities and 62 per cent of all houses destroyed occurred within the city of Kobe.[69] It therefore became apparent there was a pressing need to research and understand the uneven distribution of the earthquake's impact, and to determine the human elements that contributed to risk alongside the natural hazards and geological structure of the area.[70]

Ten years later, the international community returned to Kobe with the stated aim of developing international, regional and domestic strategies to promote a 'substantial reduction of disaster losses, in lives and in the social, economic and environmental assets of communities and

[65] For examination of the early international structures for humanitarian action, see: MacAlister-Smith, *International Humanitarian Assistance*, above n 34; R Kent, *Anatomy of Disaster Relief: The International Network in Action* (Pinter, 1987).

[66] Cabinet Office, Government of Japan, *A Disaster Prevention White Paper* (2007), cited in E Yamamura, 'Natural Disasters and Social Capital Formation: The Impact of the Great Hanshin-Awaji Earthquake' (2016) 95 (S1) *Papers in Regional Science* 43, 44.

[67] UN, *Yokohama Strategy and Plan of Action for a Safer World: Guidelines for Natural Disaster Prevention, Preparedness and Mitigation*, adopted at the World Conference on Natural Disaster Reduction, Yokohama, Japan, 23–27 May 1994.

[68] L Smith, 'Kobe Earthquake 20th Anniversary: Facts about the Devastating 1995 Great Hanshin Earthquake', *International Business Times* (16 January 2015).

[69] Yamamura, 'Natural Disasters', above n 66, 47.

[70] For discussion of the historical development of the concept of DRR, see E Valencia-Ospina, *Sixth Report on the Protection of Persons in the Event of Disasters* (3 May 2013) A/CN.4/662, pp 5–12.

countries' over the next 10 years.[71] In an unforeseen coincidence of timing, the Hyogo Framework for Action (HFA) 2005–2015 was finalised on 22 January 2005, less than a month after the massive loss of life, injury and destruction wrought by the 2004 Indian Ocean Tsunami. This no doubt focused the minds of the conference delegates on the devastating impact that natural hazards can have on human populations. The central aim of the non-binding Hyogo Framework was to reduce risk and build resilience to disasters within communities, and acknowledged the grave consequences for the survival, dignity and livelihood of individuals, particularly the poor, caused by disasters.[72] Key to the strategy was the adoption by individual states of national institutional and legislative frameworks for DRR.[73] However, while the Hyogo Framework provided detailed guidance for states, regional institutions and international organisations on activities such as networking, advocacy and coordination, it did not set up a process for monitoring state responses to the risks and threats posed by disasters.[74] Indeed, Luca Corredig has noted that the HFA was simply a 'collection of guidelines, a set of standards, and as a whole it denotes a declaration of intention rather than formal obligations'.[75]

The Mid-Term Review of the HFA, conducted in 2010, likewise highlighted that although the voluntary self-reporting mechanism managed by the UN Office for Disaster Risk Reduction (UNISDR)[76] provided an opportunity for states to apply internal quality control measures to their risk assessment methods, it lacked a focus on internal accountability mechanisms.[77] The Mid-Term Review concluded that there was therefore a need to implement effective accountability measures at the international,

[71] UNISDR, Hyogo Framework for Action 2005–2015: Building the Resilience of Nations and Communities to Disasters, as adopted at the World Conference on Disaster Reduction, 18–22 January 2005, Kobe, Hyogo, Japan (A/CONF.206/6), Section II(B)(11).

[72] ibid, Section I(A)(2). See also UNISDR, *Hyogo Framework for Action 2005–2015: Building Resilience of Nations and Communities to Disasters: Mid-Term Review 2010–2011* (March 2011).

[73] UNISDR, Hyogo Framework, above n 71, Section III(B)(1).

[74] ibid, Section IV(A).

[75] L Corredig, 'Effectiveness and Accountability of Disaster Risk Reduction Practices: An Analysis through the Lens of IN-LAW' in A Berman et al (eds), *Informal International Lawmaking: Case Studies* (Torkel Opsahl Academic Epublisher, 2012) 474.

[76] The UN Office for Disaster Risk Reduction (UNISDR) was established in 1999 as the dedicated secretariat to facilitate the implementation of the International Strategy for Disaster Reduction (ISDR), which was the successor to the International Decade of Natural Disaster Reduction. The UNISDR is mandated via UNGA Resolution 56/195 (21 January 2002) to serve as the 'main forum within the UN system for devising strategies and policies for disaster reduction and ensuring complementarity of action by agencies involved in disaster reduction, mitigation and preparedness'.

[77] UNISDR, *Mid-Term Review*, above n 72, 60. The Overseas Development Institute likewise noted the weakness of domestic accountability and evaluation mechanisms for monitoring the HFA. See *Disaster Risk Management in Post-2015 Policy Frameworks: Forging a More Resilient Future*, Briefing Paper, Overseas Development Institute, June 2012, 2.

regional, national and local levels.[78] The Mid-Term Review also noted that while many states had made significant progress, three areas required particular focus, namely: strategic and holistic implementation of the HFA; local implementation; and integrating climate change.[79] Reflecting the increasing global concern regarding the impacts of anthropogenic climate change, Nicola Ranger and Susannah Fisher stressed the need for greater DRR measures in the post-2015 HFA framework, alongside the more traditional focus on disaster response and humanitarian assistance.[80]

B. Sendai Framework for Action 2015–2030

In preparation for the conclusion of the Hyogo Framework in 2015, UNISDR conducted over 125 regional consultative events to gather feedback and input into the proposed post-2015 framework.[81] The Global Platform Consultations held in May 2013 provided an opportunity for stakeholders to synthesise and reflect on the constituent elements which should be included in the new agreement, in advance of the third World Conference on Disaster Risk Reduction to be held in March 2015.[82] Moreover, reflecting the interconnected nature of global challenges and the international legal and policy frameworks to tackle them, the discussions on the post-2015 DRR framework occurred simultaneously to the renegotiation of the Kyoto Protocol to the UNFCCC on climate change and the follow-on to the Millennium Development Goals.[83] The interconnections between these three parallel processes were clearly flagged in the Rio+20 Conference on Sustainable Development in June 2012, which called on states, the UN, international financial institutions, sub-regional, regional and international organisations and civil society 'to accelerate implementation of the [Hyogo] Framework and the achievement of its goals',[84] while

[78] UNISDR, *Mid-Term Review*, above n 72, 61.

[79] ibid, 43–52.

[80] N Ranger and S Fisher, *Incorporating Climate Change and Growth into the Post-2015 Framework for Disaster Risk Reduction*, Policy Paper, LSE Centre for Climate Change Economics and Policy and Grantham Research Institute on Climate Change and the Environment, April 2013, 15.

[81] UNISDR, *Proposed Elements for Consideration in the Post-2015 Framework for Disaster Risk Reduction* (December 2013).

[82] UNISDR, *Post-2015 Framework for Disaster Risk Reduction (HFA2): Report from 2013 Global Platform Consultations* (October 2013).

[83] See: D Cubie, 'Promoting Dignity for All: Human Rights Approaches in the Post-2015 Climate Change, Disaster Risk Reduction and Sustainable Development Frameworks' (2014) 8 *Human Rights and International Legal Discourse* 1.

[84] UNGA, *Outcome Statement of the Rio+20 Conference: The Future We Want* (24 July 2012) A/66/L.56, para 186.

emphasising that 'adaptation to climate change represents an immediate and urgent global priority'.[85]

The Sendai Framework for Action 2015–2030,[86] adopted in March 2015, follows the previous Yokohama and Hyogo formats as a non-binding instrument, rather than a binding international legal text. However, recognising the identified gaps in the HFA, the Sendai Framework states that it is 'an action-oriented framework' that governments and relevant stakeholders can implement in a supportive and complementary manner, to identify disaster risks to be managed and guide investment to improve resilience. The expected outcome is a substantial reduction of disaster risk and losses, while the overarching goal is to prevent new and reduce existing disaster risk.[87] As a means of measuring effectiveness and implementation, the Framework sets out seven global targets (to be subsequently complemented by more detailed indicators) which national DRR strategies should aim to support. These targets are:

1. Substantially reduce global disaster ***mortality*** by 2030.
2. Substantially reduce the number of ***affected people*** globally by 2030.
3. Reduce direct disaster ***economic loss*** in relation to global gross domestic product (GDP) by 2030.
4. Substantially reduce disaster ***damage to critical infrastructure*** and disruption of basic services, among them health and educational facilities, including through developing their resilience by 2030.
5. Substantially increase the number of countries with national and local ***DRR strategies*** by 2020.
6. Substantially enhance ***international co-operation*** to developing countries through adequate and sustainable support to complement their national actions for implementation of this framework by 2030.
7. Substantially increase the availability of and access to ***multi-hazard early warning systems*** and disaster risk information and assessments by 2030.

The introduction of these voluntary targets and indicators mirrors the approach taken in the Sustainable Development Goals, which specifically cite the Sendai Framework. Table 8.3 below sets out the specific targets in the SDGs which directly reference disasters and DRR.[88]

[85] ibid, para 190.

[86] UN, Sendai Framework, above n 2. For a variety of perspectives, see the June 2015 edition of the *International Journal of Disaster Risk Science* which focused exclusively on the Sendai Framework.

[87] ibid, Section II.

[88] Taken from UNGA, *Transforming Our World: The 2030 Agenda for Sustainable Development* (21 October 2015) A/RES/70/1.

Table 8.3: Summary of targets in the Sustainable Development Goals (2015–2030) relating to disasters

Goal	Target
1. End poverty in all its forms everywhere	**1.5** By 2030, build the resilience of the poor and those in vulnerable situations and reduce their exposure and vulnerability to climate-related extreme events and other economic, social and environmental shocks and disasters.
2. End hunger, achieve food security and improved nutrition and promote sustainable agriculture	**2.4** By 2030, ensure sustainable food production systems and implement resilient agricultural practices that increase productivity and production, that help maintain ecosystems, that strengthen capacity for adaptation to climate change, extreme weather, drought, flooding and other disasters and that progressively improve land and soil quality.
11. Make cities and human settlements inclusive, safe, resilient and sustainable	**11.5** By 2030, significantly reduce the number of deaths and the number of people affected and substantially decrease the direct economic losses relative to global gross domestic product caused by disasters, including water-related disasters, with a focus on protecting the poor and people in vulnerable situations. **11.b** By 2020, substantially increase the number of cities and human settlements adopting and implementing integrated policies and plans towards inclusion, resource efficiency, mitigation and adaptation to climate change, resilience to disasters, and develop and implement, in line with the Sendai Framework for Disaster Risk Reduction 2015–2030, holistic disaster risk management at all levels.
13. Take urgent action to combat climate change and its impacts	**13.1** Strengthen resilience and adaptive capacity to climate-related hazards and natural disasters in all countries.

However, as non-binding instruments, there are no hard legal obligations set out in either the Sendai Framework or the Sustainable Development Goals. As with the Hyogo Framework before it, the aim of the Sendai Framework is to encourage and support states to adopt national legislative and policy measures, and to promote international co-operation, rather than create specific legal obligations.[89] It therefore remains a

[89] For example, the Framework calls on the international community to 'promote the strengthening of … international *voluntary* mechanisms for monitoring and assessment of disaster risks'. UN, Sendai Framework, above n 2, Section IV(28)(f) [emphasis added].

non-binding normative text, albeit an authoritative one. One of the key challenges identified in the HFA was the accountability gap between the general commitments to DRR endorsed by states, and their actual implementation on the ground. Therefore, the global targets and supplemental indicators are intended to provide greater precision in what is expected of governments, and also a more effective means of measuring whether or not any actions taken have actually reduced the human and financial impacts of disasters. As noted at an expert meeting in Rome in June 2015, the accountability measures set out in the Sendai Framework which promote the setting of standards and mechanisms, elaboration of laws, legislation and plans, as well as the reporting duties and disclosure provisions are 'extraordinarily strong'.[90] Moreover, it was argued that the Sendai Framework reinforced the position taken in the ILC draft articles on the protection of persons in the event of disasters that states have a duty to reduce the risk of disasters, even if the Sendai Framework does not expressly identify a particular legal obligation.[91]

The Sendai Framework additionally elaborates a series of Guiding Principles for implementation, including reiterating a state's primary responsibility to prevent and reduce disaster risk, and the importance of international co-operation.[92] Unlike the HFA, the Sendai Framework includes a specific reference to the international obligation to promote and protect all human rights, and the need to ensure an all-of-society approach that promotes community empowerment, participation and non-discrimination, including for vulnerable and marginalised groups. However, while the Guiding Principles contain a reference to human rights, it is noticeable that within the body of recommended actions, despite express references to 'financial protection', 'protection of cultural institutions' and 'protection of livelihoods and productive assets' there is no reference to the protection of persons.[93] Considering the need for coherence between international instruments, and the extensive work undertaken by the ILC on the protection of persons in disasters, this is an unfortunate omission. Recommended actions are focused on four priority areas: i) understanding disaster risk; ii) strengthening disaster risk governance to manage disaster risk; iii) investing in DRR for resilience; and

[90] G Bartolini, T Natoli and A Riccardi, *Report of the Expert Meeting on the ILC's Draft Articles on the Protection of Persons in the Event of Disasters, Roma Tre University Department of Law, 8–9 June 2015*, International Law and Disasters Working Papers Series 03 (2015), 43.

[91] ibid. For further discussion of the ILC draft articles and DRR, see Section II.C below.

[92] UN, Sendai Framework, above n 2, Section III.

[93] For discussion of the need to integrate human rights language and principles into various post-2015 frameworks, see Cubie, 'Promoting Dignity', above n 84, in particular 43–45 discussing the planned successor to the Hyogo Framework for Action.

iv) enhancing disaster preparedness for effective response and to 'Build Back Better' in recovery, rehabilitation and reconstruction.

Close to 100 specific action points are set out across these four priority areas, broken down between national and local actions, and global and regional actions. It is not possible to discuss each action point contained in the Framework; however, a few key points will be highlighted.[94] In the context of information provision, the Framework highlights the need for states to provide information both to local communities regarding known disaster risks and prevention and response strategies,[95] and to the international community. Likewise, at a global and regional level states should promote and enhance access, sharing and use of non-sensitive data and other information.[96] Of particular relevance is the call for states to 'review and promote the coherence and further development, as appropriate, of national and local frameworks of laws, regulations and public policies'.[97] At the national accountability level, states are urged to promote public scrutiny and encourage institutional debates, including by parliamentarians and other relevant officials, on local and national plans for DRR,[98] while also undertaking comprehensive public and community consultations during the development of laws and regulations to support their implementation.[99] Reflecting the non-binding nature of many texts addressing DRR activities, it is perhaps no surprise that the Sendai Framework also explicitly promotes:

> the further development and dissemination of instruments, such as standards, codes, operational guides and other guidance instruments to support coordinated action in disaster preparedness and response and facilitate information sharing on lessons learned and best practices for policy practice and post-disaster reconstruction programmes.[100]

The multi-faceted nature of DRR is highlighted in the variety of sectors which are mentioned in the Sendai Framework. In addition to the global frameworks on climate change and sustainable development, states need to consider how key policies and infrastructure may be affected or require to be strengthened. Sectors covered include rural development planning,

[94] The IFRC and UNDP published a *Handbook on Law and Disaster Risk Reduction* in December 2015 which aims to 'provide practical guidance to lawmakers, officials, and practitioners on how to review and improve laws and regulations to ensure DRR is prioritized in all sectors and at all levels with clear mandates and accountability frameworks', 4.

[95] UN, Sendai Framework, above n 2, Section IV(24)(a–f).

[96] ibid, Section IV(25)(c).

[97] ibid, Section IV(27)(a).

[98] ibid, Section IV(27)(e).

[99] ibid, Section IV(27)(f).

[100] ibid, Section IV(34)(b).

management of areas prone to droughts and flooding, building codes, and the preservation of historical, cultural or religious sites. Moreover, the financial impact of disasters, as well as the need to ensure on-going delivery of supplies in an emergency situation, requires states to consider business resilience and the protection of livelihoods and productive assets throughout supply chains, and for the international community to encourage coordination between global and regional financial institutions to assess and anticipate potential impacts of disasters.

The Sendai Framework therefore provides a comprehensive roadmap for states and the international community to achieve the expected outcome of substantial reduction of disaster risk and losses by 2030. However, the issues which plagued the domestic implementation of the preceding Hyogo Framework for Action remain. As a non-binding instrument, there are limited accountability mechanisms should states not develop or implement national or local disaster risk management plans. Moreover, the overall approach taken in the Sendai Framework can be classified as a state-centric technical or operational approach. The lack of a more explicit focus on human rights, beyond the brief reference in the Guiding Principles, is a lost opportunity to more fully integrate human rights principles into a key international instrument for humanitarian action.[101] Arielle Tozier de la Poterie and Marie-Ange Baudoin have charted a 'concerning shift away from valuing local community input and toward promoting technological advances' between the Yokohama and Sendai frameworks, and argue that community actors have gone from being valued partners to 'aid recipients'.[102] Finally, the need to ensure coherence across the various legal and policy frameworks is particularly evident when one considers that the Sendai Framework does not even reference the ILC draft articles on the protection of persons in the event of disasters, despite the ILC draft articles including an operative article on disaster risk reduction. This omission is particularly glaring when it has been argued that the Sendai Framework and the ILC draft articles should be considered as a coherent whole due to their complementarity.[103] It is therefore to the ILC draft articles that we turn to next.

[101] The UN Human Rights Council has explicitly highlighted the human rights implications of disasters; see HRC, *Report on Human Rights*, above n 7.

[102] A Tozier de la Poterie and M-A Baudoin, 'From Yokohama to Sendai: Approaches to Participation in International Disaster Risk Reduction Frameworks' (June 2015) 6(2) *International Journal of Disaster Risk Science* 128, 137.

[103] Bartolini, Natoli and Riccardi, *Report of Expert Meeting*, above n 90, 43.

C. ILC Draft Articles on the Protection of Persons in the Event of Disasters

Following the preceding discussion of the Sendai Framework, it is pertinent to briefly consider the current text of the ILC draft articles on the protection of persons in the event of disasters as they relate to the issue of disaster risk reduction.[104] The International Law Commission has engaged in a comprehensive examination of the protection of persons in disasters since 2008,[105] and the Special Rapporteur, Eduardo Valencia-Ospina, has produced eight detailed reports on various aspects of international law pertaining to disasters, including international solidarity and co-operation,[106] humanitarian principles,[107] duties of affected states,[108] and disaster risk reduction.[109] The ILC completed the first full version of the draft articles in May 2014, with 21 operative articles and associated commentaries. Following a period of consultation with states and relevant inter-governmental organisations, the Special Rapporteur introduced his eighth report in March 2016.[110] In May 2016, the ILC Drafting Committee adopted the second reading version of the draft articles, reducing them from 21 to 18 operative articles, and introducing a preamble.[111] Subsequently in August 2016, the ILC adopted this second reading text and recommended its transmission to the UN General Assembly for elaboration into a convention. The text set out below therefore reflects this final ILC text, although subsequent changes may be made should states commence negotiations for the conclusion of a binding international convention at some future date.[112]

[104] For discussion, see R Connolly, E Flaux and A Wu, 'Working Paper on the ILC Draft Articles on the Protection of Persons in the Event of Disasters', Human Rights Centre, Queen's University Belfast, February 2016, 33.

[105] ILC, *Secretariat Memorandum on the Protection of Persons in the Event of Disasters*, 60th Session of the ILC (11 December 2007) A/CN.4/590.

[106] E Valencia-Ospina, *Second Report on the Protection of Persons in the Event of Disasters* (7 May 2009) A/CN.4/615.

[107] E Valencia-Ospina, *Third Report on the Protection of Persons in the Event of Disasters* (31 March 2010) A/CN.4/629.

[108] E Valencia-Ospina, *Fourth Report on the Protection of Persons in the Event of Disasters* (11 May 2011) A/CN.4/643.

[109] Valencia-Ospina, *Sixth Report*, above n 70.

[110] E Valencia-Ospina, *Eighth Report on the Protection of Persons in the Event of Disasters* (17 March 2016) A/CN.4/697.

[111] For the final text of the preamble, draft articles and commentaries adopted by the ILC, see Official Records of the General Assembly, Seventy-first Session, *Supplement No 10* (A/71/10), Chapter IV: Protection of Persons in the Event of Disasters (2016), pp 13–17.

[112] For analysis of the ILC's evolving work on the protection of persons in the event of disasters, see: D Cubie, 'An Enchanted Tool? Humanitarian Assistance and the ILC Draft Articles on the Protection of Persons in the Event of Disasters' (2009–2010) IV-V *Irish Yearbook of International Law* 119; A Pronto, 'Consideration of the Protection of Persons in the Event of

Reflecting the original focus on disaster response, as opposed to the broader disaster cycle, it was only in 2013 that the Special Rapporteur focused exclusively on the international legal principles relating to DRR. In his Sixth Report the Special Rapporteur noted the duality of the horizontal rights and obligations states have in relation to each other and the international community as a whole, and the vertical rights and obligations states have in relation to persons within their territory and control.[113] Moreover, the report highlighted that the existence of an international legal obligation to prevent harm, both in its horizontal and vertical dimensions, was supported by international human rights law and environmental law.[114] The Special Rapporteur's Eighth Report therefore included one article addressing the horizontal rights and obligations of states to international co-operation, and another addressing the obligation on the state to undertake proactive measures to reduce the risk of disasters for persons in their territory or control.[115] However, significant changes were made between the first and second reading of the draft articles, with these two operative articles on DRR being reduced to only one. As a result, a specific reference to a duty on states to co-operate in disaster risk reduction has been omitted from the current draft, although draft Article 7 does require states to co-operate 'in the application of the present draft articles' which the Chairperson of the Drafting Committee confirmed includes the provisions on DRR in draft Article 9(2).[116] Even before the deletion of the article on co-operation for DRR, the Commentaries had noted:

> the extent of any international legal duty relating to any … measures that may be taken in order to reduce the risk of disasters is to be determined by way of the relevant specific agreements or arrangements each State has entered into with other actors with which it has the duty to cooperate.[117]

Draft Article 7 notes that states have a general duty to co-operate among themselves, with the UN, the components of the Red Cross and Red

Disasters by the International Law Commission' (2008–2009) 15 *ILSA Journal of International and Comparative Law* 449; J Benton Heath, 'Disasters, Relief, and Neglect: The Duty to Accept Humanitarian Assistance and the Work of the International Law Commission' (2010–2011) 43 *NYU Journal of International Law and Politics* 419; F Giustiniani, 'The Works of the International Law Commission on "Protection of Persons in the Event of Disasters": A Critical Appraisal' in A de Guttry, M Gestri and G Venturini (eds), *International Disaster Response Law* (TMC Asser Press 2012) 65–84.

[113] Valencia-Ospina, *Sixth Report*, above n 70, 12.

[114] ibid, 14.

[115] For text of the draft articles as proposed by the Special Rapporteur, see Valencia-Ospina, *Eighth Report*, above n 110, 101–05.

[116] ILC, *Protection of Persons in the Event of Disasters: Statement of the Chairman of the Drafting Committee* (3 June 2016) 16.

[117] For text of the Commentary to draft Art 9 (formerly draft Art 11), see Official Records of the General Assembly, A/71/10, above n 17, 42–50.

Crescent Movement and other assisting actors (which are defined in draft Article 3(d) as 'a competent intergovernmental organisation, or a relevant non-governmental organisation or entity, providing assistance to an affected State with its consent').[118] However, some states have been sceptical regarding the existence of a general international duty to co-operate in disasters. The representative from China argued in the UNGA Sixth Committee that the concepts of solidarity and co-operation should be included as moral values only, and that 'their inclusion could in no way be construed as an obligation on the part of the disaster-affected states to accept relief or on the part of states providing relief to satisfy requests for assistance'.[119] The Czech Republic meanwhile argued that a distinction should be made between the duty to co-operate with the UN as opposed to other organisations.[120] Conversely, France clearly acknowledged the duty to co-operate as a principle of general international law.[121]

Draft Article 9—Reduction of the risk of disasters

1. Each State shall reduce the risk of disasters by taking appropriate measures, including through legislation and regulations, to prevent, mitigate, and prepare for disasters.
2. Disaster risk reduction measures include the conduct of risk assessments, the collection and dissemination of risk and past loss information, and the installation and operation of early warning systems.

Draft Article 9 is premised on the concept of due diligence on the part of each state. In other words, while a state cannot guarantee that no harm will arise from disasters on its territory, it has an obligation of conduct to ensure that it has taken all necessary and appropriate measures to prevent such harm occurring in the first place or to minimise the impacts of a disaster when it occurs. Drawing on decisions of the European Court of Human Rights as well as national and regional agreements on DRR, the Commentaries to draft Article 9 stress the legal nature of the obligation to reduce the risk of disasters that rests on all states.[122] Moreover, the article highlights the need for domestic legislation and regulatory frameworks to be introduced or developed to specifically reduce the risk of harm caused by natural or human-made hazards in the state. As noted by the Commentaries, this imports into the draft articles 'a reference to ensuring that

[118] Draft Art 3(d), ibid, p 14.

[119] UNGA Sixth Committee, *Summary record of the 20th meeting* (30 October 2009) A/C.6/64/SR.20, para 24 (China).

[120] ibid, para 42 (Czech Republic).

[121] UNGA Sixth Committee, *Summary record of the 21st meeting* (30 October 2009) A/C.6/64/SR.21, para 24 (France).

[122] Official Records of the General Assembly, A/71/10, above n 17, 42–50.

mechanisms for implementation and accountability for non-performance be defined within domestic *legal* systems'.[123]

Likewise, implicit in subsection 2 is the recognition of the differential types and levels of risk and hazards that states face, and so the need for domestic authorities to undertake risk assessments and other specific measures aimed at prevention, mitigation and preparation for disasters. The non-exhaustive list tracks the type of measures states should engage in: from risk assessments to the collection and dissemination of information and the establishment of early warning mechanisms. However, the removal of specific references to states' duty to co-operate in DRR appears to fly in the face of the Sendai Framework and the recognised legal obligations that states have to institute adequate preparation and risk reduction measures as noted by the European Court of Human Rights in the cases of *Öneryildiz, Budayeva, Kolyadenko* and *Hadzhiyska*.[124] Moreover, it represents a worrying re-assertion of state sovereignty in regard to the draft articles, which is also now clearly stressed in the preamble to the draft articles. The statement by the Chairperson of the Drafting Committee that 'The reference to sovereignty provides the background against which the entire draft articles are to be understood' appears to neglect the fact that the objective of the topic is the protection of persons, not the protection of states.[125]

III. HUMANITARIAN RESPONSE AND RECOVERY

A. ILC Draft Articles on the Protection of Persons in the Event of Disasters

The express purpose of the ILC draft articles is 'to facilitate the adequate and effective response to disasters, and reduction of the risk of disasters, so as to meet the essential needs of the persons concerned, with full respect for their rights'.[126] As can be seen by the structure of this article, the primary objective relates to response, while the secondary objective is the reduction of risk. However, the draft articles remain a work-in-progress, and their final form has yet to be conclusively determined. While the ILC Secretariat and the Special Rapporteur have recommended

[123] ibid [emphasis added].

[124] For analysis of DRR by the European Court of Human Rights, see ch 5, Section II.C.i.

[125] ILC, *Protection of Persons in the Event of Disasters: Statement of the Chairman of the Drafting Committee* (3 June 2016) 3.

[126] Draft Art 2, Official Records of the General Assembly, A/71/10, above n 17, p 14.

that they should form the basis of a binding international convention,[127] states have disagreed as to the most appropriate format. Certain states, such as the United Kingdom, the Czech Republic, India, the Russian Federation and Spain, have expressed a preference for their adoption as non-binding guidelines or a framework of principles.[128] Conversely, Mexico and Poland, along with the IFRC, have supported a binding framework convention format.[129]

Considering the potential for future changes to be made to the text of the draft articles, as well as uncertainty surrounding their final form (and therefore legal status), it is not possible to analyse in-depth each of the relevant key articles.[130] Nevertheless, they have the potential to form the basis of a global legally binding instrument for disasters, akin to the 1947 Geneva Conventions for humanitarian protection and assistance in armed conflicts or the 1951 Convention for refugees. Moreover, even if they remain as non-binding guidelines or principles, it is highly likely they will have legal impacts. As noted by James Crawford in the context of the ILC draft articles on state responsibility, despite their non-binding status, those draft articles were cited by courts and tribunals and therefore influenced the development of international law even prior to their formal conclusion.[131] Likewise, Robert Rosenstock, former Chairperson of the ILC, has stated that 'codification of *lex lata* may be no less effective if contained in a paragraph of a report rather than in an article of a multilateral treaty'.[132] It is foreseeable that whatever form the draft articles finally take, they will be used as the basis for regional and bilateral binding agreements between states, and even in the absence of formal agreement they will influence state practice. Therefore, following our earlier discussion of draft Article 9 relating to disaster risk reduction, the text of key provisions relating to humanitarian response and recovery is set out in Table 8.4 below.

[127] At the conclusion of the second reading of the draft articles in August 2016, the ILC formally recommended that the General Assembly should elaborate a convention on the basis of the draft articles: Official Records of the General Assembly, Seventy-first Session, *Supplement No 10* (A/71/10), Chapter IV: Protection of Persons in the Event of Disasters (2016), 13.

[128] ibid, 97–98.

[129] ibid, 98.

[130] For analysis of the first-reading text, see: Bartolini, Natoli and Riccardi, *Report of Expert Meeting*, above n 90; Connolly, Flaux and Wu, 'ILC Draft Articles', above n 104.

[131] J Crawford, 'The ILC's Articles on Responsibility of States for Internationally Wrongful Acts: A Retrospect' (2002) 96 *American Journal of International Law* 874.

[132] R Rosenstock, 'The ILC and State Responsibility' (2002) 96 *American Journal of International Law* 792, 792. See also: D Caron, 'The ILC Articles on State Responsibility: The Paradoxical Relationship Between Form and Authority' (2002) 96 *American Journal of International Law* 857.

Table 8.4: Key provisions of the ILC draft articles regarding humanitarian response and recovery

i. Key Provisions Regarding Humanitarian Response and Recovery[133]

Article 7—Duty to cooperate

In the application of the present draft articles, States shall, as appropriate, cooperate among themselves, with the United Nations, with the components of the Red Cross and Red Crescent Movement, and with other assisting actors.

Article 8—Forms of cooperation in the response to disasters

Cooperation in the response to disasters includes humanitarian assistance, coordination of international relief actions and communications, and making available relief personnel, equipment and goods, and scientific, medical and technical resources.

Article 10—Role of the affected State

1. The affected State has the duty to ensure the protection of persons and provision of disaster relief assistance in its territory, or in territory under its jurisdiction or control.
2. The affected State has the primary role in the direction, control, coordination and supervision of such relief assistance.

Article 11—Duty of the affected State to seek external assistance

To the extent that a disaster manifestly exceeds its national response capacity, the affected State has the duty to seek assistance from, as appropriate, other States, the United Nations, and other potential assisting actors.

Article 12—Offers of external assistance

1. In the event of disasters, States, the United Nations, and other potential assisting actors may offer assistance to the affected State.
2. When external assistance is sought by an affected State by means of a request addressed to another State, the United Nations, or other potential assisting actor, the addressee shall expeditiously give due consideration to the request and inform the affected State of its reply.

Article 13—Consent of the affected State to external assistance

1. The provision of external assistance requires the consent of the affected State.
2. Consent to external assistance shall not be withheld arbitrarily.

(continued)

[133] Final text as adopted by the ILC in August 2016: Official Records of the General Assembly, A/71/10, above n 17, 13–17.

Table 8.4: (*Continued*)

3. When an offer of external assistance is made in accordance with the present draft articles, the affected State shall, whenever possible, make known its decision regarding the offer in a timely manner.

Article 14—Conditions on the provision of external assistance

The affected State may place conditions on the provision of external assistance. Such conditions shall be in accordance with the present draft articles, applicable rules of international law and the national law of the affected State. Conditions shall take into account the identified needs of the persons affected by disasters and the quality of the assistance. When formulating conditions, the affected State shall indicate the scope and type of assistance sought.

Article 15—Facilitation of external assistance

1. The affected State shall take the necessary measures, within its national law, to facilitate the prompt and effective provision of external assistance, in particular regarding:
   (a) relief personnel, in fields such as privileges and immunities, visa and entry requirements, work permits, and freedom of movement; and
   (b) equipment and goods, in fields such as customs requirements and tariffs, taxation, transport, and the disposal thereof.
2. The affected State shall ensure that its relevant legislation and regulations are readily accessible, to facilitate compliance with national law.

Article 16—Protection of relief personnel, equipment and goods

The affected State shall take the appropriate measures to ensure the protection of relief personnel and of equipment and goods present in its territory, or in territory under its jurisdiction or control, for the purpose of providing external assistance.

Article 17—Termination of external assistance

The affected State, the assisting State, the United Nations, or other assisting actor may terminate external assistance at any time. Any such State or actor intending to terminate shall provide appropriate notification. The affected State and, as appropriate, the assisting State, the United Nations, or other assisting actor shall consult with respect to the termination of external assistance and the modalities of termination.

Ultimately, whether or not the draft articles are sent forward for consideration at a diplomatic conference depends on the wishes of states in the UN General Assembly.[134] As David Fidler pessimistically noted prior

[134] For discussion of the final form of the ILC draft articles, see Cubie, 'An Enchanted Tool', above n 112, 137–49.

to the commencement of the ILC consideration of the topic: 'states typically craft international law where their interests converge on the need to regulate sovereignty. With natural disasters, the interests of both the victim and assisting states converge on maintaining as much sovereignty as possible—a convergence that does not stimulate the robust development of international law.'[135] The explicit reference to sovereignty in the preamble to the draft articles may justify Fidler's concerns. At a minimum, it highlights the fundamental importance of reading the text of the draft articles with the Commentaries and statements by the Drafting Committee to understand the nuances and caveats placed on particular phrases within the draft articles. Nevertheless, the extent of engagement by states and international organisations in developing the current text of the ILC draft articles is significant. Considerable political and diplomatic effort has already gone into the draft articles, no doubt based on states' dual motivation of improving potential responses to disasters that may occur within their own territory, while protecting their ability to control who enters their state and which activities are undertaken should a disaster occur. This has significantly advanced our understanding of the international legal obligations and consequences of natural and human-made disasters, and has promoted the development of a coherent body of international disaster laws, policies and practices, as opposed to a piecemeal or sectoral approach. While the final form of the draft articles is yet to be decided, they may well create an international chapeau which will be drawn from by more specialised international instruments and regional and sub-regional frameworks. We therefore now turn to examine some examples of specific and general international conventions relating to aspects of disaster preparation and response, before concluding with an examination of some key non-binding normative instruments.

B. Selected International Conventions

i. Tampere Convention on Telecommunications in Disasters (1998)

The adoption of the Tampere Convention on the Provision of Telecommunication Resources for Disaster Mitigation and Relief Operations[136] in June 1998 represented a major advance in the global regulation of humanitarian

[135] Fidler, 'Disaster Relief', above n 22, 461.

[136] Tampere Convention on the Provision of Telecommunication Resources for Disaster Mitigation and Relief Operations (adopted 18 June 1998, entered into force 8 January 2005) 2296 UNTS 5 ('Tampere Convention'). The Tampere Convention is open for signature by all member states of the UN and the International Telecommunications Union.

operations. Effective telecommunications is a vital tool for humanitarian agencies in disasters—when working in an emergency context the national or local telecommunications infrastructure may be damaged or non-existent due to the remoteness of the affected communities. While mobile phone and broadband technology and coverage has advanced considerably in recent years, many agencies still require VHF, UHF or digital radio capacities to ensure communications between their office and personnel working in the field as a means of assisting their operational programmes and for safety reasons. Yet operating licences and access to radio frequencies are generally strictly regulated at the domestic level. So in the aftermath of a disaster, the ability to obtain the necessary permission to legally establish communications networks can be fraught with regulatory, bureaucratic and logistical challenges, leading to delays in the commencement of life-saving assistance.

The role of NGOs is expressly recognised in the Tampere Convention, which regulates not just the relationship between an affected and donor state, but also the relationship between the affected state and humanitarian agencies operating on its territory.[137] The principal aim of the Convention is to simplify and regulate the types of organisations which can gain priority access to telecommunications infrastructure in disasters, while maintaining the affected state's right to reject all or part of any telecommunication assistance offered in accordance with their existing national law and policy.[138] The Convention revolves around three cardinal themes: respecting state sovereignty; removing barriers to the entry and use of telecommunications equipment; and establishing privileges and immunities for humanitarian personnel.[139] Telecommunications is defined as: 'any transmission, emission, or reception of signs, signals, writing, images, sounds or intelligence of any nature, by wire, radio, optical fibre or other electromagnetic system.'[140] State parties may request assistance through the UN Emergency Relief Coordinator, who is the Operational Coordinator under the Convention, and who then forwards the requests to relevant state parties and non-state organisations.[141] Crucially, the requesting state must specify the scope and type of assistance required, as well as any potential regulatory barriers and the facilities in place for humanitarian

[137] ES Oh, 'Information and Communication Technology in the Service of Disaster Mitigation and Humanitarian Relief', *Proceedings of the 9th Asia-Pacific Conference on Communications*, 21–24 September 2003, vol 2, 730, 731.

[138] ibid, Art 4(5).

[139] IFRC, *IDRL Factsheet: Regulation of Emergency Telecommunications* (Geneva 2005). See also A Rahrig, 'Love Thy Neighbor: The Tampere Convention as Global Legislation' (Summer 2010) 17(2) *Indiana Journal of Global Legal Studies* 273.

[140] Art 1(15) Tampere Convention, above n 136.

[141] ibid, Art 2.

personnel.[142] The Convention currently has 60 signatories and 48 state parties, and entered into force in early January 2005, just days after the 2004 Indian Ocean Tsunami. Perhaps reflecting the recent nature of its entry into force, Victoria Bannon and David Fisher noted that:

> Despite the fact that Sri Lanka had ratified the Tampere Convention, there is no indication that any of its provisions were specifically invoked during the relief operation. In fact, some organisations reported that radio equipment was a particularly difficult item to have processed quickly through customs.[143]

Nevertheless, the Tampere Convention presents some far-reaching provisions for the coordination and management of a vital aspect of humanitarian operations between states and between states and humanitarian organisations. A robust international framework for co-operation is therefore required, not least due to the constant development and evolution of telecommunications technology. Ei Sun Oh has highlighted how the convergence of the policy objectives of the Tampere Convention and technological advancements can assist in alleviating human suffering and reducing property damage due to disasters, while simultaneously linking relief and rehabilitation to sustainable development objectives by strengthening sustainable information and communications technologies.[144]

ii. Framework Convention on Civil Defence Assistance (2000)

The origins of national civil defence organisations in the early twentieth century were to protect civilians from military attack, and their particular status and distinctive emblem of a blue equilateral triangle on an orange background was acknowledged in the 1977 Additional Protocol I for international armed conflicts.[145] Such objectives intensified following the Second World War and the advent of Cold War nuclear threats. Consequently, most civil defence structures (variously called Civil Defence, civil protection, civil safety, or emergency management) are part of the official state first responders' apparatus, either as statutory bodies or as auxiliaries to the military and emergency services. Due to changing threats, increasingly civil defence organisations have focused on protecting and assisting civilians from the threat of natural and human-made disasters. Irrespective of the source of the threats to the civilian population, civil

[142] ibid, Art 4(2).
[143] Bannon and Fisher, 'Legal Lessons', above n 9.
[144] Oh, 'Information and Communication Technology', above n 137, 733.
[145] Art 66 Protocol Additional to the Geneva Conventions of 12 August 1949 and relating to the Protection of Victims of International Armed Conflicts (adopted 8 June 1977, entered into force 7 December 1978) 1125 UNTS 4. For discussion, see ch 7, Section II.B.

defence organisations are charged with three key objectives: to protect and assist the population; to safeguard property; and to safeguard the environment.[146]

The Framework Convention on Civil Defence Assistance[147] was developed by the International Civil Defence Organisation in the late 1990s to improve collaboration between states for cross-border deployment of national civil defence assets. In other words, the Convention focuses specifically on reducing or eliminating technical and regulatory obstacles between states, and a mechanism for affected states to request the assistance of civil defence organisations from other countries.[148] The Convention has two limited, but important, objectives: a) promoting co-operation between Civil Defence Services, particularly with regard to training of personnel and exchange of information and expertise; and b) reducing obstacles to assistance and delays in intervention.[149] The Convention clearly establishes that all offers of assistance shall 'respect the sovereignty, independence and territorial integrity of the Beneficiary State as well as the principle of non-intervention in the internal affairs of this State and should be carried out with due respect for its ways and customs' and shall be undertaken in a spirit of humanity, solidarity and impartiality.[150] The key responsibilities of the beneficiary state are to simplify and minimise administrative and customs' formalities relating to the entry and stay of external Civil Defence Units, and as per their national law, to grant all privileges, immunities, and facilities necessary for carrying out the assistance and to provide protection for personnel and for property belonging to external Civil Defence Units.[151]

While providing an important mechanism for co-operation between civil defence units of different states, there has been limited uptake of the Convention, which has only 26 state parties covering a limited geographic spread.[152] Moreover, it is noticeable that while a follow-up international conference was held in Geneva in October 2002 to promote the Framework Convention,[153] since then there has been less visible engagement by civil

[146] ICDO, *Commentary on the Framework Convention on Civil Defence Assistance, 22 May 2000*, 23.

[147] ICDO Framework Convention on Civil Defence Assistance (adopted 22 May 2000, entered into force 23 September 2001) 2172 UNTS 213 ('Framework Convention').

[148] ICDO, *Commentary*, above n 416, 2.

[149] Art 2 Framework Convention, above n 147.

[150] ibid, Art 3(b) and (d).

[151] ibid, Art 4(3) and (5).

[152] PC Parisetti, 'The Use of Civil and Military Defence Assets in Emergency Situations' in Guttry, Gestri and Venturini, *International Disaster Response Law*, above n 112, 559.

[153] *Protection and Assistance for All*, First International Conference for the follow-up of the Framework Convention on Civil Defence Assistance of 22 May 2000, Geneva, 3 October 2002.

defence organisations than had been expected. One potential reason may be the growth of regional approaches to civil protection. A good example is the EU Civil Protection Mechanism, which was established in 2001 to coordinate and facilitate the exchange of national civil defence units between the member states of the European Union, and subsequently expanded to facilitate EU civil defence units responding to natural and human-made disasters anywhere in the world.[154] The EU Civil Protection Mechanism comprises the European Emergency Response Capacity (EERC), which is a pool of trained voluntary experts available for deployment at short notice, coordinated by the operational Emergency Response Coordination Centre (ERCC) and facilitated by the Common Emergency Communication and Information System (CECIS). Since its establishment, the EU Civil Protection Mechanism has received over 200 requests for assistance. Despite the comprehensive structures and procedures in place, the challenges facing the global Framework Convention have also been seen in the EU system. While recognising that an impressive level of solidarity has been shown by various EU member states in supporting civil defence units to respond to disasters abroad, Magnus Ekengren et al have highlighted that the countervailing focus on national sovereignty means that many EU states continue to use alternative, bilateral arrangements to provide assistance.[155] This tension between solidarity and sovereignty is reflected throughout state practice and policy towards humanitarian action and the important but limited uptake of the Framework Convention and the EU Civil Protection Mechanism would imply that bilateral connections continue to dominate state responses to disasters.

C. Selected Non-Binding Normative Instruments

As noted previously, there are a wide range of non-binding sources of the *acquis humanitaire* which play an important normative role in humanitarian theory and practice.[156] From an operational perspective, humanitarian organisations have attempted to advance their management of humanitarian programmes through the elaboration of technical standards

[154] The external component of the EU's humanitarian activities are governed by: Art 214 of the Treaty on the Functioning of the European Union (TFEU—Lisbon Treaty); the 2007 European Consensus on Humanitarian (2008/C 25/01); and updated 2009 EU Guidelines on Promoting Compliance with International Humanitarian Law (16841/09). For analysis, see Caritas Europa, *Bridging the Gap Between Policy and Practice: The European Consensus on Humanitarian Aid and Humanitarian Principles* (October 2011).

[155] M Ekengren et al, 'Solidarity or Sovereignty? EU Cooperation in Civil Protection' (2006) 28(5) *Journal of European Integration* 457, 472–73.

[156] See, eg, Cubie, 'Analysis of Soft Law', above n 46.

and humanitarian principles. The first key instrument adopted was the *Code of Conduct for the International Red Cross and Red Crescent Movement and NGOs in Disaster Relief* in 1994, which established non-binding common standards for relief agencies responding to humanitarian crises.[157] This was quickly followed by the *Sphere Handbook: Humanitarian Charter and Minimum Standards in Humanitarian Response* in 1998, which aimed to improve performance and increase the accountability of non-governmental humanitarian agencies through self-regulation. As noted by Peter Walker, one of the original authors: 'any set of "industry" standards must first be prefaced by a set of "consumer rights"; a beneficiaries or claimants charter, which highlights what, under existing international law and declarations, a person should have a "right" to in a humanitarian crisis.'[158] This approach permeates the *Sphere Handbook*, which contains four interconnected sections: the Humanitarian Charter, Protection Principles, Core Standards and Minimum Standards.

Within the UN and inter-governmental sector, the IASC acts as the principal inter-agency forum for coordination, policy development and decision-making, under the direction of the UN Emergency Relief Coordinator.[159] The IASC *Operational Guidelines on the Protection of Persons in Situations of Natural Disasters*[160] are intended to provide practical advice to humanitarian agencies to implement a human rights-based approach to humanitarian assistance. This conceptual basis ensures that those affected by disasters are viewed as 'individual rights-holders who can claim rights from particular duty-bearers rather than simply being passive beneficiaries and recipients of charity'.[161] Considering the diversity of technical and operational minimum standards and guidelines relating to humanitarian action in disasters, it is not possible to explore all such sources of the *acquis humanitaire* here. However, following our review of selected existing international conventions addressing aspects of humanitarian response and recovery in disasters, three specific non-binding instruments will also be examined, namely: the IFRC 'IDRL Guidelines' as a leading exposition of domestic responsibilities; the IFRC model act on disaster relief as an example of domestic legislation which can be adopted by states to

[157] Interestingly, empirical research conducted in 2004 found that 70 per cent of respondents from humanitarian agencies viewed the Code's articles as binding principles. See D Hilhorst, 'A Living Document? The Code of Conduct of the Red Cross and Red Crescent Movement and NGOs in Disaster Relief', Research paper produced for the conference *Ten Years Code of Conduct: Principles in Practice*, Disaster Studies Wageningen University, 2004, 36.

[158] Quoted in J Darcy, 'Locating Responsibility: The Sphere Humanitarian Charter and Its Rationale' (2004) 28(2) *Disasters* 112, 117.

[159] *Strengthening of the Coordination of Humanitarian Emergency Assistance of the United Nations*, UNGA Res 46/182, 19 December 1991.

[160] IASC, *Operational Guidelines*, above n 40.

[161] ibid, 2.

facilitate humanitarian responses; and the INSARAG search and rescue guidelines as an example of a highly technical and skilled framework for disaster response activities.

i. IFRC IDRL Guidelines (2007)

Following the publication of the *World Disasters Report 2000*, and the establishment of the International Disaster Response Law (IDRL) Programme in 2001, the IFRC commenced a series of research projects to map existing disaster laws.[162] This culminated in 2007 with the publication of the *Guidelines for the Domestic Facilitation and Regulation of International Disaster Relief and Initial Recovery Assistance*, the so-called 'IDRL Guidelines'. The IDRL Guidelines were developed with the express aim of assisting states to develop their national disaster-preparedness and response plans.[163] As such, the Guidelines provide a practical approach to legal issues relating to the affected state's response, setting out their primary responsibility for disaster risk reduction, relief and recovery assistance, and reiterate the accepted international law position that assistance by other humanitarian actors should only be initiated with the consent of the state and in principle on the basis of an appeal by the State.[164] The Guidelines are split into five sections:

1. Core responsibilities
2. Early warning and preparedness
3. Initiation and termination of international disaster relief and initial recovery assistance
4. Eligibility for legal facilities
5. Legal facilities for entry and operations.

Reflecting the operational focus of the IDRL Guidelines, they elaborate eligibility requirements for the granting of legal facilities to humanitarian actors by affected states, and a range of practical and logistical areas where states should review their national laws to ensure humanitarian assistance is not unnecessarily delayed or restricted. Such areas include: granting

[162] Publications of relevance include: H Fischer, *International Disaster Response Law: A Preliminary Overview and Analysis of Existing Treaty Law*, IFRC (Geneva 2003); IFRC, *International Disaster Response Laws, Principles and Practice: Reflections, Prospects and Challenges* (Geneva 2003); IFRC, *Law and Legal Issues in International Disaster Response: A Desk Study* (Geneva 2007).

[163] IFRC, *Introduction to the Guidelines for the Domestic Facilitation and Regulation of International Disaster Relief and Initial Recovery Assistance* (Geneva, reprinted 2011) 3.

[164] ibid, *Introduction*, point 1.1, and *Part III: Initiation and termination of international disaster relief and initial recovery assistance*, point 10.1. For discussion of cross-border aid without the consent of the affected state in armed conflicts, see ch 6, Section III.A.i.

visas for international relief personnel; ensuring relief goods and equipment are exempt from customs duties, taxes and tariffs; reducing legal and administrative importation barriers for telecommunications equipment and medical supplies; and ensuring vehicles involved in humanitarian response can transit and enter affected and neighbouring states.[165]

The purpose of the IDRL Guidelines is therefore to assist governments, and to promote disaster planning and preparation through a proactive approach to examining national laws that may unintentionally hinder humanitarian operations. As such, they can be seen as a continuation of the approach taken by UNGA Resolution 2816 (XXVI) of 1972, which called on governments to examine their own domestic legal arrangements for disaster response, and the 1982 UNITAR Model Rules for Disaster Relief Operations, which provided a framework for governments to adapt based on their own national requirements. In light of this, it is perhaps not surprising that the first words of the IDRL Guidelines are: 'These Guidelines are non-binding.' By setting out a series of recommendations to governments on the minimum quality standards and legal facilities that humanitarian actors require to undertake their work effectively, the IDRL Guidelines do not attempt to expand international law or create new rights and obligations for states.[166] The IDRL Guidelines therefore fall squarely into the category of 'technical guidelines'.

Notwithstanding the technical nature of the IDRL Guidelines, they are a highly persuasive source of non-binding norms. Not only are the Guidelines directed at states themselves, but 194 states and the International Red Cross Movement formally adopted the Guidelines at the 30th International Conference of the Red Cross and Red Crescent in November 2007. While recognising the non-binding nature of the Guidelines, states acknowledged their importance and encouraged all governments to make use of them to strengthen their national legal, policy and institutional frameworks for disaster preparation and response. Indeed, between their publication and November 2015, 23 countries across all continents formally adopted new laws, rules or procedures drawing on the IDRL Guidelines, while a further 12 states are in the process of finalising legislation or draft rules.[167] Moreover, the IDRL Guidelines have been utilised

[165] ibid, *Part V: Legal facilities for entry and operations*, points 16–24.

[166] Point 1.4 states that the IDRL Guidelines are 'not intended to recommend any changes to, or affect the meaning and implementation of, any existing international law or agreements', 10.

[167] IFRC, *Ready or Not? Third Progress Report on the Implementation of the Guidelines for the Domestic Facilitation and Regulation of International Disaster Relief and Initial Recovery Assistance* (November 2015). The Report notes that some of these 23 countries (namely Burkina Faso, Cambodia, Seychelles, Viet Nam) have included extensive sections drawing on the IDRL Guidelines in their national disaster management acts. Others (Colombia, Indonesia, Namibia, Peru, Philippines) have referenced the IDRL Guidelines in legislation but intend

by inter-governmental organisations such as the ILC and World Customs Organisation, and at a regional level to develop or strengthen regional frameworks and mechanisms for disaster management.[168]

ii. IFRC Model Act on Disaster Relief (2013)

As the IDRL Guidelines are intended as a baseline of legal issues and challenges which states should consider in advance of a disaster occurring, the IFRC and national Red Cross and Red Crescent Societies have engaged with national authorities to review states' disaster risk profile and existing prevention and response capacities. Since 2007, detailed reports have been conducted for 31 states, while technical assistance has been provided in 53 states to support domestic authorities to use the IDRL Guidelines to evaluate and strengthen their relevant laws, rules or procedures.[169] However, there was a noticeable drop in the level of engagement by national authorities over the course of the three progress reports on the IDRL Guidelines (published in 2009, 2011 and 2015), and the IFRC has warned of the danger of 'issue fatigue' in the area of disaster laws.[170] Nevertheless, reflecting the domestic focus of the IDRL Guidelines, the IFRC has worked in conjunction with UNOCHA and the Inter-Parliamentary Union to develop detailed legislative guidance for governments in the form of a *Model Act for the Facilitation and Regulation of International Disaster Relief and Initial Recovery Assistance*. A pilot version was initially prepared in November 2011, before the final version was published in March 2013.[171]

The comprehensive Model Act is intended to act as a voluntary reference tool for states to integrate the IDRL Guidelines into their domestic legislation, regulations or procedures.[172] Reflecting the advisory nature of the Model Act, the Commentaries highlight that a state's disaster risk profile and legal system may influence how the Model Act is best utilised. For some countries, the Model Act may form the basis of a comprehensive, stand-alone disaster management legislation. Alternatively, specific provisions may be incorporated into existing legislation, rules and procedures.[173] For example, the provisions on granting humanitarian visas for

to introduce implementing regulations. Other states have included individual provisions in sectoral laws or regulations, such as: immigration (Mexico, Norway), customs (Tajikistan), aviation (Ecuador) and medicines (Mozambique). Finally, some states have adopted less formal instruments, such as operating procedures or manuals (Cook Islands, New Zealand, Netherlands), 7.

168 ibid, 10–15.
169 ibid, 8.
170 ibid, 8–9.
171 IFRC, Model Act, above n 44.
172 ibid, 6.
173 ibid, 9.

foreign humanitarian personnel may be better suited within the immigration legislation of the state, while financial provisions covering waiver of taxes and import duties for humanitarian goods and equipment may be placed in existing taxation instruments. In addition to setting out suggested language for new or amended national legislation, the Commentaries provide detailed examples of legal provisions from domestic law and policy. For example, on the question of registration of foreign non-governmental organisations, the Commentaries note that in Nepal the Social Welfare Act 1992 established a separate system for registration of foreign NGOs. While this Act does not contain a specific waiver for humanitarian organisations, there is an established practice to allow assisting international actors entry without registration during disasters.[174] Meanwhile, China only allows foreign NGOs to provide humanitarian assistance if they are already established as legal entities under Decree No 400 of the State Council of the People's Republic of China, the Regulations on Administration of Foundations, which can create difficulties for organisations wishing to respond to a disaster if they are not already present in China.[175]

iii. INSARAG Guidelines (2014)

One highly specialised area of expertise which can be essential in the aftermath of a major earthquake or industrial accident is urban search and rescue teams. For many countries, the complexities of locating and extracting survivors from inherently unstable collapsed buildings, and the equipment required for such extractions, are outside their domestic capabilities. This was starkly highlighted in the 1980s during the 1985 Mexico City earthquake and 1988 Armenian earthquake. Following an earthquake, speed is of the essence. Yet the challenges of obtaining the required approvals for the entry of personnel, trained search and rescue dogs, and heavy machinery led to crucial delays and lack of coordination for foreign search and rescue teams.[176]

The establishment of the International Search and Rescue Advisory Group (INSARAG) in 1991 represents a valuable example of the role that non-binding instruments can have on state practice and for professional

[174] ibid, 108; although humanitarian access during the 2015 Nepalese earthquake was still challenging. See X Castellanos, 'A Year on from Nepal's Earthquake, Red Cross Urges Overhaul of Disaster Laws', *Thomson Reuters Foundation News*, 22 April 2016.

[175] ibid.

[176] For analysis of the Mexico City and Armenian earthquakes, see KN Bookmiller, 'The International Law of 96 Hours: Urban Search and Rescue Teams and the Current State of International Disaster Response Law' in D Caron, M Kelly and A Telesetsky (eds), *The International Law of Disaster Relief* (Cambridge University Press, 2014) 115–21.

accountability. INSARAG is a global professional network of independent urban search and rescue teams (USAR) based in 59 countries, ranging from small-scale 'light' USAR teams which are able to assist with search and rescue of victims in the immediate aftermath of a sudden-onset structural collapse disaster but generally do not deploy to international disasters, to 'heavy' USAR teams which have the operational capability for multiple complex technical search and rescue operations in collapsed or failed structures, particularly those involving structures reinforced or built with structural steel.[177] INSARAG's secretariat is based in the offices of UNOCHA in Geneva.[178]

The INSARAG Guidelines were originally developed to promote common standards and the coordination of USAR teams, both with the national authorities of affected countries, and between themselves. The Guidelines were endorsed by the UN General Assembly in Resolution 57/150 of 2002[179] and are now regarded as a constituent part of international disaster laws.[180] Reflecting on-going advances in technology and science, the Guidelines and associated Methodology are viewed as a living instrument, with the most recent updates concluded in late 2014. Of note, despite earlier calls for the adoption of an international convention on urban search and rescue, the non-binding nature of the INSARAG Guidelines has benefited the development of international common standards and co-operation in the sector. As recalled by Arjun Katoch, former head of the INSARAG Secretariat:

> [I]t became fairly clear that the Governments of most countries were extremely unlikely to accept any legal framework that possibly involved ratification and amendment of their own laws ... The group took a wise decision to go for the achievable rather than the ideal.[181]

The INSARAG model of creating a professional network of independent actors and non-binding common technical standards for highly specialised professions has also been adopted by the World Health Organisation in developing standards for Foreign Medical Teams (FMT) which respond to disasters.[182] As with urban search and rescue teams, while large

[177] UNOCHA, *INSARAG Guidelines, vol 1: Policy* (December 2014) 20.

[178] See generally www.insarag.org. For a historical retrospective, see: UNOCHA, *The Story of INSARAG 20 Years On...* (Geneva, 2010).

[179] *Strengthening the Effectiveness and Coordination of International Urban Search and Rescue Assistance*, UNGA Res 57/150 (27 February 2003) A/Res/57/150.

[180] KN Bookmiller, 'Can International Law Save Us from Disasters? Urban Search and Rescue and Foreign Medical Teams are Counting on It!' (2014) 108 *ASIL Proceedings* 173, 176.

[181] Quoted in Bookmiller, ibid, 175.

[182] For detailed analysis of the evolving legal framework for Foreign Medical Teams, see KN Bookmiller, 'Professional Standards and Legal Standard Setting: INSARAG, FMTs, and International Disaster Relief Volunteers' (2015) 48(4) *Vanderbilt Journal of Transnational Law* 957.

numbers of highly trained experts in a particular field may be crucial in an emergency situation, uncoordinated or inexperienced volunteers arriving into a crisis may actually exacerbate the situation by placing additional pressure on scarce resources. For example, 44 foreign field hospitals from more than 18 middle- and high-income countries were deployed in the immediate aftermath of the 2010 Haitian earthquake. Yet detailed analysis of these interventions concluded there was no control or coordination of their activities.[183] Moreover, the impossibility of determining the outcome of such medical activities in Haiti raises serious questions regarding the legal and professional accountability of such FMT. Therefore, the WHO has developed guidelines in the form of a simple classification system and registration form to define type, capacities, services, and minimum deployment standards for FMTs.[184]

IV. CONCLUSION: DEVELOPING COHERENCE

The range of legal and non-legal instruments developed in recent years reflects the context-specific and rapidly changing nature of humanitarian responses to different forms of natural and human-made disasters, and the highly technical nature of some humanitarian interventions. International legal instruments can help to set benchmarks for national and regional instruments, as well as clarifying the rights and responsibilities of key actors. Meanwhile, the flexibility of non-binding, yet authoritative, texts should be welcomed as a means of improving the quality and coordination of humanitarian actors. However, as seen in the Haitian medical interventions, the question of accountability remains a key consideration. Large numbers of well-meaning individuals and organisations may react when a major disaster occurs—from globally recognised international organisations to small 'mom and pop' groups specifically focused on a particular country or event.

As argued in chapter three, there is space for a diversity of actors within the field of humanitarian action due to the extent of potential needs and division of labour between different types of organisation. However, first and foremost, the needs and wishes of the local affected communities must be taken into consideration.[185] Their need for material assistance and

[183] M Gerdin, A Wladis and J von Schreeb, 'Foreign Field Hospitals after the 2010 Haiti Earthquake: How Good Were We?' (2013) 30 *Emergency Medicine Journal* 1, 3.

[184] WHO, *Classification and Minimum Standards for Foreign Medical Teams in Sudden Onset Disasters* (2013) Foreign Medical Team Working Group under the Global Health Cluster.

[185] See, eg, MG Pietropaolo, 'Observations on Strengthening Community Participation in Disaster Risk Reduction in Disaster Law and Policy', IFRC Disaster Law Working Paper Series No 5, September 2015.

humanitarian protection should not be left to ad hoc and uncoordinated responses. While states retain the primary responsibility to ensure the protection of persons on their territory, the international community of states and humanitarian agencies can and should assist affected communities whenever possible, to fulfil the humanitarian imperative. The development of a coherent body of international disaster laws can support such interventions, and the ever-expanding body of law, policy and practice pre- and post-disasters forms a core component of the *acquis humanitaire*. Yet, as has been consistently argued throughout this book, one cannot look at each branch of law in isolation. As with armed conflicts, major natural or human-made disasters can lead to large-scale population movements. Such forced displacement may occur across an international border or within the borders of the affected state. The well-established body of refugee and displacement persons law therefore is of direct relevance in both disaster and conflict settings, as will be seen in the following chapter.

9

Refugee and Displaced Persons Law

I. INTRODUCTION

THE FINAL BODY of law which contributes to the normative content of the *acquis humanitaire* is also one of the most highly developed at the international, regional and domestic levels. Conflict and humanitarian crises often provide the catalyst for people to uproot from their homes and communities to search for protection and an improved life elsewhere. It is therefore no surprise that the first High Commissioner for Refugees, the Norwegian explorer Fridtjof Nansen, was appointed in the aftermath of the First World War. Indeed, Nansen's initial task focused specifically on the millions of Russians who were not only displaced by the war and Soviet revolution, but also by massive crop failures in the summer of 1921.[1] The subsequent famine remains a stark reminder of the interplay between environmental conditions, armed conflict and population movements.

Despite Nansen's untimely death in 1930, the work of his office continued and with the conclusion of the UN Convention relating to the Status of Refugees[2] in 1951 was re-established as the Office of the UN High Commissioner for Refugees (UNHCR). Throughout the second half of the twentieth century, in the face of Cold War rivalry, the popular perception of a 'refugee' solidified into that of an individual fleeing political persecution across an international border.[3] However, it was not until the 1990s that the material assistance and protection needs of persons displaced within the borders of their own country were identified, in large part due to the ground-breaking work of Roberta Cohen and Francis Deng in the Brookings Institution.[4] Moreover, the international normative frameworks

[1] See B Cabanes, *The Great War and the Origins of Humanitarianism 1918–1924* (Cambridge University Press, 2014), ch 3, 'The Tragedy of Being Stateless: Fridtjof Nansen and the Rights of Refugees'.

[2] Convention relating to the Status of Refugees (adopted 28 July 1951, entered into force 22 April 1954) 189 UNTS 137 ('Refugee Convention').

[3] For two of the definitive accounts of international refugee law, see: JC Hathaway and M Foster, *The Law of Refugee Status* 2nd edn (Cambridge University Press, 2014); GS Goodwin-Gill and J McAdam, *The Refugee in International Law* 3rd edn (Oxford University Press, 2007).

[4] R Cohen and F Deng, *Masses in Flight: The Global Crisis of Internal Displacement* (Washington, DC: The Brookings Institution, 1998).

for refugees and internally displaced persons (IDPs) have been further developed at a regional level, such as through the African Union's Kampala Convention on internal displacement, and through states' domestic refugee and immigration laws and policies.

At the close of the Cold War, James Hathaway, one of the leading refugee law academics of the past 30 years, differentiated between refugee law paradigms based on humanitarianism and on human rights. Hathaway argued that a refugee law inspired by humanitarianism would require 'a general commitment to, at the least, meeting the basic human needs of refugees, whether by the provision of temporary material assistance, the facilitation of return to their country, or the grant of asylum abroad'.[5] Such an approach would cover all involuntary migrants, irrespective of the reasons for their flight. Conversely, a human rights approach to refugee law would entail a narrower focus in which, at a minimum, the most basic elements of human liberty and need would be protected, alongside an examination of the reasons for the individual's flight.[6] However, Hathaway concluded that the current refugee law framework was a mixture of these two approaches and that its purpose: 'is not specifically to meet the needs of the refugees themselves … but rather is to govern disruptions of regulated international migration in accordance with the interests of states.'[7]

Since Hathaway wrote those words in 1990, the world has faced multiple upheavals and forced population movements which have challenged states' willingness to accept those fleeing persecution into their territory and the coherence of the global refugee law framework itself; and witnessed the abject failure of the international community and states to provide even a minimum level of protection to people in places such as Srebrenica, Rwanda and Syria. In June 2016, UNHCR recorded the highest number ever of globally displaced persons, with 65.3 million people displaced by conflict or persecution in 2015.[8] Of these, 21.3 million were refugees and 40.8 million were IDPs, plus 3.2 million asylum seekers currently awaiting determination on their claim to be recognised as a refugee.[9]

Considering the depth of international, regional and domestic law, policy and practice relating to refugees and displacement since the conclusion of the 1951 Refugee Convention, this chapter will focus specifically on aspects of international refugee and displaced persons law from

[5] JC Hathaway, 'A Reconsideration of the Underlying Premise of Refugee Law' (1990) 31 *Harvard International Law Journal* 129, 131.
[6] ibid.
[7] ibid, 133.
[8] UNHCR, *Global Trends: Forced Displacement in 2015* (June 2016) 5.
[9] ibid, 2.

the perspective of the *acquis humanitaire*, namely protection and material assistance at all stages of the displacement cycle. Examples of current and emerging challenges in displacement will be examined, such as tackling sexual and gender-based violence in protracted camp settings, and displacement arising from natural disasters and climate change. The chapter commences by examining the pre-eminent global instrument covering refugees, the 1951 Refugee Convention, before examining more recent moves to provide a normative framework to protect and assist IDPs. The chapter then discusses the emerging recognition of climate change and disasters as a cause of forced displacement, exemplified by the Nansen Initiative's Protection Agenda. The chapter concludes by examining an example of regional approaches to refugee and displaced persons, namely regional and sub-regional binding frameworks within Africa.

II. GLOBAL INSTRUMENTS

A. UN Convention Relating to the Status of Refugees (1951)

The 1951 UN Convention relating to the Status of Refugees was drawn up in the same post-war environment as the 1948 Universal Declaration of Human Rights and 1949 Geneva Conventions, and was intended to provide an additional avenue of protection for those fleeing the effects of persecution. The fundamental basis of legal protection within the Refugee Convention (and its subsequent Protocol)[10] is the concept of *non-refoulement*. In other words, an individual should not be returned against their wishes to a country where there is a real risk that they will face persecution or serious human rights violations. Elihu Lauterpacht and Daniel Bethlehem's detailed submission to UNHCR examining the status of *non-refoulement* in international law concluded that as a rule of customary international law:

1. No person shall be rejected, returned, or expelled in any manner whatever where this would compel him or her to remain in or return to a territory where substantial grounds can be shown for believing that he or she would face a real risk of being subjected to torture or cruel, inhuman or degrading treatment or punishment. This principle allows of no limitation or exception.
2. In circumstances which do not come within the scope of paragraph 1, no person seeking asylum may be rejected, returned, or expelled in any manner

[10] UNGA, Protocol relating to the Status of Refugees (16 December 1966) A/RES/2198. The Protocol removed the geographic and temporal limitations of the Refugee Convention, which was originally restricted to events occurring within Europe before 1 January 1950 (reflecting the Eurocentric bias of the original Convention).

whatever where this would compel him or her to remain in or to return to a territory where he or she may face a threat of persecution or a threat to life, physical integrity, or liberty. Save as provided in paragraph 3, this principle allows of no limitation or exception.

3. Overriding reasons of national security or public safety will permit a State to derogate from the principle expressed in paragraph 2 in circumstances in which the threat of persecution does not equate to and would not be regarded as being on a par with a danger of torture or cruel, inhuman or degrading treatment or punishment and would not come within the scope of other non-derogable customary principles of human rights. The application of these exceptions is conditional on the strict compliance with principles of due process of law and the requirement that all reasonable steps must first be taken to secure the admission of the individual concerned to a safe third country.[11]

The customary international law status of the principle of *non-refoulement* has been widely recognised, and forms the core legal protection for both recognised refugees and persons who may face torture or other serious human rights violations in their country of origin.[12] However, while the Refugee Convention establishes the definition of a refugee as an individual with a 'well-founded fear of persecution' for one of five enumerated grounds[13] and protection from *non-refoulement* for individuals falling within this definition, it does not elaborate standards or mechanisms for the provision of humanitarian assistance to refugees. The underlying rationale was that refugees present in the territory of a host state would receive access to services and support at least as favourably as other (non-refugee) foreign nationals. For example, Chapter III on gainful employment obliges state parties to: 'accord to refugees lawfully staying in their territory the most favourable treatment accorded to nationals of a foreign country in the same circumstances, as regards the right to engage in wage earning employment.'[14] Similar provisions are in place for self-employment by refugees. Meanwhile, Chapter IV provides that refugees should be allowed to access national welfare schemes such as rationing, housing, public relief and assistance, and education in a manner the same as or no less favourably than nationals of the country of asylum.[15]

[11] E Lauterpacht and D Bethlehem, 'The Scope and Content of the Principle of *Non-refoulement*: Opinion' in E Feller, V Türk and F Nicholson (eds), *Refugee Protection in International Law: UNHCR's Global Consultations on International Protection* (Cambridge University Press, 2003).

[12] See, eg, UNHCR, *Advisory Opinion on the Extraterritorial Application of Non-refoulement Obligations under the 1951 Convention relating to the Status of Refugees and its 1967 Protocol* (26 January 2007); A Duffy, 'Expulsion to Face Torture? *Non-refoulement* in International Law' (2008) 20(3) *International Journal of Refugee Law* 373.

[13] Art 1(A) Refugee Convention.

[14] ibid, Art 17(1).

[15] ibid, Arts 20–24.

This approach neglected to consider the likelihood that refugees would be housed in dedicated camp settings, as has been the experience of countless millions of refugees since the conclusion of the Convention.

Despite this omission within the Convention, from an operational perspective UNHCR has been acutely aware of the multiple needs of refugees. Peter MacAlister-Smith has argued that the rapid expansion of UNHCR material assistance programmes in the 1950s stemmed from recognition that durable solutions could not be found simply by addressing refugees' legal protection concerns. Consequently, UNHCR had to engage in operational activities to provide material assistance to refugees.[16] Indeed, the Convention on the Rights of the Child, adopted nearly 40 years after the Refugee Convention, recognised this reality by clearly guaranteeing the rights of refugee children to receive 'appropriate protection and humanitarian assistance'.[17] Guglielmo Verdirame has argued that due to UNHCR's operational and institutional expertise, humanitarian assistance for refugees has 'often offered the blueprint for all humanitarian operations'.[18]

Owing to the lack of specific provisions within the Refugee Convention, the vast majority of sources of information and normative standards regarding protection activities and material assistance for refugees are found in non-binding texts. For example, the *Sphere Handbook* articulates minimum standards for technical areas of humanitarian operations such as water supplies and food security, alongside a Humanitarian Charter and Protection Principles.[19] Other core humanitarian texts of direct relevance for refugee protection and assistance emanate from the IASC, such as their *Policy Statement on Gender Equality in Humanitarian Action*[20] or *Guidelines on Mental Health and Psychosocial Support in Emergency Settings*.[21] Likewise, UNHCR regularly provides policy guidance and updates on areas of global concern, such as refugee status determination[22] or refugee protection and solutions in urban areas.[23] Reflecting UNHCR's

[16] P MacAlister-Smith, *International Humanitarian Assistance: Disaster Relief Actions in International Law and Organization* (Martinus Nijhoff, 1985) 38–45.

[17] Art 22(1) Convention on the Rights of the Child (adopted 20 November 1989, entered into force 2 September 1990) 1577 UNTS 3.

[18] G Verdirame, 'Compliance with Human Rights in UN Operations' (2002) 2(2) *Human Rights Law Review* 265, 271.

[19] The Sphere Project, *Humanitarian Charter and Minimum Standards in Humanitarian Response* 3rd edn, April 2011). For discussion of the *Sphere Handbook*, see ch 3, Section I.C.i.

[20] IASC, *Policy Statement: Gender Equality in Humanitarian Action* (20 June 2008).

[21] IASC, *Guidelines on Mental Health and Psychosocial Support in Emergency Settings* (2007).

[22] UNHCR, *Handbook and Guidelines on Procedures and Criteria for Determining Refugee Status under the 1951 Convention and the 1967 Protocol relating to the Status of Refugees* (Reissued Geneva, December 2011).

[23] UNHCR, *Policy on Refugee Protection and Solutions in Urban Areas* (September 2009).

operational activities, UNHCR also produces key texts to support humanitarian operations, from global guidelines such as the *Handbook for Emergencies*[24] to highly context-specific guidance, such as feeding support of children under two in transit settings in Europe.[25] As noted in chapter two, such norms may be highly authoritative and directly influence state and humanitarian actors' practice, irrespective of their non-legal and non-binding status.[26] Moreover, the harsh reality is that for the vast majority of the world's refugees, the opportunity for them to enforce even existing rights via judicial or other legal mechanisms is limited. Accountability for the protection of refugees therefore must be integrated into the operational activities of humanitarian agencies, and overseen by the national authorities of the host state. An example of the challenges of protecting refugees from harm, and the limited options for legal accountability, can be seen by the response to sexual and gender-based violence in the Bhutanese refugee camps in eastern Nepal in the early 2000s.

i. Nepal: Sexual and Gender-based Violence in Bhutanese Refugee Camps[27]

Background: In late 1992 and early 1993, large numbers of ethnic Nepali-speaking Hindus started fleeing their homes in southern Bhutan, arriving in eastern Nepal citing a policy of violence and serious human rights abuses against them by the Bhutanese government. The Nepalese government, with the support of UNHCR, established several refugee camps to host the arrivals and by mid-1994 approximately 86,000 refugees were living in the camps.[28] The Bhutanese government consistently denied that the vast majority of the refugees were even Bhutanese citizens, claiming they were in fact illegal migrants, and so Bhutan had no responsibility to accept them back into Bhutan. The Nepalese government, while willing to support the refugees in camps, was unenthusiastic about promoting their local integration. The resulting stalemate and

[24] UNHCR, *Handbook for Emergencies* 4th edn (2015).

[25] UNHCR, *Interim Operational Considerations for the Feeding Support of Infants and Young Children under 2 years of age in Refugee and Migrant Transit Settings in Europe* (1 October 2015).

[26] See ch 2, Section II.A.

[27] In the interest of transparency, I should note that I arrived in Nepal in early 2003 as part of the UNHCR response. As UNHCR protection staff, our role was to respond to all protection needs within the camps, with a significant focus on addressing historic and on-going cases of SGBV, in particular by working with the refugees, UNHCR's NGO implementing partners and Nepalese authorities to prevent future cases.

[28] Human Rights Watch, *Trapped by Inequality: Bhutanese Refugee Women in Nepal* (September 2003) 20.

lack of durable solutions led to one of Asia's largest protracted refugee situations.

Over the course of the next 10 years, the seven refugee camps developed into self-contained communities of over 100,000 people, with schools and healthcare facilities primarily staffed by refugee volunteers, supported by UNHCR and its NGO implementing partners including the Lutheran World Federation, Caritas and the Nepalese Red Cross.[29] The Nepalese government administered the camps with the support of UNHCR. There was a high level of refugee participation in the day-to-day running of the camps via the refugee Camp Management Committee (CMC), resulting in the camps being cited as a model of good practice. However, in October 2002, allegations of serious sexual and gender-based violence (SGBV) within the camps came to light. The cases included rape, sexual assault, child marriage, domestic violence and other serious forms of abuse, primarily committed by other refugees within the camps. It also transpired that the Camp Management Committees had taken it upon themselves to impose sanctions, often without the knowledge of the relevant Nepalese authorities or UNHCR. For example, rape victims were forced to marry the rapist to preserve their 'honour'. Serious shortfalls were identified in UNHCR's knowledge of the level of cases within the camps and subsequent response when cases had been identified. Following an internal UNHCR investigation, a series of immediate and longer-term responses were instituted during 2003, drawing from UNHCR's SGBV Guidelines, which were first published in May 2003.[30] Independently of UNHCR, Human Rights Watch conducted research into SGBV in the camps and critically analysed the responses of the Nepalese authorities and UNHCR.[31]

Legal response: One of the challenges identified was that the domestic Nepalese law on sexual assault, including rape, contained a 30-day statute of limitations. In other words, if a rape or sexual assault was not reported to the police within 30 days, there was no possibility of prosecuting the alleged offender. Considering the nature of sexual offences in general, plus the understandable reticence of refugees to report sexual assaults, this presented an insurmountable barrier to criminal sanctions

[29] For a description of the camps, see ibid, 20–22. See also D Hilhorst et al, 'Doing Good / Being Nice? Aid Legitimacy and Mutual Imaging of Aid Workers and Aid Recipients' in D Hilhorst (ed), *Disaster, Conflict and Society in Crises: Everyday Politics of Crisis Response* (Routledge, 2013) 265–67.

[30] UNHCR, *Sexual and Gender-Based Violence against Refugees, Returnees and Internally Displaced Persons: Guidelines for Prevention and Response* (May 2003). For discussion of the Nepalese authorities and UNHCR's shortfalls, see HRW, *Trapped by Inequality*, above n 28, 41–44.

[31] HRW, *Trapped by Inequality*, above n 28. See generally J Ward, *If Not Now, When? Addressing Gender-based Violence in Refugee, Internally Displaced, and Post-conflict Settings: A Global Overview* (2002) Reproductive Health for Refugees Consortium.

in most cases. Moreover, at the time there was no specific offence of domestic violence in Nepalese law.[32] To support the victims, UNHCR signed an agreement with the Nepalese Bar Association to provide legal advice to all victims of SGBV in the camps. Through awareness raising with the Camp Management Committees and NGO implementing partners, and a more proactive response by the Nepalese authorities, successful criminal prosecutions were brought in some cases, resulting in long prison sentences for the offenders.[33]

Despite improvements in the level of awareness of SGBV, and recognition that victims need to be fully supported, a follow-up visit by Human Rights Watch in 2007 found that the overall levels of SGBV within the camps had remained consistent between 2003 and 2007.[34] While women refugees acknowledged that progress had been made in changing perceptions, including perceptions of domestic violence, financial cutbacks by the international community had led to worsening conditions in the camps resulting in additional strains within families thereby contributing to domestic violence. As an elderly refugee woman stressed to HRW:

> This [SGBV] problem is due to so many people being packed so tightly together. As long as we are in these camps, in such cramped conditions, such problems will exist. No amount of social awareness training will be able to deal with this. To remove this problem, there has to be a permanent solution for the refugees.[35]

Durable solutions: The Bhutanese refugee camps in Nepal, which were in place for over 20 years, are now largely disbanded. In recognition that the optimal solution of voluntary return to Bhutan was as distant as ever for the majority of refugees in the camps, in October 2006 the US announced that it would accept 60,000 Bhutanese refugees under their resettlement programme. Other traditional countries of resettlement, including Canada, Australia and New Zealand, also accepted large numbers from the camps as part of a coordinated response to the protracted refugee setting. A major milestone was reached in November 2015 when the 100,000th refugee was resettled from the camps.[36] Of the original seven camps, only two currently remain operational hosting fewer than 20,000 refugees. The experience in Nepal highlights that sexual and gender-based violence is a constant threat in any refugee or displaced

[32] For discussion of domestic violence in the camps, see HRW, ibid, 54–57.

[33] For discussion of problems in the administration of justice in Nepal, see ibid, 61–63.

[34] Human Rights Watch, *Last Hope: The Need for Durable Solutions for Bhutanese Refugees in Nepal and India* (May 2007) 23–26.

[35] ibid, 26.

[36] DD Shrestha, 'Resettlement of Bhutanese Refugees Surpasses 100,000 Mark', *UNHCR Press Release*, 19 November 2015 www.unhcr.org/564dded46.html.

persons camp, and must be tackled with a range of immediate actions including education, awareness raising and criminal sanctions. But ultimately, finding a durable solution to the displacement itself, whether voluntary return, local integration or resettlement to a third country, is the best way to remove the threats created by cramped camp settings.[37]

B. UN Guiding Principles on Internal Displacement (1998)

i. Development of the Guiding Principles

Arguably it is a non-binding international text that has had one of the greatest impacts on establishing minimum standards of material assistance and protection to persons in humanitarian crises.[38] While international refugee law is based on the 1951 Refugee Convention, the rights and protection available to persons displaced within a country's borders are covered by the UN Guiding Principles on Internal Displacement.[39] The Guiding Principles were drafted at the request of the UN Commission on Human Rights by a group of international legal experts convened by the Representative of the UN Secretary-General on the Human Rights of Internally Displaced Persons[40] in 1996. The original request was to develop 'an appropriate framework … for the protection of internally displaced persons', although the request was careful to avoid the term 'legal' when referring to the expected framework.[41] The Guiding Principles were subsequently revised in 2004, and were welcomed and endorsed by the UN Secretary-General, General Assembly and Security Council, as well as specialised UN agencies including UNHCR, UNICEF, UNOCHA and UNHCHR. However, despite the normative format of the Guiding Principles, they are not an international treaty, so do not carry the binding force

[37] For discussion of sexual violence in IDP sites in Haiti, see L Davis, 'Still Trembling: State Obligation Under International Law to End Post-Earthquake Rape in Haiti' (2010–2011) 65 *University of Miami Law Review* 867.

[38] See D Fisher, 'The Right to Humanitarian Assistance' in W Kälin et al (eds), *Incorporating the Guiding Principles on Internal Displacement into Domestic Law: Issues and Challenges*, ASIL and Brookings-Bern Project on Internal Displacement, Studies in Transnational Legal Policy, No 41 (2010) 48.

[39] UN Commission on Human Rights, *Guiding Principles on Internal Displacement*, E/CN.4/1998/53/Add.2 (1998) ('Guiding Principles').

[40] Hereinafter 'Representative of the Secretary-General'.

[41] W Kälin, 'How Hard is Soft Law? The Guiding Principles on Internal Displacement and the Need for a Normative Framework', presentation at Roundtable Meeting, Ralph Bunche Institute for International Studies, 19 December 2001; R Cohen, 'The Guiding Principles on Internal Displacement: An Innovation in International Standard Setting' (2004) 10 *Global Governance* 459.

of the Refugee Convention.[42] In his Preface to the annotated version of the Guiding Principles in 2008, Walter Kälin noted:

> These Principles, although not a binding legal instrument, have … gained considerable authority. The Heads of State and Government assembled … for the September 2005 World Summit unanimously recognized them as an 'important international framework for the protection of internally displaced persons', and the General Assembly has not only welcomed 'the fact that an increasing number of States, United Nations agencies and regional and non-governmental organisations are applying them as a standard' but also encouraged 'all relevant actors to make use of the Guiding Principles when dealing with situations of internal displacement'.[43]

It has been argued that their widespread acceptance by states stems from the fact that the Guiding Principles represent a restatement of existing international law, rather than creating new rights for IDPs.[44] Roberta Cohen, one of the principal drafters, has noted that a strength of the Guiding Principles is that 'although not a binding document per se, they are based on already binding law'.[45] Indeed, at least 20 states and regional organisations have adopted national laws or policies based on the Guiding Principles,[46] and as such they provide a global framework for the protection of individuals affected by humanitarian crises who have not been able to cross an international border.[47] Owing to their genesis through an expert consultative process, rather than the usual deliberative procedures of the General Assembly, ILC or Security Council, one might expect that states would be wary of endorsing international norms they had limited influence drafting.[48] As Kälin has observed: 'where the Guiding Principles were met with resistance, it was not because of their content but because of a suspicion that they might be binding regardless of all assertions to the contrary.'[49] Therefore, a key element of the process to promote the Guiding

[42] See C Beyani, *Mapping the Response to Internal Displacement: The Evolution of Normative Developments* (October 2014) Brookings-LSE Project on Internal Displacement.

[43] W Kälin, *Guiding Principles on Internal Displacement: Annotations*, ASIL and Brookings-Bern Project on Internal Displacement, Studies in Transnational Legal Policy, No 38 (2008) vii [references omitted].

[44] *Response from the Representative of the UN Secretary-General on Internally Displaced Persons, Francis M Deng, to Questions Posed by the Delegate of Algeria*, Third Committee of the General Assembly, 12 November 2001, quoted in Cohen, 'Guiding Principles', above n 41, 473–74.

[45] R Cohen, 'Lessons Learned from the Development of the Guiding Principles on Internal Displacement' (October 2013) Working Paper, Institute for the Study of International Migration, Georgetown University, 7.

[46] R Cohen, 'Reconciling R2P with IDP Protection' (March 2010) Brookings-LSE Project on Internal Displacement, 8.

[47] Beyani, *Mapping the Response*, above n 42, 7.

[48] Cohen 'Lessons Learned', above n 45, 2.

[49] Kälin 'Annotations', above n 41, 7.

Principles has been to encourage states to adopt their own national laws and policies to protect and assist IDPs, thereby internalising the Guiding Principles.

To this end, in 2005 the Brookings-Bern Project on Internal Displacement (which has hosted the Representative of the Secretary-General since its inception) published *Addressing Internal Displacement: A Framework for National Responsibility*, which sets out a series of benchmarks to assist governments to develop effective national policies for preventing, responding to and resolving internal displacement situations.[50] Complementing the normative framework of the Guiding Principles, in 2010 the Global Protection Cluster published a comprehensive *Handbook for the Protection of Internally Displaced Persons* to assist humanitarian personnel, particularly field staff, to implement the Guiding Principles and related protection activities.[51] In the same year, the IASC endorsed the *Framework for Durable Solutions for Internally Displaced Persons*, which sets out three options for sustainable solutions for IDPs, namely: return to their place of origin; local integration in an area of refuge; or integration in another part of the country.[52] Such global guidance and operational texts help provide context and advice for governments and humanitarian agencies to implement international standards at the local level. The experience of Colombia provides an interesting example of how a domestic legal system can internalise such an international normative framework.

ii. Colombia: Internalisation of the Guiding Principles

Background: As a result of persistent internal armed conflict within Colombia dating back to the 1960s, for many years Colombia held the dubious record of the country with the highest number of IDPs. While figures vary, up to 5 million people were displaced due to the conflict over more than 50 years, resulting in multi-generational impacts, with children born into families living in protracted displacement.[53] After four years of negotiations, in August 2016 the Government of Colombia and

[50] *Addressing Internal Displacement: A Framework for National Responsibility* (April 2005) Brookings-Bern Project on Internal Displacement. The Framework was utilised for a detailed survey of the national implementation of the Guiding Principles in: E Ferris, E Mooney and C Stark, *From Responsibility to Response: Assessing National Approaches to Internal Displacement*, Brookings-LSE Project on Internal Displacement, November 2011, in particular 63–73.

[51] IASC, *Handbook on the Protection of Internally Displaced Persons*, Global Protection Cluster Working Group (2010). For discussion, see ch 3, Section I.C.i.

[52] IASC, *Framework for Durable Solutions for Internally Displaced Persons* (April 2010).

[53] 'IDPs in Protracted Displacement: Is Local Integration a Solution?' Report from the Second Expert Seminar on Protracted Internal Displacement, 19–20 January 2011, Geneva, Brookings-LSE Project on Internal Displacement/Internal Displacement Monitoring Centre (IDMC) 25–29.

the FARC (*Fuerzas Armadas Revolucionarias de Colombia*—Revolutionary Armed Forces of Colombia) signed a comprehensive peace agreement, potentially removing one of the primary root causes of the internal displacement.[54] Due to the complex nature of the conflict, concerns had been expressed in advance that, at least in the short term, such a peace agreement may even lead to an increase in violence. Such concerns may be well founded, as the Colombian public rejected the peace agreement by a narrow margin in a national referendum in October 2016, in part due to the limited sanctions placed on FARC members.[55] Whether modifications to the existing peace agreement would be feasible or acceptable to the public remains to be seen.[56]

Legal framework: Reflecting this long-standing experience of internal displacement, in 1994 the Colombian government invited the Representative of the Secretary-General, Francis Deng, along with domestic civil society groups to assist in drafting Law 387 of 1997 to provide specific rights for IDPs.[57] The government's proactive stance, even before the conclusion of the UN Guiding Principles in 1998, arguably created 'the world's most comprehensive legal system for IDPs'.[58] In her case study of the Colombian displacement, Elizabeth Ferris notes that in contrast to countries such as Somalia or the Democratic Republic of Congo, there are no IDP camps in Colombia and the government does not rely on external humanitarian organisations to provide material assistance to IDPs.[59]

Over the past 20 years, the protection of IDPs in Colombia has developed through the interplay between domestic legislation, civil society activism highlighting allegations of inconsistent application of the law, and judicial examination of claims brought by IDPs. For example, in 2004 the Constitutional Court issued a landmark judgment in the case *T-025*[60] which held that IDPs faced 'grave, massive and systemic' violations of their constitutional rights. The Court held that this had arisen

[54] 'Colombians Celebrate as Peace Deal is Reached with Farc Rebels', *BBC News Online*, 25 August 2016 www.bbc.com/news/world-latin-america-37180752.

[55] 'Colombia Referendum: Voters Reject Farc Peace Deal', *BBC News Online*, 3 October 2016 www.bbc.com/news/world-latin-america-37537252.

[56] E Ferris, *Changing Times: The International Response to Internal Displacement in Colombia* (December 2014) Brookings-LSE Project on Internal Displacement 10–11.

[57] E Fadnes and C Horst, 'Responses to Internal Displacement in Colombia: Guided by What Principles?' (2009) 26(1) *Refuge* 111, 113–14.

[58] Ferris, *Changing Times*, above n 55, 4. See also Fadnes and Horst, above n 56, 111.

[59] Ferris, above n 55, 10–11.

[60] Colombian Constitutional Court, *Decision T-025 of 2004*, adopted by the third chamber of the Court, composed by Manuel José Cepeda-Espinosa, Jaime Córdoba-Triviño and Rodrigo Escobar-Gil.

due to structural failures across government departments compounded by insufficient funding.[61] As a result, a permanent monitoring group, the *Comisión de Seguimiento*, was established to oversee progress in the realisation of the rights of IDPs.

Crucially, a series of legal developments over the past 10 years have created mechanisms for accountability and restitution for victims of the conflict. In 2005, Law 975 (*Ley de Justicia y Paz*—the Law of Justice and Peace) was introduced, inter alia, to guarantee the rights of victims (including many IDPs) to truth, justice and reparations. A subsequent Constitutional Court ruling, *Sentence C-370 of 2006*, held that while perpetrators of crimes committed in the conflict had the primary responsibility to provide compensation to victims, the government must assume responsibility if they are unable to pay. Consequently, administrative systems required to implement Law 975 as per the Constitutional Court's ruling were established by Presidential Decree 1290 of 2008 which created a programme of individual reparations for victims of armed groups. Most recently, Law 1448 (*Ley de Víctimas y Restitución de Tierras*—the Victims and Land Restitution Law) was adopted in July 2011 setting out the registration process so that IDPs can access stabilisation assistance, that is, bridging assistance going beyond emergency humanitarian assistance to support their transition to self-reliance through accessing public services such as education, training and employment.[62]

Internalisation of norms: Considering the complex legal and historical backdrop, it would appear that the UN Guiding Principles on Internal Displacement have, to a large extent, been socially, politically and legally internalised within Colombia. However, Fadnes and Horst have argued that the focus on technocratic solutions to displacement has masked the political root causes of the displacement; as can be seen by the recourse to humanitarian assistance programmes, at the expense of preventative measures or searching for durable solutions.[63] In other words, while the Colombian law on paper addresses all stages of the displacement cycle, in practice there is an unnecessary focus on

[61] For analysis, see CE Reales, 'Design and Implementation of the Orders Issued in Decision T-025 of 2004: An Assessment of the Process' in RA Rivadeneira (ed), *Judicial Protection of Internally Displaced Persons: The Colombian Experience* (November 2009) Brookings-Bern Project on Internal Displacement.

[62] For detailed discussion, see Ferris, *Changing Times*, above n 55, 18–22. See also 'Annex 8: IDPs' Livelihoods and Self-reliance Interventions in Colombia' in N Crawford et al, *Protracted Displacement: Uncertain Paths to Self-reliance in Exile* (2015) Humanitarian Policy Group, Overseas Development Institute.

[63] Fadnes and Horst, 'Internal Displacement', above n 58, 112.

humanitarian assistance during displacement, to the exclusion of pro-active measures to prevent displacement from occurring or to promote durable solutions such as an IDP's right to return to their place of origin or permanently settle elsewhere.

Moreover, following a country visit in his capacity of Representative of the Secretary-General, Walter Kälin expressed his concern regarding: 'the clear gap between the policies decided in the capital Bogotá and their often ineffective implementation at the departmental and municipal levels. The actual implementation of national policies seemed to depend too much on efforts the individual civil servants are willing to undertake in order to make the system work.'[64] Robert Goldman therefore concludes that 'the government's implementation of measures designed to prevent displacement and to meet the urgent protection needs of its displaced citizens to date have been woefully inadequate'.[65] This highlights that the internalisation of international norms, such as those contained within the Guiding Principles, is an on-going process.[66] Despite the internationally recognised quality of their domestic legislation, continual pressure from civil society combined with judicial interpretations of national and international obligations is required to ensure that there is consistent political internalisation of the norms set out in the Guiding Principles at all levels of the state.

iii. Substantive Content of the Guiding Principles

Robert Goldman, who helped develop the Guiding Principles with Francis Deng and Walter Kälin in the mid-1990s, has explained that the preliminary study into internal displacement produced in 1995[67] adopted a needs-based approach, which first required: 'identifying the basic needs of IDPs and then determining the extent to which international human

[64] HRC, *Report of the Representative of the Secretary-General on the Human Rights of Internally Displaced Persons, Walter Kälin. Addendum: Mission to Colombia* (24 January 2007) A/HRC/4/38/Add.3, para 27.

[65] RK Goldman, 'Internal Displacement, the Guiding Principles on Internal Displacement, the Principles Normative Status, and the Need for their Effective Domestic Implementation in Colombia' (2009) 2 *Colombian Yearbook of International Law* 59, 83.

[66] For an analysis of the Guiding Principles utilising Finnemore and Sikkink's theory of a norm life-cycle, see H Entwisle, 'Tracing Cascades: The Normative Development of the UN Guiding Principles on Internal Displacement' (2004–2005) 19 *Georgetown Immigration Law Journal* 369.

[67] UN, *Compilation and Analysis of Legal Norms, Report of the Representative of the Secretary-General on Internally Displaced Persons* (5 December 1995) E/CN.4/1996/52/Add.2. This was followed in 1998 by *Part II, Legal Aspects Relating to Protection Against Arbitrary Displacement* (11 February 1998) E/CN.4/1998/53/Add.1.

rights law, international humanitarian law and refugee law, by analogy, meet those needs in three recognized situations in international law.'[68]

The final text of the Guiding Principles adopted a merged needs-based and rights-based approach, setting out 30 principles covering the life-cycle of displacement, namely: protection from displacement *ab initio*; protection of fundamental rights during displacement; the provision of humanitarian assistance; and durable solutions of return, resettlement or reintegration. Reflecting Kälin's concept of a cycle of protection, this approach can be distilled down into prevention, protection, assistance and solutions.[69] The Guiding Principles have, over a relatively short period of time, become a hugely authoritative global framework, despite their initially non-binding nature. For example, the ICRC has cited them as evidence of customary international law rules regarding the prohibition of forcible displacement and the treatment of civilian displacees during international and non-international armed conflicts.[70] Moreover, the Inter-American Court of Human Rights has highlighted the role of the Guiding Principles as rules for interpretation of Article 22 of the Inter-American Convention on Human Rights covering freedom of movement and residence.[71] Such invocations of the Guiding Principles in turn reinforce the authoritative status of their substantive content, and advance the transnational legal process of interactions, interpretation and internalisation at the national and international levels.

Article 2—Introduction: Scope and Purpose

> For the purposes of these Principles, internally displaced persons are persons or groups of persons who have been forced or obliged to flee or to leave their homes or places of habitual residence, in particular as a result of or in order to avoid the effects of armed conflict, situations of generalised violence, violations of human rights or natural or human-made disasters, and who have not crossed an internationally recognised State border.

As evident from the description of an 'internally displaced person' set out in Article 2, the Guiding Principles are intended to provide protection to much broader categories of people than the 1951 Refugee Convention, which requires an individual who has fled their country of nationality or

[68] Goldman, 'Internal Displacement', above n 65, 64.

[69] W Kälin, 'Report of the Representative of the Secretary-General on the Human Rights of Internally Displaced Persons: Addendum on Protection of Internally Displaced Persons in Situations of Natural Disasters' (5 March 2009) A/HRC/10/13/Add.1, para 21. For discussion of the full cycle of protection, see ch 3, Section II.A.

[70] JM Henckaerts and L Doswald-Beck, *Customary International Humanitarian Law: Rules and Practice* (Cambridge University Press, 2005), Rules 129–33.

[71] See, eg, *Case of the Moiwana Community v Suriname*, Judgment of June 15, 2005 (Preliminary Objections, Merits, Reparations and Costs), para 111; *Case of the 'Mapiripán Massacre' v Colombia*, Judgment of September 15, 2005 (Merits, Reparations and Costs), para 171.

habitual residence to have a well-founded fear of persecution for reasons of race, religion, nationality, membership of a particular social group or political opinion.[72] As such, they avoid some of the definitional problems faced by UNHCR and national authorities in the refugee determination process, and through the use of the words 'in particular' provide an element of flexibility for the internalisation of the description of an IDP into domestic legislation or policy based on the specific context of the country concerned.

Principle 3

1. National authorities have the primary duty and responsibility to provide protection and humanitarian assistance to internally displaced persons within their jurisdiction.
2. Internally displaced persons have the right to request and to receive protection and humanitarian assistance from these authorities. They shall not be persecuted or punished for making such a request.

While a non-binding text, the authoritative nature of the Guiding Principles means that Principle 3(2) provides one of the strongest sources of a general right for individuals to request and receive humanitarian assistance.[73] The Guiding Principles continue by setting out a series of guarantees for all IDPs, whether as a result of conflict, generalised violence or disasters. Drawing on international human rights law, the Guiding Principles address key civil and political rights as well as economic, social and cultural rights for IDPs, such as: Principle 12(3) on protection from discriminatory arrest and detention resulting from displacement; Principle 18 on the right to an adequate standard of living; Principle 21 on the protection of property; and Principle 23 on the right to education. Section IV of the Guiding Principles then sets out a series of principles specifically covering the provision of humanitarian assistance. In particular, the Guiding Principles outline that:

— **Principle 24:** All humanitarian assistance shall be carried out in accordance with the principles of humanity and impartiality, without discrimination, and shall not be diverted (in particular for political or military reasons).

— **Principle 25:** The primary duty and responsibility for providing humanitarian assistance to IDPs lies with the national authorities. However, international humanitarian organisations and other appropriate actors have the right to offer their services. Such offers shall not be regarded as an unfriendly act or interference in a state's internal affairs, so consent shall not be arbitrarily withheld.[74]

[72] Art 1A(2) Refugee Convention.

[73] Fisher, 'Right to Humanitarian Assistance', above n 38, 48.

[74] See K Luopajärvi, 'Is there an Obligation on States to Accept International Humanitarian Assistance to Internally Displaced Persons under International Law?' (2003) 15(4) *International Journal of Refugee Law* 678.

- **Principle 26:** Humanitarian personnel, equipment and supplies shall be respected and protected, and shall not be the object of attack or other acts of violence.
- **Principle 27:** Without prejudice to the specific protection mandates of some international organisations,[75] international humanitarian organisations and other appropriate actors should give due regard to the protection needs and human rights of IDPs, and should respect relevant international standards and codes of conduct.

By reaffirming the primary duty and responsibility of the affected state, while simultaneously acknowledging the right of international humanitarian organisations and other appropriate actors to offer their services, the Guiding Principles represent a balancing of state sovereignty with humanitarian imperatives. Roberta Cohen has explained that a philosophical foundation behind the principles was the concept of sovereignty as responsibility, and argues that although the primary responsibility for the welfare and safety of IDPs rests with national authorities, the international community has a corresponding obligation to provide material assistance and protection if a national government is unable to fulfil their responsibilities.[76]

However, it should be noted that the Guiding Principles do not contain an integral monitoring or enforcement mechanism. Francis Deng and then Walter Kälin substantially advanced the normative framework and reporting of internal displacement through country visits and global reports during their tenures as Representative of the Secretary-General. In 2010, Chaloka Beyani was appointed the Special Rapporteur on the Human Rights of Internally Displaced Persons under the UN Human Rights Council, thereby mainstreaming the rights of IDPs, and by extension the Guiding Principles, into the broader UN human rights monitoring and enforcement mechanisms. As per HRC Resolution 23/8 of 2013, the Special Rapporteur's mandate includes promoting the rights of IDPs through continuous dialogue with governments, strengthening the international response to internal displacement, integrating a gender perspective throughout the mandate, and mainstreaming the rights of IDPs throughout the UN system.[77] While the Guiding Principles provide a clear example of the progression of non-binding norms into binding national,

[75] For discussion of the protection mandates of UNHCR, UNICEF, OHCHR, and ICRC, see ch 3, Section I.B.i.

[76] R Cohen, 'The Guiding Principles on Internal Displacement: An Innovation in International Standard Setting' (2004) 10 *Global Governance* 459, 466. See also R Cohen and F Deng, 'Sovereignty as Responsibility: Building Block for R2P' in A Bellamy and T Dunne (eds), *The Oxford Handbook of the Responsibility to Protect* (Oxford University Press, 2016).

[77] HRC, Res 28/3 Mandate of the Special Rapporteur on the Human Rights of Internally Displaced Persons (20 June 2013) A/HRC/RES/23/8, para 14.

regional and customary law rules, the fact that there are over 40 million IDPs in the world today highlights the on-going challenges of ensuring that the protection of persons is a reality on the ground, not just an assertion in legal or academic texts.

C. Climate Change and Disasters: The Nansen Initiative's Protection Agenda

The large number of internally displaced persons in the world stems in part from the difficulties most people face in financing or physically undertaking a potentially hazardous cross-border journey, not least those who are vulnerable due to infirmity or personal circumstance. These difficulties have been exacerbated by a series of emerging trends which have gained increasing prominence in recent years. The threat posed by global climate change has been recognised since the early 1990s, most noticeably with the conclusion of the UN Framework Convention on Climate Change (UNFCCC).[78] However, it is only in the past few years that the reality of forced displacement arising from climate change, for example as a result of flooding of river deltas, sea level rise, or desertification, has received serious attention.[79] At the same time, the human rights implications of natural and human-made disasters have been highlighted, not least by the UN High Commissioner for Human Rights.[80] Owing to its role as the Global Protection Cluster lead, UNHCR reviewed its operational capacities to respond to population displacements caused by natural disasters in 2010.[81] It is reported that between 2008 and 2014, over 184 million people were displaced by sudden-onset disasters, equating to over 26 million people a year. Of these, an annual average of 22.5 million people were displaced by weather- and climate-related hazards.[82]

[78] UN Framework Convention on Climate Change (adopted 9 May 1992, entered into force 21 March 1994) 1771 UNTS 107.

[79] See, eg, J McAdam, *Climate Change, Forced Migration, and International Law* (Oxford University Press, 2012). For analysis of the impact of extreme weather events, see IPCC, CB Field et al (eds), 'Summary for Policymakers' in IPCC, *Managing the Risks of Extreme Events and Disasters to Advance Climate Change Adaptation: Special Report of the Intergovernmental Panel on Climate Change* (Cambridge University Press, 2012) 6–7 (known as the 'SREX Report').

[80] UN, *Report of the Office of the United Nations High Commissioner for Human Rights on the Relationship between Climate Change and Human Rights* (15 January 2009) A/HRC/10/61. See also the work of former UN High Commissioner for Human Rights Mary Robinson on climate justice: www.mrfjc.org.

[81] B Deschamp et al, *Earth, Wind and Fire: A Review of UNHCR's Role in Recent Natural Disasters*, UNHCR Policy Development and Evaluation Service (June 2010).

[82] Nansen Initiative, *Agenda for the Protection of Cross-border Displaced Persons in the Context of Disasters and Climate Change* (December 2015) 6.

There has been considerable academic and practitioner debate as to whether or not a new international convention is required to address such emerging forms of forced displacement, or whether so-called 'climate refugees' should be included within the Refugee Convention.[83] Meanwhile humanitarian agencies have argued that international law does not currently cover the 'chaotic diversity' of people fleeing complex emergencies, including environmental disasters, resulting in a lack of protection and humanitarian aid.[84] However, the difficulties in determining a causal link between global climate change and an individual's decision to move are evident, and from a refugee law perspective identifying the agent of persecution is even harder.[85] Therefore, inspired by the 2010 Cancún Agreement on Climate Change Adaptation[86] that called for '[m]easures to enhance understanding, coordination and cooperation with regard to climate change induced displacement, migration and planned relocation,' in 2012 the Norwegian and Swiss governments commenced the 'Nansen Initiative' to examine the protection gap for people displaced across borders as a result of disasters and the effects of climate change.[87] Led by Walter Kälin, between 2012 and 2015 this inter-governmental initiative explored the connections between refugees, forced displacement, disasters, and climate change through research, case studies and policy papers.[88] In October 2015, a 'Protection Agenda' was finalised with the aim of building consensus on the policy and legal implications of such cross-border displacement,[89] which was subsequently endorsed by the World Humanitarian Summit in May 2016 through the establishment of the inter-governmental Platform on Disaster Displacement.[90]

The initial draft of the Protection Agenda, published in April 2015 in advance of the final conference, set out the rationale behind the initiative:

> Rather than calling for a new binding international convention on cross-border disaster-displacement, this Protection Agenda supports an approach

[83] See, eg, J McAdam, 'Swimming against the Tide: Why a Climate Change Displacement Treaty is Not the Answer' (2011) 23(1) *International Journal of Refugee Law* 2.

[84] Trócaire, *Migration*, Learning for Livelihoods Series No 2 (2007) 21.

[85] For a detailed analysis of the issues at stake, see *AF (Kiribati)* [2013] NZIPT 800413 before the Immigration and Protection Tribunal of New Zealand.

[86] Para 14(f), UNFCCC, Cancún Agreement on Climate Change Adaptation (15 March 2011) FCCC/CP/2010/7/Add.1.

[87] See *The Nansen Conference: Climate Change and Displacement in the 21st Century*, report of a conference held in Oslo, Norway, 5–7 June 2011, Norwegian Refugee Council.

[88] See W Kälin and N Schrepfer, *Protecting People Crossing Borders in the Context of Climate Change: Normative Gaps and Possible Approaches*, UNHCR Division of International Protection (February 2012); J McAdam, *Climate Change Displacement and International Law: Complementary Protection Standards*, UNHCR Division of International Protection (May 2011). See also R Cohen and M Bradley, 'Disasters and Displacement: Gaps in Protection' (2010) 1 *Journal of International Humanitarian Legal Studies* 95.

[89] Nansen Initiative, *Global Consultation Conference Report* (Geneva, 12–13 October 2015).

[90] For information see http://disasterdisplacement.org.

> that focuses on the integration of such effective practices by States and (sub-) regional organizations into their own normative frameworks in accordance with their specific situations and challenges.[91]

This approach was adopted in the final text, which states that the Protection Agenda does 'not aim to create new legal standards but may, where appropriate, inspire and facilitate the elaboration of such standards at, in particular, domestic and (sub-) regional levels'.[92] Adopting the IASC definition of 'protection', the Agenda itself is split into three sections, covering: i) protecting cross-border disaster-displaced persons; ii) managing disaster displacement risk in the country of origin; and iii) priority areas for future action. The Agenda notes that there are two distinct forms of protection that states can provide to such displaced individuals. First, they can allow people fleeing disasters or climate change to enter their territory, at least temporarily. Second, states can refrain from returning people already on their territory to areas affected by severe disasters or climate change (thereby introducing the principle of *non-refoulement* into states' responses to disaster and climate change displacement).[93] The Agenda reflects Kälin's own concept of the cycle of protection, highlighting the need to reduce vulnerability and build resilience through risk reduction and prevention measures,[94] as well as promoting durable solutions, including planned relocations. Cross-cutting all actions is the concept of migration with dignity.[95] It remains to be seen what the normative and operational impact of the Protection Agenda will be; however, the focus on cross-border movements arising from disasters and climate change reflects the changing humanitarian crises which states and humanitarian agencies need to address now and in the coming years.

III. REGIONAL APPROACHES: THE AFRICAN EXPERIENCE

Regional organisations, such as the European Union (EU), the Council of Europe, the Organisation of American States (OAS) and the Association

[91] Nansen Initiative, *Cross-border Displacement in the Context of Disasters and Climate Change: A Protection Agenda*, Draft for Consultation (8 April 2015) iv.

[92] Nansen Initiative, *Protection Agenda*, above n 82, 7.

[93] ibid, 7–8.

[94] For discussion of a human rights-based approach to prevention measures in the context of climate change, see D Cubie, 'In-Situ Adaptation: Non-Migration as a Coping Strategy for Vulnerable Persons' in A Baldwin et al, *Climate Change, Migration and Human Rights: Law and Policy Perspectives* (Routledge, forthcoming).

[95] 'Facilitating Migration with Dignity' in Nansen Initiative, *Protection Agenda*, above n 82, 47–48. See also J McAdam and B Saul, 'Displacement with Dignity: International Law and Policy Responses to Climate Change Migration and Security in Bangladesh' (2010) Sydney Law School, Legal Studies Research Paper No.10/113.

of Southeast Asian Nations (ASEAN), have generally developed comprehensive legal and normative frameworks for international co-operation and regulation in regard to cross-border population movement. The complex structure of the EU's common European asylum system is a case in point.[96] Moreover, regional judicial bodies such as the Inter-American Court of Human Rights and the European Court of Human Rights have reaffirmed the rights of migrants, including the importance of the UN Guiding Principles, within their jurisprudence.[97] Likewise, regional intergovernmental organisations have called on their constituent member states to protect and assist IDPs, as seen in Resolution 2229 (XXXVI-O/06) passed by the General Assembly of the OAS in June 2006.[98] In the context of this book, it is not possible to outline all the regional law, non-binding norms and non-law relating to the protection of and assistance for refugee and displaced persons. Therefore, this final section examines one specific region of the world, Africa, as an example of overlapping regional legal instruments for the provision of material assistance and protection for refugees and displaced persons.

A. OAU Convention Governing the Specific Aspects of Refugee Problems in Africa (1969)

Africa has a strong tradition of adopting regional legal instruments addressing humanitarian, refugee and displacement issues, such as the African Union Charter on the Rights and Welfare of the Child which specifically provides that state parties shall take all feasible measures to ensure the protection and care of children affected by all forms of armed conflict.[99] Likewise, as a statement of solidarity with those fleeing the struggle against colonialism, the Convention Governing the Specific Aspects of Refugee Problems in Africa,[100] adopted by the Organisation of

[96] See, eg, H Lambert, 'Transnational Judicial Dialogue, Harmonization and the Common European Asylum System' (2009) 58(3) *International and Comparative Law Quarterly* 519; S Velluti, *Reforming the Common European Asylum System—Legislative Developments and Judicial Activism of the European Courts* (Springer, 2014).

[97] See, eg, IACHR, *'Mapiripán Massacre' case*, above n 71; *Soltanov and Others v Azerbaijan*, ECtHR, Applications 41177/08, 41224/08, 41226/08, 41245/08, 41393/08, 41408/08, 41424/08, 41688/08, 41690/08 and 43635/08, judgment of 13 January 2011; *Isayeva v Russia*, ECtHR, Application 6846/02, judgment of 15 November 2007.

[98] OAS General Assembly, *Internally Displaced Persons*, AG/RES. 2229 (XXXVI-O/06) (Adopted by the Plenary at its fourth session, held on 6 June 2006).

[99] Art 22(3) OAU, African Charter on the Rights and Welfare of the Child (adopted 11 July 1990, entered into force 29 November 1999) CAB/LEG/24.9/49.

[100] OAU, Convention Governing the Specific Aspects of Refugee Problems in Africa (adopted 10 September 1969, entered into force 20 June 1974) UNTS 14691 ('1969 OAU Convention'). For analysis see JO Moses Okello, 'The 1969 OAU Convention and the Continuing Challenge for the African Union' (November 2014) 48 *Forced Migration Review* 70.

African Unity (the precursor to the African Union) in 1969, expanded the definition of a refugee in the 1951 Refugee Convention to also apply to:

> every person who, owing to external aggression, occupation, foreign domination or events seriously disturbing public order in either part or the whole of his country of origin or nationality, is compelled to leave his place of habitual residence in order to seek refuge in another place outside his country of origin or nationality.[101]

Despite including provisions covering practical issues such as the issuance of travel documents, and non-discrimination in the application of the Convention, the 1969 OAU Convention does not include the minimal guarantees of equal treatment in regard to welfare and employment set out in the 1951 Refugee Convention. Therefore, the primary importance of the Convention is that it incorporates protection from *non-refoulement* into regional law. However, in the spirit of African solidarity and international co-operation, the Convention does stipulate that if a Member State faces difficulties in continuing to grant asylum to refugees, they can call on other Member States to take appropriate measures to 'lighten the burden'.[102]

B. ICGLR Pact on Security, Stability and Development in the Great Lakes (2006)

The African region has also been proactive in concluding agreements on the question of internal displacement. This is understandable considering that several countries, particularly around the Great Lakes Region, have seen massive numbers of IDPs in the recent past.[103] As noted by Moses Okello, former UNHCR Representative in Ethiopia, 'while Africa succeeded in freeing itself from the yoke of colonialism, the continent has yet to free itself from its own transgressions'.[104] Over 5 million IDPs have been created as a result of the various conflicts within Sudan, while the conflict in northern Uganda resulted in 1.7 million IDPs, and the Democratic Republic of Congo saw 1.1 million IDPs arising from conflict and natural disasters.[105] Therefore, in 2006 the Member States of the International

101 1969 OAU Convention, Art I(2). As per Art VIII(2), the 1969 Convention is deemed to be: 'the effective regional complement in Africa of the 1951 United Nations Convention on the Status of Refugees.'

102 ibid, Art II(4).

103 See, eg, L Moffett, 'Accountability for Forced Displacement in Democratic Republic of Congo and Uganda before the International Criminal Court' (2015) 1(2) *African Journal of International Criminal Justice* 129.

104 Okello, 'OAU Convention', above n 100, 70.

105 W Kälin, 'The Great Lakes Protocol on Internally Displaced Persons: Responses and Challenges', paper presented at *Symposium on International Law in Post Conflict Situations: The Great Lakes Process*, LSE-International Humanitarian Law Project, 27 September 2007.

Conference on the Great Lakes Region (ICGLR)[106] internalised the UN Guiding Principles into regional law via the binding Pact on Security, Stability and Development in the Great Lakes.[107] The Pact, as amended in November 2012, contains 10 Protocols and four programmes of action encompassing 33 priority projects. One of the key objectives of the Pact is to provide a legal framework governing relations between the Member States.[108] The Protocols therefore take the form of articles within the Pact, with two of particular relevance in the context of displacement. The Protocol on the Protection and Assistance to Internally Displaced Persons (Article 12) requires Member States to provide special protection and assistance to IDPs and in particular to adopt and implement the UN Guiding Principles, while the Protocol on Property Rights of Returning Persons (Article 13) requires Member States to adopt legal principles and create a legal framework to ensure that returning refugees and IDPs are able to recover their property on their return.[109] The Pact also contains a Programme of Action on Humanitarian, Social and Environmental Issues which requires Member States to 'find lasting solutions to guarantee protection and assistance to populations affected by political conflicts in the Great Lakes Region' and to promote 'relevant policies to guarantee access to basic social services by the populations affected by conflicts and effects of natural disasters'.[110]

C. AU Convention for the Protection and Assistance of Internally Displaced Persons in Africa (2009)

The most developed binding legal framework addressing humanitarian crises in Africa is the African Union's 2009 Convention for the Protection and Assistance of Internally Displaced Persons in Africa (known as the 'Kampala Convention'), which incorporates key aspects of the UN Guiding Principles, including the broad description of 'internally displaced

[106] The International Conference on the Great Lakes Region is an inter-governmental organisation currently composed of: Angola, Burundi, Central African Republic, Republic of Congo, Democratic Republic of Congo, Kenya, Uganda, Rwanda, Republic of South Sudan, Sudan, Tanzania and Zambia. For more information see www.icglr.org.

[107] ICGLR, *The Pact on Security, Stability and Development for the Great Lakes Region* (December 2006, amended November 2012).

[108] ibid, Art 2(a).

[109] The *Protocol for the Prevention and the Punishment of the Crime of Genocide, War Crimes and Crimes against Humanity and all forms of Discrimination* (Art 8) and *Protocol on the Prevention and Suppression of Sexual Violence Against Women and Children* (Art 11) are applicable in all contexts and so are also of direct relevance for refugees and IDPs.

[110] ibid, Art 20.

persons' found in Article 2 of the Guiding Principles.[111] This is perhaps not surprising as Walter Kälin, then Representative of the Secretary-General on IDPs, assisted the African Union in the drafting of the Convention.[112] Reflecting the on-going development of international law and practice, the Convention expands the enumerated causes of flight to include climate change as a form of natural or human-made disaster.[113] Of note, Article 3(1)(j) provides that: 'States Parties shall … ensure assistance to internally displaced persons by meeting their basic needs as well as allowing and facilitating rapid and unimpeded access by humanitarian organisations and personnel.' Complementing the right of humanitarian organisations to provide assistance is an individual right for IDPs to 'peacefully request or seek protection and assistance … a right for which they shall not be persecuted, prosecuted or punished'.[114]

Reflecting Kälin's cycle of protection, the Convention requires State Parties to: 'Devise early warning systems … in areas of potential displacement, establish and implement disaster risk reduction strategies, emergency and disaster preparedness and management measures and, where necessary, provide immediate protection and assistance to internally displaced persons.'[115] Such protection and assistance should be provided 'to the fullest extent practicable and with the least possible delay'.[116] Utilising mandatory language, Article 9(2)(b) provides that 'such assistance *shall* include food, water, shelter, medical care and other health services, sanitation, education, and any other necessary social services'.[117] In another innovation for a binding international convention, Article 9(2)(b) provides that 'where appropriate, [Member States shall] extend such assistance to local and host communities'. This is particularly important as perceived inequalities between displaced populations, who may be receiving international assistance, and the local and host communities, who often are not, can be a source of tension and conflict.[118] Indeed, the inter-governmental

[111] Art 1(k), African Union, Convention for the Protection and Assistance of Internally Displaced Persons in Africa (adopted 22 October 2009, entered into force 6 December 2012) ('Kampala Convention'). See AM Abebe, 'The African Union Convention on Internally Displaced Persons: Its Codification Background, Scope, and Enforcement Challenges' (2010) 29(3) *Refugee Survey Quarterly* 28; F Giustiniani, 'New Hopes and Challenges for the Protection of IDPs in Africa: The Kampala Convention for the Protection and Assistance of Internally Displaced Persons in Africa' (2010–2011) 39 *Denver Journal of International Law and Policy* 347.

[112] AM Abebe, 'Special Rapporteurs as Law Makers: The Developments and Evolution of the Normative Framework for Protecting and Assisting Internally Displaced Persons' (2011) 15(2) *International Journal of Human Rights* 286, 295.

[113] Kampala Convention, above n 111, Art 5(4).

[114] ibid, Art 5(9).

[115] ibid, Art 4(2).

[116] ibid, Art 9(2)(b).

[117] ibid [emphasis added].

[118] See, eg, L Berry, 'The Impacts of Environmental Degradation on Refugee-Host Relations' (2008) 17(3) *African Security Review* 125.

draft political statement prepared in advance of the 2016 High-level Meeting of the UN General Assembly expressly noted:

> We are committed to providing humanitarian assistance to refugees so as to ensure essential support in key life-saving sectors, eg healthcare, shelter, food, water and sanitation. We commit to supporting host countries and communities in this regard, including by using locally available knowledge and capacities. We will support community-based development programmes that benefit both refugees and host communities.[119]

Stephane Ojeda has highlighted the interaction between regional and international instruments, arguing that the Kampala Convention's reliance on the UN Guiding Principles has contributed to their 'evolution from soft law to hard law standards'.[120] Yet, as seen globally, the domestic application of international obligations often trails states' willingness to sign up to them on the international stage.[121] Even after its entry into force in December 2012, there have been regular breaches of compliance with the provisions of the Convention, which potentially reduces the value of such international commitments. Nevertheless, the Convention remains one of the few international binding texts to include such strong normative commitments to humanitarian assistance and protection, and it remains to be seen the impact that such a regionally binding document will have on future humanitarian actions for IDPs in Africa.[122]

IV. CONCLUSION: EVALUATING THE NORMATIVE CONTENT OF THE *ACQUIS HUMANITAIRE*

The conflict in Syria provides a tragic example of how massive humanitarian suffering leads directly to large-scale population movements, which in turn can exacerbate that human suffering due to the risks people face as they undertake perilous journeys by road or sea, or end up in cramped and inadequate camp settings. As reported by UNHCR, nearly 5 million people have fled Syria since the start of the conflict, and nearly 9 million

[119] Point 4.17, *Outcome Document for 19 September 2016 High-level Meeting to address large movements of refugees and migrants*, draft for adoption by the UN General Assembly (29 July 2016).

[120] S Ojeda, 'The Kampala Convention on Internally Displaced Persons: Some International Humanitarian Law Aspects' (2010) 29(3) *Refugee Survey Quarterly* 58, 59.

[121] See, eg, H Koh, 'Why do Nations Obey International Law?' (June 1997) 106(8) *Yale Law Journal* 2599; O Hathaway, 'Do Human Rights Treaties Make a Difference?' (2001–2002) 111 *Yale Law Journal* 1935; Okello, 'OAU Convention', above n 100.

[122] For jurisprudence from the African Commission on Human and Peoples' Rights regarding the rights of IDPs, see: *Centre for Minority Rights Development (Kenya) and Minority Rights Group International on behalf of Endorois Welfare Council v Kenya*, Communication 276/2003; *Malawi Association and Others v Mauritania*, Communication 54/91.

people remain displaced within the country's borders.[123] Considering UNHCR's operational experience over the past 70 years, it is not surprising that Guglielmo Verdirame has noted that UNHCR has provided 'the blueprint for all humanitarian operations'.[124] It is particularly noticeable that UNHCR's operational experience in humanitarian action developed notwithstanding the limited express legal provisions on such assistance in the 1951 Refugee Convention.

UNHCR's operational experience also reflects the interconnected nature of the different branches of international law where elements of the *acquis humanitaire* are located. Humanitarian operations often incorporate aspects of international human rights, refugee, criminal or disaster laws. Humanitarian personnel must navigate situations where armed conflicts, population displacement, international criminal acts and natural disasters are occurring simultaneously. Drawing from a range of binding and non-binding sources therefore strengthens their arguments for humanitarian access to populations in need whether with state officials or non-state armed groups. However, it can be harder to undertake preventative actions to increase the resilience and decrease the vulnerability of at-risk populations in advance of a crisis occurring, not least because of resource constraints for risk reduction measures resulting from an overemphasis on funding response activities. Determining the legal rights and obligations arising from different branches of international law therefore requires an understanding of the interconnected nature of humanitarian crises, and a coherent framework for grouping together the relevant legal provisions and non-legal normative texts.

The preceding five chapters have provided an overview of some of the key legal and non-legal sources relating to the international legal protection of persons in humanitarian crises. From this analysis, it is clear that while there are extensive provisions which create binding legal obligations on states, there are also fundamental gaps in the web of international legal protection. The different levels of protection for civilians between international and non-international armed conflicts is a case in point. While the ICRC has argued that customary international law fills many of these gaps, the consent of the parties to a conflict is essential to effectively undertake humanitarian action and this can be harder to obtain in an internal armed conflict such as in Syria. Yet conversely, the UN Guiding Principles on Internal Displacement have provided one of the clearest examples of normative guidance for states and humanitarian actors, despite the fact that internal displacement was originally seen as a matter falling within state sovereignty. The non-binding nature of the Guiding Principles has

[123] UNHCR, *Syria Emergency* www.unhcr.org/syria-emergency.html.
[124] Verdirame, 'Compliance with Human Rights', above n 18, 271.

not prevented their internalisation into both domestic and regional legally binding frameworks. Indeed, one could argue that it has helped to promote their acceptance as they were presented as a restatement of international law, rather than the creation of new international obligations.[125] This highlights the potential positive impact on state and humanitarian actors' practice of non-binding norms.

Therefore, drawing on the conceptual framework and substantive content of the *acquis humanitaire* set out over the preceding chapters, the final Part of this book provides some concluding observations on the future development of the *acquis humanitaire*. The next chapter draws together strands from international human rights law and the other key branches of international law to determine whether or not a specific 'right to humanitarian assistance' currently exists in international law, applicable in all humanitarian contexts. The concluding chapter then provides a brief summary of the core arguments presented in this monograph before identifying some next steps for the potential future development of the *acquis humanitaire*.

[125] See Cohen, 'Guiding Principles', above n 41, 473–74.

Part III

Concluding Observations

10

Crystallisation of a General Right to Humanitarian Assistance

I. INTRODUCTION

> As a general rule, it appears that at the present time there is no right *de lege lata* to render humanitarian assistance. There is only a right to offer such assistance, but its exercise is contingent on consent by the State concerned … As long as consent by the State concerned lies at the root of humanitarian assistance, one cannot speak of a genuine right to provide or receive such assistance.
>
> Yoram Dinstein, 1995[1]

The question of whether or not a general right to humanitarian assistance[2] currently exists in international law has been posed for more than 20 years, with Professor Dinstein arguing against the legal concept in the context of armed conflicts back in 1995. Conversely, the non-binding Bruges Resolution on Humanitarian Assistance from 2003 argued: 'Leaving the victims of disaster without humanitarian assistance constitutes a threat to human life and an offence to human dignity and therefore a violation of fundamental human rights.'[3] Moreover, a large number of non-state actors have socially internalised a general right to humanitarian assistance in all humanitarian crises, for example through their adherence to the Sphere Standards and/or the RCRC Code of Conduct.[4] Even so,

[1] Y Dinstein, 'The Legal Consequences of Infringing upon the Right to Humanitarian Assistance', paper presented at the International Colloquium on the Right to Humanitarian Assistance, Paris, 25–27 January 1995, para 3. See also Y Dinstein, 'The Right to Humanitarian Assistance' (Autumn 2000) *Naval War College Review* 77.

[2] It should be noted that the terminology of a 'right to humanitarian assistance' is used in many of the relevant texts. I understand the right to humanitarian assistance to include the right to protection and material assistance as set out in ch 1, Section II.

[3] Arts II.1 and II.2 Resolution on Humanitarian Assistance, Institute of International Law, Bruges Session, September 2003.

[4] As of August 2016, 618 NGOs have formally signed the Red Cross Red Crescent Code of Conduct for the International Red Cross and Red Crescent Movement and NGOs in Disaster Relief, see www.ifrc.org/Global/Publications/general/Code%20of%20Conduct%20UPDATED_August%202016.pdf. Meanwhile, over 400 NGOs from more than 80 countries

such assertions of the right explicitly recognise that it is not formulated in the same terms under international law, and while such texts may aim to reflect international law, they are primarily premised on the non-binding concept of humanity. Furthermore, only a small minority of states have expressly supported the existence of a right to humanitarian assistance in non-armed conflict settings,[5] and the ILC has noted that 'existing positive law on the subject remains unclear'.[6]

Therefore, to analyse the existence of a general right to humanitarian assistance in humanitarian crises, one has to separate the arguments into two strands. The first line of argument posits that despite the lack of explicit references to a binding right to humanitarian assistance in disaster settings, by drawing analogies from the law of armed conflict, international human rights law, and other relevant branches of international law, a legal right to humanitarian assistance in all humanitarian crises already exists.[7] The second line of argument highlights the positive legal obligations for the protection of persons in the law of armed conflict, supported by specific provisions in international criminal law, human rights law and international refugee and displaced persons law, but concurrently notes the lack of equivalent legal rights in disaster settings. Nevertheless, while a general right to humanitarian assistance may not currently exist in international law, this approach argues that there is the potential for the creation of such a right or that such a right may be in the process of crystallisation.[8]

This chapter adopts this second strand of argument. In particular, for determining whether or not a general right to humanitarian assistance is in the process of crystallisation, a specific analysis and focus on the right to humanitarian assistance during armed conflicts and displacement provides an important comparison and reference point for discussion. By examining the humanitarian motivations and legal obligations to ensure a minimum standard of protection and material assistance for civilians in times of armed conflict or displacement, one can better understand

provided input for the 2011 revision of the Sphere Project's Humanitarian Charter and Minimum Standards in Humanitarian Response, April 2011. See L McDougal and J Beard, 'Revisiting Sphere: New Standards of Service Delivery for New Trends in Protracted Displacement' (2011) 35(1) *Disasters* 87, 90.

[5] For a summary of states' views, see: Official Records of the General Assembly, Sixty-fourth Session, Report of the International Law Commission, *Supplement No 10* (A/64/10), Chapter IX, paras 241–46; *Secretariat Memorandum on the Protection of Persons in the Event of Disasters*, 60th Session of the ILC (11 December 2007) A/CN.4/590, 20–24.

[6] ILC, *Secretariat Memorandum*, above para 5, 152–53.

[7] D Fisher, 'The Right to Humanitarian Assistance', in W Kälin et al (eds), *Incorporating the Guiding Principles on Internal Displacement into Domestic Law: Issues and Challenges*, ASIL and Brookings-Bern Project on Internal Displacement, Studies in Transnational Legal Policy, No 41 (2010) 51–52.

[8] Dinstein, 'Legal Consequences', above n 1, para 3.

the rights and responsibilities of states and humanitarian agencies in all humanitarian preparation and response activities. Nevertheless, the concept of an *acquis humanitaire* is intended as a means of understanding the differential provisions of law, policy and practice relating specifically to the protection of persons in all humanitarian crises, without constraining its normative content per se. Therefore, the concept of an *acquis humanitaire* is not contingent on the crystallisation of a right to humanitarian assistance, and contains a spectrum of technical and operational approaches to humanitarian action alongside more normative ones.

As discussed in chapter three and visualised in Figure 10.1 below, one can separate these different approaches into needs-based and rights-based approaches. This monograph has consistently argued that these two approaches are not mutually exclusive and that both approaches can and should incorporate human rights principles into operational decision making.[9] However, rights-based approaches can be further split into approaches which are premised on the application of existing human rights provisions (such as the right to food, housing or physical integrity) in humanitarian crises,[10] and approaches premised on a specific right to humanitarian assistance. Moreover, a specific 'right to humanitarian assistance' entails two separate components: an individual or group's right to request or receive assistance, and an organisational right to offer their services (the so-called right of initiative for humanitarian organisations).

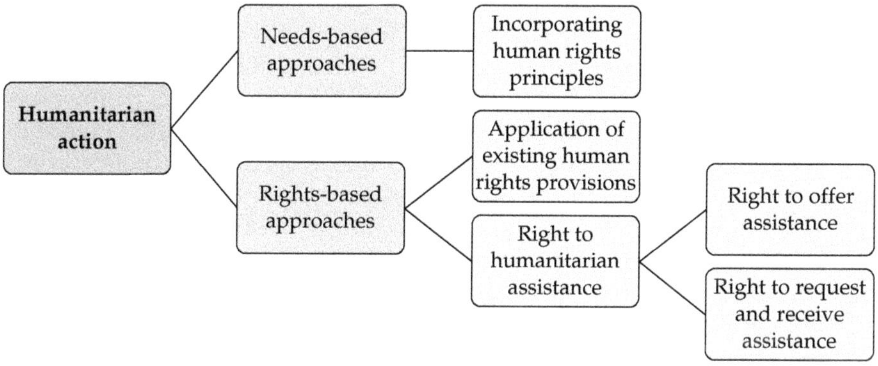

Figure 10.1: Approaches to humanitarian action

[9] See ch 3, Section II.B.

[10] For example, draft Art 5 of the ILC draft articles on the protection of persons in the event of disasters states that: 'Persons affected by disasters are entitled to the respect for and protection of their human rights in accordance with international law.' For the final text of the preamble, draft articles and commentaries adopted by the ILC, see Official Records of the General Assembly, Seventy-first Session, *Supplement No 10* (A/71/10), Chapter IV: Protection of Persons in the Event of Disasters (2016). See also A Vandenbogaerde, 'The Right to Development in International Human Rights Law: A Call for its Dissolution' (2013) 31(2) *Netherlands Quarterly of Human Rights* 187.

Ruth Stoffels has stressed the coherence between these two components of a right to humanitarian assistance, noting that the law of armed conflict provides humanitarian organisations 'the right to offer victims the relief supplies that they need and the right for the offer of aid not to be unreasonably refused when the needs of the victims are not met in some other way. This right should be regarded as a corollary to the right of victims to humanitarian assistance, without which it lacks a solid justificatory basis'.[11] Likewise, UNICEF has noted that: 'The humanitarian imperative implies a right to receive humanitarian assistance and a right to offer it.'[12] If the right to receive humanitarian assistance is directly linked to the right to offer humanitarian assistance in this way, then one can think of a universal or general 'right to humanitarian assistance'. However, the ILC Special Rapporteur on the Protection of Persons in the Event of Disasters highlighted the definitional challenges a potential right to humanitarian assistance in disaster settings may pose:

> In international humanitarian law [the] right [to humanitarian assistance] has been recognised as a matter of law. In disaster situations, however, it appears that no legal instruments explicitly acknowledge the existence of such a right. At most, it could be said to be implicit in international human rights law. The nature of such a right is, however, unclear. Would it be a human right or just a right of those affected by a disaster? Would it be a human right or a collective right? Against whom, if at all, would it be enforceable? After all, the criteria to determine the existence and status of a human right are subject to controversy.[13]

Yet this analysis does not sufficiently distinguish between the right of third states and humanitarian organisations to offer assistance and an individual's right to request and receive assistance. Indeed, Stoffels has highlighted that UNSC Resolutions calling for humanitarian assistance in specific armed conflicts usually make reference to 'the duties of the parties to the conflict and the rights of humanitarian organizations and personnel, and not to the right of victims to humanitarian assistance'.[14] Therefore, one needs to separate any potential rights that accrue to humanitarian organisations from that of the individual victims to determine the substantive content of these twin components of a general right to humanitarian assistance.

[11] R Stoffels, 'Legal Regulation of Humanitarian Assistance in Armed Conflict: Achievements and Gaps' (September 2004) 86(855) *International Review of the Red Cross* 515, 521.

[12] UNICEF, *UNICEF's Humanitarian Principles*, July 2003 www.unicef.org/pathtraining/Documents/Session%204%20Humanitarian%20Principles/Participant%20Manual/4.2%20UNICEF%20Humanitarian%20Principles.doc.

[13] E Valencia-Ospina, *Preliminary Report*, 8 May 2008, A/CN.4/598, para 54.

[14] Stoffels, 'Legal Regulation', above n 11, 522, fn 16.

II. INDIVIDUAL RIGHT TO REQUEST OR RECEIVE HUMANITARIAN ASSISTANCE

A. During Armed Conflicts

Yoram Dinstein argued strongly against a general individual right to humanitarian assistance in armed conflicts when he noted: 'Surely, civilians do not have an absolute right to demand relief from the outside, applicable *erga omnes* (that is, vis-à-vis the entire international community) … [I]t would be absurd to contend that every state in the world is duty bound to come up, on demand, with relief aid to civilians embroiled in any armed conflict, wherever it is raging.'[15] Indeed, although Article 30 Geneva Convention IV expressly contains a right for individuals to request humanitarian assistance, this is constrained as Contracting Parties' may respond 'within the bounds set by military or security considerations' and only need to facilitate access to protected persons 'as much as possible'.[16] The ICRC clearly acknowledges that military considerations are part and parcel of decisions surrounding the provision of humanitarian assistance to civilians in conflict zones.[17] Furthermore, humanitarian access in war zones is a highly contentious issue, and can present serious dangers for both humanitarian personnel and civilians. Nevertheless, while the parameters of a binding international legal right to humanitarian assistance are contested, the fact remains that the law of armed conflict does provide specific rights to protection and assistance for individuals during armed conflicts. Moreover, an individual's right to request and receive humanitarian assistance may be bolstered by binding regional instruments, such as the AU Kampala Convention which is applicable during both international and non-international armed conflicts.

Within the context of international armed conflicts, Article 70 Additional Protocol I (API) utilises non-discretionary language: 'If the civilian population … is not adequately provided … relief actions which are humanitarian and impartial in character and conducted without any adverse distinction *shall* be undertaken.'[18] Despite this mandatory language, Article 70 then introduces specific limitations—first and foremost that humanitarian assistance must be 'subject to the agreement of the Parties concerned'. Additionally, the Parties have the right to prescribe technical

[15] Dinstein, 'Right to Humanitarian Assistance', above n 1, 78.

[16] Art 30 Geneva Convention IV relative to the Protection of Civilian Persons in Times of War (1949).

[17] ICRC, *Commentary: Fourth Geneva Convention relative to the Protection of Civilian Persons in Time of War*, J Pictet (ed) (1958) 180.

[18] Art 70 Protocol relating to the Protection of Victims of International Armed Conflicts (1977) [emphasis added].

arrangements, including search procedures, under which the passage of humanitarian supplies is permitted. Meanwhile, although Article 71 API provides that humanitarian personnel shall be respected and protected in the discharge of their functions, it also stresses that '[u]nder no circumstances may relief personnel exceed the terms of their mission … In particular they shall take account of the security requirements of the Party in whose territory they are carrying out their duties'.[19]

Internal armed conflicts present specific challenges for humanitarian access, yet Additional Protocol II (APII) does not contain the same level of detail regarding relief activities for civilian populations. Article 18(1) only provides that 'relief societies located in the territory of the High Contracting Party … may offer their services for the performance of their traditional functions in relation to the victims of the armed conflict'.[20] Yet Article 18(2) uses mandatory language in proscribing that '[i]f the civilian population is suffering undue hardship owing to a lack of the supplies essential for its survival … relief actions for the civilian population … shall be undertaken'.[21] However, once again, offers of assistance are subject to the consent of the High Contracting Party concerned. Therefore, one of the parties to an internal conflict can legitimately deny humanitarian activities for civilians, for example due to military necessity. Nevertheless, although Article 18 does not impose an obligation on parties to accept external humanitarian assistance, this does not absolve the party of their obligation to provide some form of relief for civilian populations to prevent and alleviate suffering. The provisions of humane treatment set out in Common Article 3 apply in all internal armed conflicts, and the ICRC has determined that the provision of humanitarian assistance to civilian populations in armed conflicts is part of customary international law.

Under Customary International Law Rule 55, the parties to a conflict must allow and facilitate the rapid and unimpeded passage of humanitarian relief for civilians in need,[22] while Rule 56 states that Parties to a conflict must ensure the freedom of movement of authorised humanitarian personnel.[23] Crucially, only in the case of imperative military necessity may their movements be temporarily restricted. Nevertheless, all

[19] ibid, Art 71.

[20] Art 18(1) Protocol II relating to the Protection of Victims of Non-International Armed Conflicts (1977).

[21] ibid, Art 18(2). See also Stoffels, 'Legal Regulation', above n 11, 519.

[22] The ICRC *Customary International Humanitarian Law Project* Rule 55 (Access for Humanitarian Relief for Civilians in Need). See JM Henckaerts and L Doswald-Beck, *Customary International Humanitarian Law: Rules and Practice* (Cambridge University Press, 2005).

[23] The ICRC *Customary International Humanitarian Law Project* Rule 56 (Freedom of Movement of Humanitarian Relief Personnel).

these provisions reflect the recognition throughout the law of armed conflict that while parties to a conflict have explicit responsibilities towards civilians and those *hors de combat* under their control, individual rights may be legitimately constrained, either for military necessity, security reasons or due to insufficient resources.

B. During Other Humanitarian Crises

The legal obligations in place regarding an individual's right to request or receive humanitarian assistance in non-conflict situations are less well defined. For example, the 1951 Refugee Convention is premised on the equal treatment of recognised refugees in the territory of a host state, allowing refugees access to employment, training and welfare on at least the same basis as other foreign nationals. However, in recognition of the challenges refugees and those fleeing persecution face, and the practice of establishing large-scale refugee camps in the face of mass displacement, UNHCR's operational protection mandate has encompassed the provision of both legal protection and material assistance activities since its establishment. Yet there are wide divergences between state practice in different humanitarian crises, which indicates a lack of legal compulsion felt by state and humanitarian organisations in their responses. While the humanitarian imperative may be based on the desire to prevent and alleviate human suffering wherever it may be found, the reality is that for a range of political, financial and practical reasons not all victims of armed conflict, forced displacement or natural disaster receive adequate protection and assistance commensurate with their needs.[24] This does not negate the possibility that an individual right to request and receive humanitarian assistance exists—many economic, social and cultural rights are based on progressive realisation rather than immediate implementation,[25] and the rights to protection and assistance in the law of armed conflict may also be constrained due to military or financial reasons.[26] Moreover, a legally binding right to protection and assistance does exist for one specific group of refugees, namely refugee children.[27]

[24] B Schweizer, 'Moral Dilemmas for Humanitarianism in the Era of "Humanitarian" Military Interventions' (September 2004) 86(855) *International Review of the Red Cross* 547, 551.

[25] M Dennis and D Stewart, 'Justiciability of Economic, Social and Cultural Rights: Should There be an International Complaints Mechanism to Adjudicate the Rights to Food, Water, Housing and Health?' (2004) 98 *American Journal of International Law* 462.

[26] See, eg, Art 55(1) GCIV, above n 16; Art 69(1) API, above n 18, 'To the fullest extent of the means available to it …'

[27] Art 22(1) Convention on the Rights of the Child (1989).

Likewise, the non-binding UN Guiding Principles on Internal Displacement clearly state:

> Internally displaced persons have the *right to request and to receive* protection and humanitarian assistance from these [national] authorities. They shall not be persecuted or punished for making such a request.[28]

However, the challenge of determining the substantive content of any proposed individual right to humanitarian assistance remains. An individual's right to request assistance is meaningless without a corresponding right to receive. Echoing Stoffels' argument, Walter Kälin's Annotations to the Guiding Principles state that the right to request and receive assistance is the corollary to a state's duty to protect and assist IDPs.[29] Indeed, one can argue that if a state is unable or unwilling to provide assistance to persons on its territory, it has an obligation to accept international humanitarian assistance. Yet the enforceability of a request for assistance is not elaborated within the Guiding Principles. Even within the African Union's Kampala Convention, which also includes an individual's right to request and receive humanitarian assistance,[30] if a state does not have sufficient resources to provide humanitarian assistance to IDPs their obligations are simply to co-operate with other state parties to seek assistance from international humanitarian organisations.[31] In the absence of explicit compliance and accountability mechanisms, an individual's 'right' to assistance, either from their national authorities or from an international source, risks becoming an empty promise. So despite the authoritative non-binding influence of the UN Guiding Principles and regional importance of the Kampala Convention, and their potential internalisation into the domestic legal systems of specific states, pending the emergence of a broad-based international consensus on the implications of a binding right for individuals to request and receive humanitarian assistance, it is hard to argue that a general individual right to humanitarian assistance currently exists in all humanitarian crises.

[28] UN, Commission on Human Rights, *The Guiding Principles on Internal Displacement*, E/CN.4/1998/53/Add.2 (1998), Principle 3(2) [emphasis added].

[29] W Kälin, *Guiding Principles on Internal Displacement: Annotations*, ASIL and Brookings-Bern Project on Internal Displacement, Studies in Transnational Legal Policy, No 38 Revised Edition (2008) 20.

[30] Art 5(9) African Union Convention for the Protection and Assistance of Internally Displaced Persons in Africa ('Kampala Convention') (adopted 22 October 2009, entered into force 6 December 2012).

[31] ibid, Art 5(6). State parties have obligations to organise, enable and facilitate international humanitarian assistance subject to their right to prescribe technical arrangements for the delivery of assistance, Art 5(7). However, the Kampala Convention does not proscribe or propose an individual compliance mechanism to allow enforcement of an individual's right to assistance in Art 5(9).

III. ORGANISATIONAL RIGHT TO OFFER HUMANITARIAN SERVICES

Conversely, one can argue that both customary and general international law already recognises a right of initiative, or the right of humanitarian organisations to offer their services to affected states in certain circumstances. During armed conflicts, Common Article 3 provides a general provision for impartial humanitarian bodies to offer their services to the Parties to the conflict.[32] Meanwhile, Article 63 GCIV and Article 18 APII allow humanitarian organisations to conduct humanitarian activities for civilians, with Article 70(1) API highlighting that '[o]ffers of such relief shall not be regarded as interference in the armed conflict or as unfriendly acts'. Therefore express provisions for impartial humanitarian organisations to offer humanitarian assistance, subject to certain limitations, exist in both international and non-international armed conflicts. Similarly, the non-binding Guiding Principles on Internal Displacement utilise rights-based language by proposing a specific right for international humanitarian organisations and other appropriate actors in the context of internal displacement.[33]

It is noticeable that the original text of Article 12 of the ILC draft articles on the protection of persons in the event of disasters distinguished between a 'right to offer' for states and inter-governmental organisations, and weaker wording covering relevant non-governmental organisations who 'may also offer' their services.[34] The reluctance of states to expand a specific right of initiative to NGOs reflects on-going concerns regarding sovereignty and non-interference in domestic affairs, despite the fact that non-governmental humanitarian actors equally need legal certainty and standing commensurate to the role that they play in humanitarian activities.[35] Moreover, the final wording removed the 'right' to offer altogether and now simply states: 'In the event of disasters, States, the United Nations, and other potential assisting actors may offer assistance to the affected State.'[36] The reduction of language from a general 'right to offer' for all organisations, to a right only for states and inter-governmental organisations, to finally a reference only to offers of assistance implies a

[32] Common Art 3(2) Geneva Conventions: 'An impartial humanitarian body, such as the International Committee of the Red Cross, may offer its services to the Parties to the conflict.'

[33] Principle 25(2), *Guiding Principles*, above n 28.

[34] For discussion, see G Bartolini, T Natoli and A Riccardi, *Report of the Expert Meeting on the ILC's Draft Articles on the Protection of Persons in the Event of Disasters*, Roma Tre University Department of Law, 8–9 June 2015, International Law and Disasters Working Papers Series 03 (2015) 63–67. Note, Art 12 was originally Art 16.

[35] For comments by states expressing caution regarding an organisational right to humanitarian assistance, see: Greece (A/C.6/67/SR.19, para 57); Malaysia (A/C.6/67/SR.19, para 107); USA (A/C.6/67/SR.19, para 116); Iran (A/C.6/67/SR.20, para 15); Pakistan (A/C.6/67/SR.20, para 32).

[36] Draft Art 12(1). See Official Records of the General Assembly, A/71/10, above n 10, 15.

move away from a rights-based approach, even on the less contentious or onerous organisational right to offer as opposed to an individual right to request and receive humanitarian assistance.

A fundamental issue for any organisation offering their assistance is whether or not an affected state has the power to refuse their offer, and on what grounds. The Annotations to the UN Guiding Principles note that a state cannot withhold their consent arbitrarily,[37] while the ICRC has noted: 'It is nonetheless self-evident that a humanitarian organisation cannot operate without the consent of the party concerned. However, such consent must not be refused on arbitrary grounds.'[38] Likewise, the ILC draft articles propose that an affected state has a duty to seek assistance from other states and humanitarian agencies if a disaster exceeds its domestic capacities. While highlighting the requirement for such agencies to receive consent from the affected state, the draft articles similarly propose that such consent shall not be withheld arbitrarily.[39]

The general convergence of opinions across these binding and non-binding texts, covering all types of humanitarian crises, suggests that a right for humanitarian and impartial organisations to offer their services to an affected state may exist in general international law. However, the revised wording of the ILC draft articles in the context of disasters may reflect a move away from rights-based approaches to humanitarian action, at least on the part of state representatives. Moreover, any such organisational right to offer is constrained by the requirement to obtain the affected state's consent before assistance is provided, although the affected state cannot withhold their consent arbitrarily. Considering the 'soft' nature of such a right, whereby sovereignty is maintained as states may accept or reject an offer of assistance, the determination of whether an offer is being refused 'arbitrarily' will be hard to make, particularly in the midst of a complex humanitarian crisis and in the absence of any legal accountability mechanisms that a humanitarian agency could call upon beyond moral and political arguments to prove their good intentions for assisting victims in an affected state.[40] As noted by the Overseas Development Institute: 'whatever the duties imposed by international law, it is humanitarian organisations' persuasive power and relevance on the ground that matter most in the end.'[41]

[37] Kälin, *Annotations*, above n 29, 118–19.

[38] Henckaerts and Doswald-Beck, *Customary IHL*, above n 22, Rule 55.

[39] Draft Art 11 (Duty of the affected state to seek external assistance) and draft Art 13 (Consent of the affected state to external assistance). See Official Records of the General Assembly, A/71/10, above n 10, 15–16.

[40] For discussion of this point, see E Valencia-Ospina, *Fourth Report*, 11 May 2011, A/CN.4/643, paras 51–77.

[41] S Collinson and S Elhawary, 'Humanitarian Space: A Review of Trends and Issues', Overseas Development Institute, Humanitarian Policy Group Report No 32, April 2012, 2.

IV. THE CRYSTALLISATION OF A GENERAL RIGHT TO HUMANITARIAN ASSISTANCE

Based on the above observations, one can summarise the current legal situation as follows. There is a limited individual right to request and receive assistance from impartial humanitarian organisations in armed conflicts, although there are no compliance mechanisms for individuals to enforce their rights to assistance in a war zone, and these rights differ between international and non-international armed conflicts. There is not yet a comparable individual right during peace-time humanitarian crises, although binding international law provides such a general right for refugee children, and non-binding global texts and regional binding texts have proposed such a right for all internally displaced persons. Furthermore, there is a right for impartial humanitarian organisations to offer their services to affected states in both international and non-international armed conflicts, and the affected state should not refuse such offers arbitrarily. However, the practical implications and application of such a right need further elaboration. Moreover, the status of a right for humanitarian organisations to offer their services in other types of humanitarian crisis is not yet evident and the language in the ILC draft articles appears to be moving away from an express invocation of such a right, even for states and inter-governmental organisations.

Therefore, it is clear that international law is currently in the process of developing, interpreting and refining a range of individual and organisational rights to humanitarian assistance in both conflict and non-conflict settings. Yet there is limited international consensus on the boundaries and limitations of each of these rights. Explicit references to a right to humanitarian assistance in authoritative and diverse documents emanating from the UN, Red Cross Movement,[42] respected academics and humanitarian agencies may mean that a general right to humanitarian assistance covering armed conflicts, forced displacement and natural and human-made disasters is in the process of formation. There are compelling arguments to justify such a stance based on the importance of humanity and human dignity in international law, which are further strengthened by extensive state practice in undertaking humanitarian action and authoritative non-binding norms endorsing a right to humanitarian assistance.

However, if a general right to humanitarian assistance encompassing both the right of individuals to request and receive assistance and for

[42] It has been argued that the Red Cross itself contributes to the formation of international law, both by its activities and by the drafting of legal instruments submitted to diplomatic conferences. See F Bugnion, 'Red Cross Law' (September–October 1995) 308 *International Review of the Red Cross* 491, 492.

organisations to offer assistance is already in existence, why are states reticent to adopt rights-based language when discussing the concept of humanitarian action? The removal of the reference to a right to humanitarian assistance in the 2011 IASC Operational Guidelines for Natural Disasters would seem to be at odds with the 2009 AU Kampala Convention and 2011 edition of the *Sphere Handbook*, which both incorporate such a right. This is even more striking considering that the 2002 IASC publication, Growing the Sheltering Tree, clearly stated: 'The right to receive humanitarian assistance—and the right to offer it—are fundamental humanitarian principles underpinned by international law.'[43] Furthermore, the ILC's work on the protection of persons in the event of disasters has contained limited references to a 'right to humanitarian assistance',[44] and it is noticeable that even in the context of offers of assistance, the Special Rapporteur's original proposal for draft Article 12 entitled 'Right to Offer Assistance' has been modified to simply 'Offers of Assistance'. Nevertheless, the inclusion of substantive articles on human dignity and human rights by the ILC, even in the absence of specific references to an individual right to receive or request assistance or organisational right to offer their services, clearly ties the emerging international legal framework for disasters into the broader international human rights mechanisms.[45]

Thus, while the law of armed conflict has formalised an individual's right to assistance in certain situations, a more general right for individuals to request and receive assistance and for organisations to provide assistance (as opposed to simply offering their services) in all humanitarian crises does not yet exist in international law due to the continuing reliance on respect for state sovereignty. This means that claims for assistance are generally dependent on domestic mechanisms, which often lack enforcement procedures.[46] On this basis, it is clear that Professor Dinstein's view is as applicable today as it was 20 years ago; namely, 'there is no right *de lege lata* to render humanitarian assistance. There is only a right to offer such assistance, but its exercise is contingent on consent by the State concerned.'[47]

[43] IASC, *Growing the Sheltering Tree: Protecting Rights through Humanitarian Action* (2002) 5.

[44] The 158-page ILC Secretariat background Memorandum of 2008 only devoted six pages to the question of a right to humanitarian assistance and existing human rights law applicable in the event of disasters. See ILC, *Secretariat Memorandum*, above n 5, 149–54.

[45] Draft Art 4 reads: 'The inherent dignity of the human person shall be respected and protected in the event of disasters'; while draft Art 5 states: 'Persons affected by disasters are entitled to the respect for and protection of their human rights in accordance with international law.' See Official Records of the General Assembly, A/71/10, above n 10, 14–15.

[46] Fisher, 'Right to Humanitarian Assistance', above n 6, 48–49.

[47] Dinstein, 'Legal Consequences', above n 6, para 3.

Yet despite this pessimistic conclusion, arguably a right to humanitarian assistance is in the process of crystallisation. The increased attention and analysis of international law, policy and practice surrounding humanitarian crises, signified by the expanding normative content of the *acquis humanitaire*, highlights the norm life-cycle that a general right to humanitarian assistance may be engaged in. The increasing focus on the human rights implications of humanitarian crises is recasting the debate about humanitarian responses into the language of rights. A broad range of non-binding sources developed by both inter-governmental and non-governmental actors have proclaimed the existence of a right to humanitarian assistance, while the African Union's Kampala Convention provides the first binding multilateral convention which expressly provides for a general right to humanitarian assistance in displacement settings. It follows that the transnational legal process of on-going interactions between states, humanitarian actors, affected communities and academics will lead to increasing interpretations of what a general right to humanitarian assistance may entail for both rights-holders and duty-bearers, leading to increased internalisation of the right(s) by individual states, regional organisations, and the international community. However, while providing a strong moral and ethical call for action, until sufficient states accept the legal obligations which arise from a general right to humanitarian assistance, its applicability as a legal concept remains limited.

11

Future Development of the Acquis Humanitaire

THE CONCEPT OF an *acquis humanitaire* elaborated over the course of this monograph is intended to highlight the wide range of materials that relate specifically to the legal protection of persons in humanitarian crises. Many of these sources are non-binding, and so from a strictly legal positivist perspective are not of direct relevance in determining the legal rights and obligations at play in armed conflicts, forced displacement or disaster settings. However, the extensive practice of states and humanitarian organisations (both inter-governmental and non-governmental) is evidence of the priority placed on assisting those most in need, irrespective of the source of suffering or the origins of those affected. Despite the multitude of wars and disasters in the 150 years since Henri Dunant passionately recounted his experiences on the battlefield of Solferino, the humanitarian imperative remains strong.

Such humanitarian actions need to be planned, managed and regulated to ensure a high and consistent standard of appropriate material assistance alongside fundamental activities to protect people from mistreatment and abuse, whether at the hands of armed groups or as a result of inadequate living conditions in a refugee camp. It follows that guiding principles, codes of conduct and minimum standards are fundamental for the efficient and respectful implementation of the humanitarian imperative. Experience has shown that appeals to moral or ethical standards may provide protection as forcefully as appeals to legal obligations. However, there is a need for legal and non-legal accountability mechanisms at all stages of the protection cycle. States must be accountable to other states, and to persons in their territory. Assisting states must be accountable to ensure that they support the primary responsibility of the affected state, rather than working at cross-purposes or for their own self-interest. Likewise, humanitarian organisations, from large UN agencies to small NGOs must ensure that they comply with the highest ethical and legal standards and most importantly 'do no harm'.

However, the concept of an *acquis humanitaire* elaborated in Part I of this book is conceived as a broad tent. By highlighting the various branches of international law which can contribute to our better understanding of the protection and assistance of persons in humanitarian crises, the *acquis humanitaire* represents a flexible and dynamic framework. It is a positive sign that only a selection of key legal and non-binding texts could be included in Part II due to space constraints. The *acquis humanitaire* encompasses a rich and varied normative content from the international, regional and domestic levels, although this in itself may raise questions of coherence across and within the applicable branches of international law. Some may argue against the inclusion or exclusion of particular legal or non-legal texts, or case examples, within this exposition of the *acquis humanitaire*. Such interactions and dialogue are to be welcomed and, as with any attempt to systematise a vast breadth of information, choices needed to be made. However, my overall objective in advancing the concept of an *acquis humanitaire* was to identify normative sources which put those most affected by humanitarian crises, namely civilians caught up in the crossfire of war or individuals whose lives and livelihoods are destroyed by natural disasters or forced displacement, at the forefront of our legal consciousness.

Scholars such as Michael Barnett and Thomas Weiss have undertaken extensive research to advance our conceptual understandings of what 'humanitarianism' means in theory and in practice. From the forces of destruction comes the humanitarian imperative which motivates the forces of production and salvation to prevent and alleviate suffering wherever it may be found. Hugo Slim, amongst many others, has reminded us of the fundamental importance of the humanitarian principles of impartiality, neutrality and above all humanity. Likewise, Ruti Teitel has highlighted the existence of 'humanity's law' as a means of reconceiving security in terms of protection and preservation of persons and peoples. Meanwhile, the Brookings Institute in Washington, DC has supported numerous committed academics and practitioners who have challenged and progressed the law and practice relating to displacement and humanitarianism—from Francis Deng and Roberta Cohen's original insights into the importance of an international framework for the protection of and assistance for internally displaced persons to Elizabeth Ferris's call for a clearer understanding of the promise, and risks, associated with physical, humanitarian and human rights protection. The Brookings Institute has also hosted Walter Kälin, who has advanced our understanding of the cycle of protection required at all stages of preparation, prevention, response and recovery. The importance and practical utility of this protection cycle is evidenced by Kälin's application of it to new and emerging global threats such as cross-border displacement arising from disasters and climate change.

Meanwhile, around the world countless volunteers and staff of domestic and international humanitarian organisations work to assist those most in need. From a legal perspective, the Red Cross Movement has been at the forefront of providing guidance and support for developing national, regional and international legal frameworks for armed conflicts and disasters. Notably, David Fisher has led the drive for improved domestic and international disaster laws, alongside the work of Eduardo Valencia-Ospina and members of the International Law Commission. In armed conflicts, the ICRC Customary International Humanitarian Law study provides a fundamental baseline for discussions about the universality of specific provisions of the law of armed of conflict. One should also not forget the extensive role played by civil servants and government officials in countless countries, both those affected and those co-operating with them, to ameliorate the worst effects of humanitarian crises for people in their territories. Most importantly, as witnessed every day, it is local communities that provide the first line of protection and assistance to those facing war, displacement or disaster.

Yet law is only words on paper if it is not implemented on the ground. Harold Koh has explained the process whereby rules of law can be created via multiple international interactions between transnational actors, leading to a range of interpretations of an emerging norm before ultimately it is internalised (socially, politically and/or legally) into domestic law, policy and practice or the internal rules of non-state actors. Such internalisation is facilitated by effective accountability mechanisms to promote compliance with and enforcement of the rights and obligations arising from humanitarian action. As Mark Bovens has highlighted, such accountability mechanisms may be political, legal, administrative, professional or social, and provide a fundamental avenue to hold responsible actors to account. International judicial structures such as the International Criminal Court and the European Court of Human Rights provide a key form of legal accountability, alongside domestic legal systems, while professional accountability arises from guidelines, minimum standards and codes of conduct for humanitarian actors.

As argued in this monograph, a rights-based approach to humanitarian action entails a procedural requirement for humanitarian actors to respect the wishes of the local community in all their activities by incorporating the human rights principles of empowerment, participation, non-discrimination and accountability into all forms of humanitarian programming. While one must recognise the divergent approaches of humanitarian organisations, incorporating such obligations of conduct into humanitarian programming is conceptually valid and operationally achievable even within so-called 'traditional' needs-based approaches to humanitarian activities. Meanwhile, certain duty-bearers will have a legal obligation to respect, protect and fulfil specific rights, and other actors may choose to undertake human rights-based activities and advocacy to address the substantive content of human rights law. This division of labour between humanitarian activities and human rights activities reflects the differences between humanitarian and human rights protection. Both have an important role to play in the complex and challenging setting of a major humanitarian crisis.

As evidenced by the variety of international and regional legal and non-legal instruments examined in Part II of this book, it is clear that the normative content of the *acquis humanitaire* is derived from a multitude of sources. Each chapter has therefore attempted to provide an overview of key international legal instruments, judicial decisions and non-binding norms of relevance to the *acquis humanitaire* in their respective body of law, policy and practice. To provide additional clarity, a variety of country and thematic case examples have been analysed to highlight specific aspects of the *acquis humanitaire*. While the phrase 'the law of humanitarian assistance' may lack the necessary legal precision, it is clear that the extensive physical and financial support for humanitarian activities provided between countries, whether directly from governments or through private and philanthropic donations, requires a coherent and comprehensive legal framework.

Therefore, how can the future development of the *acquis humanitaire* help to strengthen the web of international legal protection for persons in humanitarian crises? As noted above, only a selection of legal and non-legal instruments could be examined within the confines of this monograph. It follows that identifying the overlaps and gaps in protection for persons in humanitarian crises needs continual work—laws, policies and practices change over time, and new crises emerge or develop. In particular, the normative content of the *acquis humanitaire* set out in this monograph has been predominantly focused on international instruments and texts. This is not to diminish the role and importance of regional and national laws, policies and practices, but reflects the difficulty of balancing critical analysis with substantive depth. Consequently, further in-depth thematic, country and region-specific case studies may provide additional understanding and interpretations of the relevant norms for the legal protection of persons in humanitarian crises.

Moreover, despite my conclusion regarding the limited nature of existing legal rights to humanitarian assistance set out in chapter ten, I also believe that international law can and should be working towards the crystallisation of a general right to humanitarian assistance in all forms of humanitarian crises. The first step must be a more consistent application of existing international human rights law to humanitarian crises. Such consistency can be promoted via non-binding normative texts, such as joint General Comments from UN human rights treaty bodies and special rapporteurs elaborating the potential violations, and necessary preventative actions, for duty-bearers in all forms of humanitarian crisis. The UN Human Rights Council research into the human rights implications of post-disaster and post-conflict settings provides one example which can be drawn upon.[1] Concurrently, legal accountability mechanisms can apply international, regional and domestic human rights law to situations of humanitarian crisis.

Existing legal obligations in armed conflicts and internal displacement likewise provide a basis for expanding our understanding of the rights and obligations of all humanitarian actors. While many non-governmental actors have internalised and promote a general right to humanitarian assistance, states have been more reticent—both in their legal interpretations and in their practice. This requires states to reassess their positions on state sovereignty and non-interference in domestic affairs in the face of major humanitarian crises, for example by ensuring genuine and consistent access for impartial humanitarian organisations, as well as fulfilling their legal responsibilities to persons in their territory. Concomitantly, assisting states and humanitarian actors must work with the relevant authorities and local communities to ensure that appropriate types of assistance and protection are provided before, during and after a humanitarian crisis. Promoting legal certainty for all actors through a greater understanding of the evolving and expanding normative content of the *acquis humanitaire* will provide a crucial step towards strengthening the international legal protection of persons, and therefore greater humanity and human dignity in humanitarian crises.

[1] HRC, *Final research-based report of the Human Rights Council Advisory Committee on best practices and main challenges in the promotion and protection of human rights in post-disaster and post-conflict situations*, 28th Session of the HRC (10 February 2015) A/HRC/28/76.

Index

www.ingramcontent.com/pod-product-compliance
Ingram Content Group UK Ltd.
Pitfield, Milton Keynes, MK11 3LW, UK
UKHW020132290926
15471UKWH00003B/433

9 781509 931316